6th Workshop on Innovative Use of NLP for Building Educational Applications 2011

Held at ACL HLT 2011

Portland, Oregon, USA
24 June 2011

ISBN: 978-1-61839-251-0

Printed from e-media with permission by:

Curran Associates, Inc.
57 Morehouse Lane
Red Hook, NY 12571

Some format issues inherent in the e-media version may also appear in this print version.

Printed by Curran Associates, Inc. (2011)

For permission requests, please contact the Association for Computational Linguistics at the address below.

Association for Computational Linguistics
209 N. Eighth Street
Stroudsburg, Pennsylvania 18360

Phone: 1-570-476-8006
Fax: 1-570-476-0860

acl@aclweb.org

Additional copies of this publication are available from:

Curran Associates, Inc.
57 Morehouse Lane
Red Hook, NY 12571 USA
Phone: 845-758-0400
Fax: 845-758-2634
Email: curran@proceedings.com
Web: www.proceedings.com

Table of Contents

Introduction

Research in NLP applications for education continues to progress using innovative NLP techniques. New technologies have made it possible to include speech in both assessment and in Intelligent Tutoring Systems (ITS). NLP techniques are also being used to generate assessments and tools for curriculum development of reading materials, as well as tools to support assessment and test development. As a community, we continue to improve existing capabilities and to identify and generate innovative and creative ways to use NLP in applications for writing, reading, speaking, critical thinking, and assessment.

In this workshop, we focus on contributions to core educational problem spaces: development of curriculum and assessment (e.g., applications that help teachers develop reading materials), delivery of curriculum and assessments (e.g., applications where the student receives instruction and interacts with the system), and reporting of assessment outcomes (e.g., automated essay scoring). The need for, and the rapid development of, language-based capabilities have been driven by increased requirements for state and national assessments and a growing population of foreign and second language learners.

This is the sixth in a series of workshops on Building NLP Applications for Education that began at NAACL/HLT 2003 (Edmonton), and continued at ACL 2005 (Ann Arbor), ACL/HLT 2008 (Columbus), NAACL/HLT 2009 (Boulder), NAACL/HLT 2010 (Los Angeles), and now ACL/HLT 2011 (Portland). Research in this area continues to grow, and there is ever-increasing interest and practical application that was evidenced this year, again, by the large number of submissions.

We received a record 35 submissions and accepted 8 full papers as oral presentations and 14 papers as poster presentations. Each paper was carefully reviewed by at least three members of the Program Committee. We selected reviewers most appropriate for each paper so as to give more helpful feedback and comments. This workshop offers an opportunity to present and publish work that is highly relevant to ACL, but is also specialized, so the workshop is often a more appropriate venue. The decision to have a poster session this year was made so as to offer more breadth in terms of topics related to NLP and education and to reinstate the original concept of a workshop as a venue for fully developed work as well as work in progress. Also, we continue to have a strong policy with respect to conflicts of interest and made a concerted effort to not assign papers to reviewers if the paper had an author from their institution.

The papers accepted to this workshop were selected on the basis of several factors: the relevance to a core educational problem space, the novelty of the approach or domain, and the strength of the research. The final set of papers fall under several main themes.

Assessing Speech – Five papers focus on assessing spoken language of non-native speakers of English (Chen and Yoon; Cook, et al; Downey, et al; Yoon and Higgins; and Yoon, et al).

Grammatical Error Detection – Five papers deal with grammatical error detection for non-native speakers, ranging from new paradigms and methodologies (Gamon; Dickinson, et al; West, et al), to CALL applications (Huang, et al), to using grammar checking to measure language development (Hassanali and Liu).

Generation – Five papers address different aspects of generating questions, exercises and examples for students (Agarawal, et al; Agarawal and Mannem; Mostow and Duan; Olney, et al; and Theune, et al).

Intelligent Tutoring – Three papers discuss issues concerning intelligent tutoring systems (Chen, et al; Ward and Crowley; and Ward, et al).

Finally, we also have four papers on other topics. Xiong and Litman use NLP techniques to determine the effectiveness of peer-review. Van Oosten and Hoste investigate the efficacy of using experts and crowdsourcing for readability assessment. Dela Rosa and Eskenazi investigate the effect of word complexity on vocabulary learning for language learners. Yang and Heines apply NLP techniques to the novel task of determining the best transfer course equivalencies.

We wish to thank everyone who showed interest and submitted a paper, all of the authors for their contributions, the members of the Program Committee for their thoughtful reviews, and everyone who attends this workshop. All of these factors contribute to a truly rich and successful event. And, the informal post-workshop dinner is getting more crowded every year!

Joel Tetreault, Educational Testing Service
Jill Burstein, Educational Testing Service
Claudia Leacock, Butler Hill Group

Organizers:

Joel Tetreault, Educational Testing Service
Jill Burstein, Educational Testing Service
Claudia Leacock, Butler Hill Group

Program Committee:

Delphine Bernhard, LIMSI-CNRS, France
Jared Bernstein, Pearson, USA
Chris Brockett, MSR, USA
Lei Chen, ETS, USA
Martin Chodorow, Hunter College, CUNY, USA
Mark Core, Institute for Creative Technologies
Barbara Di Eugenio, University of Illinois at Chicago, USA
Markus Dickinson, Indiana University, USA
Bill Dolan, Microsoft, USA
Maxine Eskenazi, Carnegie Mellon University, USA
Keelan Evanini, ETS, USA
Peter Foltz, Pearson Knowledge Technologies, USA
Jennifer Foster, Dublin City University, Ireland
Horacio Franco, SRI, USA
Michael Gamon, Microsoft, USA
Caroline Gasperin, TouchType Ltd., UK
Kallirroi Georgila, Institute for Creative Technologies
Iryna Gurevych, University of Darmstadt, Germany
Na-Rae Han, University of Pittsburgh, USA
Trude Heift, Simon Frasier University, Canada
Derrick Higgins, ETS, USA
Emi Izumi, Kyoto University of Foreign Studies, Japan
Heng Ji, Queens College, USA
Pamela Jordan, University of Pittsburgh, USA
Ola Knutsson, KTH Nada, Sweden
John Lee, City University of Kong, USA
Jackson Liscombe, SpeechCycle, Inc., USA
Diane Litman, University of Pittsburgh, USA
Annie Louis, University of Pennsylvania
Nitin Madnani, ETS, USA
Montse Maritxalar, University of the Basque Country, Spain
James Martin, University of Colorado
Aurelien Max, LIMSI-CNRS, France
Detmar Meurers, University of Tübingen, Germany
Lisa Michaud, Merrimack College, USA

Rada Mihalcea, University of North Texas
Michael Mohler, University of North Texas
Jack Mostow, CMU, USA
Smaranda Muresan, Rutgers University, USA
Ani Nenkova, University of Pennsylvania, USA
Mari Ostendorf, University of Washington, USA
Ted Pedersen, University of Minnesota, USA
Patti Price, PPRICE Speech and Language Technology, USA
Andrew Rosenberg, Queens College, CUNY, USA
Mihai Rotaru, TextKernel, the Netherlands
Dan Roth, UIUC, USA
Alla Rozovskaya, UIUC, USA
Mathias Schulze, University of Waterloo, Canada
Stephanie Seneff, MIT, USA
Izhak Shafran, Oregon Health & Science University, USA
Jana Sukkarieh, ETS, USA Svetlana Stenchikova, Open University, UK
Helmer Strik, Radboug University Nijmegen, the Netherlands
Joseph Tepperman, Rosetta Stone, USA
Nai-Lung Tsao, National Central University, Taiwan
Monica Ward, Dublin City University, Ireland
Pete Whitelock, Oxford University Press, UK
David Wible, National Central University, Taiwan
Klaus Zechner, ETS, USA

Automatic Question Generation using Discourse Cues

Manish Agarwal*, **Rakshit Shah*** and **Prashanth Mannem**
Language Technologies Research Center
International Institute of Information Technology
Hyderabad, AP, India - 500032
{manish.agarwal, rakshit.shah, prashanth}@research.iiit.ac.in

Abstract

In this paper, we present a system that automatically generates questions from natural language text using discourse connectives. We explore the usefulness of the discourse connectives for Question Generation (QG) that looks at the problem beyond sentence level. Our work divides the QG task into content selection and question formation. Content selection consists of finding the relevant part in text to frame question from while question formation involves sense disambiguation of the discourse connectives, identification of question type and applying syntactic transformations on the content. The system is evaluated manually for syntactic and semantic correctness.

1 Introduction

Automatic QG from sentences and paragraphs has caught the attention of the NLP community in the last few years through the question generation workshops and the shared task in 2010 (QGSTEC, 2010). Previous work in this area has concentrated on generating questions from individual sentences (Varga and Ha, 2010; Paland et al., 2010; Ali et al., 2010). Sneiders and E. (2002) used question templates and Heilman et al. (2009) used general-purpose rules to transform sentences into questions. A notable exception is Mannem et al. (2010) who generated questions of various scopes (general, medium and specific) * [1] from paragraphs instead of individual sentences. They boil down the *QG from paragraphs* task into first identifying the sentences in the paragraph with general, medium and specific scopes and then generating the corresponding questions from these sentences using semantic roles of predicates.

Discourse connectives play a vital role in making the text coherent. They connect two clauses or sentences exhibiting discourse relations such as *temporal*, *causal*, *elaboration*, *contrast*, *result*, etc. Discourse relations have been shown to be useful to generate questions (Prasad and Joshi, 2008) but identifying these relations in the text is a difficult task (Pitler et al., 2009). So in this work, instead of identifying discourse relations and generating questions using them, we explore the usefulness of discourse connectives for QG. We do this by analyzing the senses of the connectives that help in QG and propose a system that makes use of this analysis to generate questions of the type *why*, *when*, *give an example* and *yes/no*.

The two main problems in QG are identifying the content to ask a question on and finding the corresponding question type for that content. We analyze the connectives in terms of the content useful for question generation based on the senses they exhibit. We show that the senses of the connectives further help in choosing the relevant question type for the content.

In this paper, we present an end-to-end QG system that takes a document as input and outputs all the questions generated using the selected discourse connectives. The system has been evaluated manually by two evaluators for syntactic and semantic

*First two authors contributed equally to this work

[1]General scope - entire or almost entire paragraph, Medium scope - multiple clauses or sentences, and Specific scope - sentence or less

Proceedings of the Sixth Workshop on Innovative Use of NLP for Building Educational Applications, pages 1–9,
Portland, Oregon, 24 June 2011.

correctness of the generated questions. The overall system has been rated 6.3 out of 8 for QGSTEC development dataset and 5.8 out of 8 for Wikipedia dataset.

2 Overview

Question Generation involves two tasks, content selection (the text selected for question generation) and question formation (transformations on the content to get the question). Question formation further has the subtasks of (i) finding suitable question type (wh-word), (ii) auxiliary and main verb transformations and (iii) rearranging the phrases to get the final question.

There are 100 distinct types of discourse connectives listed in PDTB manual (PDTB, 2007). The most frequent connectives in PDTB are *and*, *or*, *but*, *when*, *because*, *since*, *also*, *although*, *for example*, *however* and *as a result*. In this paper, we provide analysis for four subordinating conjunctions, *since, when, because* and *although*, and three adverbials, *for example, for instance* and *as a result*. Connectives such as *and*, *or* and *also* showing *conjunction* relation have not been found to be good candidates for generating *wh*-type questions and hence have not been discussed in the paper. Leaving aside *and, or* and *also*, the selected connectives cover 52.05 per cent of the total number of the connectives in QGSTEC-2010 [2] dataset and 41.97 per cent in Wikipedia articles. Connective-wise coverage in both the datasets is shown in Table 1. Though *but* and *however* denoting *contrast* relation occur frequently in the data, it has not been feasible to generate wh-questions using them.

	QGSTEC-2010 Dev. Data		Wikipedia Dataset	
Connective	**count**	**%**	**count**	**%**
because	20	16.53	36	10.28
since	9	7.44	18	5.14
when	23	19.00	35	10.00
although	4	3.30	22	6.28
as a result	5	4.13	6	1.71
for example	2	1.65	30	8.28
for instance	0	0.00	1	0.28
Total	121	52.05	350	41.97

Table 1: Coverage of the selected discourse connectives in the data

The system goes through the entire document and identifies the sentences containing at least one of the seven discourse connectives. In our approach, suitable *content* for each discourse connective which is referred to as *target argument* is decided based on the properties of discourse connective. The system finds the question type on the basis of discourse relation shown by discourse connective.

[2] QGSTEC 2010 data set involves Wikipedia, Yahoo Answers and OpenLearn articles.

3 Discourse connectives for QG

In this section, we provide an analysis of discourse connectives with respect to their target arguments and the question types they take.

3.1 Question type identification

The sense of the discourse connective influences the question-type (*Q-type*). Since few discourse connectives such as *when, since* and *although* among the selected ones can show multiple senses, the task of sense disambiguation of the connectives is essential for finding the question type.

Since: The connective can show *temporal, causal* or *temporal + causal* relation in a sentence. Sentence exhibits *temporal* relation in presence of keywords like time(7 am), year (1989 or 1980s), start, begin, end, date(9/11), month (January) etc. If the relation is *temporal* then the question-type is *when* whereas in case of *causal* relation it would be *why*.

1. *Single wicket has rarely been played* ***since*** *limited overs cricket* ***began****.*
   Q-type: **when**

2. *Half-court games require less cardiovascular stamina ,* ***since*** *players need not run back and forth a full court.*
   Q-type: **why**

In examples 1 and 2, 1 is identified to show *temporal* relation because it has the keyword *began* whereas there is no keyword in the context of example 2 that gives the hint of *temporal* relation and so the relation here is identified as *causal*.

When: Consider the sentences with connective *when* in Figure 1. Although *when* shows multiple senses (*temporal, temporal+causal* and *conditional*), we can frame questions by a single question type, *when*. Given a new instance of the connective, finding the correct sense of *when*

Sentence:	The San–Francisco earthquake hit when resources in the field already were stetched. (Temporal)
Question:	When did San–Francisco earthquake hit ?
Sentence:	Venice's long decline started in the 15th century, when it first made an unsuccessful attempt to hold Thessalonica against the Ottomans (1423–1430). (Temporal + Causal)
Question:	When did Venice's long decline start in the 15th century ?
Sentence:	Earthquake mainly occurs when the different blocks or plates that make up the Earth's surface move relative to each other, causing distortion in the rock. (Conditional)
Question:	When do earthquake mainly occur ?

Figure 1: Questions for discourse connective ***when***

Discourse connectives	Sense	Q-type
because	causal	why
since	temporal causal	when why
when	causal + temporal temporal conditional	when
although	contrast concession	yes/ no
as a result	result	why
for example	instantiation	give an example where
for instance	instantiation	give an instance where

Table 2: Question type for discourse connectives

becomes unnecessary as a result of using discourse connectives.

Although: The connective can show *concession* or *contrast* discourse relations. It is difficult to frame a *wh*-question on *contrast* or *concession* relations. So, system generates a *yes/no* type question for *although*. Moreover, *yes/no* question-type adds to the variety of questions generated by the system.

3. *Greek colonies were not politically controlled by their founding cities , although they often retained religious and commercial links with them .*
   Q-type: **Yes/No**

A yes/no question could have been asked for connectives *but* and *however* denoting a *contrast* relation but it was not done to preserve the question-type variety in the final output of the QG system. Yes/no questions have been asked for occurrences of $although$ since they occur less frequently than *but* and $however$.

Identifying the question types for other selected discourse connectives is straight forward because they broadly show only one discourse relation (Pitler and Nenkova, 2009). Based on the relations exhibited by these connectives, Table 2 shows the question types for each discourse connective.

3.2 Target arguments for discourse connectives

A discourse connective can realize its two arguments, Arg1 and Arg2, structurally and anaphorically. Arg2 is always realized structurally whereas Arg1 can be either structural or anaphoric (PDTB, 2007; Prasad et al., 2010).

4. *[Arg1 Organisms inherit the characteristics of their parents]* ***because*** *[Arg2 the cells of the offspring contain copies of the genes in their parents' cells.](Intra-sentential connective because)*

5. *[Arg1* The scorers are directed by the hand signals of an umpire.*]* ***For example****, [Arg2 the umpire raises a forefinger to signal that the batsman is out (has been dismissed); he raises both arms above his head if the batsman has hit the ball for six runs.](Inter-sentential connective for example)*

Consider examples 4 and 5. In 4, Arg1 and Arg2 are the structural arguments of the connective *because* whereas in 5, Arg2 is the structural argument and Arg1 is realized anaphorically.

The task of content selection involves finding the *target argument* (either Arg1 or Arg2) of the discourse connective. Since both the arguments are potential candidates for QG, we analyze the data to identify which argument makes better content for each of the connectives. Our system selects one of the two arguments based on the properties of the discourse connectives. Table 3 shows the *target argu-*

Discourse connective	Target argument
because	Arg1
since	Arg1
when	Arg1
although	Arg1
as a result	Arg2
for example	Arg1
for instance	Arg1

Table 3: Target argument for discourse connectives

ment i.e. either Arg1 or Arg2, which is used as *content* for QG.

4 Target Argument Identification

Target argument for a discourse connective can be a clause(s) or a sentence(s). It could be one or more sentences in case of *inter-sentential*[3] discourse connectives, whereas one or more clauses in case of *intra-sentential*[4] connectives.

Discourse connectives *for example* and *for instance* can realize its Arg1 anywhere in the prior discourse (Elwell and Baldridge, 2008). So the system considers only those sentences in which the connectives occur at the beginning of the sentence and the immediate previous sentence is assumed to be the Arg1 of the connective (which is the *target argument* for QG).

In case of intra-sentential connectives (*because, since, although* and *when*) and *as a result* (*target argument* is Arg2 which would be a clause), identification of *target argument* is done in two steps. The system first locates the syntactic head or head verb of the *target argument* and then extracts it from the dependency tree of the sentence.

4.1 Locate syntactic head

Approach for locating the syntactic head of *target argument* is explained with the help of Figure 2 (generic dependency trees) and an example shown in Figure 3. Syntactic head of Arg2 is the first finite verb while percolating up in the dependency tree starting from the discourse connective. In case of intra-sentential connectives where Arg1 is the *target argument*, the system percolates up until it gets the second finite verb which is assumed to be target head

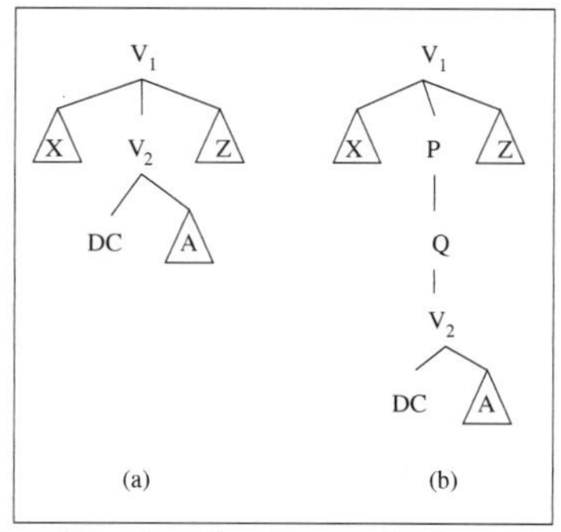

Figure 2: Head selection of the *target argument* for intra-sentential connectives (V_1, V_2: *finite verbs*; X,Z: *subtrees of* V_1; A: *subtree of* V_2; P,Q:*Not verbs*; DC:*discourse connective(child of* V_2*))*

of Arg1. Number of percolations entirely depend on structure and complexity of the sentence. Figure 2 shows two dependency trees (a) and (b). Starting from the discourse connective *DC* and percolating up, the system identifies that the head of Arg2 is V_2 and that of Arg1 is V_1.

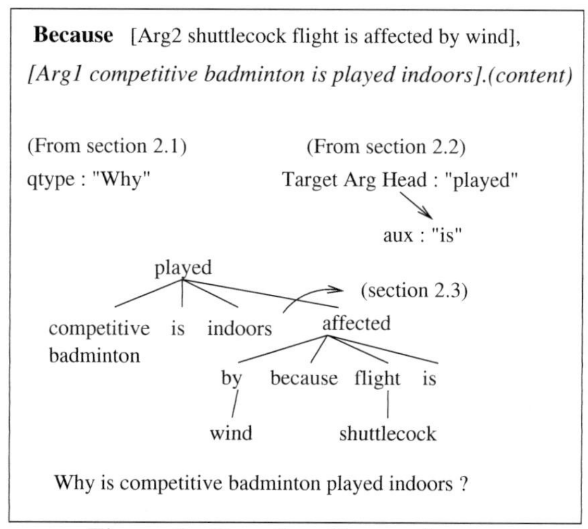

Figure 3: Question Generation process

Since the discourse connective in the example of Figure 3 is *because*, the *target argument* is Arg1 (from Table 2). By percolating up the tree starting from *because*, the head of Arg2 is *affected* and that of Arg1 is *played*. Once we locate the head of the *target argument*, we find the auxiliary as Mannem et al. (2010) does. For the example in Figure 3, the auxiliary for question generation is *is*.

4.2 Target Argument Extraction

The extraction of the *target argument* is done after identifying its syntactic head. For *as a result*, the *target argument*, Arg2, is the subtree with head

[3]Connectives that realize its Arg1 anaphorically and Arg2 structurally

[4]Connectives that realize both of its arguments structurally

Score	Description	Example
4	The question is grammatically correct and idiomatic/natural.	In which type of animals are phagocytes highly developed?
3	The question is grammatically correct but does not read as fluently as we would like.	In which type of animals are phagocytes, which are important throughout the animal kingdom, highly developed?
2	There are some grammatical errors in the question.	In which type of animals is phagocytes, which are important throughout the animal kingdom, highly developed?
1	The question is grammatically unacceptable.	On which type of animals is phagocytes, which are important throughout the animal kingdom, developed?

Table 4: Evaluation guidelines for syntactic correctness measure

as the head of the connective. For intra-sentential connectives, the *target argument*, Arg1, is the tree remaining after removing the subtree that contains Arg2.

In Figures 2 (a) and (b) both, a tree with head V_1 and its children, X and Z, is left after removing Arg2 from dependency trees, which is the *content* required for generating the question. Note that in the tree of Figure 2(b), the child P of the head verb V_1 is removed with its entire subtree that contains Arg2. Thus, subtree with head V_2 is the unwanted part for the tree in Figure 2(a) whereas subtree with head P is the unwanted part for the tree in Figure 2(b) when the target argument is Arg1.

In Figure 3, after removing the unwanted argument Arg2 (subtree with head *affected*), the system gets *competitive badminton is played indoors* which is the required clause (*content*) for question generation. The next section describes how the *content* is transformed into a question.

5 Syntactic Transformations and Question Generation

The syntactic transformations used in this work are similar to those by Mannem et al. (2010). At this stage, the system has the question type, auxiliary and the *content*. The following set of transformations are applied on the *content* to get the final question. (1) If the auxiliary is present in the sentence itself then it is moved to the beginning of the sentence; otherwise auxiliary is added at the beginning of the sentence. (2) If a wh-question is to be formed, the question word is added just before the auxiliary. In case of Yes/No questions, the question starts with the auxiliary itself as no question word is needed. (3) A question-mark(*?*) is added at the end to complete the question.

Consider the example in Figure 3. Here the *content* is *competitive badminton is played indoors*. Applying the transformations, the auxiliary is first moved at the start of the sentence to get *is competitive badminton played indoors*. Then the question type *Why* is added just before the auxiliary *is*, and a question-mark is added at the end to get the final question, *Why is competitive badminton played indoors ?*

Scope: In QGSTEC 2010 the question had to be assigned a scope, specific, medium or general. The scope is defined as: *general* - entire input paragraph, *medium* - one or more clauses or sentences and *specific* - phrase or less. Questions generated using discourse connectives are usually of the scope specific or medium. Mannem et al. (2010) assigned medium scope to the questions generated using the semantic roles such as ARGM-DIS (result), ARGM-CAU (causal) and ARGM-PNC (purpose) given by the SRL. However, most of the times, the scope of the answer to these questions is just a clause or a sentence and should have been assigned specific scope instead of medium.

6 Evaluation and Results

Automatic evaluation of any natural language generated text is difficult. So, our system is evaluated manually. The evaluation was performed by two graduate students with good English proficiency. Evaluators were asked to rate the questions on the scale of 1 to 4 (4 being the best score) on syntactic and semantic correctness (Evalguide, 2010) of the question and an overall rating on the scale of 8 (4+4) is assigned to each question.

The syntactic correctness is rated to ensure that the system can generate grammatical output. In addition, those questions which read fluently are given greater score. The syntactic correctness and fluency is evaluated using the following scores: 4 - gram-

Discourse Connective	Example
because	One-handed backhand players move to the net with greater ease than two-handed players **because** the shot permits greater forward momentum and has greater similarities in muscle memory to the preferred type of backhand volley (one-handed, for greater reach). *Why do one-handed backhand players move to the net with greater ease than two-handed players ?* (**Causal**)
since	Half-court games require less cardiovascular stamina, **since** players need not run back and forth a full court. *Why do half-court games require less cardiovascular stamina ?* (**Causal**) Single wicket has rarely been played **since** limited overs cricket began. *Since when has single wicket rarely been played ?* (**Temporal**)
when	A one-point shot can be earned **when** shooting from the foul line after a foul is made. *When can a one-point shot be earned ?* (**Conditional**)
although	A bowler cannot bowl two successive overs, **although** a bowler can bowl unchanged at end for several overs. *Can a bowler bowl unchanged at the same end for several overs?* (**Contrast, concession**)
as a result	In the United States sleep deprivation is common with students because almost all schools begin early in the morning and many of these students either choose to stay up awake late into the night or cannot do otherwise due to delayed sleep phase syndrome. **As a result**, students that should be getting between 8.5 and 9.25 hours of sleep are getting only 7 hours. *Why are students that should be getting between 8.5 and 9.25 hours of sleep getting only 7 hours?* (**Result**) **As a result** of studies showing the effects of sleep-deprivation on grades , and the different sleep patterns for teenagers , a school in New Zealand , changed its start time to 10:30, in 2006, to allow students to keep to a schedule that allowed more sleep. *Why did a school in New Zealand change its start time ?* (**Result**)
for example	Slicing also causes the shuttlecock to travel much slower than the arm movement suggests. **For example**, a good cross court sliced drop shot will use a hitting action that suggests a straight clear or smash, deceiving the opponent about both the power and direction of the shuttlecock. *Give an example where slicing also causes the shuttlecock to travel much slower than the arm movement suggests.* (**Instantiation**)
for instance	If the team that bats last scores enough runs to win, it is said to have "won by n wickets", where n is the number of wickets left to fall. **For instance** a team that passes its opponents' score having only lost six wickets would have won "by four wickets". *Give an instance where if the team that bats last scores enough runs to win, it is said to have "won by n wickets",where n is the number of wickets left to fall.* (**Instantiation**)

Table 5: Examples

matically correct and idiomatic/natural, 3 - grammatically correct, 2 - some grammar problems, 1 - grammatically unacceptable. Table 4 shows syntactic correctness measure with examples.

The semantic correctness is evaluated using the following scores: 4 - semantically correct and idiomatic/natural, 3 - semantically correct and close to the text or other questions, 2 - some semantic issues, 1 - semantically unacceptable.

Table 5 shows questions generated by the system for each connective. The results of our system on QGSTEC-2010 development dataset are shown in Table 6. The overall system is rated 6.3 out of 8 on this dataset and the total number of questions generated for this dataset is 61. The instances of the connectives were less in the QGSTEC-2010 development dataset. So, the system is further tested on five Wikipedia articles (football, cricket, basketball, badminton and tennis) for effective evaluation. Results on this dataset are presented in Table 7. Overall rating of the system is 5.8 out of 8 for this dataset and 150 are the total number of questions generated for this dataset. The ratings presented in the Tables 6 and 7 are the average of the ratings given by both the evaluators. The inter-evaluator agreement (Cohen's kappa coefficient) for the QGSTEC-2010 development dataset for syntactic correctness measure is 0.6 and is 0.5 for semantic correctness measure, and in case of Wikipedia articles the agreement is 0.7 and 0.6 for syntactic and semantic correctness measures respectively.

Discourse connective	No. of questions	Syntactic Correctness(4)	Semantic Correctness(4)	Overall Rating(8)
because	20	3.6	3.6	7.2
since	9	3.8	3.2	7
when	23	2.3	2.2	4.5
although	4	4	3.8	7.8
as a result	5	4	4	8
Overall	61	3.2	3.1	6.3

Table 6: Results on QGSTEC-2010 development dataset

Discourse connective	No. of questions	Syntactic Correctness(4)	Semantic Correctness(4)	Overall Rating(8)
because	36	3.3	3.2	6.5
since	18	3.1	3	6.1
when	35	2.4	2.0	4.4
although	22	3.1	2.8	5.9
as a result	6	3.6	3.2	6.8
for example	16	3.1	2.9	6.0
for instance	2	4	3	7
Overall	135	3.0	2.8	5.8

Table 7: Results on the Wikipedia data(cricket, football, basketball, badminton, tennis)

On analyzing the data, we found that the Wikipedia articles have more complex sentences (with unusual structure as well as more number of clauses) than QGSTEC-2010 development dataset. As a result, the system's performance consistently drops for all the connectives in case of Wikipedia dataset.

No comparable evaluation was done as none of the earlier works in QG exploited the discourse connectives in text to generate questions.

7 Error Analysis

An error analysis was carried out on the system's output and the four most frequent types of errors are discussed in this section.

7.1 Coreference resolution

The system doesn't handle coreference resolution and as a result of this, many questions have been rated low for semantic correctness by the evaluators. Greater the number of pronouns in the question, lesser is the semantic rating of the question.

6. *They grow in height* ***when*** *they reach shallower water, in a wave shoaling process.*
   Question: *When do* ***they*** *grow in height?*

Although the above example 6 is syntactically correct, such questions are rated semantically low because the context is not sufficient to answer the question due to the pronouns in it. 13.54% of the generated questions on the Wikipedia dataset have pronouns without their antecedents, making the questions semantically insufficient.

7.2 Parsing Errors

Sometimes the parser fails to give a correct parse for the sentences with complex structure. In such cases, the system generates a question that is unacceptable. Consider the examples below.

7. *In a family who know that both parents are carriers of CF ,* ***either because*** *they already have a CF child* ***or as a result*** *of carrier testing , PND allows the conversion of a probable risk of the disease affecting an unborn child to nearer a certainty that it will or will not be affected.*
   Question: *Why do in a family who know that both parents are carriers of CF , either or will not be affected ?*

In example 7 above, the sentence has a complex structure containing paired connective, either-or, where the argument of *either* has *because* and that of *or* has *as a result* in it. Here the question is formed using *because* which is correct neither syntactically nor semantically due to the complex nature of the sentence. 9.38% sentences in the datasets are complex with either three or more discourse connectives.

7.3 Errors due to the inter-sentential connectives

For inter-sentential connectives, system considers only those sentences in which the connectives occur at the beginning of the sentence and the immediate previous sentence is assumed to be the Arg1 of the connective (which is the target argument for QG). But this assumption is not always true. Of the total number of instances of these connectives, 52.94% (for Wikipedia dataset) connectives occur at the beginning of the sentences. Consider the paragraph below.

8. *A game point occurs in tennis whenever the*

player who is in the lead in the game needs only one more point to win the game. The terminology is extended to sets (set point), matches (match point), and even championships (championship point). *For example, if the player who is serving has a score of 40-love, the player has a triple game point (triple set point, etc.) as the player has three consecutive chances to win the game.*

Here in example 8, the third sentence in which the example is specified is related to the first sentence but not the immediately previous sentence. For these connectives, the assumption that immediate previous sentence is Arg1 is false 14.29% of the times.

7.4 Fluency issues

The system does not handle the removal of predicative adjuncts. So the questions with optional phrases in it are rated low for syntactic correctness measure.

8 Conclusions and Future Work

Our QG system generates questions using discourse connectives for different question types. In this work, we present an end-to-end system that takes a document as input and outputs all the questions for selected discourse connectives. The system has been evaluated for syntactic and semantic soundness of the question by two evaluators. We have shown that some specific discourse relations are important such as *causal*, *temporal* and *result* than others from the QG point of view. This work also shows that discourse connectives are good enough for QG and that there is no need for full fledged discourse parsing. In the near future, we plan to implement coreference resolution and sentences with more than two connectives. We aim to improve the system with respect to the sentence complexity and also incorporate other discourse connectives.

Acknowledgements

We would like to thank Suman Yelati and Sudheer Kolachina from LTRC, IIIT-Hyderabad for their helpful discussions and pointers during the course of this work. Thanks also to the anonymous reviewers for useful feedback.

References

2010 *Question generation shared task and evaluation challenge*, http://questiongeneration.org/QG2010

Andrea Varga and Le An Ha 2010 *WLV: A Question Generation System for the QGSTEC 2010 Task B*, Proceedings of QG2010: The Third Workshop on Question Generation

Santanu Paland Tapabrata Mondal, Partha Pakray, Dipankar Das and Sivaji Bandyopadhyay 2010 *QGSTEC System Description JUQGG: A Rule based approach* , Proceedings of QG2010: The Third Workshop on Question Generation

Husam Ali, Yllias Chali, and Sadid A. Hasan 2010 *Automation of Question Generation From Sentences*, Proceedings of QG2010: The Third Workshop on Question Generation

Eriks Sneiders 2002. *Automated question answering using question templates that cover the conceptual model of the database.* In Proceedings of the 6th International Conference on Applications of Natural Language to Information Systems (pp. 235-239).

Michael Heilman, Noah A. Smith. 2009 *Question generation via overgenerating transformations and ranking* Technical Report CMU-LTI-09-013, Carnegie Mellon University.

Prashanth Mannem, Rashmi Prasad and Aravind Joshi 2010 *Question Generation from Paragraphs at UPenn: QGSTEC System Discription*, Proceedings of QG2010: The Third Workshop on Question Generation

Rashmi Prasad and Aravind Joshi 2008 *A Discourse-based Approach to Generating why-Questions from text*, Proceedings of the Workshop on the Question Generation Shared Task and Evaluation Challenge Arlington, VA, September 2008

Emily Pitler, Annie Louis and Ani Nenkova 2009 *Automatic sense prediction for implicit discourse relations in text* , ACL '09 Proceedings of the Joint Conference of the 47th Annual Meeting of the ACL and the 4th International Joint Conference on Natural Language Processing of the AFNLP: Volume 2 - Volume 2

2007 *PDTB 2.0 Annotation Manual*, http://www.seas.upenn.edu/ pdtb/PDTBAPI/pdtb-annotation-manual.pdf

Emily Pitler and Ani Nenkova 2009 *Using syntax to Disambiguate Explicit Discourse Connectives in Text*, ACLShort '09 Proceedings of the ACL-IJCNLP 2009 Conference Short Papers

Rashmi Prasad and Aravind Joshi and Bonnie Webber 2010 *Exploiting Scope for Shallow discourse Parsing*, LREC2010

Robert Elwell and Jason Baldridge 2008 *Discourse connective argument identification with connective specific rankers*, In Proceedings of ICSC-2008

Evaluation guidelines 2010 *In QGSTEC-2010 Task B evaluation guidelines*, http://www.question generation.org/QGSTEC2010/ uploads/QG-fromSentences-v2.doc

Understanding Differences in Perceived Peer-Review Helpfulness using Natural Language Processing

Wenting Xiong
University of Pittsburgh
Department of Computer Science
Pittsburgh, PA, 15260
wex12@cs.pitt.edu

Diane Litman
University of Pittsburgh
Department of Computer Science &
Learning Research and Development Center
Pittsburgh, PA, 15260
litman@cs.pitt.edu

Abstract

Identifying peer-review helpfulness is an important task for improving the quality of feedback received by students, as well as for helping students write better reviews. As we tailor standard product review analysis techniques to our peer-review domain, we notice that peer-review helpfulness differs not only between students and experts but also between types of experts. In this paper, we investigate how different types of perceived helpfulness might influence the utility of features for automatic prediction. Our feature selection results show that certain low-level linguistic features are more useful for predicting student perceived helpfulness, while high-level cognitive constructs are more effective in modeling experts' perceived helpfulness.

1 Introduction

Peer review of writing is a commonly recommended technique to include in good writing instruction. It not only provides more feedback compared to what students might get from their instructors, but also provides opportunities for students to practice writing helpful reviews. While existing web-based peer-review systems facilitate peer review from the logistic aspect (e.g. collecting papers from authors, assigning reviewers, and sending reviews back), there still remains the problem that the quality of peer reviews varies, and potentially good feedback is not written in a helpful way. To address this issue, we propose to add a peer-review helpfulness model to current peer-review systems, to automatically predict peer-review helpfulness based on features mined from textual reviews using Natural Language Processing (NLP) techniques. Such an intelligent component could enable peer-review systems to 1) control the quality of peer reviews that are sent back to authors, so authors can focus on the helpful ones; and 2) provide feedback to reviewers with respect to their reviewing performance, so students can learn to write better reviews.

In our prior work (Xiong and Litman, 2011), we examined whether techniques used for predicting the helpfulness of product reviews (Kim et al., 2006) could be tailored to our peer-review domain, where the definition of helpfulness is largely influenced by the educational context of peer review. While previously we used the average of two expert-provided ratings as our gold standard of peer-review helpfulness[1], there are other types of helpfulness rating (e.g. author perceived helpfulness) that could be the gold standard, and that could potentially impact the features used to build the helpfulness model. In fact, we observe that peer-review helpfulness seems to differ not only between students and experts (example 1), but also between types of experts (example 2).

In the following examples, students judge helpfulness with discrete ratings from one to seven; experts judge it using a one to five scale. Higher ratings on both scales correspond to the most helpful reviews.

Example 1:

Student rating = 7, Average expert rating = 2 *The*

[1] Averaged ratings are considered more reliable since they are less noisy.

Proceedings of the Sixth Workshop on Innovative Use of NLP for Building Educational Applications, pages 10–19,
Portland, Oregon, 24 June 2011.

author also has great logic in this paper. How can we consider the United States a great democracy when everyone is not treated equal. All of the main points were indeed supported in this piece.

Student rating = 3, Average expert rating = 5 *I thought there were some good opportunities to provide further data to strengthen your argument. For example the statement "These methods of intimidation, and the lack of military force offered by the government to stop the KKK, led to the rescinding of African American democracy." Maybe here include data about how . . . (126 words)*

Example 2:

Writing-expert rating = 2, Content-expert rating = 5 *Your over all arguements were organized in some order but was unclear due to the lack of thesis in the paper. Inside each arguement, there was no order to the ideas presented, they went back and forth between ideas. There was good support to the arguements but yet some of it didnt not fit your arguement.*

Writing-expert rating = 5, Content-expert rating = 2 *First off, it seems that you have difficulty writing transitions between paragraphs. It seems that you end your paragraphs with the main idea of each paragraph. That being said, . . . (173 words) As a final comment, try to continually move your paper, that is, have in your mind a logical flow with every paragraph having a purpose.*

To better understand such differences and investigate their impact on automatically assessing peer-review helpfulness, in this paper, we compare helpfulness predictions using our many different possibilities for gold standard ratings. In particular, we compare the predictive ability of features across gold standard ratings by examining the most useful features and feature ranks using standard feature selection techniques. We show that paper ratings and lexicon categories that suggest clear transitions and opinions are most useful in predicting helpfulness as perceived by **students**, while review length is generally effective in predicting **expert** helpfulness. While the presence of praise and summary comments are more effective in modeling **writing-expert** helpfulness, providing solutions is more useful in predicting **content-expert** helpfulness.

2 Related Work

To our knowledge, no prior work on peer review from the NLP community has attempted to automatically predict peer-review helpfulness. Instead, the NLP community has focused on issues such as highlighting key sentences in papers (Sandor and Vorndran, 2009), detecting important feedback features in reviews (Cho, 2008; Xiong and Litman, 2010), and adapting peer-review assignment (Garcia, 2010). However, many NLP studies have been done on the helpfulness of other types of reviews, such as product reviews (Kim et al., 2006; Ghose and Ipeirotis, 2010), movie reviews (Liu et al., 2008), book reviews (Tsur and Rappoport, 2009), etc. Kim et al. (2006) used regression to predict the helpfulness ranking of product reviews based on various classes of linguistic features. Ghose and Ipeirotis (2010) further examined the socio-economic impact of product reviews using a similar approach and suggested the usefulness of subjectivity analysis. Another study (Liu et al., 2008) of movie reviews showed that helpfulness depends on reviewers' expertise, their writing style, and the timeliness of the review. Tsur and Rappoport (2009) proposed RevRank to select the most helpful book reviews in an unsupervised fashion based on review lexicons.

To tailor the utility of this prior work on helpfulness prediction to educational peer reviews, we will draw upon research on peer review in cognitive science. One empirical study of the nature of peer-review feedback (Nelson and Schunn, 2009) found that feedback implementation likelihood is significantly correlated with five feedback features. Of these features, *problem localization* —pinpointing the source of the problem and/or solution in the original paper— and *solution* —providing a solution to the observed problem— were found to be most important. Researchers (Cho, 2008; Xiong and Litman, 2010) have already shown that some of these constructs can be automatically learned from textual input using Machine Learning and NLP techniques. In addition to investigating what properties of textual comments make peer-review helpful, researchers also examined how the comments produced by students versus by different types of experts differ (Patchan et al., 2009). Though focusing on differences between what students and experts produce, such work sheds light on our study of students' and experts' helpfulness ratings of the same student comments (i.e. what students and experts value).

Our work in peer-review helpfulness prediction integrates the NLP techniques and cognitive-science approaches mentioned above. We will particularly focus on examining the utility of features motivated by related work from both areas, with respect to different types of gold standard ratings of peer-review helpfulness for automatic prediction.

3 Data

In this study, we use a previously annotated peer-review corpus (Nelson and Schunn, 2009; Patchan et al., 2009) that was collected in an introductory college history class using the freely available web-based peer-review SWoRD (Scaffolded Writing and Rewriting in the Discipline) system (Cho and Schunn, 2007). The corpus consists of 16 papers (about six pages each) and 189 reviews (varying from twenty words to about two hundred words) accompanied by numeric ratings of the papers. Each review was manually segmented into idea units (defined as contiguous feedback referring to a single topic) (Nelson and Schunn, 2009), and these idea units were then annotated by two independent annotators for various coding categories, such as feedback type (*praise, problem, and summary*), *problem localization*, *solution*, etc. For example, the second case in Example 1, which only has one idea unit, was annotated as $feedbackType = problem$, $problemlocalization = True$, and $solution = True$. The agreement (Kappa) between the two annotators is 0.92 for FeedbackType, 0.69 for localization, and 0.89 for solution.[2]

Our corpus also contains author provided back evaluations. At the end of the peer-review assignment, students were asked to provide back evaluation on each review that they received by rating review helpfulness using a discrete scale from one to seven. After the corpus was collected, one writing expert and one content expert were also asked to rate review helpfulness with a slightly different scale from one to five. For our study, we will also compute the average ratings given by the two experts, yielding four types of possible gold-standard ratings of peer-review helpfulness for each review. Figure 1 shows the rating distribution of each type. Interestingly, we observed that expert ratings roughly follow a normal distribution, while students are more likely to give higher ratings (as illustrated in Figure 1).

4 Features

Our features are motivated by the prior work introduced in Section 2, in particular, NLP work on predicting product-review helpfulness (Kim et al., 2006), as well as work on automatically learning cognitive-science constructs (Nelson and Schunn, 2009) using NLP (Cho, 2008; Xiong and Litman, 2010). The complete list of features is shown in Table 3 and described below. The **computational linguistic features** are automatically extracted based on the output of syntactic analysis of reviews and papers[3]. These features represent structural, lexical, syntactic and semantic information of the textual content, and also include information for identifying certain important cognitive constructs:

- **Structural features** consider the general structure of reviews, which includes review length in terms of tokens (*reviewLength*), number of sentences (*sentNum*), the average sentence length (*sentLengthAve*), percentage of sentences that end with question marks (*question%*), and number of exclamatory sentences (*exclams*).

- **Lexical features** are counts of ten lexical categories (Table 1), where the categories were learned in a semi-supervised way from review lexicons in a pilot study. We first manually created a list of words that were specified as signal words for annotating *feedbackType* and *problem localization* in the coding manual; then we supplemented the list with words selected by a decision tree model learned using a Bag-of-Words representation of the peer reviews.

[2]For Kappa value interpretation, Landis and Koch (1977) propose the following agreement standard: 0.21-0.40 = "Fair"; 0.41-0.60 = "Moderate"; 0.61-0.80 = "Substantial"; 0.81-1.00 = "Almost Perfect". Thus, while localization signals are more difficult to annotate, the inter-annotator agreement is still substantial.

[3]We used MSTParser (McDonald et al., 2005) for syntactic analysis.

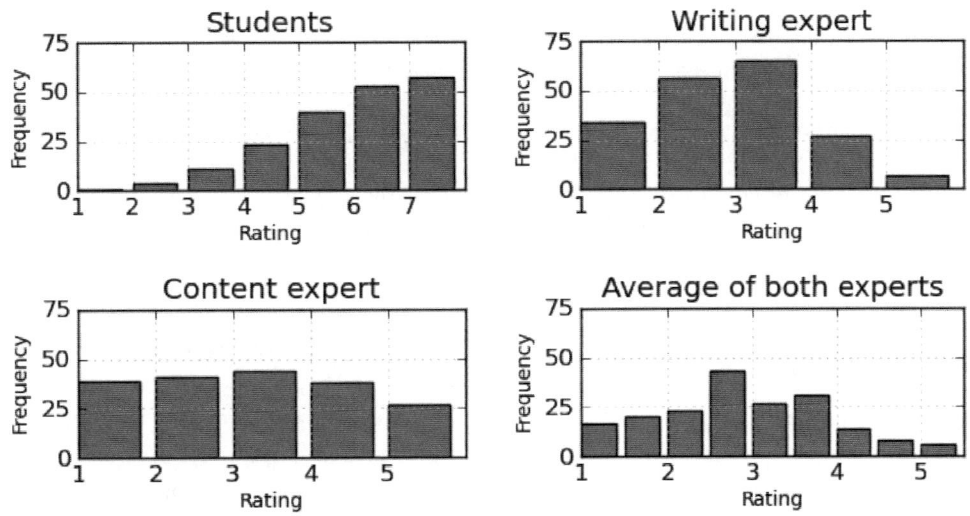

Figure 1: Distribution of peer-review helpfulness when rated by students and experts

Tag	Meaning	Word list
SUG	suggestion	should, must, might, could, need, needs, maybe, try, revision, want
LOC	location	page, paragraph, sentence
ERR	problem	error, mistakes, typo, problem, difficulties, conclusion
IDE	idea verb	consider, mention
LNK	transition	however, but
NEG	negative words	fail, hard, difficult, bad, short, little, bit, poor, few, unclear, only, more
POS	positive words	great, good, well, clearly, easily, effective, effectively, helpful, very
SUM	summarization	main, overall, also, how, job
NOT	negation	not, doesn't, don't
SOL	solution	revision specify correction

Table 1: Ten lexical categories

Compared with commonly used lexical unigrams and bigrams (Kim et al., 2006), these lexical categories are equally useful in modeling peer-review helpfulness, and significantly reduce the feature space.[4]

- **Syntactic features** mainly focus on nouns and verbs, and include percentage of tokens that are nouns, verbs, verbs conjugated in the first person (*1stPVerb%*), adjectives/adverbs, and open classes, respectively.

- **Semantic features** capture two important peer-review properties: their relevance to the main topics in students' papers, and their opinion sentiment polarities. Kim et al. (2006) extracted product property keywords from external resources based on their hypothesis that helpful product reviews refer frequently to certain product properties. Similarly, we hypothesize that helpful peer reviews are closely related to domain topics that are shared by all students papers in an assignment. Our domain topic set contains 288 words extracted from the collection of student papers using topic-lexicon extraction software[5]; our feature (*domainWord*)

[4]Lexical categories help avoid the risk of over-fitting, given only 189 peer reviews in our case compared to more than ten thousand Amazon.com reviews used for predicting product review helpfulness (Kim et al., 2006).

[5]The software extracts topic words based on topic signatures (Lin and Hovy, 2000), and was kindly provided by Annie Louis.

Feature	Description
regTag%	The percentage of problems in reviews that could be matched with a localization pattern.
soDomain%	The percentage of sentences where any domain word appears between the subject and the object.
dDeterminer	The number of demonstrative determiners.
windowSize	For each review sentence, we search for the most likely referred window of words in the related paper, and windowSize is the average number of words of all windows.

Table 2: Localization features

counts how many words of a given review belong to the extracted set. For sentiment polarities, we extract positive and negative sentiment words from the General Inquirer Dictionaries [6], and count their appearance in reviews in terms of their sentiment polarity (*posWord, negWord*).

- **Localization features** are motivated by linguistic features that are used for automatically predicting problem localization (an important cognitive construct for feedback understanding and implementation) (Nelson and Schunn, 2009), and are presented in Table 2. To illustrate how these features are computed, consider the following critique:

  The section of the essay on African Americans needs more careful attention to the timing and reasons for the federal governments decision to stop protecting African American civil and political rights.

  The review has only one sentence, in which one regular expression is matched with "the section of" thus $regTag\% = 1$; no demonstrative determiner, thus $dDeterminer = 0$; "African" and "Americans" are domain words appearing between the subject "section" and the object "attention", so *soDomain* is true for this sentence and thus $soDomain\% = 1$ for the given review.

In addition to the low-level linguistic features presented above, we also examined **non-linguistic features** that are derived from the ratings and prior manual annotations of the corpus, described in Section 3.

- **Cognitive-science features** are motivated by an empirical study (Nelson and Schunn, 2009) which suggests significant correlation between certain cognitive constructs (e.g. *feedbackType, problem localization, solution*) and review implementation likelihood. Intuitively, helpful reviews are more likely to get implemented, thus we introduced these features to capture desirable high-level characteristics of peer reviews. Note that in our corpus these cognitive constructs are manually coded at the idea-unit level (Nelson and Schunn, 2009), however, peer-review helpfulness is rated at the review level.[7] Our cognitive-science features aggregate the annotations up to the review-level by reporting the percentage of idea-units in a review that exhibit each characteristic: the distribution of review types (*praise%, problem%, summary%*), the percentage of problem-localized critiques (*localization%*), as well as the percentage of solution-provided ones (*solution%*).

- **Social-science features** introduce elements reflecting interactions between students in a peer-review assignment. As suggested in related work on product review helpfulness (Kim et al., 2006; Danescu-Niculescu-Mizil et al., 2009), some social dimensions (e.g. customer opinion on related product quality) are of great influence in the perceived helpfulness of product reviews. Similarly, in our case, we introduced related paper ratings (*pRating*) — to consider whether and how helpfulness ratings are affected by the rating that the paper receives[8] — and the absolute difference between the rat-

[6] http://www.wjh.harvard.edu/ inquirer/homecat.htm

[7] Details of different granularity levels of annotation can be found in (Nelson and Schunn, 2009).

[8] That is, to examine whether students give higher ratings to peers who gave them higher paper ratings in the first place.

ing and the average score given by all reviewers (*pRatingDiff*) — to measure the variation in perceived helpfulness of a given review.

5 Experiments

We take a machine learning approach to model different types of perceived helpfulness (student helpfulness, writing-expert helpfulness, content-expert helpfulness, average-expert helpfulness) based on combinations of linguistic and non-linguistic features extracted from our peer-review corpus. Then we compare the different helpfulness types in terms of the predictive power of features used in their corresponding models. For comparison purpose, we consider the linguistic and non-linguistic features both separately and in combination, which generates three set of features: 1) linguistic features, 2) non-linguistic features, and 3) all features. For each set of features, we train four models, each corresponding to a different kind of helpfulness rating. For each learning task (three by four), we use two standard feature selection algorithms to find the most useful features based on 10-fold cross validation. First, we perform Linear Regression with Greedy Stepwise search (stepwise LR) to select the most useful features when testing in each of the ten folds, and count how many times each features is selected in the ten trials. Second, we use Relief Feature Evaluation[9] with Ranker (Relief) (Kira and Rendell, 1992; Witten and Frank, 2005) to rank all used features based on their average merits (the ability of the given feature to differentiate between two example pairs) of ten trials.[10]

Although both methods are supervised, the wrapper is "more aggressive" because its feature evaluation is based on the performance of the regression model and thus the resulting feature set is tailored to the learning algorithm. In contrast, Relief does not optimize feature sets directly for classifier performance, thus it takes into account class information in a "less aggressive" manner than the Wrapper method. We use both methods in our experiment to provide complementary perspectives. While the former can directly tell us what features are most useful, the latter gives feature ranks which provide more detailed information about differences between features. To compare the feature selection results, we examine the four kind of helpfulness models for each of the three feature sets separately, as presented below. Note that the focus of this paper is comparing feature utilities in different helpfulness models rather than predicting those types of helpfulness ratings. (Details of how the average-expert model performs can be found in our prior work (Xiong and Litman, 2011).)

5.1 Feature Selection of Linguistic Features

Table 4 presents the feature selection results of computational linguistic features used in modeling the four different types of peer-review helpfulness. The first row lists the four sources of helpfulness ratings, and each column represents a corresponding model. The second row presents the most useful features in each model selected by stepwise LR, where "# of folds" refers to the number of trials in which the given feature appears in the resulting feature set during the 10-fold cross validation. Here we only report features that are selected by no less than five folds (half the time). The third row presents feature ranks computed using Relief, where we only report the top six features due to the space limit. Features are ordered in descending ranks, and the average merit and its standard deviation is reported for each one of the features.

The selection result of stepwise LR shows that reviewLength is most useful for predicting expert helpfulness in general, while specific lexicon categories (i.e. *LNK*, and *NOT*) and positive words (*posWord*) are more useful in predicting student helpfulness. When looking at the ranking result, we observe that transition cues (*LNK*) and *posWord* are also ranked high in the student-helpfulness model, although *question%* and suggestion words (*SUG*) are ranked highest. For expert-helpfulness models, *windowSize* and *posWord*, which are not listed in the selected features for expert helpfulness (although they are selected for students), are actually ranked high for modeling average-expert helpfulness. While exclamatory sentence number (*exclams*) and summarization cues are ranked top for the writing expert,

[9]Relief evaluates the worth of an attribute by repeatedly sampling an instance and changing the value of the given attribute based on the nearest instance of the same and different class.

[10]Both algorithms are provided by Weka (http://www.cs.waikato.ac.nz/ml/weka/).

Type	Features
Structural	reviewLength, sentNum, sentLengthAve, question%, exclams
Lexical	SUG, LOC, ERR, IDE, LNK, NEG, POS, SUM, NOT, SOL (Table 1)
Syntactic	noun%, verb%, 1stPVerb%, adj+adv%, opClass%
Semantic	domainWord, posWord, negWord
Localization	regTag%, soDomain%, dDeterminer, windowSize (Table 2)
Cognitive-science	praise%, problem%, summary%, localization%, solution%
Social-science	pRating, pRatingDiff

Table 3: Summary of features

Source	Students		Writing expert		Content expert		Expert average	
	Feature	# of folds	Feature	# of folds	Feature	# of folds	Feature	# of folds
Stepwise LR	LNK	9	reviewLength	8	reviewLength	10	reviewLength	10
	posWord	8			question%	6	sentNum	8
	NOT	6			sentNum	5	question%	8
	windowSize	6			1stPVerb%	5		
					POS	5		
	Feature	Merit	Feature	Merit	Feature	Merit	Feature	Merit
Relief	question%	$.019 \pm .002$	exclams	$.010 \pm .003$	question%	$.010 \pm .004$	exclams	$.010 \pm .003$
	SUG	$.015 \pm .003$	SUM	$.008 \pm .004$	ERR	$.009 \pm .003$	question%	$.011 \pm .004$
	LNK	$.014 \pm .003$	NEG	$.006 \pm .004$	SUG	$.009 \pm .004$	windowSize	$.008 \pm .002$
	sentLengthAve	$.012 \pm .003$	negWord	$.005 \pm .002$	posWord	$.007 \pm .002$	posWord	$.006 \pm .002$
	POS	$.011 \pm .002$	windowSize	$.004 \pm .002$	exclams	$.006 \pm .001$	reviewLength	$.004 \pm .001$
	posWord	$.010 \pm .001$	sentNum	$.003 \pm .001$	1stPVerb%	$.007 \pm .004$	sentLengthAve	$.004 \pm .001$

Table 4: Feature selection based on linguistic features

the percentage of questions (*question%*) and error cues (*ERR*) are ranked top for the content-expert. In addition, the percentage of words that are verbs conjugated in the first person (*1stPVerb%*) is both selected and ranked high in the content-expert helpfulness model. Out of the four models, *SUG* are ranked high for predicting both students and content-expert helpfulness. These observations indicate that both students and experts value questions (*question%*) and suggestions (*SUG*) in reviews, and students particularly favor clear signs of logic flow in review arguments (*LNK*), positive words (*posWord*), as well as reference of their paper content which provides explicit context information (*windowSize*). In addition, experts in general prefer longer reviews (*reviewLength*), and the writing expert thinks clear summary signs (*SUM*) are important indicators of helpful peer reviews.

5.2 Feature Selection of non-Linguistic Features

When switching to the high-level non-linguistic features (Table 5), we find that *solution%* is always selected (in all ten trials) as a most useful feature for predicting all four kind of helpfulness, and is also ranked high for content-expert and student helpfulness. Especially for the content-expert, *solution%* has a much higher merit (0.013) compared to all the other features ($\leq$ 0.03). This agrees with our observation in section 5.1 that SUG are ranked high in both cases. *localization%* is selected as one of the most useful features in the content-expert helpfulness model, which is also ranked top in the student model (though not selected frequently by stepwise LR). For modeling the writing-expert helpfulness, praise (*praise%*) is more important than problem and summary, and the paper rating (*pRating*) loses its predictive power compared to how it works in the other models. In contrast, *pRating* is both selected and ranked high for predicting students' perceived helpfulness.

5.3 Feature Selection of All Features

When considering all features together as reported in Table 6, *pRating* is only selected in the student-helpfulness model, and still remains to be the most important feature for predicting students' perceived helpfulness. As for experts, the structural feature

Source	Students		Writing expert		Content expert		Expert average	
	Feature	# of folds	Feature	# of folds	Feature	# of folds	Feature	# of folds
Stepwise LR	pRating	10	solution%	10	localization%	10	solution%	10
	solution%	10			solution%	10	pRating	10
	problem%	9			pRating	10	localization%	9
	Feature	Merit	Feature	Merit	Feature	Merit	Feature	Merit
Relief	localization%	.012 ± .003	praise%	.008 ± .002	solution%	.013 ± .005	problem%	.004 ± .002
	pRatingDiff	.010 ± .002	problem%	.007 ± .002	pRating	.003 ± .002	localization%	.004 ± .006
	pRating	.007 ± .002	summary%	.001 ± .004	praise%	.001 ± .002	praise%	.003 ± .003
	solution%	.006 ± .005	localization%	.001 ± .005	localization%	.001 ± .004	solution%	.002 ± .004
	problem%	.004 ± .002	pRating	.004 ± .004	problem%	.001 ± .002	pRating	.005 ± .003
	summary%	.004 ± .003	pRatingDiff	.007 ± .002	pRating	.002 ± .003	pRatingDiff	.006 ± .005

Table 5: Feature selection based on non-linguistic features

Source	Students		Writing expert		Content expert		Expert average	
	Feature	# of folds	Feature	# of folds	Feature	# of folds	Feature	# of folds
Stepwise LR	pRating	10	reviewLength	10	reviewLength	10	reviewLength	10
	dDeterminer	7			problem%	8	problem%	6
	pRatingDiff	5						
	sentNum	5						
	Feature	Merit	Feature	Merit	Feature	Merit	Feature	Merit
Relief	pRating	.030 ± .006	exclams	.016 ± .003	solution%	.025 ± .003	exclams	.015 ± .004
	NOT	.019 ± .004	praise%	.015 ± .003	domainWord	.012 ± .002	question%	.012 ± .004
	pRatingDiff	.019 ± .005	SUM	.013 ± .004	regTag%	.012 ± .007	LOC	.007 ± .002
	sentNum	.014 ± .002	summary%	.008 ± .003	reviewLength	.009 ± .002	sentNum	.007 ± .002
	question%	.014 ± .003	problem%	.009 ± .003	question%	.010 ± .003	reviewLength	.007 ± .001
	NEG	.013 ± .002	reviewLength	.004 ± .001	sentNum	.008 ± .002	praise%	.008 ± .004

Table 6: Feature selection based on all features

reviewLength stands out from all other features in both the writing-expert and the content-expert models. Interestingly, it is the number of sentences (*sentNum*) rather than review length of structure features that is useful in the student-helpfulness model. And demonstrative determiners (*dDeterminer*) is also selected, which indicates that having a clear sign of comment targets is considered important from the students' perspective. When examining the model's ranking result, we find that more lexicon categories are ranked high for students compared to other kind of helpfulness. Specifically, *NOT* appears high again, suggesting clear expression of opinion is important in predicting student-helpfulness. Across four types of helpfulness, again, we observed that the writing expert tends to value praise and summary (indicated by both *SUM* and *summary%*) in reviews while the content-expert favors critiques, especially solution provided critiques.

5.4 Discussion

Based on our observations from the above three comparisons, we summarize our findings with respect to different feature types and provide interpretation: 1) review length (in tokens) is generally effective in predicting expert perceived helpfulness, while number of sentences is more useful in modeling student perceived helpfulness. Interestingly, there is a strong correlation between these two features ($r = 0.91, p \leq 0.001$), and why one is selected over the other in different helpfulness models needs further investigation. 2) Lexical categories such as transition cues, negation, and suggestion words are of more importance in modeling student perceived helpfulness. This might indicate that students prefer clear expression of problem, reference and even opinion in terms of specific lexicon clues, the lack of which is likely to result in difficulty in their understanding of the reviews. 3) As for cognitive-science features, solution is generally an effective indicator of helpful peer reviews. Within the three feedback types of peer reviews, praise is valued high by the writing expert. (It is interesting to notice that although praise is shown to be more important than problem and summary for modeling the writing-expert helpfulness, positive sentiment words do not appear to be more predictive than negative sentiments.) In contrast, problem is more desirable from the content expert's point of view. Although students assign less importance to the problem themselves, solution provided peer reviews could be helpful for them with respect to the learning goal of peer-review assignments. 4) Paper rating is a very effective feature for predicting review helpfulness perceived by students, which is not the case for either expert. This supports the argument of social aspects in people's perception of review helpfulness, and it also reflects the fact that students tend to be nice to each other in such peer-review interactions. However, this dimension might not correspond with the real helpfulness of the reviews, at least from the perspective of both the writing expert and content expert.

6 Conclusion and Future Work

We have shown that the type of helpfulness to be predicted does indeed influence the utility of different feature types for automatic prediction. Low-level general linguistic features are more predictive when modeling students' perceived helpfulness; high-level theory supported constructs are more useful in experts' models. However, in the related area of automated essay scoring (Attali and Burstein, 2006), others have suggested the need for the use of validated features related to meaningful dimensions of writing, rather than low-level (but easy to automate) features. In this perspective, our work similarly poses challenge to the NLP community in terms of how to take into account the education-oriented dimensions of helpfulness when applying traditional NLP techniques of automatically predicating review helpfulness. In addition, it is important to note that predictive features of perceived helpfulness are not guaranteed to capture the nature of "truly" helpful peer reviews (in contrast to the perceived ones).

In the future, we would like to investigate how to integrate useful dimensions of helpfulness perceived by different audiences in order to come up with a "true" helpfulness gold standard. We would also like to explore more sophisticated features and other NLP techniques to improve our model of peer-review helpfulness. As we have already built models to automatically predict certain cognitive constructs (problem localization and solution), we will replace the annotated cognitive-science features used here with their automatic predictions, so that we can build our helpfulness model fully automatically. Finally, we would like to integrate our helpfulness model into a real peer-review system and evaluate its performance extrinsically in terms of improving students' learning and reviewing performance in future peer-review assignments.

Acknowledgments

This work was supported by the Learning Research and Development Center at the University of Pittsburgh. We thank Melissa Patchan and Chris Schunn for generously providing the manually annotated peer-review corpus. We are also grateful to Michael Lipschultz and Chris Schunn for their feedback while writing this paper.

References

Yigal Attali and Jill Burstein. 2006. Automated essay scoring with e-rater v.2. *The Journal of Technology, Learning and Assessment (JTLA)*, 4(3), February.

Kwangsu Cho and Christian D. Schunn. 2007. Scaffolded writing and rewriting in the discipline: A web-based reciprocal peer review system. *Computers and Education*, 48:409–426.

Kwangsu Cho. 2008. Machine classification of peer comments in physics. In *Proceedings of the First International Conference on Educational Data Mining (EDM2008)*, pages 192–196.

Cristian Danescu-Niculescu-Mizil, Gueorgi Kossinets, Jon Kleinberg, and Lillian Lee. 2009. How opinions are received by online communities: A case study on Amazon.com helpfulness votes. In *Proceedings of WWW*, pages 141–150.

Raquel M. Crespo Garcia. 2010. Exploring document clustering techniques for personalized peer assessment in exploratory courses. In *Proceedings of Computer-Supported Peer Review in Education (CSPRED) Workshop in the Tenth International Conference on Intelligent Tutoring Systems (ITS 2010)*.

Anindya Ghose and Panagiotis G. Ipeirotis. 2010. Estimating the helpfunless and economic impact of product reviews: Mining text and reviewer characteristics. *IEEE Transactions on Knowledge and Data Engineering*, 99.

Soo-Min Kim, Patrick Pantel, Tim Chklovski, and Marco Pennacchiotti. 2006. Automatically assessing review helpfulness. In *Proceedings of the 2006 Conference on Empirical Methods in Natural Language Processing (EMNLP2006)*, pages 423–430, Sydney, Australia, July.

Kenji Kira and Larry A. Rendell. 1992. A practical approach to feature selection. In Derek H. Sleeman and Peter Edwards, editors, *ML92: Proceedings of the Ninth International Conference on Machine Learning*, pages 249–256, San Francisco, CA, USA. Morgan Kaufmann Publishers Inc.

J. R. Landis and G. G. Koch. 1977. The measurement of observer agreement for categorical data. *Biometrics*, 33:159–174.

Chin-Yew Lin and Eduard Hovy. 2000. The automated acquisition of topic signatures for text summarization. In *Proceedings of the 18th conference on Computational linguistics*, volume 1 of *COLING '00*, pages 495–501, Stroudsburg, PA, USA. Association for Computational Linguistics.

Yang Liu, Xiangji Guang, Aijun An, and Xiaohui Yu. 2008. Modeling and predicting the helpfulness of online reviews. In *Proceedings of the Eighth IEEE International Conference on Data Mining*, pages 443–452, Los Alamitos, CA, USA.

Ryan McDonald, Koby Crammer, and Fernando Pereira. 2005. Online large-margin training of dependency parsers. In *Proceedings of the 43rd Annual Meeting on Association for Computational Linguistics*, ACL '05, pages 91–98, Stroudsburg, PA, USA. Association for Computational Linguistics.

Melissa M. Nelson and Christian D. Schunn. 2009. The nature of feedback: how different types of peer feedback affect writing performance. *Instructional Science*, 37(4):375–401.

Melissa M. Patchan, Davida Charney, and Christian D. Schunn. 2009. A validation study of students' end comments: Comparing comments by students, a writing instructor, and a content instructor. *Journal of Writing Research*, 1(2):124–152.

Agnes Sandor and Angela Vorndran. 2009. Detecting key sentences for automatic assistance in peer-reviewing research articles in educational sciences. In *Proceedings of the 47th Annual Meeting of the Association for Computational Linguistics and the 4th International Joint Conference on Natural Language Processing of the Asian Federation of Natural Language Processing (ACL-IJCNLP)*, pages 36–44.

Oren Tsur and Ari Rappoport. 2009. Revrank: A fully unsupervised algorithm for selecting the most helpful book reviews. In *Proceedings of the Third International AAAI Conference on Weblogs and Social Media (ICWSM2009)*, pages 36–44.

IH Witten and E. Frank. 2005. *Data Mining: Practical Machine Learning Tools and Techniques, Second Edition*. Morgan Kaufmann, San Francisco, CA.

Wenting Xiong and Diane Litman. 2010. Identifying problem localization in peer-review feedback. In *Proceedings of Tenth International Conference on Intelligent Tutoring Systems (ITS2010)*, volume 6095, pages 429–431.

Wenting Xiong and Diane Litman. 2011. Automatically predicting peer-review helpfulness. In *Proceedings 49th Annual Meeting of the Association for Computational Linguistics: Human Language Technologies (ACL/HLT)*, Portland, Oregon, June.

Generating Varied Narrative Probability Exercises

Mariët Theune[1] **Roan Boer Rookhuiszen**[1] **Rieks op den Akker**[1] **Hanneke Geerlings**[2]
Department of Computer Science[1]
Department of Research Methodology, Measurement and Data Analysis[2]
University of Twente
Enschede, The Netherlands
m.theune@utwente.nl, a.r.boerrookhuiszen@alumnus.utwente.nl,
h.j.a.opdenakker@utwente.nl, h.geerlings@gw.utwente.nl

Abstract

This paper presents Genpex, a system for automatic generation of narrative probability exercises. Generation of exercises in Genpex is done in two steps. First, the system creates a specification of a solvable probability problem, based on input from the user (a researcher or test developer) who selects a specific question type and a narrative context for the problem. Then, a text expressing the probability problem is generated. The user can tune the generated text by setting the values of some linguistic variation parameters. By varying the mathematical content of the exercise, its narrative context and the linguistic parameter settings, many different exercises can be produced. Here we focus on the natural language generation part of Genpex. After describing how the system works, we briefly present our first evaluation results, and discuss some aspects requiring further investigation.

1 Introduction

Narrative exercises (also called word problems or story problems) are mathematical exercises embedded in a story or text. They are commonly used as test items, to assess or train a student's understanding of the underlying mathematical concepts. When solving a narrative exercise, the student is required to derive the underlying mathematical question from the story and to calculate the correct answer to this mathematical problem.

This paper presents Genpex, a system for generating narrative exercises expressing probability problems. Genpex was created in the context of an international project on item generation for testing student competencies in solving probability problems. Automatic item generation is an effective way of constructing many items with controlled difficulties, based on a set of predefined task parameters (Enright et al., 2002; Deane and Sheehan, 2003; Arendasy et al., 2006; Holling et al., 2009). The goal of our item generation project is to develop a model to support optimal problem and test construction. A large collection of narrative exercises is needed to test the developed models in field trials. All of these narrative exercises should be different, but the properties that define the difficulty of the exercise should be known. Genpex was designed to enable easy creation of new exercises meeting these requirements.

Figure 1 shows a narrative probability exercise generated by Genpex. The text of the exercise is in German, because the target group of our project are German high school students. The texts produced by Genpex are based on a set of example narrative exercises that were created earlier within the project (Zeuch, In preparation).

A property that sets Genpex apart from other narrative exercise generation systems is that it was specifically designed to support variation in the generated exercises. Unlike other systems, it not only changes the context of the narrative exercise (e.g., instead of bikes, the example exercise could also have been about hotel rooms with different properties) but it also varies the way the texts are formulated. Most existing systems for narrative exercise generation use fixed sentence templates to express mathematical content, which means that the same content is always expressed in the same way (Fa-

Proceedings of the Sixth Workshop on Innovative Use of NLP for Building Educational Applications, pages 20–29,
Portland, Oregon, 24 June 2011.

In einer großen Halle ist eine Mischung von Fahrrädern. Es gibt insgesamt 100 Fahrräder.	In a big hall there are a variety of bicycles. There are 100 bicycles in total.
Es gibt 30 grüne Fahrräder und es gibt 70 weiße. 40 Fahrräder sind Mountainbikes, 50 sind Rennräder und es gibt 10 Hollandräder. 70 Fahrräder sind billiger als 500 Euro und 30 Fahrräder teurer als 500 Euro. 41 Fahrräder sind billiger als 500 Euro und sind Rennräder.	There are 30 green bicycles and there are 70 white ones. 40 bicycles are mountain bikes, 50 are road bikes, and there are 10 Dutch bikes. 70 bicycles are less expensive than 500 Euros and 30 bicycles more expensive than 500 Euros. 41 bicycles are less expensive than 500 Euros and are road bikes.
Fahrradtyp und Preis sind abhängig voneinander und alle anderen Merkmale sind unabhängig voneinander.	Bicycle type and price are dependent on each other and all other properties are independent of each other.
Wie groß ist die Wahrscheinlichkeit, dass ein Fahrrad nicht sowohl ein Mountainrad als auch grün ist?	What is the probability that a bicycle is not both a mountain bike and green?
Wie groß ist die Wahrscheinlichkeit, dass ein Fahrrad entweder billiger als 500 Euro oder ein Rennrad ist?	What is the probability that a bicycle is either cheaper than 500 Euros or a road bike?

Figure 1: The text of an exercise generated by Genpex. (Left: German original, right: English translation.)

iron and Williamson, 2002; Arendasy et al., 2006; Holling et al., 2009). A system that uses a linguistically sophisticated approach, thus in principle allowing for similar text variations as Genpex, is Model-Creator (Deane and Sheehan, 2003; Higgins et al., 2005). However, this system focuses on semantic factors influencing the expression of events with different participants (e.g., different types of vehicles) rather than on generating linguistic variations.

Below, we first describe how a probability problem is constructed by Genpex, based on input by the user. Then we explain in some detail how the natural language generation (NLG) module of Genpex creates a text expressing the probability problem, focusing on the creation of variation in the generated texts. We end with a brief discussion of our first evaluation results and some pointers to future work.

2 Probability Problems

Figure 2 presents the probability problem underlying the narrative exercise of Figure 1. It specifies the context, the total number of entities (*numEntities*), and the distribution of (combinations of) attribute values over the entities. Number information may be suppressed so as not to give the answer away; this is done by inserting a question mark in the place of the number (e.g., *colour[green] = ?*). Explicitly listing such 'hidden' information in the probability problem ensures that all possible values of each attribute are mentioned in the text of the exercise. A basic assumption in creating the probability problems is that all entities have exactly one value for each attribute. For example, all bikes must have some colour, and they cannot have two colours at the same time.

In addition to the number statements, the probability problem also lists which pairs of attributes are dependent on each other. In the example, these are *type* and *price*. This means that if we look at the subset of bikes of a specific type, the probability that one of these bikes has a certain price is not the same as when we look at the entire collection of bikes (and vice versa). If a pair of attributes is not specified as being dependent, it is independent.

Q delineates the question part of the probability problem; we refer to the other parts (except *Context*) as 'statements'. All questions require the calculation of a probability. A question of the form *Q: P(A)* asks for the probability of **event** A, which can be described as "Someone randomly draws one entity out of a (sub)set of entities and this entity has property A". For example, the question could be to calculate the probability that a bike is black if we randomly pick one bike from the set of all bikes. We equate the probability of event A with the relative frequency of the set A of objects that satisfy property A, computed as $|A|/|U|$, where U is the set of all entities (that is, $|U|$ = *numEntities*). In general, the set we draw from is the entire set of entities, but this set can be limited by a conditional statement: the event $A|B$ can be described as "Someone randomly draws one entity with property A from a subset of entities that have property B". In this case, the

Context: bikes

numEntities: 100

colour[green] = 30
colour[white] = 70
type[mountainbike] = 40
type[sportsbike] = 50
type[hollandbike] = 10
price[<500] = 70
price[>500] = 30
price[<500] ∧ type[sportsbike] = 41

dependentAttributes: price & type

Q: P(¬(type[mountainbike] ∧ colour[green]))
Q: P(price[<500] ∨ type[sportsbike])

Figure 2: The probability problem underlying Figure 1.

probability $P(A|B)$ is computed as $|A \cap B|/|B|$. All events involve a single draw of exactly one entity.

Probability problems such as the one in Figure 2 are automatically created by Genpex; the only thing the user has to do is to select one or more question types (defining the difficulty of the exercise) and a context for the exercise. All available question types are of the form *P(A)* or *P(A|B)*, where A (but not B) can be a complex event, i.e., involving a conjunction or disjunction of properties. For example, *Q: P(A ∧ B)* asks for the probability that an entity has both property A and property B. Moreover, parts of a question can be negated.

Currently, Genpex can handle 25 different question types. Some restrictions we put on the available questions are the following. Each question involves at most two different attributes, to avoid complex dependencies. There are no recursive questions (e.g., double negations) and no conditional questions about independent attributes. Finally, we exclude questions that are likely to result in ambiguous language. For example, if we try to express the question *Q: P(¬(colour[white]) ∧ type[sportsbike])* in English, it will be something like "What is the probability that a bike is not white and a road bike?". Due to scope ambiguity of the negation, this sentence may be misinterpreted as "What is the probability that a bike is not white and also *not* a road bike?". The same ambiguity is found in the German sentence expressing this question.[1] Excluding these types of questions does not simplify the task for Genpex; the excluded questions are not more difficult to generate than the included ones. The main reason to exclude certain question types was to avoid creating exercises that might be unclear to the reader.

In addition to selecting one or more question types as input for Genpex, the user also selects a context for the exercise. As a resource, Genpex uses a repository of context files[2] with information concerning the entities that the exercise should be about ('bikes' in our example) and the properties they may have. Each attribute in the context file is linked to a lexical lemma for the word that expresses its relation to the entity (e.g., bikes *are* of a certain colour or type but *have* a certain price). Similarly, for each attribute, a list of possible attribute values and the words expressing them is provided. For example, the type attribute in the bikes context can have the values 'mountainbike', 'sportsbike', 'hollandbike' and 'seniorbike', respectively associated with the words "Mountainbike" (mountain bike), "Rennrad" (road bike), "Hollandrad" (Dutch bike) and "Seniorenrad" (senior bike). Other NLG-related information in the context files is discussed in Section 3. The context file also specifies world knowledge such as the range of *numEntities* (a context about rooms in a hotel will involve fewer entities than a context about books in a bookshop) and possible dependencies between attributes (in the bikes context, price is more likely to be dependent on type than on colour).

Taking the selected question type(s) and context as input, Genpex automatically constructs a probability problem. This involves selecting a number of attributes and values, depending on the question or questions that need to be answered, and creating a correct and complete **world**: an internal representation of the situation in which all entities are fully defined (all their properties are known), and there are no inconsistencies. A part of this world is reflected in the statements of the probability problem. Currently, all statements provide information that is

[1]Genpex does include a re-ordered, mathematically equivalent version of the same question: *Q: P(type[sportsbike] ∧ ¬(colour[white]))*. Because the generated questions follow the order of the attributes in the question specification, this version can be expressed without ambiguity as "What is the probability that a bike is a road bike and not white?"

[2]In the current Genpex prototype, five different contexts are available. The system comes with an editor for the creation of new context files.

required to solve the exercise; redundant information is not included. If the user manually edits the generated probability problem, Genpex reconstructs the world, and tries to solve the exercise using the information in the edited problem. The user is warned in case of inconsistencies or missing information. A warning is also issued if the edited problem contains properties for which no lexical information is available. See Boer Rookhuiszen (2011) for more details on how probability problems are constructed.

3 Language Generation

The NLG process of Genpex has two goals: generating a correct textual representation of a given probability problem, and enabling variation, so that multiple runs will result in different texts. The generated texts should be in grammatically correct German, and they must be unambiguous: the formulation of the text should not leave the reader uncertain about the underlying mathematical exercise.

An overview of the NLG component of Genpex is given in Figure 3. Its architecture reflects the language generation pipeline of Reiter and Dale (2000), with three modules: Document Planner, Microplanner and Surface Realizer. Information between the modules is exchanged in the form of a list of **sentence trees**, each defining the content and grammatical structure of a sentence. The Document Planner creates basic sentence trees. These are manipulated by the Microplanner to create variations. The microplanning stage can in principle be skipped, but that will result in very monotonous texts. Finally, the Surface Realizer applies the correct morphology to the sentence trees and creates the layout of the text. Below, we discuss each module in turn.

3.1 Document Planning: Creating Basic Sentence Structures

The input of the Document Planner is a probability problem, which defines the content and the structure of the narrative exercise. The output is a document plan: a structured list of sentence trees expressing the statements and questions in the probability problem. The document plan also includes an introduction: a simple 'canned' text specified in the context file. If multiple introduction texts are available, one is randomly selected.

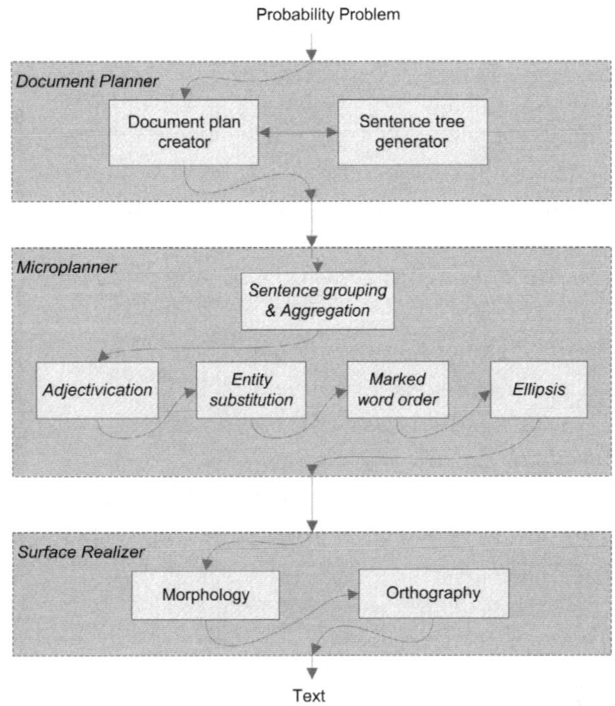

Figure 3: The NLG module of Genpex.

The sentences included in the document plan are all very simple, with the same basic structure. Take for example the statement *colour[white] = 70*. The Document Planner first creates a subject NP expressing the number of entities involved, e.g., "70 Fahrräder" (70 bicycles). Then it creates a VP expressing the relation and the attribute value, e.g., "sind weiß" (are white). The relevant words and their parts of speech are looked up in the context file. For the example statement, this process results in the following basic tree, shown in a simplified notation. Note that the words in the tree have not yet been inflected.

```
[s]
  [np grammaticalRole=su]
     [det grammaticalRole=num]70[/det]
     [noun grammaticalRole=hd]Fahrrad[/noun]
  [/np]
  [vp]
     [verb grammaticalRole=hd]sind[/verb]
     [adj grammaticalRole=predc]weiss[/adj]
  [/vp]
[/s]
```

All sentence trees for questions start with the phrase "Wie groß ist die Wahrscheinlichkeit dass" (What is the probability that), included as canned text in a tree node with syntactic category 'clause'.

This main clause is followed by an indefinite NP referring to the type of entities discussed in the exercise, e.g., "ein Fahrrad" (a bicycle). The structure of the rest of the sentence tree depends on the question type. Sentence tree templates are available for all possible question types. They can be used recursively: slots in the templates can be filled with an expression for an attribute value, or with one of the other templates.

Figure 4 shows the construction of a sentence tree for a fairly complex question of type $P(A \vee B \mid \neg C)$, using multiple question templates. For questions about conditional probabilities Genpex uses the slightly formal "vorausgesetzt" (given that), because simpler phrasings are likely to be ambiguous. For example, assume we want to ask the question *Q: P(type[mountainbike] | colour[green])*. A simple way to ask this question would be "Wie groß ist die Wahrscheinlichkeit dass ein grünes Fahrrad ein Mountainbike ist?" (What is the probability that a green bike is a mountain bike?). However, such a question could be mistakenly interpreted as asking for a joint probability: *Q: P(colour[green]* $\wedge$ *type[mountainbike])*. For this reason, the more complex formulation is preferred.

3.2 Microplanning: Creating Variation

The Microplanner modifies the sentence trees produced by the Document Planner by applying a number of **variation techniques**. These techniques place specific requirements on the sentences to which they can be applied, and therefore not every technique can be applied to all sentence trees.

When introducing variation in the narrative form of the exercise, it is important that variations of the same exercise should all have the same meaning and approximately the same difficulty. According to Deane and Sheehan (2003), it is possible to change the wording of a text without changing its difficulty. Reiter and Dale (2000) state that for example aggregating multiple sentences does not change the information they express, but improves the readability and fluency of the text. This is what we want to achieve: adding variation to the text without affecting its interpretation. Genpex therefore uses aggregation as well as a number of text variation techniques, assuming that they do not influence the meaning or difficulty of an exercise.

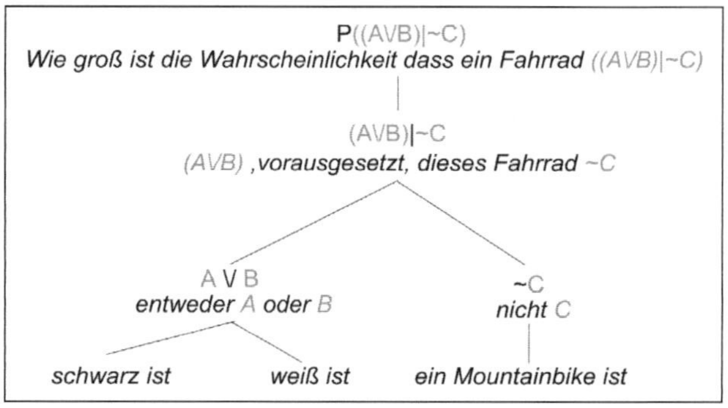

Figure 4: Construction of a question combining multiple templates. Translation, with brackets marking the template boundaries: "What is the probability that a bicycle [[is either black or white] given that this bicycle [is not a mountainbike]]?"

Below we discuss the operations applied to basic sentence trees in the Microplanner. They are only applied to sentences expressing statements, even though it would be practically possible to apply some of the variations to the questions too. Given that understanding the question is crucial for solving the exercise, and that varying the way the questions are asked might cause confusion, we chose to adhere to a fixed format for the questions, cf. Fairon and Williams (2002).

Aggregation. As a first step, the Microplanner applies aggregation: grouping multiple simple sentences and combining them into one complex sentence. This process leaves the original order of the sentences in the Document Plan intact. Sentences referring to different attributes are never grouped together, to avoid possible misinterpretations. For example, a complex sentence such as "70 bicycles are white and 40 bicycles are mountain bikes" might suggest that the 40 mountain bikes are different entities than the 70 white bikes, excluding the possibility of white mountain bikes. Since this is not the intended meaning, we avoid creating this kind of complex sentences. Sentences referring to the same attribute can be grouped together without risk, because there can never be any overlap between the sets of entities mentioned in these sentences (an entity cannot have multiple values for the same attribute).

Aggregation is performed on a maximum of three sentences to prevent the generation of overly large conjunctions. Groups of four basic sentences are aggregated into two new complex sentences. This way we avoid creating unbalanced texts like example 1 below, preferring to generate sentences that are similar in both length and complexity, as in example 2.

1. 42 Fahrräder sind Mountainbikes, 168 Fahrräder sind Rennräder und 200 Fahrräder sind Hollandräder. 10 Fahrräder sind Seniorenräder.

   (42 bicycles are mountain bikes, 168 bicycles are road bikes, and 200 bicycles are Dutch bikes. 10 bicycles are senior bikes.)

2. 42 Fahrräder sind Mountainbikes und 168 Fahrräder sind Rennräder. 200 Fahrräder sind Hollandräder und 10 Fahrräder sind Seniorenräder.

   (42 bicycles are mountain bikes and 168 bicycles are road bikes. 200 bicycles are Dutch bikes and 10 bicycles are senior bikes.)

Aggregation in Genpex is not optional; it is always applied under the assumption that this will make the generated texts more coherent and pleasant to read. Moreover, it enables variation through ellipsis, as discussed later in this section. Variations in aggregation can be achieved by manually reordering the statements in the probability problem. This will lead to a different Document Plan and as a consequence, to different aggregations, within the restrictions stated above.

Adjectivication. The text variation technique we call 'adjectivication' changes the position and grammatical role of the adjective (if any) expressing the attribute value in a sentence. In basic sentence trees, attribute values expressed by adjectives are included as predicative complements in the VP. If we apply adjectivication to a sentence, the adjective is instead added as a modifier to the subject NP, and the original verb is removed. To make the sentence tree complete again, the words "Es gibt" (There are') are added in front. For example, the sentence "30 Fahrräder sind grün" (30 bicycles are green) will be changed to "Es gibt 30 grüne Fahrräder" (There are 30 green bikes). In German, adjectivication may cause the inflection of the adjective to change, because it gets a different grammatical role: when used as a modifier its inflection reflects the gender and case of the noun it modifies. This is taken care of by the Surface Realizer.

Entity substitution. In case an attribute value is expressed as a noun, e.g., "Rennrad" (road bike) the text variation technique we call 'entity substitution' can be applied. It involves replacing the noun that represents the entity in a basic sentence with the noun that represents the attribute value. As with adjectivication, the original verb is removed and instead "Es gibt" (There are) is added to the sentence. For example, entity substitution changes the basic sentence "50 Fahrräder sind Rennräder" (50 bicycles are road bikes) to "Es gibt 50 Rennräder" (There are 50 road bikes).

Marked word order. Another source of variation is topicalizing the phrase expressing the attribute value by moving it to the front of the sentence. Applying this variation technique changes the basic sentence "30 Fahrräder sind teurer als 500 Euro" (30 bicycles are more expensive than 500 Euros) to "Teurer als 500 Euro sind 30 Fahrräder" (More expensive than 500 Euros are 30 bicycles). Since using such a marked word order may come across as unnatural in a neutral discourse context, this type of variation should be applied with caution.

Ellipsis. This is the removal of duplicate words from sentences, which typically applies to aggregated sentences (Harbusch and Kempen, 2009). Genpex can apply different types of ellipsis, such as Gapping and Conjunction Reduction. Gapping is the removal of all except the first verb in an aggregated sentence. An example from Figure 1 is the sentence "70 Fahrräder sind billiger als 500 Euro und 30 Fahrräder teurer als 500 Euro" (70 bicycles are less expensive than 500 Euros and 30 bicycles more expensive than 500 Euros), where the verb "sind" (are) has been deleted from the second clause. (Forward) Conjunction Reduction deletes the subject of subsequent clauses if it is identical to the subject of the first clause. The following sentence is an example: "40 Fahrräder sind Mountainbikes und 50 sind Rennräder" (40 bicycles are mountain bikes and 50 are road bikes). It is possible to combine Gapping and Conjunction Reduction, e.g., "40 Fahrräder sind Mountainbikes und 50 Rennräder" (40 bicycles are mountain bikes and 50 road bikes).

Ellipsis is also possible in sentences with marked word order. For example, "Grün sind 30 Fahrräder und weiß sind 40 Fahrräder"(Green are 30 bicycles and white are 40 bicycles) could be reduced to "Grün sind 30 Fahrräder und weiß sind 40" (Green are 30 bicycles and white are 40). However, in this sentence, the verb cannot be removed from the last clause. Genpex currently allows aggregated sentences in which some of the clauses have marked word order. In these cases, ellipsis is not applied, because it will most likely result in grammatically incorrect sentences. For example, in the sentence "30 Fahrräder sind grün und Weiß sind 40 Fahrräder" (30 bicycles are green and white are 40 bicycles) the system will not apply ellipsis.

For every sentence in the document plan, the system will check which of the variation techniques described above can be applied to it, by analyzing the structure of the sentence tree. If a technique is in principle applicable, the probability of it being actually applied depends on information in the context file, and on parameters set by the user through the GUI of Genpex. For every attribute in the context file, the author of the file can prevent Genpex from applying a specific technique by giving it a probability of 0, if it is never suitable in the case of this specific attribute. For example, applying marked word order to a sentence expressing the 'type' attribute in the bikes context would lead to odd sentences such as "Mountainbikes sind 40 Fahrräder" (Mountainbikes are 40 bicycles). Though grammatically correct, such sentences would be hard to interpret and therefore are best avoided.

During generation, the user can directly influence the probability that certain variations are applied through sliders in the GUI; see Figure 5. The probability holds for every sentence that satisfies the structural requirements of the variation technique in question, unless the technique is excluded based on the information in the context file, as explained above. After having set the variation probabilities, the user can click 'Update Text' to see the effect. The user can also choose to have the text automatically updated every time a slider is moved.

When the user saves a generated exercise, information about the variation techniques that have been applied is logged and saved together with the exercise. If further research shows that a certain variation technique has an unintended influence on exercise difficulty, it will be easy to exclude this technique from the creation of new exercises by setting its probability to 0 in the GUI.

3.3 Surface Realisation: the Final Polish

The main task of the Surface Realizer is to convert the sentence trees that have been manipulated by the Microplanner to actual text, applying correct morphology and orthography.

Information about German morphology is retrieved from a lexicon listing the possible word forms of each lemma in the context files. German has a rich inflectional system compared to English, with suffixes reflecting the gender, number and case of determiners, adjectives and nouns. Gender can be masculine, feminine or neuter, number is singular or plural, and case is nominative, accusative, dative or genitive. In the type of exercises currently generated by Genpex, all words are in nominative case. Number information for nouns and verbs is given in the sentence tree, while the inflection of determiners and adjectives in an NP depends on the properties of the noun. For the inflection of adjectives, Genpex also has to consider the determiner that is used before the adjective. In German, so-called 'strong inflection' has to be used after a cardinal number, 'weak inflection' after a definite determiner and 'mixed inflection' after an indefinite determiner. We currently use canoonet[3] as the source for German morphological information in Genpex.

Orthography is the process that converts the sentence trees to text. This is quite easy, because the word order is already defined by the tree structure. All values of the nodes in the tree can be joined together in a sentence in that order, separated by white spaces. The clauses in aggregated sentences are joined by a comma, except for the last conjunction where the word 'und' is used. A characteristic of German is that all nouns are capitalized. The Surface Realiser takes care of this, and also of the capitalization of the first word in each sentence, punctuation and the placement of paragraph boundaries. The generated texts are marked up with HTML for easy display in web browsers.

4 Evaluation

Potential users of Genpex (researchers working on test design) have been involved at different stages of development of the system, such as requirements specification and usability testing. Field trials with

[3] http://www.canoo.net/

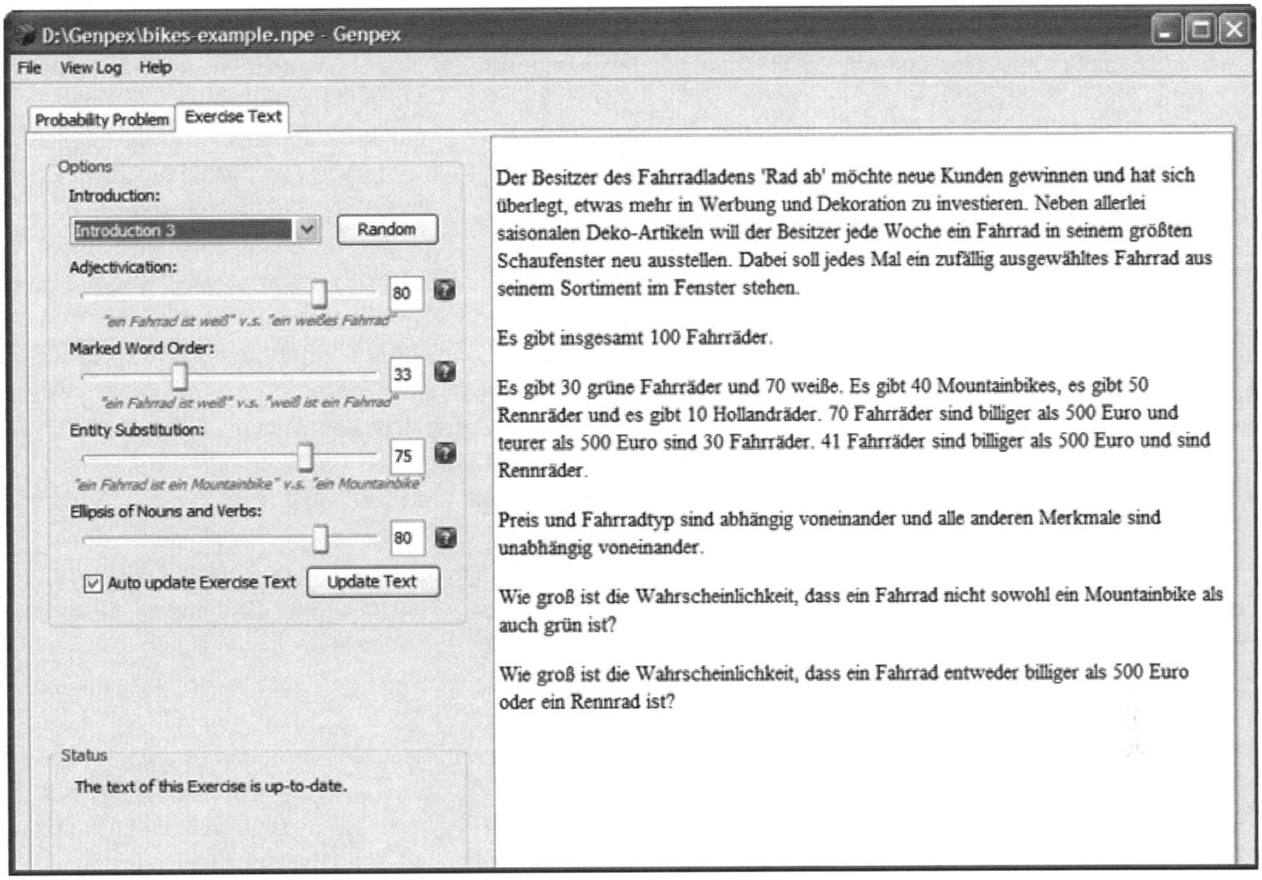

Figure 5: Screenshot of the GUI of Genpex, showing a variation of the narrative exercise in Figure 1. The introductory text was taken from Zeuch (In preparation).

students are future work, but we did carry out some preliminary, qualitative evaluations with a few native speakers of German (including one item generation expert) to test the grammaticality and understandability of the generated exercises. This revealed some small mistakes that have since been corrected, but also a few bigger problems with some of the variation techniques and other NLG aspects.

One of the things noted by the native speakers was that applying ellipsis sometimes leads to slightly unnatural sentences. The preferred type and degree of ellipsis is different for each type of sentence, but this is not taken into account by Genpex. As a consequence, the system frequently applies too much or too little ellipsis to the generated sentences, with less than ideal (though not ungrammatical) results. The existence of such preferred formulations is in line with the results of Cahill and Forst (2010), who carried out an experiment in which native speakers of German evaluated a number of alternative realisations of the same sentence. Their subjects accepted some variation in word order, but showed a clear preference for some of the alternatives.

Some of the generated question sentences also sounded a bit forced to the native speakers. For example, the question template for joint probabilities ($A \wedge B$) uses the formal phrasing "sowohl... als auch" (both ... and), whereas a simple "und" (and) would be the more natural choice for most questions. However, in some question contexts, in particular those involving negations, using the simpler formulation might lead to the kind of scope ambiguities mentioned in Section 2. Therefore, the choice was made to use "sowohl... als auch" in all cases, even in those where it is not strictly necessary. Similarly, questions asking for a conditional probability were found to be somewhat difficult to understand. For these questions, readability might be improved by using two sentences to express them, along the lines of "Consider the set of bicycles that are not mountain bikes. What is the probability that one of those bicycles is either black or white?" as an alternative to the more complex formulation given in Figure 4.

The comments by the native speakers suggest that in some cases, Genpex goes too far in its "one size fits all" approach, and that we should try to add more flexibility to the NLG component, allowing it to make finer distinctions in the application of variation techniques to specific sentences and of question templates to specific question types.

5 Discussion

The texts currently being generated by Genpex are grammatical, but our native speakers reported that some sentences had to be studied carefully before it was possible to get the information needed to solve the problem. No actual misinterpretations occurred, but the increased reading time (as compared to more preferred formulations) may still increase the difficulty of the exercise. A thorough investigation into the effect of textual variations on item difficulty is therefore necessary. Genpex supports this type of research by enabling the systematic application of different variations, while logging all textual operations that have been applied and saving them together with the generated text. The underlying probability problem is saved together with the text as well, so all factors that certainly or potentially influence item difficulty are known. This makes it relatively easy to test the influence of those factors on the difficulty of the exercise, for example by carrying out the kind of statistical and cognitive analysis advocated by Graf et al. (2005).

The effect of the main parameters of the probability problems in Genpex (i.e., the type of question being asked) was already statistically analyzed by Holling et al. (2009) and Zeuch (In preparation). They used automatically generated items similar to the exercises generated by Genpex, except that their exercises did not have variations in wording apart from context-related ones. Also, the exercises used by Holling et al. (2009) mentioned probabilities instead of counts in the statements.

Once we know more about the effects of the textual variations, Genpex can be of great value to test developers, given that there exists a great need for large amounts of learning and assessment materials with a controlled level of difficulty (Enright et al., 2002; Fairon and Williamson, 2002; Deane and Sheehan, 2003; Arendasy et al., 2006; Holling et al., 2008; Holling et al., 2009). The initial development and testing of the system is a one-time investment, which we expect will pay off afterward when large amounts of test items can be created with little effort. In particular, we think Genpex can be very useful in combination with Computerized Adaptive Testing (CAT). The system could be used for on-the-fly generation of new items for each individual student, adapted to that student's skill level estimated from his or her previous answers. Because every student gets custom exercises, the risk of frequently used items becoming known among students is reduced, thus increasing test security.

In principle, given that the factors influencing item difficulty are known, generating difficult items is not more complicated than generating easy ones. However, as illustrated in Section 2, combining multiple difficulty factors such as negation and joint probability may lead to textual formulations that are ambiguous or hard to understand, and which – if not successfully prevented in advance – may need to be filtered out or corrected by hand. For that reason, Genpex seems most suitable for the generation of exercises up to a moderate level of complexity. Still, even if the need for hand-crafting will not be completely eliminated, reducing it to complex items that require particularly careful wording already represents a big gain in efficiency.

Acknowledgements

We thank our anonymous reviewers and everybody who helped testing Genpex. Special thanks go to our colleagues from the University of Münster for providing the reference exercises on which the Genpex output was modelled. This research was funded by the Deutsche Forschungsgemeinschaft (DFG), Schwerpunktprogramm "Kompetenzmodelle zur Erfassung individueller Lernergebnisse und zur Bilanzierung von Bildungsprozessen" (SPP 1293), project "Rule-based Item Generation of Algebra Word Problems Based upon Linear Logistic Test Models for Item Cloning and Optimal Design".

References

Martin Arendasy, Markus Sommer, Georg Gittler, and Andreas Hergovich. 2006. Automatic generation of quantitative reasoning items: A pilot study. *Journal of Individual Differences*, 27(1):2–14.

Roan Boer Rookhuiszen. 2011. Generation of German narrative probability excercises. Master's thesis, University of Twente.

Aiofe Cahill and Martin Forst. 2010. Human evaluation of a German surface realisation ranker. In E. Krahmer and M. Theune, editors, *Empirical Methods in Natural Language Generation*, volume 5790 of *Lecture Notes in Computer Science*, pages 201–221. Springer, Berlin / Heidelberg.

Paul Deane and Kathleen Sheehan. 2003. Automatic item generation via frame semantics: Natural language generation of math word problems. Educational Testing Service, Princeton. Paper presented at the Annual Meeting of the National Council on Measurement in Education (Chicago, IL, April 22-24, 2003).

Mary K. Enright, Mary Morley, and Kathleen M. Sheehan. 2002. Items by design: The impact of systematic feature variation on item statistical characteristics. *Applied Measurement in Education*, 15(1):49–74.

Cédrick Fairon and David M. Williamson. 2002. Automatic item text generation in educational assessment. In *Proceedings of TALN 2002*, pages 395–401.

Edith Aurora Graf, Stephen Peterson, Manfred Steffen, and René Lawless. 2005. Psychometric and cognitive analysis as a basis for the design and revision of quantitative item models. Technical Report RR-05-25, Educational Testing Service, Princeton.

Karin Harbusch and Gerard Kempen. 2009. Generating clausal coordinate ellipsis multilingually: A uniform approach based on postediting. In *Proceedings of the 12th European Workshop on Natural Language Generation*, pages 138–145.

Derrick Higgins, Yoko Futagi, and Paul Deane. 2005. Multilingual generalization of the ModelCreator software for math item generation. Technical Report RR-05-02, Educational Testing Service, Princeton.

Heinz Holling, Helen Blank, Karoline Kuchenbäcker, and Jörg-Tobias Kuhn. 2008. Rule-based item design of statistical word problems: A review and first implementation. *Psychology Science Quarterly*, 50(3):363–378.

Heinz Holling, Jonas P. Bertling, and Nina Zeuch. 2009. Automatic item generation of probability word problems. *Studies In Educational Evaluation*, 35(2-3):71–76.

Ehud Reiter and Robert Dale. 2000. *Building Natural Language Generation Systems*. Cambridge University Press, Cambridge, UK.

Nina Zeuch. In preparation. *Rule-based item construction: Analysis with and comparison of linear logistic test models and cognitive diagnostic models with two item types*. Ph.D. thesis, University of Münster.

Elicited Imitation for Prediction of OPI Test Scores

Kevin Cook
Brigham Young University
Department of Computer Science
kevincook13@gmail.com

Jeremiah McGhee, Deryle Lonsdale
Brigham Young University
Department of Linguistics
{jlmcghee, lonz}@byu.edu

Abstract

Automated testing of spoken language is the subject of much current research. Elicited Imitation (EI), or sentence repetition, is well suited for automated scoring, but does not directly test a broad range of speech communication skills. An Oral Proficiency Interview (OPI) tests a broad range of skills, but is not as well suited for automated scoring. Some have suggested that EI can be used as a predictor of more general speech communication abilities. We examine EI for this purpose. A fully automated EI test is used to predict OPI scores. Experiments show strong correlation between predicted and actual OPI scores. Effectiveness of OPI score prediction depends upon at least two important design decisions. One of these decisions is to base prediction primarily on acoustic measures, rather than on transcription. The other of these decisions is the choice of sentences, or EI test items, to be repeated. It is shown that both of these design decisions can greatly impact performance. It is also shown that the effectiveness of individual test items can be predicted.

1 Introduction

1.1 Background

Learning to speak a second language is an important objective for many people. Assessing progress in oral proficiency is often expensive and time-consuming. The development of automated systems promises to significantly lower costs and increase accessibility.

Elicited imitation (EI) has been used for nearly half a century to measure abnormal language development (Fujiki and Brinton, 1987) and the performance of second language learners (Chaudron et al., 2005; Vinther, 2002). As a method for assessing oral proficiency it consists of a person listening to a test item, typically a full sentence, and then doing their best to repeat it back correctly. This method is also referred to as sentence repetition, or more simply as repeats. One motivation for using EI, as opposed to some other form of test, is that it is relatively inexpensive to administer. An EI test can be effectively scored by non-experts in a relatively short amount of time. It is also well suited for automated scoring (Graham et al., 2008), since correct responses are predictable.

1.2 Motivation

The language skills directly measured by an EI test are those involved in repeating back what one has just heard. In order to directly measure a broader set of language skills, other tests must be used. One of these is the Oral Proficiency Interview (OPI).

The OPI is face-to-face interview conducted to assess language proficiency. The interview tests different types of relevant skills and lasts for about 30 minutes. Additionally, a validated OPI requires a second review of a recording created during the initial interview with arbitration if necessary. This process is expensive ($150 U.S.) and time-consuming with a turn-around of several weeks before finalized results are received.

A fully automated OPI test does not seem to be practical. This is especially the case when the in-

Proceedings of the Sixth Workshop on Innovative Use of NLP for Building Educational Applications, pages 30–37,
Portland, Oregon, 24 June 2011. ©2011 Association for Computational Linguistics

terpersonal aspects of a face-to-face interview are considered. There have been several efforts to automatically score the type of speech which might be spoken by an OPI test-taker, spontaneous non-native speech (Zechner and Xi, 2008). It has been shown that current automatic speech recognition (ASR) systems, used to transcribe such speech, have error rates which make it challenging to use transcripts for testing purposes.

The argument has been made that although EI does not directly measure communicative skills, such as the ability to converse with another person, it can be used to infer such skills (Henning, 1983). Part of the theory behind EI is that people typically are not able to memorize the sounds of an utterance the length of a full sentence. Rather, people build a mental model of the meaning of an utterance, and are then able to remember the model. People who cannot understand the utterance are not able to build a mental model, and are therefore unable to remember or repeat the utterance. If it is true that EI can be used to infer more general speech communication abilities, even if only to a limited extent, then EI may be useful for predicting test scores which are designed to directly measure that ability.

Bernstein et al. (2000) describe a system which elicits short predictable responses, such as readings, repeats (EI), opposites, and short answers, for automated testing. A similar system is discussed later in Bernstein et al. (2010). It is evident that EI is used in these systems, as part of a greater whole. The argument is made that although the skills directly tested are limited, the scores produced may be useful for inferring more general language abilities. It is shown that automated scores correlate well with scores from conventional tests, such as the OPI. One aspect which may not be as clear is the role that EI plays as compared to other methods used in the automated test.

We are interested in the use of a fully automated EI test as a means to predict more general ability in spoken language communication. Since the OPI test is specifically designed to measure such general ability we use it as a gold standard, in spite of the fact that we do not expect it to be a perfect measure. We are interested in learning the extent to which OPI scores can be predicted using an EI test. We are also interested in learning how to design an automated system such that prediction of OPI scores is most effective. We evaluate system performance based on how highly correlated OPI score predictions are with actual OPI scores.

Several design decisions must be made in the development of such a system. One, is which method to use for converting spoken responses to OPI score predictions. Another, is the choice of sentences, or EI test items, to be repeated. We address both of these issues.

There are at least two approaches to scoring spoken responses. One, is to score based on transcriptions, generated by a speech recognizer. Another, is to score based on acoustic measures alone, such as pronunciation and fluency (Cincarek et al., 2009). The primary difference between these two approaches is what is assumed about the textual content of a spoken response. Acoustic measures are based on the assumption that the textual content of each spoken response is known. Speech recognition is based on the assumption that the content is not known. We explore the effect of this assumption on OPI prediction.

The selection of effective EI test items has been the subject of some research. Tomita et al. (2009) outline principles for creating effective EI test items. Christensen et al. (2010) present a tool for test item creation. We explore the use of OPI scores as a means to evaluate the effectiveness of individual test items.

2 Related Work

The system described by Bernstein et al. (2010) uses EI as part of the automated test. Sentences range in length from two to twenty or more syllables. If fewer than 90% of natives can repeat the sentence verbatim, then the item is not used. An augmented ASR system is used which has been optimized for non-native speech. The ASR system is used to transcribe test-taker responses. Transcriptions are compared to the word string recited in the prompt. Word errors are counted and used to calculate a score. Fluency and pronunciation of spoken responses are also scored.

Graham et al. (2008) report on a system which uses EI for automated assessment. Results show that automated scores are strongly correlated with manual EI scores. ASR grammars are specific to each test item. Our work is based on this system.

Müller et al. (2009) compare the effectiveness of reading and repeating (EI) tasks for automated testing. Automated scores are compared with manual scores for the same task. It is found that repeating tasks provide a better means of automatic assessment than reading tasks.

3 Experiments

In this section we describe experiments, including both an OPI test and an automated EI test. We detail the manner of automated scoring of the EI test, together with the method used to predict OPI scores.

3.1 Setup

We administer an ACTFL-OPI (see www.actfl.org) and an automated EI test to each of 85 English as a Foreign Language learners of varying proficiency levels. This group of speakers (test-takers) is randomly divided into a 70%/30% training/testing split, with 60 speakers forming the training set and the remaining 25 forming the test set. Training data consists of OPI scores and EI responses for each speaker in the training set. Test data consists of OPI scores and EI responses for each speaker in the test set.

An OPI is a face-to-face interview conducted by a skilled, certified human evaluator. (We do not expect that this interview results in an ideal evaluation of oral proficiency. We use the OPI because it is designed to directly test speech communication skills which are not directly tested by EI.) OPI proficiency levels range across a 10-tiered nominal scale from Novice Low to Superior. We convert these levels to an integer score from 1 to 10 ($NoviceLow = 1$, $Superior = 10$).

The EI test consists of 59 items, each an English sentence. An automated system plays a recording of each sentence and then records the speaker's attempt to repeat the sentence verbatim. A fixed amount of time is allotted for the speaker to repeat the sentence. After that fixed time, the next item is presented, until all items are presented and all responses recorded. The choice of which items to include in the test is somewhat arbitrary; we select those items which we believe might work well, given past experimentation with EI. We expect that improvement could be made in both the manner of administration of the test, and in the selection of test items.

Responses are scored using a Sphinx 4 (Walker et al., 2004) ASR system, version 1.0 beta 4, together with the supplied 30-6800HZ WSJ acoustic model. ASR performance is affected by various system parameters. For our experiments, we generally use default parameters found in configuration files for Sphinx demos. The ASR system has not been adapted for non-native speech.

3.2 Language Models

We vary the language model component of the ASR system in order to evaluate the merit of assuming that the content of spoken responses is known. Speech recognizers use both an acoustic model and a language model, to transcribe text. The acoustic model is used to estimate a probability corresponding to how well input speech sounds like output text. The language model is used to estimate a probability corresponding to how well output text looks like a target language, such as English. Output text is determined based on a joint probability, using both the acoustic and the language models. We vary the degree to which it is assumed that the content of spoken responses is known. This is done by varying the degree to which the language model is constrained to the text of the expected response.

When the language model is fully constrained, the assumption is made that the content of each spoken response is known. The language model assigns all probability to the text of the expected response. All other output text has zero probability. The acoustic model estimates a probability for this word sequence according to how well the test item is pronounced. If the joint probability of the word sequence is below a certain rejection threshold, then there is no output from the speech recognizer. Otherwise, the text of the test item is the output of the speech recognizer. With this fully constrained language model, the speech recognizer is essentially a binary indicator of pronunciation quality.

When the language model is fully unconstrained, there is no relationship between the language model and test items, except that test items belong to the English language. In this case, the speech recognizer functions normally, as a means to transcribe spoken responses. Output text is the best guess of the ASR system as to what was said.

A partially constrained language model is one that is based on test items, but also allows variation in output text.

We perform experiments using the following five language models:

1. **WSJ20K** The 20K word Wall Street Journal language model, supplied with Sphinx.

2. **WSJ5K** The 5K word Wall Street Journal language model, supplied with Sphinx.

3. **EI Items** A custom language model created from the corpus of all test items.

4. **Item Selection** A custom language model constraining output to any one of the test items.

5. **Forced Alignment** A custom language model constraining output to only the current test item.

The first two language models, WSJ20K and WSJ5K, are supplied with Sphinx and have no special relationship to the test items. The training corpus used to build these models is drawn from issues of the Wall Street Journal. These models are fully unconstrained.

The third model, EI Items, is a conventional language model with the exception that the training corpus is very limited. The training corpus consists of all test items; no other text is included in the training corpus. The fourth model, Item Selection, is not a conventional language model. It assigns a set probability to each test item as a whole. That probability is equal to one divided by the total number of test items. Such a simple language model is sometimes referred to as a grammar (Walker et al., 2004; Graham et al., 2008). Both the EI Items and Item Selection models are partially constrained. The Item Selection model is much more highly constrained than the EI Items model.

The last model, Forced Alignment, is fully constrained. It assigns all probability to item text. These five language models are chosen for the purpose of evaluating the effectiveness of constraining the language model to the text of the expected response.

i	Item
I	Number of items
s	Speaker (test-taker)
S	Number of speakers
x_{is}	Score for item i, speaker s
y_s	Predicted OPI score for speaker s
o_s	Actual OPI score for speaker s
MSE_i	Mean squared error for item i

Figure 1: Notation used in this paper.

3.3 Scoring

Each response is scored using a two-step process. First, the spoken response is transcribed by the ASR system. Second, word error rate (WER) is calculated by comparing the transcription to the item text. WER is converted to an item score x_{is} for item i and speaker s in the range of 0 to 1 using the following formula:

$$x_{is} = \begin{cases} 1 - \frac{WER}{100} & \text{if } WER < 100\% \\ 0 & \text{otherwise} \end{cases} \quad (1)$$

A list of notation used in this paper is shown in Figure 1.

3.4 Prediction

In order to avoid over-fitting, a simple linear model is trained (Witten and Frank, 2005) to predict an OPI score y_s, given items scores x_{is} together with model parameters a and b. The mean of item scores for speaker s is multiplied by parameter a. This product plus parameter b is the OPI score prediction: (I is the total number of items.)

$$y_s = \frac{1}{I} \sum_i x_{is} \cdot a + b \quad (2)$$

Correlation is calculated between predicted and actual OPI scores for all speakers in the test set.

4 Results

Correlation for each of the language models using all 59 test items is shown in Figure 2. Correlation for both of the unconstrained language models was relatively poor. Performance improved significantly as the language model was constrained to the expected response. These results suggest that it is effective to assume that the content of spoken responses is known.

Fully constraining the language model to the text of the expected response results in an item score which is a binary indicator (because, in this case, WER is either 100% or 0%) of how well the spoken response sounds like the expected response. In this case, prediction is based on the output of the acoustic model of the speech recognizer, an acoustic measure. Prediction is not based on transcription, since a specific transcription is assumed prior to processing the spoken response. When the language model is fully unconstrained, an item score is an indicator of how well ASR transcription matches the text of the expected response. In this case, prediction is based on transcription, the speech recognizer's best guess of which words were spoken. Results indicate that correlation between predicted and actual OPI scores improves as prediction is based on acoustic measures, rather than on transcription.

Language Model	Constrained	Corr.
WSJ20K	Not	0.633
WSJ5K	Not	0.600
EI Items	Partial	0.737
Item Selection	Partial	0.805
Forced Alignment	Full	0.799

Figure 2: Correlation with OPI scores, for all 5 language models, using all 59 test items. Language models are unconstrained, partially constrained, or fully constrained to the text of the expected response.

4.1 Item MSE

The effectiveness of individual test items is explored by defining a measure of item quality. If each item score x_{is} were ideally linearly correlated with the actual OPI score o_s for speaker s then the equality shown below would hold: (o_s is an integer from 1 to 10. x_{is} is a real number from 0 to 1.)

$$IDEAL \Longrightarrow o_s = x_{is} * 9 + 1 \tag{3}$$

We calculate the difference between this ideal and the actual OPI score:

$$(x_{is} * 9 + 1) - o_s \tag{4}$$

This difference can be seen as a measure of how useful the item is as a predictor OPI scores. For better items, this difference is closer to zero. The mean of the squares of these differences for a particular item, over all S speakers in the training set, is a measure of item quality MSE_i:

$$MSE_i = \frac{1}{S}\sum_{s}((x_{is} * 9 + 1) - o_s)^2 \tag{5}$$

Because we expect improved results by assuming that the content of expected responses is known, we use the Forced Alignment language model to calculate an MSE score for each test item. A sample of items and their associated MSE are listed in Figure 3.

MSE	Item text
9.28	He should have walked away before the fight started.
10.48	We should have eaten breakfast by now.
...	
14.53	She dove into the pool gracefully, and with perfect form.
14.68	If her heart were to stop beating, we might not be able to help her.
...	
25.78	She ought to learn Spanish.
26.09	Sometimes they go to town.

Figure 3: Sample EI items with corresponding MSE scores.

Item MSE scores are used to define various subsets of test items, better items, worse items, and so on. Better items have lower MSE scores. These subsets are used to compute a series of correlations for each of the five language models. First, correlation is computed using only one test item. That item is the item with the lowest (best) MSE score. Then, correlation is computed again using only two test items, the two items with the lowest MSE scores. This process is repeated until correlation is computed using all test items. Results are shown in Figure 4. These results show even more convincingly that OPI prediction improves by assuming that the content of spoken responses is known.

4.2 OPI Prediction

Figure 4 also gives an idea of how effectively EI can be used to predict OPI scores. Correlation over 0.80 is achieved using the Forced Alignment language

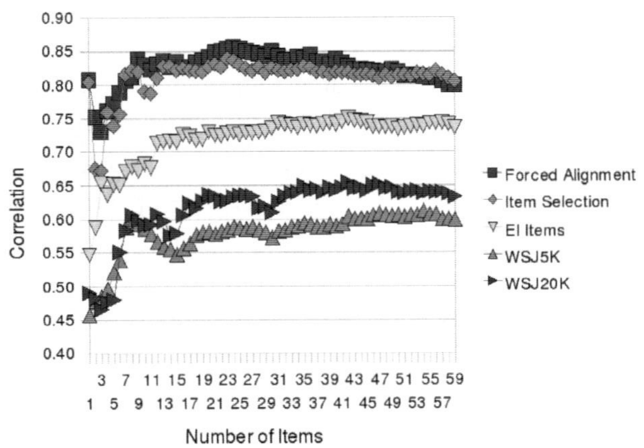

Figure 4: Correlation with OPI scores, for all 5 language models, using varying numbers of test items.

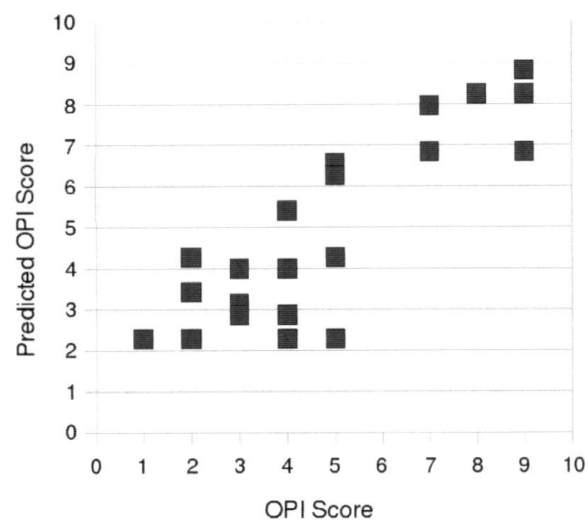

Figure 5: Plot of predicted OPI scores as a function of actual OPI scores, using the Forced Alignment language model and the best 24 test items.

model for all but 7 of the 59 subsets of test items. Correlation is over 0.84 for 11 of the subsets (best 20 - best 31). Correlation is above 0.85 for 3 subsets (best 23 - best 25). Predicted OPI scores correlate strongly with actual OPI scores.

Figure 5 shows a plot of predicted OPI scores as a function of actual OPI scores, using the Forced Alignment language model and only the best 24 test items. Correlation is 0.856. Interestingly, two of the outliers (OPI=5, predicted OPI=2.3) and (OPI=4, predicted OPI=2.3) were for speakers whose responses contained only silence, indicating those participants may have experienced technical difficulties or may have been uncooperative during their test session. The inferred model used to calculate OPI predictions for Figure 5 is shown below:

$$y_s = \frac{1}{I}\sum_i x_{is} * 6.8 + 2.3 \qquad (6)$$

(Given this particular model, the lowest possible predicted OPI score is 2.3, and the highest possible predicted score is 9.1. The ability to predict OPI scores 1 and 10 is lost, but the objective is to improve overall correlation.)

4.3 Item Selection

To see more clearly the effect that the choice of test items has on OPI prediction, we compute a series of correlations similar to before, except that the order of test items is reversed: First, correlation is computed using only the test item with the highest (worst) MSE score. Then, correlation is computed again using only the two worst items, and so on. This series of correlations is computed for the Forced Alignment language model only. It is shown together with the original ordering for the Forced Alignment language model from Figure 4.

These two series are shown in Figure 6. The series with generally high correlation is computed using best items first. The series with generally low correlation is computed using worst items first. At the end of both series all items are used, and correlation is the same. As mentioned earlier, correlation using only the best 24 items is 0.856. By contrast, correlation using only the worst 24 items is 0.679. The choice of test items can have a significant impact on OPI score prediction.

Figure 6 also shows that the effectiveness of individual test items can be predicted. MSE scores were calculated using only training data. Correlations were calculated for test data.

4.4 Rejection Threshold

Since the Forced Alignment language model is found to be so effective, we experiment further to learn more about its behavior. Using this language model, item scores are either zero or one, depending upon whether ASR output text is the same as item text, or there is no output text. If joint probability, for a spoken response, is below a certain rejection threshold, no text is output. We perform experiments

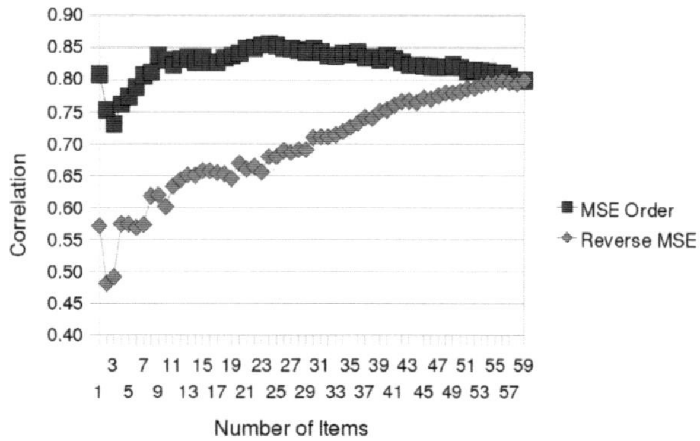

Figure 6: Correlation with OPI scores, showing the difference between best and worst items, using the Forced Alignment language model.

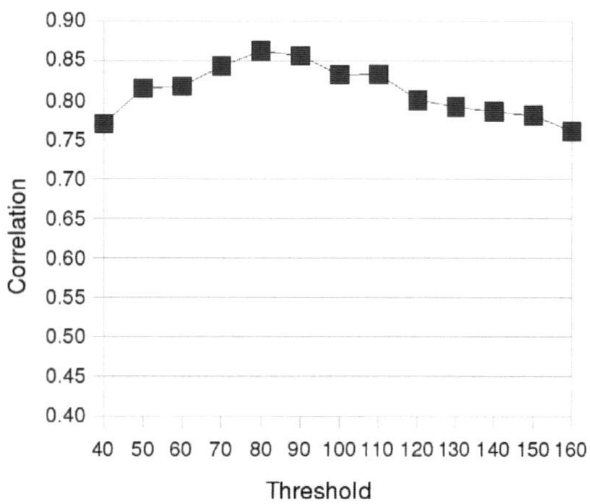

Figure 7: Correlation with OPI scores versus rejection threshold.

to see how sensitive OPI predictions are to the setting of this threshold.

Any ASR system parameter which affects probability estimates of word sequences can affect the rejection threshold. We make the arbitrary decision to vary the Sphinx $relativeBeamWidth$ parameter. For all previous experiments, the value of this parameter was fixed at $1E - 90$. The $wordInsertionProbability$ parameter, which also affects the rejection threshold, was fixed at $1E - 36$.

Correlation is computed for various values of the $relativeBeamWidth$ parameter. Results are shown in Figure 7. Good results are obtained over a wide range of rejection thresholds. Correlation peaks at $1E - 80$. OPI prediction does not appear to be overly sensitive to the setting of this threshold.

5 Discussion

We conclude that a fully-automated EI test can be used to effectively predict more general language ability than those abilities which are directly tested by EI. Such an EI test is used to predict the OPI scores of 25 test-takers. Correlation between predicted and actual OPI scores is strong.

Effectiveness of OPI score prediction depends upon at least two important design decisions. One of these decisions is to base prediction primarily on acoustic measures, rather than on transcription. The other of these decisions is the choice of sentences, or EI test items, to be repeated. It is shown that both of these design decisions can greatly impact performance. It is also shown that the effectiveness of individual test items can be predicted.

We quantify the effectiveness of individual test items using item MSE. It may be possible to use item MSE to learn more about the characteristics of effective EI test items. Developing more effective test items may lead to improved prediction of OPI test scores. In this paper, we do not attempt to address how linguistic factors (such as sentence length, syntactic complexity, lexical difficulty, and morphology) affect test item effectiveness for OPI prediction. However, others have discussed similar questions (Tomita et al., 2009; Christensen et al., 2010).

It may be possible that a test-taker could learn strategies for doing well on an EI test, without developing more general speech communication skills. If test-takers were able to learn such strategies, it may affect the usefulness of EI tests. Bernstein et al. (2010) suggest that, as yet, no conclusive evidence has been presented on this issue, and that automated test providers welcome such research.

It is possible that other automated systems are found to be more effective as a means for testing speech communication skills, or as a means for predicting OPI scores. We expect this to be the case. The purpose of this research is not to design the best possible system. Rather, it is to improve understanding of how such a system might be designed. It is shown that an EI test can be used as a key component of such a system. Strong correlation between actual and predicted OPI scores is achieved without using any other language testing method.

Acknowledgments

We would like to thank the Brigham Young University English Language Center for their support. We also appreciate assistance from the Pedagogical Software and Speech Technology research group, Casey Kennington, and Dr. C. Ray Graham.

References

Jared Bernstein, John De Jong, David Pisoni, and Brent Townshend. 2000. Two experiments on automatic scoring of spoken language proficiency. In P. Delcloque, editor, *Proceedings of InSTIL2000 (Integrating Speech Technology in Learning)*, pages 57–61.

Jared Bernstein, Alistair Van Moere, and Jian Cheng. 2010. Validating automated speaking tests. *Language Testing*, 27(3):355–377.

Craig Chaudron, Matthew Prior, and Ulrich Kozok. 2005. Elicited imitation as an oral proficiency measure. Paper presented at the 14th World Congress of Applied Linguistics, Madison, WI.

Carl Christensen, Ross Hendrickson, and Deryle Lonsdale. 2010. Principled construction of elicited imitation tests. In Nicoletta Calzolari (Conference Chair), Khalid Choukri, Bente Maegaard, Joseph Mariani, Jan Odijk, Stelios Piperidis, Mike Rosner, and Daniel Tapias, editors, *Proceedings of the Seventh Conference on International Language Resources and Evaluation (LREC'10)*, Valletta, Malta. European Language Resources Association (ELRA).

Tobias Cincarek, Rainer Gruhn, Christian Hacker, Elmar Nth, and Satoshi Nakamura. 2009. Automatic pronunciation scoring of words and sentences independent from the non-native's first language. *Computer Speech and Language*, 23(1):65 – 88.

Martin Fujiki and Bonnie Brinton. 1987. Elicited imitation revisited: A comparison with spontaneous language production. *Language, Speech, and Hearing Services in the Schools*, 18(4):301–311.

C. Ray Graham, Deryle Lonsdale, Casey Kennington, Aaron Johnson, and Jeremiah McGhee. 2008. Elicited Imitation as an Oral Proficiency Measure with ASR Scoring. In *Proceedings of the 6th International Conference on Language Resources and Evaluation*, pages 1604–1610, Paris, France. European Language Resources Association.

Grant Henning. 1983. Oral proficiency testing: comparative validities of interview, imitation, and completion methods. *Language Learning*, 33(3):315–332.

Pieter Müller, Febe de Wet, Christa van der Walt, and Thomas Niesler. 2009. Automatically assessing the oral proficiency of proficient L2 speakers. In *Proceedings of the ISCA Workshop on Speech and Language Technology in Education (SLaTE), Warwickshire, UK.*

Yasuyo Tomita, Watuaru Suzuki, and Lorena Jessop. 2009. Elicited imitation: Toward valid procedures to measure implicit second language grammatical knowledge. *TESOL Quarterly*, 43(2):345–349.

Thora Vinther. 2002. Elicited imitation: a brief overview. *International Journal of Applied Linguistics*, 12(1):54–73.

Willie Walker, Paul Lamere, Philip Kwok, Bhiksha Raj, Rita Singh, Evandro Gouvea, Peter Wolf, and Joe Woelfel. 2004. Sphinx-4: A flexible open source framework for speech recognition.

Ian H. Witten and Eibe Frank. 2005. *Data Mining: Practical Machine Learning Tools and Techniques*. Morgan Kaufmann, San Francisco.

Klaus Zechner and Xiaoming Xi. 2008. Towards automatic scoring of a test of spoken language with heterogeneous task types. In *Proceedings of the Third Workshop on Innovative Use of NLP for Building Educational Applications*, pages 98–106. Association for Computational Linguistics.

Detecting Structural Events for Assessing Non-Native Speech

Lei Chen
Educational Testing Service
Princeton NJ USA
LChen@ets.org

Su-Youn Yoon
Educational Testing Service
Princeton NJ USA
SYoon@ets.org

Abstract

Structural events, (i.e., the structure of clauses and disfluencies) in spontaneous speech, are important components of human speaking and have been used to measure language development. However, they have not been actively used in automated speech assessment research. Given the recent substantial progress on automated structural event detection on spontaneous speech, we investigated the detection of clause boundaries and interruption points of edit disfluencies on transcriptions of non-native speech data and extracted features from the detected events for speech assessment. Compared to features computed on human-annotated events, the features computed on machine-generated events show promising correlations to holistic scores that reflect speaking proficiency levels.

1 Introduction

Spontaneous speech utterances are organized in a structured way and generated dynamically with optional disfluencies. In second language acquisition (SLA) research, information related to the structure of utterances and profile of disfluencies has been widely used to monitor speakers' language development processes (Iwashita, 2006). However, structural events in human conversations have not been actively used in the automated speech assessment research. For example, most research that used Automatic Speech Recognition (ASR) technology to automatically score speaking proficiency (Neumeyer et al., 2000; Zechner et al., 2007) focused on word-level cues for fluency and accuracy.

In the last decade, a large amount of research (Gotoh and Renals, 2000; Shriberg et al., 2000; Liu, 2004; Ostendorf et al., 2008) has been conducted on structural event detection (i.e., sentence and disfluency structure). This research has resulted in better models for structural event detection. The detected structural events have been found to help many of the following natural language processing (NLP) tasks: speech parsing, information retrieval, machine translation, and extractive speech summarization (Ostendorf et al., 2008).

Because structural event information: (1) is important for understanding/processing speech, (2) has been successfully used in monitoring language development, which will be summarized in Section 2, (3) has received limited attention in automated speech assessment, and (4) has been actively investigated in the speech research domain in the past decade, it is worthwhile investigating the utility of using structural event detection on automated speech assessment. Because of the fairly low word accuracy currently achieved when recognizing spontaneous non-native speech of mixed proficiency levels and native language backgrounds, this study will focus on the transcribed words rather than speech recognition outputs.

This paper is organized as follows: Section 2 reviews previous research; Section 3 reports on the data used in the paper, including the collection, scoring, transcription, and annotation processes; Section 4 discusses the methods we utilized for structural event detection; Section 5 describes the experiments of structural event detection; Section 6 described the features derived from the event sequence

Proceedings of the Sixth Workshop on Innovative Use of NLP for Building Educational Applications, pages 38–45,
Portland, Oregon, 24 June 2011. ©2011 Association for Computational Linguistics

for assessing speech and evaluation results on these features; Section 7 discusses the findings of our research and plans for future directions.

2 Previous Research

In the SLA and child language development research fields, language development is measured according to fluency, accuracy, and complexity (Iwashita, 2006). Structural events are used to derive the features measuring syntactic complexity. For example, typical metrics for measuring syntactic complexity include: length of production units (e.g., T-units[1], clauses, verb phrases, and sentences), amount of embedding, subordination and coordination, range of structural types, and structural sophistication. Iwashita (2006) investigated several measures of syntactic complexity on data generated by learners of Japanese. The author reported that some measurements (e.g., T-unit length, the number of clauses per T-unit, and the number of independent clauses per T-unit) were good at predicting learners' proficiency levels.

In addition, speech disfluencies are used to measure language development. For example, Lennon (1990) used a dozen features related to speed, pauses, and several disfluency markers, such as filled pauses per T-unit, to measure the improvement of English proficiency for four German-speaking women during a six-month study in England. He found a significant change in filled pauses per T-unit during the study process.

These two types of features derived from structural events were combined in other previous studies. For example, Mizera (2006) used fluency factors related to speed, voiced smoothness (frequency of repetitions or self-corrections), pauses, syntactic complexity (mean length of T-units), and accuracy, to measure speaking proficiency on 20 non-native English speakers. In this experiment, disfluency-related factors, such as the total number of voiced disfluencies, correlated strongly with the fluency score ($r = -0.45$); however, the syntactic complexity factor only showed a moderate correlation ($r = 0.310$).

There have been previous efforts in using NLP technology to automatically calculate syntactic complexity metrics on learners' writing data. For example, Lu (2009) and Sagae et al. (2005) used parsing to get structural information on written texts; however, such efforts have not been undertaken in assessing speech data.

Chen et al. (2010) annotated structural events (such as clause structure and disfluencies) on English language learners' speech transcriptions and extracted features based on the structural event profile. They found that the features derived from structural event profile show promising correlation to human holistic scores. Berstein et al. (2010) also computed the features related to sentence lengths and the counts of syntactic entities. They found the extracted features were highly correlated to holistic scores measuring test-takers' language proficiency in both English and Spanish.

In the speech research domain, a large amount of research has been conducted to detect structural events in speech transcriptions and recognized words using lexical and prosodic cues. Using a language model (LM) trained on words combined with the events of interest is a popular technique for using textual information for structural event detection. For example, Heeman and Allen (1999) developed a LM including part of speech (POS) tags, discourse markers (e.g., *right, anyway*), speech repairs, and intonational phrases. In this way, structural information (e.g., speech repairs), could be predicted using a traditional speech recognition approach.

Prosodic information has been widely used to further improve textual models. For example, a simple prosodic feature, pause duration between words, was used in Gotoh and Renals (2000) to detect sentence boundaries. It was found that the pause duration model alone was better than using an LM alone, and the combination of the two models further improved the performance.

More advanced prosody models were used in other research on sentence boundary and speech repair detections (Shriberg et al., 2000; Shriberg and Stolcke, 2004). A general framework was built combining textual and prosodic cues to detect various kinds of structural events in speech, including sentence boundaries, disfluencies, topic boundaries, dialog acts, emotion, etc. Shriberg and Stolcke (2004) extracted prosodic features such as pause, phone du-

[1]A T-unit is defined as essentially a main clause plus any other clauses which are dependent upon it (Hunt, 1970).

ration, rhyme duration, and F_0 features. Using all of these features, a decision tree was built to detect possible structural events. An LM augmented with structural event tokens was also used to detect structural events based on textual cues. Finally, a Hidden Markov Model (HMM) was used to combine estimations from the textual model (an augmented LM with structural events) and prosodic model (decision-tree based on prosodic features).

Research on structural event detection has been strongly affected by the DARPA EARS program (EARS, 2002). As in Shriberg et al. (2000), the structural event detection (e.g., sentence units (SUs) and speech repairs) investigated in EARS was a classification task utilizing both prosodic and textual knowledge sources. New approaches for combining the two knowledge sources, including maximum entropy (MaxEnt) and conditional random fields (CRFs), were studied to address the weaknesses of the generative HMM approach (Liu et al., 2004). Liu et al. (2005) concluded that "adding textual information, building a more robust prosodic model, using conditional modeling approaches (Maxent and CRF), and system combination all yield performance gains."

3 Non-native Structural Event Corpus

Non-native speech data were collected from the TOEFL Practice Test Online (TPO) (ETS, 2006). In each TPO test, test-takers were required to respond to six speaking test items, in which they were required to provide information or opinions on familiar topics, based on their personal experience or background knowledge. For example, the test-takers were asked to describe their opinions about living on or off campus.

A total of 1066 responses were collected from examinees. Then, a group of experienced human raters scored these items based on the scoring rubrics designed for scoring the TPO test. For each item, two human raters independently assigned 4-point holistic scores for test-takers' English proficiency levels.

The speaking content was transcribed by a professional transcribing agency. On the transcriptions, structural event annotations were added, including (1) locations of clause boundaries, (2) types of clauses (e.g., noun clauses, adjective clauses, adverb clauses, etc.), and (3) disfluencies.

Disfluencies can further be sub-classified into several groups: silent pauses, filled pauses (e.g., *uh* and *um*), false starts, repetitions, and repairs. The repetitions and repairs were denoted as "*edit disfluency*", which were comprised of a *reparandum*, an optional *editing term*, and a *correction*. The *reparandum* is the part of an utterance that a speaker wants to repeat or change, while the *correction* contains the speaker's correction. The *editing term* can be a filled pause (e.g., *um*) or an explicit expression (e.g., *sorry*). The interruption point (IP), occurring at the end of the reparandum, is where the fluent speech is interrupted to prepare for the correction.

For the research reported in this paper, we focus on two structural events: the locations of clause-ending boundaries (CBs) and interruption points (IPs) of edit disfluencies. Note that if several clauses (in different layers of a clause hierarchy) end at the same word boundary, these clause boundaries were collapsed into one CB event.

Two persons annotated the corpus separately and their annotation quality was monitored by using several Kappa computations. For CBs, κ ranges from 0.85 to 0.90; for IPs, κ ranges from 0.63 to 0.83. Generally, a κ greater than 0.8 indicates a good between-rater agreement and κ in the range of 0.6 to 0.8 indicates acceptable agreement (Landis and Koch, 1977). Therefore, we believe that our human annotations are sufficiently reliable to be used in the following experiments.

4 Methods of Structural Event Detection

4.1 Features for structural event detection

In previous research (Gotoh and Renals, 2000; Shriberg et al., 2000; Liu, 2004), prosodic cues were found to be helpful, however, such findings on native speech data may not work well with non-native speech data. Anderson-Hsieh and Venkatagiri (1994) compared the pause frequencies of three groups of speakers (native, high-scoring, and low-scoring non-native speakers). They found that pause frequency was higher for groups of speakers with lower speaking skills. For native speakers, a long pause after a word-ending boundary is an important cue for signaling the existence of a sentence or clause boundary. However, the fact that there are more frequent pauses in non-native speech obscures this relationship.

On our non-native speech corpus, we conducted a pilot study on a widely-used prosodic feature, the pause duration[2] after a word, for its predictive ability to detect clause boundaries. If the duration of the pause after a word boundary is longer than 0.15 second, we call it a *long pause*. We measured the likelihood of being a CB event on the words followed by a *long pause*. For each score level, the likelihoods are: 15% for a score of 1, 22% for a score of 2, 28% for a score of 3, and 35% for a score of 4. Clearly, for low-proficiency speakers (i.e., speakers with a score of 1), long pauses in their utterances are not tightly linked to CBs. Therefore, more research is needed to utilize prosodic cues on non-native speech; in this paper, we focus on lexical features.

4.2 Statistical models

Based on lexical features, the structural event detection task can be generalized as follows:

$$\hat{E} = arg \max_{E} P(E|W)$$

Given that E denotes the between-word event sequence and W denotes the corresponding lexical cues, the goal is to find the event sequence that has the greatest probability, given the observed features.

Recently, conditional modeling approaches were successfully used in sentence units (SUs) and speech repairs detection (Liu, 2004). Hence, we use the Maximum Entropy (MaxEnt) (Berger et al., 1996) and Conditional Random Fields (CRFs) (Lafferty et al., 2001) approaches to build statistical models for structural event detection.

5 Structural Event Detection Experiment

5.1 Setup

In our experiment, the whole corpus described in Section 3 was split into a training set (*train*), a development test set (*dev*), and testing set (*test*), without speaker overlap between any pair of sets. Table 1 summarizes the numbers of items and words, as well as structural events of each dataset.

[2]Pause durations were obtained by running forced alignment using speech and transcriptions on a tri-phone HMM speech recognizer

	train	*dev*	*test*
# item	664	101	301
# word	71523	10509	33754
# CB	6121	918	2852
# IP	1767	267	1112

Table 1: The number of items, words, and structural events of the three sets in the TPO corpus

On average, each item contains about 108.6 words, 9.3 CBs, and 3.0 IPs. 9% of the word boundaries are associated with a CB event and 3% of the word boundaries are associated with an IP event. Clearly, these CB and IP events are sparse and such a skewed distribution of structural events increases the difficulty of structural event detection.

5.2 Models

The following two conditional models were built to detect CB and IP events:

- **MaxEnt**: Given w_i as the word token at position i, the word n-gram features include: $\langle w_i \rangle$, $\langle w_{i-1}, w_i \rangle$, $\langle w_i, w_{i+1} \rangle$, $\langle w_{i-2}, w_{i-1}, w_i \rangle$, $\langle w_i, w_{i+1}, w_{i+2} \rangle$, and $\langle w_{i-1}, w_i, w_{i+1} \rangle$. Given t_i as the POS tag[3] at position i, the POS n-gram features include: $\langle t_i \rangle$, $\langle t_{i-1}, t_i \rangle$, $\langle t_i, t_{i+1} \rangle$, $\langle t_{i-2}, t_{i-1}, t_i \rangle$, $\langle t_i, t_{i+1}, t_{i+2} \rangle$, and $\langle t_{i-1}, t_i, t_{i+1} \rangle$.

  For IP detection, in addition to the n-gram features described above, another four features that capture syntactic pattern of disfluencies are utilized:

  - **filled pause adjacency**: This feature has a binary value showing whether a filled pause such as *uh* or *um* was adjacent to the current word (w_i).
  - **word repetition**: This feature has a binary value showing whether the current word (w_i) was repeated in the following 5 words or not.

[3]POS tags were obtained by tagging words using a MaxEnt POS tagger, which was implemented in the OpenNLP toolkit and trained on the Switchboard (SWBD) corpus. This POS tagger was trained on about $528K$ word/tag pairs and achieved an tagging accuracy of 96.3% on a test set of $379K$ words.

- **similarity**: This feature has a continuous value which measures the similarity between the reparandum and correction. Assuming that w_i was the end of the reparandum, the start point and the end point of the reparandum and correction were estimated, and the string edit distance between the reparandum and correction was calculated. The start point and the end point of the reparandum and correction were estimated as follows; if w_i appeared in the following 5 words, the second occurrence was defined as the end of the correction. Otherwise, w_{i+5} was defined as the end of correction. Secondly, N, the length of the correction was calculated, and w_{i-N+1} was defined as the start point of the reparandum. During the calculation of the string edit distance, a word fragment was considered to be the same as a word whose initial character sequences matched it.
- **length of correction**: This feature counts the number of words in the correction.

The first two features are similar to the features used in (Liu, 2004) while the last two features provide important keys in distinguishing edit disfluencies from fluent speech. Since the correction is composed of word sequences that are similar to the reparandum, these two features are higher than zero when the target word is a part of the edit disfluency. In addition, these two numeric features were discretized by using an equal-distance binning approach.

Using n-gram features for CB detection and all these lexical features for IP detection, we used the Maxent toolkit designed by Zhang (2005) to build MaxEnt models. The L-BFGS parameter estimation method is used, with the Gaussian-prior smoothing technique to avoid over-fitting. The Gaussian prior is estimated on the *dev* set.

- **CRF**: All features which were described in building MaxEnt models were used in the CRF model. We used the Java-based NLP package Mallet (McCallum, 2005) to build CRF models. Similar to MaxEnt models, Gaussian-prior smoothing was used with the priors estimated on the *dev* set.

These models were trained using the *train* set. Besides Gaussian priors, other parameters in the model training (i.e., the training iteration number as well as the cutting-point for event decisions) were estimated using the *dev* set. Finally, the trained models were evaluated on the *test* set.

5.3 Evaluation of event detection

Since structural event detection was treated as a classification task in this paper, four standard evaluation metrics were used:

$$
\begin{aligned}
accuracy &= \frac{TP+TN}{TP+FP+TN+FN} \\
precision &= \frac{TP}{TP+FP} \\
recall &= \frac{TP}{TP+FN} \\
F1 &= 2 \times \frac{recall \times precision}{recall + precision}
\end{aligned}
$$

where, TP and FP denote the number of true positives and false positives, and TN and FN denote the number of true negatives and false negatives. A structural event (a CB or IP boundary) is treated as a positive class. In our experiment, since we treated precision and recall as equally important, the $F1$ measurement was used.

For each model, if the estimated probability, $P(E_i|W)$, is larger than a threshold, the corresponding word boundary will be estimated to be a positive class. The threshold was chosen when a maximal $F1$ score was achieved on the *dev* set.

A model that always predicts the majority class (a no-event in this study) was treated as a baseline model. For CB detection, this type of baseline model resulted in an accuracy of 91.6%; for IP detection, this type of baseline model resulted in an accuracy of 96.7%.

5.4 Results of structural event detection

Table 2 summarizes the performance of the two models on the CB and IP detection tasks.

For CB detection, two conditional models are superior to the baseline CB detection (with an accuracy of 91.6%); they achieved relatively high $F1$ scores

	Acc.	Pre.	Rec.	$F1$
		CB		
MaxEnt	94.5	66.1	71.8	0.689
CRF	96.1	82.3	68.6	0.749
		IP		
MaxEnt	98.1	61.8	55.2	0.583
CRF	98.4	76.9	48.0	0.591

Table 2: Experimental results of the CB and IP detection measurement using accuracy (Acc.), precision (Pre.), recall (Rec.) and $F1$ measurement ($F1$) on the TPO data

ranging from 0.689 to 0.749. Between the two models, the CRF model achieved the higher $F1$ score at 0.749, The lower F-score of the MaxEnt model may be caused by the fact that the MaxEnt model does not use event history information in its decoding process.

However, these two models achieved lower performance on the task of detecting IPs for editing disfluencies. F-scores became about 0.58 to 0.59 for IP detections. The degraded performance may be caused by the extremely low IP distribution (only 3%) in our data. Between the two modeling approaches, consistent with the result shown for CB detection, the CRF model achieved a higher $F1$ score (0.591).

6 Using Detected Structural Events for Speech Assessment

6.1 Features assessing proficiency

Many previous SLA studies used the length of production units and frequency of disfluencies as metrics to measure language development (Iwashita, 2006; Lennon, 1990; Mizera, 2006). Our automated structural event detection provides the locations of CBs and IPs, which can be used to compute these features for use in speech assessment.

Using N_w to represent the total number of words in the spoken response (without pruning the reparandums and edit terms in the edit disfluencies), N_C as the total number of CBs, and N_{IP} as the total number of IPs detected on transcriptions of speech streams, the following features (i.e, *mean length of clause* (MLC), *interruption points per clause* (IPC), and *interruption points per word* (IPW)) were derived:

$$\begin{aligned} MLC &= N_w/N_C \\ IPC &= N_{IP}/N_C \\ IPW &= N_{IP}/N_w \end{aligned}$$

The IPW can be treated as the IPC normalized by the MLC. The reason for this normalization is that disfluency behavior is influenced by various factors, such as speakers' proficiency levels as well as the difficulty of utterances' structure. For example, Roll et al. (2007) found that the complexity of expression, computed based on the language's parsing-tree structure, influenced the frequency of disfluencies in their experiment on Swedish responses. Therefore, the fact that IPW is the IPC normalized by MLC (a feature related to complexity of utterances' structure) helps to reduce the impact of utterances' structure and to highlight contributions from the speaker's proficiency.

6.2 Results of measuring the derived features

On the *test* set, we produced CB and IP event sequences estimated by the MaxEnt and CRF models, respectively. These machine-generated events were evaluated by comparison with human annotations, which were denoted as REF.

The proposed features described in Section 6.1 were computed on the word/event sequence of each item. In addition, given the fact that each item only covers approximately one-minute of speech and the content is quite limited, we also extracted features on the test-taker level by combining the detected events of all of the items spoken by each test-taker. Then, according to the score handling protocol used in TPO, the human-holistic scores from the first human rater were used as item scores to compute Pearson correlation coefficients (rs) with the features. For the test-taker level evaluation, we used the average score for each test-taker from all of his/her item scores.

Table 3 reports on the evaluation results of the features derived from the structural event estimations. Compared to rs computed on the speaker level using multiple (as many as 6) items, rs computed on the item level are generally lower. This is because words and events are limited in this one-minute long response. Among the three features, the

Model	r_{MLC}	r_{IPC}	r_{IPW}
	Per item		
REF	0.003	-0.369	-0.402
MaxEnt	-0.012	-0.329	-0.343
CRF	-0.042	-0.328	-0.335
	Per speaker		
REF	0.066	-0.453	-0.516
MaxEnt	0.055	-0.396	-0.417
CRF	0.043	-0.355	-0.366

Table 3: Correlation coefficients (rs) between the features derived from structural events with human scores on the item and speaker levels

MLC shows the lowest r to human holistic scores. In contrast, the two features derived from interruption points show promising rs to human holistic scores. Between them, the IPW always shows a higher r than the IPC. Compared to the features extracted on human annotations, the features derived from structural events automatically estimated by the two NLP models show a lower but sufficiently high r. The features derived from the MaxEnt model's estimations on the test-taker level show a greater r than the features derived from the CRF model estimations.

7 Discussion

Three features measuring syntactic complexity and disfluency profile of speaking, MLC, IPC, and IPW, were extracted on the structural event sequences estimated by the developed models. Compared to the features extracted from the human-annotated structural events, the features derived from machine-generated event sequences show promisingly close correlations.

Applying automated structural event detection to spontaneous speech brings many benefits for automatic speech assessment. First, obtaining information beyond the word level, such as the structure of clauses and disfluencies, can expand and improve the construct[4] coverage of speech features. Second, knowing the structure of utterances helps to facilitate the application of more NLP processing methods (e.g., collocation detection that requires information about sentence boundaries), to speech content. In this study, using only simple word and POS based n-gram features, CBs can be detected relatively well (with an $F1$ score of approximately 0.70). More lexical features reflecting repair properties were found to help improve IP detection performance. In addition, IP-based features derived from machine-generated event sequences show promising correlation with human holistic scores. Results in detection of clause boundaries and interruption points support the approach of utilizing automated structural event detection on speech assessment.

We plan to continue our research in the following three directions. First, we will investigate integrating prosodic cues to further improve the structural event detection performance on non-native speech. Second, we will investigate estimating structural events directly on speech recognition results. Third, other aspects of syntactic complexity, such as the embedding of clauses, will be studied to provide a broader set of features for speech assessment.

[4]A construct is the set of knowledge, skills, and abilities measured by a test.

References

J. Anderson-Hsieh and H. Venkatagiri. 1994. Syllable duration and pausing in the speech of chinese ESL speakers. *TESOL Quarterly*, pages 807–812.

A. Berger, S. Pietra, and V. Pietra. 1996. A maximum entropy approach to natural language processing. *Computational Linguistics*, 22:39–72.

J. Berstein, J. Cheng, and M. Suzuki. 2010. Fluency and Structural Complexity as Predictors of L2 Oral Proficiency. In *Proc. of InterSpeech*.

L. Chen, J. Tetreault, and X. Xi. 2010. Towards using structural events to assess non-native speech. In *Fifth Workshop on Innovative Use of NLP for Building Educational Applications*, page 74.

EARS. 2002. DARPA EARS Program. `http://projects.ldc.upenn.edu/EARS/`.

ETS. 2006. TOEFL Practice Online Test (TPO).

Y. Gotoh and S. Renals. 2000. Sentence boundary detection in broadcast speech transcript. In *Proceedings of the International Speech Communication Association (ISCA) Workshop: Automatic Speech Recognition: Challenges for the new Millennium ASR-2000*.

P. Heeman and J. Allen. 1999. Speech repairs, intonational phrased and discourse markers: Modeling speakers' utterances in spoken dialogue. *Computational Linguistics*.

K. W. Hunt. 1970. Syntactic maturity in school children and adults. In *Monographs of the Society for Re-*

search in Child Development. University of Chicago Press, Chicago, IL.

N. Iwashita. 2006. Syntactic complexity measures and their relation to oral proficiency in Japanese as a foreign language. *Language Assessment Quarterly: An International Journal*, 3(2):151–169.

J. Lafferty, A. McCallum, and F. Pereira. 2001. Conditional random field: Probabilistic models for segmenting and labeling sequence data. In *Proceedings of the International Conference on Machine Learning (ICML)*.

J. R Landis and G. G Koch. 1977. The measurement of observer agreement for categorical data. *Biometrics*, pages 159–174.

P. Lennon. 1990. Investigating fluency in EFL: A quantitative approach. *Language Learning*, 40(3):387–417.

Y. Liu, A. Stolcke, E. Shriberg, and M. Harper. 2004. Comparing and combining generative and posterior probability models: Some advances in sentence boundary detection in speech. In *Proceedings of the Empirical Methods in Natural Language Processing (EMNLP)*.

Y. Liu, E. Shriberg, A. Stolcke, B. Peskin, J. Ang, Hillard D., M. Ostendorf, M. Tomalin, P. Woodland, and M. Harper. 2005. Structural Metadata Research in the EARS Program. In *Proceedings of the International Conference of Acoustics, Speech, and Signal Processing (ICASSP)*.

Y. Liu. 2004. *Structural Event Detection for Rich Transcription of Speech*. Ph.D. thesis, Purdue University.

X. Lu. 2009. Automatic measurement of syntactic complexity in child language acquisition. *International Journal of Corpus Linguistics*, 14(1):3–28.

A. McCallum. 2005. Mallet: A machine learning toolkit for language. `http://mallet.cs.umass.edu`.

G. J. Mizera. 2006. *Working memory and L2 oral fluency*. Ph.D. thesis, University of Pittsburgh.

L. Neumeyer, H. Franco, V. Digalakis, and M. Weintraub. 2000. Automatic Scoring of Pronunciation Quality. *Speech Communication*, 30:83–93.

M. Ostendorf, B. Favre, R. Grishman, D. Hakkani-Tur, M. Harper, D. Hillard, J. Hirschberg, Heng Ji, J.G. Kahn, Yang Liu, S. Maskey, E. Matusov, H. Ney, A. Rosenberg, E. Shriberg, Wen Wang, and C. Woofers. 2008. Speech segmentation and spoken document processing. *Signal Processing Magazine, IEEE*, 25(3):59–69, May.

M. Roll, J. Frid, and M. Horne. 2007. Measuring syntactic complexity in spontaneous spoken Swedish. *Language and Speech*, 50(2):227.

K. Sagae, A. Lavie, and B. MacWhinney. 2005. Automatic measurement of syntactic development in child language. In *Proc. of ACL*, volume 100.

E. Shriberg and A. Stolcke. 2004. Direct modeling of prosody: An overview of applications in automatic speech processing. In *Proceedings of the International Conference on Speech Prosody*.

E. Shriberg, A. Stolcke, D. Hakkani-Tur, and G. Tur. 2000. Prosody-based automatic segmentation of speech into sentences and topics. *Speech Communication*, 32(1-2):127–154.

K. Zechner, D. Higgins, and Xiaoming Xi. 2007. SpeechRater: A Construct-Driven Approach to Scoring Spontaneous Non-Native Speech. In *Proc. SLaTE*.

L. Zhang. 2005. Maximum Entropy Modeling Toolkit for Python and C++. `http://homepages.inf.ed.ac.uk/s0450736/maxent_toolkit.html`.

Performance of Automated Scoring for Children's Oral Reading

Ryan Downey, David Rubin, Jian Cheng, Jared Bernstein
Pearson Knowledge Technologies
299 S. California Ave.
Palo Alto, California 94306

Ryan.Downey@Pearson.com

Abstract

For adult readers, an automated system can produce oral reading fluency (ORF) scores (e.g., words read correctly per minute) that are consistent with scores provided by human evaluators (Balogh et al., 2005, and in press). Balogh's work on NAAL materials used passage-specific data to optimize statistical language models and scoring performance. The current study investigates whether or not an automated system can produce scores for young children's reading that are consistent with human scores. A novel aspect of the present study is that text-independent rule-based language models were employed (Cheng and Townshend, 2009) to score reading passages that the system had never seen before. Oral reading performances were collected over cell phones from 1st, 2nd, and 3rd grade children (n = 95) in a classroom environment. Readings were scored 1) *in situ* by teachers in the classroom, 2) later by expert scorers, and 3) by an automated system. Statistical analyses provide evidence that machine Words Correct scores correlate well with scores provided by teachers and expert scorers, with all (Pearson's correlation coefficient) r's > 0.98 at the individual response level, and all r's > 0.99 at the "test" level (i.e., median scores out of 3).

1 Introduction

Oral reading fluency (ORF), defined as "the ability to read a text quickly, accurately, and with proper expression" (National Reading Panel, 2000; p. 3.5), is a reflection of readers' decoding ability. Skilled readers can recognize words effortlessly (Rasinski and Hoffman, 2003), due to "automaticity" of processing (LaBerge and Samuels, 1974) whereby a reader's attention is no longer focused on "lower level" processing (e.g., letter to phoneme correspondence, word identification, etc.). Instead, attention can be devoted to "higher level" functions such as comprehension and expression (LaBerge and Samuels, 1974). As a means of assessing general reading ability, oral reading fluency performance is also a predictor of student success in academic areas such as reading and math (e.g., Crawford, Tindal, and Stieber, 2001). Oral reading fluency is one of the key basic skills identified in the Reading First initiative used to satisfy the standards of the No Child Left Behind Act (NCLB, 2001).

Although oral reading fluency is comprised of several abilities, due to practical constraints the most commonly reported reflection of oral reading fluency is reading rate, specifically, the words read correctly per minute (WCPM). Typically, ORF performance is measured by a classroom teacher who sits alongside a student, marking and annotating – in real time – the student's reading on a sheet of paper containing the passage to be read. Classroom testing is time-consuming and requires a teacher's full attention. In practice, teaching time is often sacrificed to "testing time" to satisfy local and federal reporting standards (e.g., NCLB). ORF scoring guidelines are specific to particular publishers; teachers must undergo training to become familiar with these guidelines, and cost, availability, and quality of training varies. Finally, despite good-faith attempts to score accurately, teachers may impose errors and inconsistencies in

Proceedings of the Sixth Workshop on Innovative Use of NLP for Building Educational Applications, pages 46–55,
Portland, Oregon, 24 June 2011. ©2011 Association for Computational Linguistics

scoring ORF performances due to unavoidable factors such as classroom distractions, varying experience with different accents/dialects, varying experience with scoring conventions, and differences in training, among others.

To address the need for a rapid and reliable way to assess oral reading fluency, a growing body of research has supported the use of automated approaches. Beginning with work by Bernstein et al. (1990) and Mostow et al. (1994), prototype systems for automatic measurement of basic components of reading have appeared. Recent projects have addressed finer event classification in reading aloud (Black, Tepperman, Lee, Price, and Narayanan, 2007), and word level reading (Tepperman et al., 2007), among others. Research has increasingly focused on systems to score passage-level reading performances (e.g., Balogh et al., 2005; Zechner, Sabatini, and Chen, 2009; Cheng and Townshend, 2009). Eskenazi (2009) presents a general historical perspective on speech processing applications in language learning, including reading.

The present automated ORF assessment was developed to deliver and score tests of oral reading fluency, allowing teachers to spend less time testing and more time teaching, while at the same time improving score consistency across time and location. Automated ORF tests are initiated by a click in a web-based class roster. Once a test is initiated, a call is placed to a local phone number and the test begins when the phone is answered. Instructions presented through the handset direct the student to read passages out loud into the cell phone, and these readings are sent to the automated ORF system for processing and scoring.

2 Present Study

The scoring models used by the automated ORF test (see **Method** below) were originally developed based on adult readings, and then optimized on large sets of data collected from students reading passages produced by AIMSweb, a publisher of Reading Curriculum-Based Measurement (R-CBM) oral reading fluency passages (www.aimsweb.com). AIMSweb passages are leveled and normed across large samples of students. Previous validation studies found that when the system was optimized using data from students reading AIMSweb passages, machine scores correlated with trained human expert score with r = 0.95 to 0.98, depending on the grade level of the student readers.

The primary question that the present studies attempt to answer is whether the automated scoring system can score newly inserted content – in this case, ORF passages offered by Sopris called "Dynamic Indicators of Basic Early Literacy Skills", or DIBELS (www.dibels.com) – accurately and at a high level of reliability. This is an evaluation of text-independent Rule Based Language Models (RBLMs) that were developed with training data from *other* readers performing on *other* passages and then applied to the new passages.

A secondary question of interest involves how different types of scorers may assign Words Correct scores differently. Two groups of human scorers were recruited: 1) teachers who were recently trained in DIBELS scoring methods who would perform scoring in the classroom, and 2) expert scorers with the ability to score reading recordings carefully and at their convenience, without classroom distractions. Answering the first part of the question involves comparing machine Words Correct scores to human scores when teachers make ratings in the classroom environment as the student reads into the phone. This analysis reveals if the machine and teachers produce systematically different scores when testing is performed in a "live" classroom with the typical attentional demands placed on a teacher scoring an ORF passage. Answering the second part of the question involves comparing machine Words Correct scores to a "consensus", or median Words Correct value, from expert scorers. These three experts, with over 14 years of combined experience scoring DIBELS passages, listened to recordings of the same readings made in the classroom. Because the recordings were digitally preserved in a database, the expert scorers were able to replay any part(s) of the recordings to determine whether each word was read correctly. The benefit of being able to replay recordings is that such scores obtained are, in theory, closer to capturing the "truth" of the student's performance, unaffected by biases or distractions encountered by scorers performing a "live" rating.

2.1 Method

2.1.1 Rule Based Language Models

The scoring models used by the automated ORF system are RBLMs such as those described by Cheng and Townshend (2009). Such models outperform traditional n-gram language models (Cheng and Shen, 2010), in part by adding intuitively simple rules such as allowing a long silence as an alternative to a short pause after every word, leading to improvements in accuracy. Also, rules like those described by Cheng and Townshend (2009) consider much longer sequential dependencies. The basic idea for this kind of language model is that each passage gets a simple directed graph with a path from the first word to the last word. Different arcs are added to represent different common errors made by the readers, such as skipping, repeating, inserting, and substituting words. For each arc, a probability is assigned to represent the chance that the arc will be chosen. Knowledge of performance on other readings produces linguistic rules, such as *she* can substitute for *he*, a single noun can replace a plural noun, the reader may skip from any place to the end, etc. All the rules used in RBLMs can be classified into five broad groups:

1. skip/repeat rules
2. rules using part-of-speech (POS) tagging information
3. rules accommodating for insertion of partial words
4. general word level rules
5. hesitation and mouth noise rules

A detailed analysis of the role of rules in RBLMs was described in Cheng and Shen (2010).

The language rules are extrapolated from transcriptions of oral reading responses to passages using four base rules: any word substitutes for any word with a low probability; any word is inserted after any word with a low probability; any word is skipped with a low probability; any word is repeated immediately with a low probability. Following Cheng and Townshend (2009), the first two are the only rules that allow out-of-vocabulary words and their probabilities are fixed to the lowest level, so their arcs will never be traversed unless there is no other choice.

General language model rules for reading can be inferred from clustering traversals of the basic models and proposing further rules that can be applied to new reading passages and used to infer underlying knowledge about the reading. Arcs are added to represent commonly observed non-canonic readings. Further analysis of rule-firing details may provide diagnostic linguistic information about children's reading habits that can be reported and analyzed.

In the present automated scoring system, new passages are automatically tagged for part-of-speech (POS) using the Penn Tree Tagger (Marcus, Santorini, and Marcinkiewicz, 1993). POS tags allow specification of certain general rules based on linguistic properties, such as:

- NN (noun, singular or mass) can become NNS (noun, plural);
- VBZ (verb, 3rd person singular present) can become VBP (verb, non-3rd person singular present); and so on.

These patterns occur quite frequently in real responses and can therefore be accounted for by rules. Sentence, clause, and end-of-line boundaries are tagged manually. Marked up passages are then inserted into the ORF scoring system, providing data regarding places in the reading that may result in pauses, hesitations, corrections, etc. If the expected response to a reading passage is highly constrained, the system can verify the occurrence of the correct lexical content in the correct sequence. It is expected that the system, using previously trained data coupled with the RBLMs from the newly inserted passages, will be able to produce Words Correct scores with high accuracy (i.e., consistent with human Words Correct scores).

Here, we make a final note on the use of Words Correct instead of words correct per minute (WCPM), when WCPM is the most common measure for quantifying oral reading performance. The automated system presents students with a 60-second recording window to read each passage, but it calculates a truer WCPM by trimming leading and trailing silence. Human scorers simply reported the number of words correct, on the assumption that the reading time is the recording window duration. Thus, Words Correct scores are the appropriate comparison values, with a fixed 60-second nominal reading time.

2.1.2 Participants

A total of 95 students were recruited from the San Jose Unified School District in San Jose,

California. The students were 20 first graders, 20 second graders, and 55 third graders, all enrolled in a summer school program. Students with known speech disorders were included in the study, as was one student with a hearing impairment. Roughly half of the participants were male and half were female. A number of English Language Learners are known to have been included in the sample, though language status was not recorded as a variable for this study. It is not known whether any of the students had been diagnosed with reading disabilities.

Four Teachers were trained to administer and score DIBELS ORF passages by an official DIBELS trainer, over the course of a two day training session. All Teachers were reading experts or teachers with experience in reading education. They were trained to navigate a web application that triggers delivery of tests over cell phones under classroom testing conditions. Evaluator qualifications are summarized in Table 1.

Evaluator	Highest degree, or relevant certification	Years assessing reading
Teacher 1	MA Education	8
Teacher 2	MA Education	7
Teacher 3	Reading Credential	15
Teacher 4	BA Education	12
Expert 1	MS, Statistics	5
Expert 2	EdS, Education	2
Expert 3	MA Education	20

Table 1. Evaluator qualifications

2.1.3 Procedure

First, nine passages – three for each of the three grades, presented together in a single test – were drawn from the DIBELS Benchmark test materials. Each DIBELS passage was tagged for parts of speech and formatting (e.g., line breaks) and inserted into the automated scoring system. Rule-based language models were produced for each passage.

During data collection, each student read the grade-appropriate DIBELS Benchmark test (3 passages) into a cellular telephone in the classroom. With three passages per student, this process yielded 285 individual reading performances.

Once a test was initiated, Teachers allowed the test to run independently and scored manually alongside the student reading into the phone. According to standard DIBELS scoring conventions, the students were allowed to read each passage for one minute. Teachers calculated and recorded the Words Correct score on a worksheet for each passage. Teachers returned the annotated score sheets for analysis.

Later, three Expert scorers logged in to a web-based interface via the Internet, where they listened to the digitized recordings of the readings. All three Expert scorers had extensive experience with DIBELS rating. One Expert was the DIBELS trainer who provided the DIBELS training to the Teachers for this study. Experts scored students' performance manually using score sheets with the instruction to use standard DIBELS scoring conventions. Each Expert entered a Words Correct score for each passage using the web interface, and the score sheets were returned for analysis.

2.1.4 Automated scoring

Incoming spoken responses were digitally recorded and sent to a speech processing system that is optimized for both native and non-native speech. Recognition was performed by an HMM-based recognizer built using the HTK toolkit (Young, et al., 2000). Acoustic models, pronunciation dictionaries, and expected-response networks were developed in-house using data from previous training studies involving many thousands of responses. The words, pauses, syllables, phones, and even some subphonemic events can be located in the recorded signal, and "words recognized" are compared with "words expected" to produce a recognized response and word count.

The acoustic models for the speech recognizer were developed using data from a diverse sample of non-native speakers of English. In addition, recordings from 57 first-grade children were used to optimize the automated scoring system to accommodate for characteristics specific to young children's voices and speech patterns. These participants produced 136 usable, individual reading samples. These samples were each rated by two expert human raters. Using this final training set, the scoring models were refined to the point that the correlation between human and machine scoring was 0.97 for WCPM.

2.1.5 Human scoring

During data preparation, it was noted that many of the teacher scores were several words longer than would be expected based on the machine scores. Further investigation revealed that teachers would occasionally continue scoring after the one minute point at which the system stopped recording a passage, perhaps because they hadn't heard the notification that the reading was complete. A total of 31 out of 285 instances (~10.8%) were found where teachers continued scoring for more than 3 words beyond the 1 minute recording window, leading to artificially inflated Teacher scores. This artifact of the testing apparatus/environment warranted making a careful correction, whereby all Teacher scores were adjusted to account for what the machine "heard". That is, words and errors which Teachers scored after the automated system stopped recording (i.e., to which the automated system did not have access) were subtracted from the original Teacher Words Correct scores. All Teacher Words Correct scores reported hereafter are thus "corrected".

For purposes of finding a "consensus" Expert score, the median of the 3 expert human scores for each passage was obtained and is referred to as $Expert_M$ in the following analyses.

Nine readings from eight separate students received no scores from teachers. Information was not provided by the teachers regarding why they failed to complete the scoring process for these readings. However, we made the following observations based on the teachers' marked-up scoring sheets. For three readings, the teacher's final score was blank when the student appeared to have skipped lines in the passage. It is possible that, despite recent scoring training, the teacher was uncertain how to score skipped lines in the readings and left the final score blank pending confirmation. For one reading, the teacher made a note that the system stopped recording well before one minute had expired because the child's reading was too quiet to be picked up, and the teacher did not record the final score on the score sheet. For one reading, the student did not hear the prompt to begin reading (confirmed by listening to the response recording) and therefore did not read the entire passage; the teacher did not enter a final score. For the four remaining readings, the teacher annotated the performance but did not write down the final score for unclear reasons.

We might have elected to fill in the teachers' final scores for these 9 readings prior to subjecting the data to analysis, especially in the cases where a teacher annotated the reading correctly on the score sheet but simply failed to record the final Words Correct score, perhaps due to oversight or not knowing how to handle unusual events (e.g., entire line of reading skipped). Excluding such readings from the analysis ensured that the teachers' scores reflected "their own" scoring – including any errors they might make – rather than our interpretation of what the Teachers *probably* would have written. In addition, to maintain the most conservative approach, whenever a single reading passage from a student lacked a teacher's score, all 3 of that student's readings were excluded. The decision to exclude all readings from students with only a single passage missing was made because relevant analyses reported below involve reporting median scores, and a median score for students lacking one or two passage scores would not be possible.[1] The final set of graded responses thus consisted of 261 responses from 87 students.[2]

2.2 Results

2.2.1 Score Group Comparisons

Words Correct scores from Teachers, $Expert_M$, and machine are displayed in Table 2. Repeated measures ANOVA with Scorer Type (machine, Teacher, $Expert_M$) as the repeated measure and Score Group as the between-subjects factor revealed a main effect of group for the 261

[1] The excluded 8 students produced 15 readings with all three (Machine, Teacher, Expert) scores. Machine scores vs. Teacher scores and Machine scores vs. $Expert_M$ scores for these 15 individual responses yielded correlations of (Pearson's) r = 0.9949 and 0.9956, respectively. Thus, excluding these responses from the larger dataset is unlikely to have significantly affected the overall results.

[2] In production, such a system would not commit these errors of omission. Readings that are unscorable for technical reasons can trigger a "*Median score not be calculated*" message and request a teacher to manually score a recording or re-administer the assessment. Also, anomalous performances where Words Correct on one passage is very different from Words Correct on the two other passages could return a message.

readings[3], $F(2, 520) = 9.912$, $p < .01$, $\omega^2 < .001$. Post-hoc pairwise comparisons [4] showed that Words Correct scores from Teachers were higher on average than both the machine and Expert_M scores (higher by 1.559 and 0.923 words correct, respectively; both p's $< .05$). On the other hand, Machine and Expert_M scores did not differ significantly from each other (diff = 0.636).

Although the ANOVA showed that the means In the above analysis were significantly different, the effect size was negligible: ω^2 was = .0002, indicating that Score Group by itself accounted for less than 1% of the overall variance in scores. These results indicate that, for all 261 passages, the Expert_M and machine scores were statistically comparable (e.g., within 1 word correct of each other), while Teachers tended to assign slightly – but not meaningfully – higher scores, on average.

Next, comparisons were made using the median value of each student's three readings. Median Words Correct scores for the 87 individual students were subjected to repeated measures ANOVA with the same factor (Scorer Group). Teachers' Words Correct scores were again higher than Expert_M scores (diff = 1.115) and Machine scores (diff = 0.851), but this was not statistically significant in the main analysis, $F(2, 172) = 3.11$, $p > .05$, $\omega^2 < .001$. Machine Words Correct scores were, on average, 0.264 words higher than Expert_M scores, but this, too, was not statistically significant. These results support the previous comparisons, in that machine scores fall well within ~1 word correct of scores from careful experts, while teachers tended to give scores of about 1 word correct higher than both experts and machine.

2.2.2 Scorer performance

To compare reliability, the Pearson's Product Moment coefficient (r) was used to estimate the correlation between paired human and machine scores, and between pairs of human raters. Two types of analyses are reported. First, analyses of Words Correct scores were conducted across scorers. Next, analyses were conducted on the basis of the median Words Correct score for each student's readings (i.e., the median score across all three passages). This score reflects the "real-life" score of DIBELS ORF tests because the median score is the one that is ultimately reported according to DIBELS scoring/reporting conventions.

2.2.2.1. Intra-rater reliability

Each Teacher scored each reading once during the live grading; intra-rater reliability could thus not be estimated for the Teacher group. During Expert rating, a randomly selected 5% of the passages were presented again for rating to each scorer. Overall Expert intra-rater reliability was 0.9998, with intra-rater reliability scores for Expert 1, Expert 2, and Expert 3 at 0.9996, 1.0, and 1.0, respectively. These results indicate that Expert human scorers are extremely consistent when asked to provide Words Correct scores for reading passages when given the opportunity to listen to the passages at a careful, uninterrupted pace. The automated scoring system would produce the exact same score (reliability = 1.0) every time it scored the same recordings, making its reliability comparable.

Score Type	Words Correct	
	261 readings Mean (*SD*)	**87 students Mean (*SD*)**
Teacher	84.3 *(42.5)*	84.0 *(42.1)*
Expert_M	83.4 *(42.3)*	82.9 *(41.8)*
Machine	82.8 *(39.6)*	83.2 *(39.3)*

Table 2. Mean Words Correct for all readings and all students.

2.2.2.2. Inter-rater reliability

Pearson's r was used to estimate the inter-rater reliability. All three Experts scored all passages, whereas any particular Teacher scored only a subset of the passages; thus, the Teacher's score was used without consideration of which teacher provided the score. Inter-rater reliability results are summarized in Table 3.

[3] For both ANOVAs, uncorrected degrees of freedom are reported but reported F values are corrected using Huynh-Feldt estimates of sphericity.

[4] Using Bonferroni adjustment for multiple comparisons.

Reliability (N = 261)			
	Teacher	Expert 1	Expert 2
Expert 1	0.998		
Expert 2	0.999	0.999	
Expert 3	0.998	0.999	0.999

Table 3. Inter-rater reliability estimates for Expert scorers.

To provide a measure of a "consensus" expert score, the median score from all 3 Experts was derived for each passage, and then compared with the Teacher score. This comparison (Teacher vs. $Expert_M$) yielded a reliability of 0.999, $p < .01$. As shown in Table 3, all inter-rater reliability estimates are extremely high, indicating, in part, that teachers in the classroom produce scores that do not differ systematically from those given by careful experts.

2.2.3 Human-machine performance

Pearson's r was computed to estimate the correlations. The different scorer groups (i.e., $Expert_M$, Teacher, and Machine) provided similarly consistent scoring, as evidenced by high correlations between scores from the three groups. These correlations were maintained even when data were broken down into individual grades. Table 4 reveals correlations between Words Correct scores provided by all 3 scoring groups, for each grade individually, for all three grades combined, and finally for the median scores for all 87 students.

Grade level (N)	Machine ~ Teacher	Machine ~ $Expert_M$	Teacher ~ $Expert_M$
1st grade (54)	0.990	0.990	0.996
2nd grade (60)	0.990	0.991	0.999
3rd grade (147)	0.964	0.962	0.997
Grades 1-3 (261)	0.989	0.988	0.999
Only medians 87	0.994	0.994	0.999

Table 4. Correlations between Words Correct scores by Experts, Teachers, and machine.

All correlations are 0.96 or higher. Correlations are highest between Teacher and $Expert_M$, but correlations between machine and both human groups are consistently 0.96 or above. The relatively lower correlations between human and machine scores seen in the third grade data may be attributed in large part to two outliers noted in the Figures below. If these outliers are excluded from the analysis, both correlations between human and machine scores in the third grade rise to 0.985. (See below for discussion of these outliers.)

2.2.4.1. Teacher vs. Machine performance

Pearson's r was used to estimate the correlation between Teacher and Machine scores. First, the Teacher-generated Words Correct score and Machine-generated Words Correct scores were obtained for each of the 261 individual recordings, where the correlation was found to be $r = 0.989$, $p < .01$.

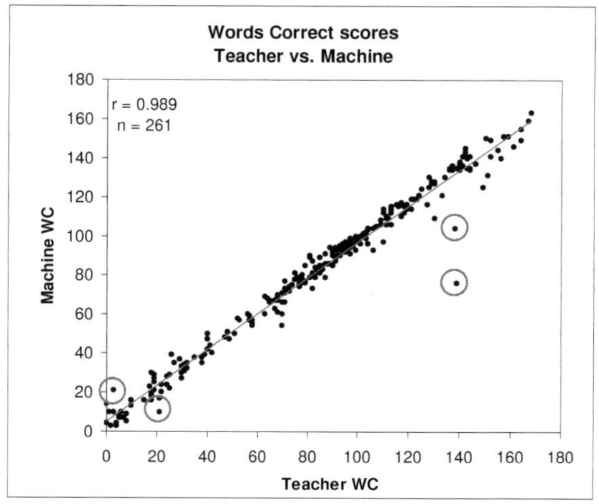

Figure 1. Words Correct (WC) scores from Teachers and Machine; response level (n = 261 responses)

Figure 1 shows a small number of outliers in the scatterplot (circled in red). One outlier (human = 3, machine = 21) came from a student whose low level of reading skill required him to sound out the letters as he read; machine scores were high for all 3 recordings from this reader. One outlier (human = 21, machine = 10) occurred because the reader had an unusually high pitched voice quality which posed a particular challenge to the recognizer. Two outliers (human = 141, machine = 76; human = 139, machine = 104) suffered from a similar recording quality-based issue whereby only some of the words were picked up by the system because the student read rapidly but quietly, making it difficult for the system to consistently pick up their voices. That is, for these calls the Teacher was close enough to hear the students' entire reading but the machine picked up only some of the words due to distance from the telephone handset.[5]

Next, median Words Correct scores for each student were computed. Median scores derived from machine and Teachers correlated at 0.994, $p < .01$ for the 87 students. These scores are presented in Figure 2.

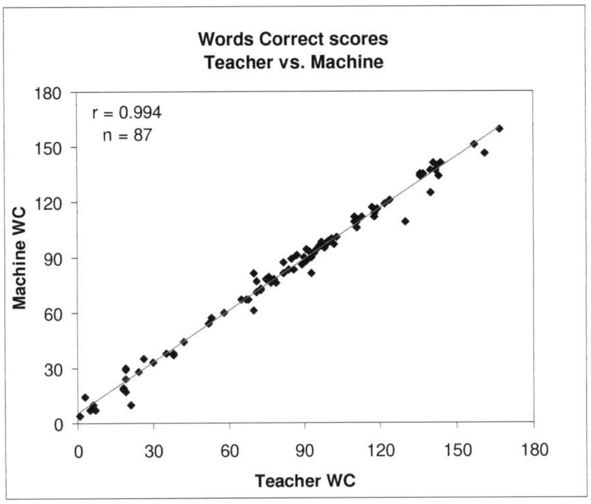

Figure 2. Words Correct (WC) scores from Teachers and Machine scoring at the reader level (n = 87).

Figure 2 shows that some of the outliers visible in the individual recording data disappear when the median score is computed for each student's reading performance, as would be expected.

2.2.4.2. Expert vs. Machine performance

The median of the 3 expert human scores for each passage (Expert$_M$) was compared to the Machine score. The correlation between machine-generated Words Correct scores and Expert$_M$-generated Words Correct scores was 0.988, $p < .01$, for the 261 individual readings, and 0.999, $p < .01$, for the median (student-level) scores. These results are displayed in Figure 3.

Figure 3 shows that two notable outliers present in the Teacher analysis were also present in the Expert$_M$ analysis. This may be due to the fact that while the recordings were of a low enough volume to present a challenge to the automated scoring system, they were of a sufficient quality for expert human scorers to "fill in the blanks" by listening repeatedly (e.g., with the ability to turn up the volume), and in some cases giving the student credit for a word spoken correctly even though they, the scorers, were not completely confident of having heard every portion of the word correctly. Though conjectural, it is reasonable to expect that the human listeners were able to interpolate the words in a "top down" fashion in a way that the machine was not.

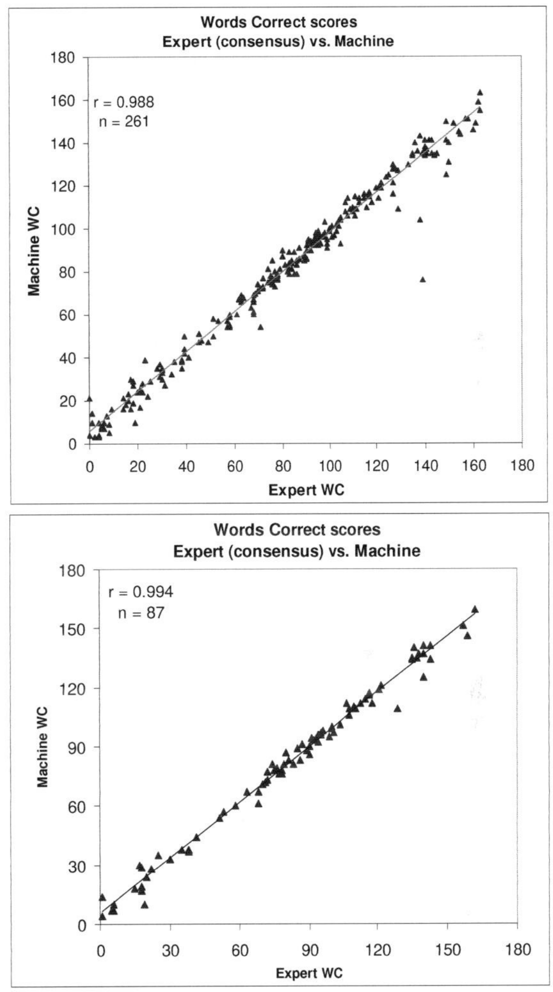

Figure 3. Words Correct (WC) Machine scores vs. Expert scores for all 261 individual responses (top) and for 87 students at test level (bottom).

2.2.5. Scoring Precision

It is reasonable to assume that careful expert scorers provide the closest possible representation of how a reading *should be scored,* particularly if the Expert score represents a "consensus" of expert opinions. Given the impracticality of having a team of experts score every passage read by a child

[5] In a production version, these recordings would return an instruction to re-administer the readings with better recording conditions or to score the recordings.

in the classroom, automated machine scoring might provide the preferred alternative if its scores can be shown to be consistent with expert scores. To explore the consistency between scores from Teachers and scores from the machine with scores provided by Experts, Teacher and Machine scores were compared against the median Expert score for each call using linear regression.

The standard error of the estimate (SE_E) for the two human groups was computed. The SE_E may be considered a measure of the accuracy of the predictions made for Teacher and Machine scores based on the (median, "consensus") Expert scores. Figure 4 below shows a scatterplot of the data, along with the R^2 and SE_E measures for both Teacher and machine scores based on Expert_M scores.

Scores from Teachers and Machine produce very similar regression lines and coefficients of determination (R^2 = 0.998 and 0.988 for Teachers and Machine, respectively). The figure also shows that, compared with the Machine scores, Teachers' scores approximate the predicted Expert_{Med} scores more closely (SE_E for Teachers = 1.80 vs. 4.25 for machine). This disparity appears to be driven by diverging scores at the upper and lower end of the distribution, as might be expected due to relatively smaller numbers of scores at the ends of the distribution.

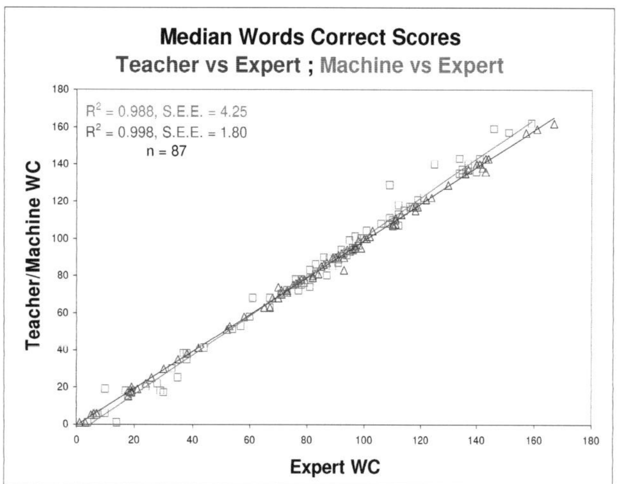

Figure 4. Median Words Correct scores from Machine (red squares) and Teachers (blue triangles) plotted against median Expert scores for 87 students. S.E.E. = Standard error of estimate.

3 Summary/Discussion

Correlations between human- and machine-based Words Correct scores were found to be above 0.95 for both individual reading passages and for median scores per student. The machine scoring was consistent with human scoring performed by teachers following along with the readings in real time (r = 0.989), and was also consistent with human scoring when performed by careful expert scorers who had the ability to listen to recorded renditions repeatedly (r = 0.988). Correlations were consistent with those between expert scorers (all r's between 0.998 and 0.999) and between Teachers and Experts (r = 0.999 and 0.988, respectively).

These results demonstrate that text-independent machine scoring of Words Correct for children's classroom reading predicts human scores extremely well (almost always within a word or two).

Acknowledgments

The authors acknowledge useful feedback from the anonymous reviewers that improved this paper.

References

Jennifer Balogh, Jared Bernstein, Jian Cheng & Brent Townshend. 2005. Ordinate Scoring of FAN in NAAL Phase III: Accuracy Analysis. Ordinate Corporation: Menlo Park, California.

Jennifer Balogh, Jared Bernstein, Jian Cheng, Alistair Van Moere, Brent Townshend, Masanori Suzuki. In press. Validation of automated scoring of oral reading. Educational and Psychological Measurement.

Jared Bernstein, Michael Cohen, Hy Murveit, Dmitry Rtischev, Dmitry, and Mitch Weintraub. 1990. Automatic evaluation and training in English pronunciation. In: Proc. ICSLP-90: 1990 Internat. Conf. on Spoken Language Processing, Kobe, Japan, pp. 1185–1188.

Matthew Black, Joseph Tepperman, Sungbok Lee, Patti Price, and Shrikanth Narayanan. 2006. Automatic detection and classification of disfluent reading miscues in young children's speech for the purpose of assessment. Proc. In INTERSPEECH/ICSLP, Antwerp, Belgium.

Jian Cheng & Jianqiang Shen. 2010. Towards Accurate Recognition for Children's Oral Reading Fluency. IEEE-SLT 2010, 91-96.

Jian Cheng & Brent Townshend. 2009. A rule-based language model for reading recognition. SLaTE 2009.

Lindy Crawford, Gerald Tindal, & Steve Stieber. 2001. Using Oral Reading Rate to Predict Student Performance on Statewide Achievement Tests. Educational Assessment, 7(4), 303-323.

Maxine Eskanazi. 2009. An overview of spoken language technology for education. Speech Communication, 51, 832-844.

David LaBerge & S. Jay Samuels. 1974. Toward a theory of automatic information processing in reading. Cognitive Psychology, 6(2), 293-323.

Mitchell P. Marcus, Beatrice Santorini, & Mary Ann Marcinkiewicz. 1993. Building a large annotated corpus of English: The Penn Treebank. Computational Linguistics 19(2):313-330.

Jack Mostow, Steven F. Roth, Alexander G. Hauptmann, & Matthew Kane. 1994. A prototype reading coach that listens. In Proc. of AAAI-94, 785–792.

National Institute of Child Health and Human Development, "Report of the national reading panel. Teaching children to read: An evidence-based assessment of the scientific research literature on reading and its implications for reading instruction," Tech. Rep. NIH Publication No. 00-4769, U.S. Government Printing Office, 2000.

Timothy V. Rasinski & . James V. Hoffman. 2003. Theory and research into practice: Oral reading in the school literacy curriculum. Reading Research Quarterly, 38, 510-522.

Joseph Tepperman, Matthew Black, Patti Price, Sungbok Lee, Abe Kazemzadeh, Matteo Gerosa, Margaret Heritage, Abeer Always, and Shrikanth Narayanan. 2007. A Bayesian network classifier for word-level reading assessment. Proceedings of ICSLP, Antwerp, Belgium.

Steve Young, D. Ollason, V. Valtchev, & Phil Woodland. 2002. The HTK Book (for HTK Version 3.2). Cambridge University Engineering Department.

Klaus Zechner, John, Sabatini, & Lei Chen. 2009. Automatic scoring of children's read-aloud text passages and word lists. Proceedings of the NAACL-HLT Workshop on Innovative Use of NLP for Building Educational Applications. Boulder, Colorado.

Automatic Gap-fill Question Generation from Text Books

Manish Agarwal and Prashanth Mannem
Language Technologies Research Center
International Institute of Information Technology
Hyderabad, AP, India - 500032
{manish.agarwal,prashanth}@research.iiit.ac.in

Abstract

In this paper, we present an automatic question generation system that can generate gap-fill questions for content in a document. Gap-fill questions are fill-in-the-blank questions with multiple choices (one correct answer and three distractors) provided. The system finds the informative sentences from the document and generates gap-fill questions from them by first blanking keys from the sentences and then determining the distractors for these keys. Syntactic and lexical features are used in this process without relying on any external resource apart from the information in the document. We evaluated our system on two chapters of a standard biology textbook and presented the results.

1 Introduction

Gap-fill questions are *fill-in-the-blank* questions, where one or more words are removed from a sentence/paragraph and potential answers are listed. These questions, being multiple choice ones, are easy to evaluate. Preparing these questions manually will take a lot of time and effort. This is where automatic *gap-fill question generation* (GFQG) from a given text is useful.

1. *A ______ bond is the sharing of a pair of valence electrons by two atoms.*
   (a) Hydrogen (b) Covalent (c) Ionic (d) Double (correct answer: Covalent)

In a gap-fill question (GFQ) such as the one above, we refer to the sentence with the gap as the *question sentence* (QS) and the sentence in the text that is used to generate the QS as the gap-fill sentence (GFS). The word(s) which is removed from a GFS to form the QS is referred to as the *key* while the three alternatives in the question are called as *distractors*, as they are used to distract the students from the correct answer.

Previous works in GFQG (Sumita et al., 2005; John Lee and Stephanie Seneff, 2007; Lin et al., 2007; Pino et al., 2009; Smith et al., 2010) have mostly worked in the domain of English language learning. Gap-fill questions have been generated to test student's knowledge of English in using the correct verbs (Sumita et al., 2005), prepositions (John Lee and Stephanie Seneff, 2007) and adjectives (Lin et al., 2007) in sentences. Pino et al. (2009) and Smith et al. (2010) have generated GFQs to teach and evaluate student's vocabulary.

In this paper, we move away from the domain of English language learning and work on generating gap-fill questions from the chapters of a biology textbook used for Advanced Placement (AP) exams. The aim is to go through the textbook, identify *informative sentences*[1] and *generate gap-fill questions* from them to aid students' learning. The system scans through the text in the chapter and identifies the *informative sentences* in it using features inspired by summarization techniques. Questions from these sentences (GFSs) are generated by first choosing a *key* in each of these and then finding appropriate *distractors* for them from the chapter.

Our GFQG system takes a document with its title as an input and produces a list of gap-fill questions as

[1]A sentence is deemed informative if it has the relevant course knowledge which can be questioned.

Proceedings of the Sixth Workshop on Innovative Use of NLP for Building Educational Applications, pages 56–64,
Portland, Oregon, 24 June 2011.

output. Unlike previous works (Brown et al., 2005; Smith et al., 2010) it doesn't use any external resource for distractor selection, making it adaptable to text from any domain. Its simplicity makes it useful not only as an aid for teachers to prepare gap-fill questions but also for students who need an automatic question generator to aid their learning from a textbook.

2 Data Used

A Biology text book *Campbell Biology, 6th Edition* has been used for work in this paper. We have reported results of our system on 2 chapters *(the structure and function of macromolecules* and *an introduction to metabolism)* of unit 1. Each chapter contains sections and subsections with their respective topic headings. Number of subsections, sentences, words per sentence in each chapter are (25, 416, 18.3) and (32, 423, 19.5) respectively. Each subsection is taken as a document. The chapters are divided into documents and each document is used for GFQG independently.

3 Approach

Given a document, the gap-fill questions are generated from it in three stages: sentence selection, key selection and distractor selection. *Sentence selection* involves identifying *informative sentences* in the document which can be used to generate a gap-fill question. These sentences are then processed in the *key selection* stage to identify the *key* on which to ask the question. In the final stage, the *distractors* for the selected *key* are identified from the given chapter by searching for words with the same context as that of the *key*.

In each stage, the system identifies a set of candidates (i.e. all sentences in the document in stage I, words in the previously selected sentence in stage II and words in the chapter in stage III) and extracts a set of features relevant to the task. *Weighted sum of extracted features* (see equation 1) is used to score these candidates, with the weights for the features in each of the three steps assigned heuristically. A small development data has been used to tune the feature weights.

$$score = \sum_{i=0}^{n} w_i \times f_i \qquad (1)$$

In equation 1, f_i denotes the feature and w_i denotes the weight of the feature f_i. The overall architecture of the system is shown in Figure 1.

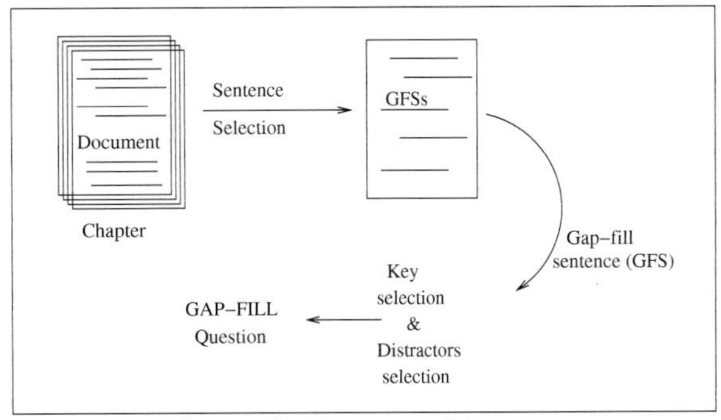

Figure 1: System architecture

In earlier approaches to generating gap-fill questions (for English language learning), the *keys* in a text were gathered first (or given as input in some cases) and all the sentences containing the *key* were used to generate the question. In domains where language learning is not the aim, a gap-fill question needs an *informative sentence* and not just any sentence with the desired *key* present in it. For this reason, in our work, *sentence selection* is performed before *key selection*.

3.1 Sentence Selection

A good GFS should be (1) *informative* and (2) *gap-fill question-generatable*. An *informative sentence* in a document is one which has relevant knowledge that is useful in the context of the document. A sentence is *gap-fill question-generatable* if there is sufficient context within the sentence to predict the *key* when it is blanked out. An *informative sentence* might not have enough context to generate a question from and vice versa.

The *sentence selection* module goes through all the sentences in the documents and extracts a set of features from each of them. These features are defined in such a way that the two criterion defined above are accounted for. Table 1 gives a summary of the features used.

First sentence: $f(s_i)$ is a binary feature to check whether the sentence s_i is the first sentence of the document or not. Upon analysing the documents in the textbook, it was observed that the first sentence in the document usually provides a summary of the document. Hence, $f(s_i)$ has been used to make use of the summarized first sentence of the document.

Feature Symbol	Description	Criterion
$f(s_i)$	Is s_i the first sentence of the document?	I
$sim(s_i)$	No. of tokens common in s_i and title / length(s_i)	I, G
$abb(s_i)$	Does s_i contain any abbreviation?	I
$super(s_i)$	Does s_i contain a word in its superlative degree?	I
$pos(s_i)$	s_i's position in the document (= i)	G
$discon(s_i)$	Is s_i beginning with a discourse connective?	G
$l(s_i)$	Number of words in s_i	G
$nouns(s_i)$	No. of nouns in s_i / length(s_i)	G
$pronouns(s_i)$	No. of pronouns in s_i / length(s_i)	G

Table 1: Feature set for *Sentence Selection* (s_i: i^{th} sentence of the document; **I**: to capture *informative sentences*; **G**: to capture the potential candidate for generating a GFQs)

Common tokens: $sim(s_i)$ is the count of words (nouns and adjectives) that the sentence and the title of the document have in common. A sentence with words from the title in it is important and is a good candidate to ask a question using the common words as the *key*.

2. *The different states of potential* ***energy*** *that* ***electrons*** *have in an atom are called* ***energy levels****, or* ***electron*** *shells.* (Title: *The Energy Levels of Electrons*)

For example sentence 2, value of the feature is 3/19 (common words:3, sentence length:19) and generating gap-fill question using *energy, levels* or *electrons* as the *key* will be useful.

Abbreviations and Superlatives: $abb(s_i)$, $super(s_i)$ features capture those sentences which contain abbreviations and words in superlative degree respectively. The binary features determine the degree of the importance of a sentence in terms of the presence of abbreviations and superlatives.

3. *In living organisms, most of the* ***strongest*** *chemical bonds are covalent ones.*

For example, in sentence 3, presence of *strongest* makes sentence more informative and useful for generating a gap-fill question.

Sentence position: $pos(s_i)$ is position of the sentence s_i, in the document (= i). Since topic of the document is elaborated in the middle of the document, the sentences occurring in the middle of the document are less important for the GFSs than those which occur either at the start or the end of the document. In order to use the above observation, the module uses this feature.

Discourse connective at the beginning: $discon(s_i)$'s value is *1* if first word of s_i is a *discourse connective*[2] and *0* otherwise. Discourse connective at the beginning of a sentence indicates that the sentence might not have enough context for a QS to be understood by the students.

4. *Because of this, it is both an* ***amine*** *and a* ***carboxylic*** *acid.*

In example 4, after selecting *amine* and *carboxylic* as a *key*, QS will be left with insufficient context to answer. Thus binary feature, $discon(s_i)$, is used.

Length: $l(s_i)$ is the number of words in the sentence. It is important to note that a very short sentence might generate an unanswerable question because of short context and a very long sentence might have enough context to make the question generated from it trivial.

Number of nouns and pronouns: Features $nouns(s_i)$ and $pronouns(s_i)$ represent the amount of context present in a sentence. More number of pronouns in a sentence reduces the contextual information, instead more number of nouns increases the number of potential *keys* to ask a gap-fill question on.

Four sample GFSs are shown in Table 3 with their document's titles.

3.2 Key Selection

For each sentence selected in the previous stage, the *key selection* stage identifies the most appropriate *key* from the sentence to ask the question on.

Previous works in this area, Smith et al. (2010) take *keys* as an input and, Karamanis et al. (2006) and Mitkov et al. (2006) select *keys* on the basis of term frequency and regular expressions on nouns. Then they search for sentences which contain that particular *key* in it. Since their approaches generate gap-fill questions only with one blank, they could end up with a trivial GFQ, especially in case of conjunctions.

[2] *because, since, when, thus, however, although, for example* and *for instance* connectives have been included.

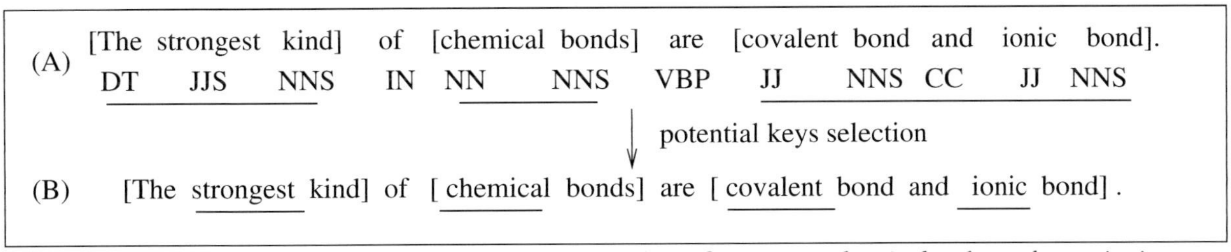

Figure 2: Generating *potential key*'s list, (*key-list*) of *strongest, chemical* and *covalent + ionic*.

5. *Somewhere in the transition from molecules to cells, we will cross the blurry boundary between* ***nonlife and life****.*

For instance in example sentence 5, selecting only one of *non-life* and *life* makes the question trivial. This is an other reason for performing sentence selection before *key* selection. Our system can generate GFQs with multiple blanks unlike previous works described above.

Our approach of *key selection* from a GFS is two step process. In the first step the module generates a list of *potential keys* from the GFS (*key-list*) and in the second step it selects the best *key* from this *key-list*.

3.2.1 Key-list formation

A list of potential keys is created in this step using the part of speech (POS) tags of words and chunks of the sentence in the following manner:

1. Each sequence of words in all the noun chunks is pushed into *key-list*. In figure 2(A), the three noun chunks *the strongest kind*, *chemical bond* and *covalent bond and ionic bond* are pushed into the *key-list*.

2. For each sequence in the *key-list*, the most important word(s) is selected as the potential *key* and the other words are removed. The most important word in a noun chunk in the context of GFQG in biology domain is a cardinal, adjective and noun in that order. In case where there are multiple nouns, the first noun is chosen as the potential *key*. If the noun chunk is a NP coordination, both the conjuncts are selected as a single potential *key* making it a case of multiple gaps in QS. In Figure 2(B) potential *keys strongest*, *chemical* and *covalent + ionic* are selected from the noun chunks by taking the order of importance into account.

An automatic POS tagger and a noun chunker has been used to process the sentences selected in the first stage. It was observed that if words of a *key* are spread across a chunk then there might not be enough context left in QS to answer the question. The noun chunk boundaries ensure that the sequence of words in the potential *keys* are not disconnected.

6. *Hydrogen has 1 valence* ***electron*** *in the first shell, but the shell's capacity is 2* ***electrons****.*

Any element of the *key-list* which occurs more than once in the GFS is discarded as a potential *key* as it more often than not generates a trivial question. For example, in sentence 6 selecting any one of the two *electron* as a *key* generates an easy gap-fill question.

7. *In contrast , trypsin , a digestive enzyme residing in the alkaline environment of the intestine , has an optimal pH of ______.*
(a) 6 (b) 7 (c) 8 (d) 9 (correct answer: 8)

If cardinals are present in a GFS, the first one is chosen as its *key* directly and a gap-fill question has been generated (see example 7).

3.2.2 Best Key selection

In this step three features, $term(key_p)$, $title(key_p)$ and $height(key_p)$, described in Table 2, are used to select the best *key* from the *key-list*.

Feature Symbol	Description
$term(key_p)$	Number of occurrences of the key_p in the document.
$title(key_p)$	Does title contain key_p ?
$height(key_p)$	height of the key_p in the syntactic tree of the sentence.

Table 2: Feature set for *key selection* (potential key, key_p is an element of *key-list*)

Term frequency: $term(key_p)$ is number of occurrences of the key_p in the document. $term(key_p)$

is considered as a feature to give preference to the potential *keys* with high frequency.

In title: $title(key_p)$ is a binary feature to check whether key_p is present in the title of the document or not. A common word of GFS and the title of the document serves as a better *key* for gap-fill question than the ones that are not present in both.

Height: $height(key_p)$ denotes the *height* [3] of the key_p in the syntactic tree of the sentence. Height gives an indirect indication of the importance of the word. It also denotes the amount of text in the sentence that modifies the word under consideration.

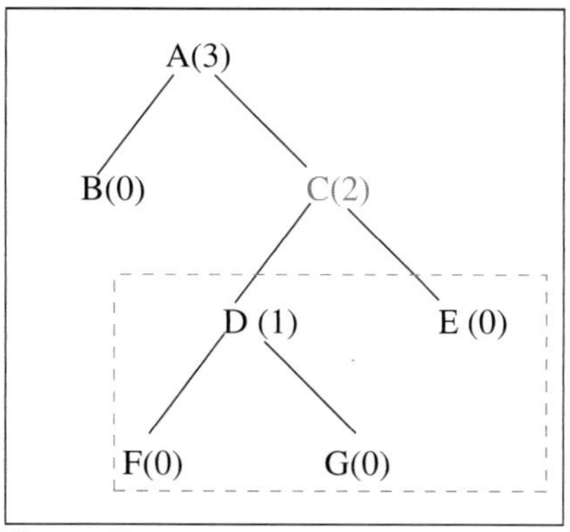

Figure 3: Height feature: node (height)

An answerable question should have enough context left after the key blanked out. A word with greater *height* in dependency tree gets more score since there is enough context from its dependent words in the syntactic tree to predict the word. For example in Figure 3, node *C*'s height is two and the words in the dashed box in its subtree provide the context to answer a question on *C*.

The score of each potential *key* is normalized by the number of words present in it and the best *key* is chosen based on the scores of potential *keys* in *key-list*. Table 3 shows the selected *keys* (red colored) for sample GFSs.

3.3 Distractor Selection

Karamanis et al. (2006) defines a *distractor* as, *an appropriate distractor is a concept semantically close to the key which, however, cannot serve as the right answer itself.*

For *distractor selection*, Brown et al. (2005) and Smith et al. (2010) used WordNet, Kunichika et al. (2002) used their in-house thesauri to retrieve similar or related words (synonyms, hypernyms, hyponyms, antonyms, etc.). However, their approaches can't be used for those domains which don't have ontologies. Moreover, Smith et al. (2010) do not select *distractors* based on the context of the *keys*. For example, in the sentences 8 and 9, the *key book* occurs in two different senses but same set of *distractors* will be generated by them.

[3]The height of a tree is the length of the path from the deepest node in the tree to the root.

No.	Selected keys (red colored)
1	An electron having a certain discrete amount of energy is something like a ball on a staircase. *(The Energy Levels of Electrons)*
2	Lipids are the class of large biological molecules that does not include polymer. *(Lipids–Diverse Hydrophobic Molecules)*
3	A DNA molecule is very long and usually consists of hundreds or thousands of genes. *(Nucleic acids store and transmit hereditary information)*
4	The fatty acid will have a kink in its tail wherever a double bond occurs. *(Fats store large amounts of energy)*

Table 3: Selected *keys* for each sample GFS

8. *Book the flight.*

9. *I read a book.*

Feature Symbol	Description
context($distractor_p$, key_s)	measure of contextual similarity of $distractor_p$ and the key_s in which they are present
sim($distractor_p$, key_s)	*Dice coefficient score* between GFS and the sentence containing the $distractor_p$
diff($distractor_p$, key_s)	difference in *term frequencies* of $distractor_p$ and key_s in the chapter

Table 4: Feature set for *distractor selection* (key_s is the selected *key* for a GFS, $distractor_p$ is the potential *distractor* for the key_s)

So a *distractor* should come from the same context and domain, and should be relevant. It is also clear from the above discussion that only *term frequency* formula alone will not work for selection of *distractors*. Our module uses features, shown in Table 4, to select three *distractors* from the set of all potential distractors. Potential distractors are the words in the chapter which have the same POS tag as that of the *key*.

Contextual similarity: *context*($distractor_p$, $keys_s$) gets the contextual similarity score of a potential $distractor$ and the $keys_s$ on the basis of context in which they occur in their respective sentences. Value of the feature depends on how similar are the *key* and the potential $distractor$ contextually. The previous two and next two words along with their POS tags are compared to calculate the score.

Sentence Similarity: $sim(distractor_p, keys_s)$ feature value represents similarity of the sentences in which the $keys_s$ and the $distractor_p$ occur in. *Dice Coefficient* (Dice, 1945) (equation 2) has been used to assign weights to those potential *distractors* which come from sentences similar to GFS because a *distractor* coming from a similar sentence will be more relevant.

$$dice\ coefficient(s_1, s_2) = \frac{2 \times commontokens}{l(s_1) + l(s_2)} \tag{2}$$

Difference in term frequencies: Feature, *diff*($distractor_p$, $keys_s$) is used to find *distractors* with comparable importance to the *key*. Term frequency of a word represents its importance in the text and words with comparable importance might be close in their semantic meanings. So, a smaller difference in the term frequencies is preferable.

key	Distractors
energy	charge, mass, water
polymer	acid, glucose, know
DNA	RNA, branch, specific
kink	available, start, method

Table 5: Selected *distractors* for selected *keys*, shown in Table 3

10. *Electrons have a negative charge, the unequal sharing of electrons in water causes the* ***oxygen*** *atom to have a partial negative charge and each* ***hydrogen*** *atom a partial positive charge.*

A word that is present in the GFS would not be selected as a *distractor*. For example in sentence 10, if system selects *oxygen* as a *key* then *hydrogen* will not be considered as a $distractor$. Table 5 shows selected three *distractors* for each selected *keys*.

4 Evaluation and Results

Two chapters of the biology book are selected for testing and top 15% candidates are selected by three modules (*sentence selection, key selection* and *distractor selection*). The modules were manually evaluated independently by two biology students with good English proficiency. Since in current system any kind of post editing or manual work is avoided, comparison of efficiency in manual and automatic generation is not needed unlike Mitkov and Ha et al. (2003).

4.1 Sentence Selection

The output of the sentence selection module is a list of sentences. The evaluators check if each of these sentences are good GFSs (*informative* and *gap-fill question-generatable*) or not and binary scoring is done. Evaluators are asked to evaluate selected sentences independently, whether they are useful for learning and answerable, or not.The coverage of the selected sentences w.r.t the document has not been evaluated.

	Chapter-5	Chapter-6	Total
No. of Sentences	390	423	813
No. of Selected Sentences	55	65	120
No. of Good GFSs (Eval-1)	51	59	110
No. of Good GFSs (Eval-2)	44	51	95

Table 6: Evaluation of Sentence Selection

Evaluator-1 and 2 rated 91.66% and 79.16% of sentences as good potential candidates for gap-fill question respectively with 0.7 inter evaluator agreement (Cohen's kappa coefficient). Table 6 shows the results of *sentence selection* for individual chapters. Upon analysing the bad GFSs, we found two different sources of errors. The first source is the feature *first sentence* and the second is lack of used in *sentence selection* module.

First sentence: Few documents in the data had either a general statement or a summary of the previous section as the first sentence and the *first sentence* feature contributed to their selection as GFS even though they aren't good GFSs.

11. *An understanding of energy is as important for students of biology as it is for students of physics, chemistry and engineering.*

For example, the system generated a gap-fill

question on example 11 which isn't a good GFS at all even though it occurs as the first sentence in the document.

Less no. of features: Features like *common tokens, superlative and abbreviation, discourse connective at the beginning* and *number of pronouns* was useful in selecting *informative sentences* from the documents. However, in absence of these features in the document, module has selected the GFSs on the basis of only two features, *length* and *position of the sentence*. In those cases Evaluators rated few GFSs as bad.

12. *Here is another example of how emergent properties result from a specific arrangement of building components.*

For example, sentence 12 rated as a *bad* GFS by the evaluators. So more features are need to be to used to avoid this kind of errors.

13. *A molecule has a characteristic* ***size*** *and* ***shape****.*

Apart from these we also found few cases where the context present in the GFS wasn't sufficient to answer the question although those sentences were informative. In the above example 13, *size* and *shape* were selected as the *key* that makes gap-fill question unanswerable because of short context.

4.2 Key Selection

Our evaluation characterizes a *key* into two categories namely *good* (*G*) and *bad* (*B*). Evaluator-1 and 2 found that 94.16% and 84.16% of the *keys* are *good* respectively with inter evaluator agreement 0.75. Table 7 shows the results of *keys selection* for individual chapters.

	Chap-5		Chap-6		Total	
	G	B	G	B	G	B
Eval-1	50	5	63	2	113	7
Eval-2	50	5	51	14	101	19

Table 7: Evaluation of Key(s) Selection: Chap: Chapter, Eval: Evaluator, G and B are for *good* and *bad key* respectively

14. *Carbon has a total of* ***6*** *electrons , with 2 in the first electron shell and 4 in the second shell.*

We observed that selection of first cardinal as *key* is not always correct. For example, in sentence 14 selection of *6* as the *key* generated trivial GFQ.

4.3 Distractors Selection

Our system generates four alternatives for each gap-fill question, out of which three are *distractors*. To evaluate the *distractors'* quality, evaluators are asked to substitute the *distractor* in the gap and check the *readability* and *semantic meaning* of the QS to classify the *distractor* as *good* or *bad*. Evaluators rate *0, 1, 2* or *3* depending on the number of *good distractors* in the GFQ (for example, questions that are rated *2* have two *good distractors* and one *bad distractor*).

15. *An electron having a certain discrete amount of ______ is something like a ball on a staircase.*
(a) charge (b) energy (c) mass (d) water
(Class: *3*)

16. *Lipids are the class of large biological molecules that does not include ______ .*
(a) acid (b)polymer (c) glucose (d) know
(Class: *2*)

17. *A ______ molecule is very long and usually consists of hundreds or thousands of genes.*
(a) DNA (b) RNA (c) specific (d) branch
(Class: *1*)

18. *The fatty acid will have a ______ in its tail wherever a double bond occurs .*
(a) available (b) method (c) kink (d) start
(Class: *0*)

Examples of gap-fill questions generated by our system are shown above (red colored alternatives are *good distractors*, blue colored ones are the correct answers for the questions and the black ones are *bad distractors*).

	Chap-5				Chap-6				Total			
Class	*0*	*1*	*2*	*3*	*0*	*1*	*2*	*3*	*0*	*1*	*2*	*3*
Eval-1	21	19	12	3	8	31	21	5	29	50	33	8
Eval-2	20	19	13	3	9	25	28	3	29	44	41	6

Table 8: Evaluation of *Distractor Selection* (Before any corrections)

Table 8 shows the human evaluated results for individual chapter. According to both evaluator-1 and evaluator-2, 75.83% of the cases the system finds *useful gap-fill questions* with 0.67 inter evaluator agreement. Useful gap-fill questions are those which have at least one *good distractor*. 60.05% and 67.72% test items are answered correctly by Evaluator 1 and 2 respectively.

We observed that when a *key* has more than one word, *distractors'* quality reduces because every token in a *distractor* must be comparably relevant. Small chapter size also effects the number of *good distractors* because *distractors* are selected from the chapter text.

In our work, as we only considered syntactic and lexical features for *distractor selection*, the selected *distractors* could be semantically conflicting with themselves or with the *key*. For example, due to the lack of semantic features in our method a hypernym of the *key* could find way into the *distractors* list thereby providing a confusing list of *distractors* to the students. In the example question 1 in section 1, *chemical* which is the hypernym of *covalent* and *ionic* could prove confusing if its one of the choices for the answer. Semantic similarity measures need to be used to solve this problem.

5 Related work

Given the distinct domains in which our system and other systems were deployed, a direct comparison of evaluation scores could be misleading. Hence, in this section we compare our approach with previous approaches in this area.

Smith et al. (2010) and Pino et al. (2009) used gap-fill questions for vocabulary learning. Smith et al. (2010) present a system, TEDDCLOG, which automatically generates draft test items from a corpus. TEDDCLOG takes the *key* as input. It finds *distractors* from a distributional thesaurus. They got 53.33% (40 out of 75) accuracy after post editing (editing either in carrier sentence (GFS) or in *distractors*) in the generated gap-fill questions.

Pino et al. (2009) describe a baseline technique to generate cloze questions (gap-fill questions) which uses sample sentences from WordNet. They then refine this technique with linguistically motivated features to generate better questions. They used the Cambridge Advanced Learners Dictionary (CALD) which has several sample sentences for each sense of a word for stem selection (GFS). The new strategy produced high quality cloze questions 66% of the time.

Karamanis et al. (2006) report the results of a pilot study on generating Multiple-Choice Test Items (MCTI) from medical text which builds on the work of Mitkov et al. (2006). Initially *key* set is enlarged with NPs featuring potential *key* terms as their heads and satisfying certain regular expressions. Then sentences having at least one *key* are selected and the terms with the same semantic type in UMLS are selected as *distractors*. In their manual evaluation, the domain experts regarded a MCTI as unusable if it could not be used in a test or required too much revision to do so. The remaining items were considered to be usable and could be post edited by the experts to improve their content and readability or replace inappropriate *distractors*. They have reported 19% usable items generated from their system and after post editing stems accuracy jumps to 54%.

However, our system takes a document and produces a list of GFQs by selecting *informative sentences* from the document. It doesn't use any external resources for *distractors selection* and finds them in the chapter only that makes it adaptable for those domains which do not have ontologies.

6 Conclusions and Future Work

Our GFQG system, selects most *informative sentences* of the chapters and generates gap-fill questions on them. Syntactic features helped in quality of gap-fill questions. We look forward to experimenting on larger data by combining the chapters. Evaluation of course coverage by our system and use of semantic features will be part of our future work.

Acknowledgements

We would like to thank Avinesh Polisetty and Sudheer Kolachina from LTRC, IIIT-Hyderabad for their helpful discussions and pointers during the course of this work. Thanks also to the anonymous reviewers for useful feedback.

References

Eiichiro Sumita, Fumiaki Sugaya, and Seiichi Yamamoto 2005. *Measuring Non-native Speakers Proficiency of English by Using a Test with Automatically-Generated Fill-in-the-Blank Questions*, 2nd Wkshop on Building Educational Applications using NLP, Ann Arbor.

John Lee and Stephanie Seneff. 2007. *Automatic Generation of Cloze Items for Prepositions*, CiteSeerX - Scientific Literature Digital Library and Search Engine [http://citeseerx.ist.psu.edu/oai2] (United States).

Lin, Y. C., Sung, L. C., Chen and M. C. 2007. *An*

Automatic Multiple-Choice Question Generation Scheme for English Adjective Understanding, CCE 2007 Workshop Proc. of Modeling, Management and Generation of Problems / Questions in eLearning, pp. 137-142.

Juan Pino, Michael Heilman and Maxine Eskenazi. 2009. *A Selection Strategy to Improve Cloze Question Quality*, Wkshop on Intelligent Tutoring Systems for Ill-Defined Domains. 9th Int. Conf. on ITS.

Simon Smith, P.V.S Avinesh and Adam Kilgarriff. 2010. *Gap-fill Tests for Language Learners: Corpus-Driven Item Generation* .

Jonathan C. Brown, Gwen A. Frishkoff, Maxine Eskenazi. 2005. *Automatic Question Generation for Vocabulary Assessment*, Proc. of HLT/EMNLP '05, pp. 819-826.

Nikiforos Karamanis, Le An Ha and Ruslan Mitkov. 2006 *Generating Multiple-Choice Test Iterms from Medical Text: A Pilot Study*, In Proceedings of INLG 2006, Sydney, Australia.

Ruslan Mitkov, Le An Ha and Nikiforos Karamanis. 2006 *A computer-aided environment for generating multiple-choice test items*, Natural Language Engineering 12(2): 177-194

Hidenobu Kunichika, Minoru Urushima,Tsukasa Hirashima and Akira Takeuchi. 2002. *A Computational Method of Complexity of Questions on Contents of English Sentences and its Evaluation*, In: Proc. of ICCE 2002, Auckland, NZ, pp. 97101 (2002).

Lee Raymond Dice. 1945. *Measures of the Amount of Ecologic Association Between Species*

Ruslan Mitkov and Le An Ha. 2003 *Computer-aided generation of multiple-choice tests*, Proceedings of the HLT/NAACL 2003 Workshop on Building educational applications using Natural Language Processing. Edmonton, Canada, 17-22.

Exploring Effective Dialogue Act Sequences in One-on-one Computer Science Tutoring Dialogues

Lin Chen, Barbara Di Eugenio
Computer Science
U. of Illinois at Chicago
lchen43,bdieugen@uic.edu

Davide Fossati
Computer Science
Carnegie Mellon U. in Qatar
davide@fossati.us

Stellan Ohlsson, David Cosejo
Psychology
U. of Illinois at Chicago
stellan,dcosej1@uic.edu

Abstract

We present an empirical study of one-on-one human tutoring dialogues in the domain of Computer Science data structures. We are interested in discovering effective tutoring strategies, that we frame as discovering which Dialogue Act (DA) sequences correlate with learning. We employ multiple linear regression, to discover the strongest models that explain why students learn during one-on-one tutoring. Importantly, we define "flexible" DA sequence, in which extraneous DAs can easily be discounted. Our experiments reveal several cognitively plausible DA sequences which significantly correlate with learning outcomes.

1 Introduction

One-on-one tutoring has been shown to be a very effective form of instruction compared to other educational settings. Much research on discovering why this is the case has focused on the analysis of the interaction between tutor and students (Fox, 1993; Graesser et al., 1995; Lepper et al., 1997; Chi et al., 2001). In the last fifteen years, many such analyses have been approached from a Natural Language Processing (NLP) perspective, with the goal of building interfaces that allow students to naturally interact with Intelligent Tutoring Systems (ITSs) (Moore et al., 2004; Cade et al., 2008; Chi et al., 2010). There have been two main types of approaches to the analysis of tutoring dialogues. The first kind of approach compares groups of subjects interacting with different tutors (Graesser et al., 2004; VanLehn et al., 2007), in some instances contrasting the number of occurrences of relevant features between the groups (Evens and Michael, 2006; Chi et al., 2010). However, as we already argued in (Ohlsson et al., 2007), this code-and-count methodology only focuses on what a certain type of tutor (assumed to be better according to certain criteria) does *differently* from another tutor, rather than on strategies that may be effective independently from their frequencies of usage by different types of tutor. Indeed we had followed this same methodology in previous work (Di Eugenio et al., 2006), but a key turning point for our work was to discover that our expert and novice tutors were equally effective (please see below).

The other kind of approach uses linear regression analysis to find correlations between dialogue features and learning gains (Litman and Forbes-Riley, 2006; Di Eugenio et al., 2009). Whereas linear regression is broadly used to analyze experimental data, only few analyses of tutorial data or tutoring experiments use it. In this paper, we follow Litman and Forbes-Riley (2006) in correlating sequences of Dialogue Acts (DAs) with learning gains. We extend that work in that our bigram and trigram DAs are not limited to tutor-student DA bigrams – Litman and Forbes-Riley (2006) only considers bigrams where one DA comes from the tutor's turn and one from the student's turn, in either order. Importantly, we further relax constraints on how these sequences are built, in particular, we are able to model DA sequences that include gaps. This allows us to discount the noise resulting from intervening DAs that do not contribute to the effectiveness of the specific sequence. For example, if we want to

Proceedings of the Sixth Workshop on Innovative Use of NLP for Building Educational Applications, pages 65–75,
Portland, Oregon, 24 June 2011.

explore sequences in which the tutor first provides some knowledge to solve the problem (DPI) and then knowledge about the problem (DDI) (DPI and DDI will be explained later), an exchange such as the one in Figure 1 should be taken into account (JAC and later LOW are the tutors, students are indicated with a numeric code, such as 113 in Figure 1). However, if we just use adjacent utterances, the *ok* from the student (113) interrupts the sequence, and we could not take this example into account. By allowing gaps in our sequences, we test a large number of linear regression models, some of which result in significant models that can be used as guidelines to design an ITS. Specifically, these guidelines will be used for further improvement of iList, an ITS that provides feedback on linked list problems and that we have developed over the last few years. Five different versions of iList have been evaluated with 220 users (Fossati et al., 2009; Fossati et al., 2010). iList is available at http://www.digitaltutor.net, and has been used by more than 550 additional users at 15 different institutions.

JAC: so we would set k equal to e and then delete. [*DPI*]
113: ok.
JAC: so we've inserted this whole list in here.[*DDI*]
113: yeah.

Figure 1: {DPI, DDI} Sequence Excerpt

The rest of the paper is organized as follows. In Section 2, we describe the CS-Tutoring corpus, including data collection, transcription, and annotation. In Section 3, we introduce our methodology that combines multiple linear regression with n-grams of DAs that allow for gaps. We discuss our experiments and results in Section 4.

2 The CS Tutoring Corpus

2.1 Data Collection

During the time span of 3 semesters, we collected a corpus of 54 one-on-one tutoring sessions on Computer Science data structures: *linked list*, *stack* and *binary search tree*. (In the following context, we will refer them as *Lists*, *Stacks* and *Trees*). Each student only participated in one session, and was randomly assigned to one of two tutors: LOW, an experienced Computer Science professor, with more than 30 years of teaching experience; or JAC, a senior undergraduate student in Computer Science, with only one semester of previous tutoring experience. In the end 30 students interacted with LOW and 24 with JAC.

Students took a pre-test right before the tutoring session, and an identical post-test immediately after. The test had two problems on Lists, two problems on Stacks, and four problems on Trees. Each problem was graded out of 5 points, for a possible maximum score of 10 points each for Lists and Stacks, and 20 points for Trees. Pre and post-test scores for each topic were later normalized to the [0..1] interval, and learning gains were computed.

Table 1 includes information on session length. Note that for each topic, the number of sessions is lower than 54. The tutor was free to tutor on what he felt was more appropriate, after he was given an informal assessment of the student's performance on the pre-test (tutors were not shown pre-tests to avoid that they'd tutor to the pre-test only). Hence, not every student was tutored on every topic.

Topic	N	Session length (minutes)				
		Min	Max	Total	μ	σ
Lists	52	3.4	41.4	750.4	14.4	5.8
Stacks	46	0.3	9.4	264.5	5.8	1.8
Trees	53	9.1	40.0	1017.6	19.2	6.6
Sessions	54	12.8	61.1	2032.5	37.6	6.1

Table 1: CS Tutoring Corpus - Descriptives

Each tutoring session was videotaped. The camera was pointing at the sheets of paper on which tutors and students were writing during the session. The videos were all transcribed. The transcripts were produced according to the rules and conventions described in the transcription manual of the CHILDES project (MacWhinney, 2000). Dialogue excerpts included in this paper show some of the transcription conventions. For example, `'+...'` denotes trailing, `'xxx'` unintelligible speech and `'#'` a short pause (see Figure 2). The CHILDES transcription manual also provides directions on utterance segmentation.

An additional group of 53 students (control group) took the pre- and post-tests, but instead of participating in a tutoring session they attended a 40 minute lecture about an unrelated CS topic. The rationale for such a control condition was to assess

LOW: what's the if? [*Prompt*]
LOW: well of course, don't do this if t two is null so if t two isn't null we can do that and xxx properly # thinking I put it in here. [*DPI*]
LOW: or else if t two is null that's telling us that this is the +... [*Prompt,FB*]

Figure 2: {Prompt,DPI,FB} sequence excerpt

whether by simply taking the pre-test students would learn about data-structures, and hence, to tease out whether any learning we would see in the tutored conditions would be indeed due to tutoring.

The learning gain, expressed as the difference between post-score and pre-score, of students that received tutoring was *significantly higher* than the learning gain of the students in the control group, for all the topics. This was showed by ANOVA between the aggregated group of tutored students and the control group, and was significant at the $p < 0.01$ for each topic. There was *no significant difference* between the two tutored conditions in terms of learning gain. The fact that students did not learn more with the experienced tutor was an important finding that led us to question the approach of comparing and contrasting more and less experienced tutors.

Please refer to (Di Eugenio et al., 2009) for further descriptive measurements of the corpus.

2.2 Dialogue Act Annotation

Many theories have been proposed as concerns DAs, and there are many plausible inventories of DAs, including for tutorial dialogue (Evens and Michael, 2006; Litman and Forbes-Riley, 2006; Boyer et al., 2010). We start from a minimalist point of view, postulating that, according to current theories of skill acquisition (Anderson, 1986; Sun et al., 2005; Ohlsson, 2008), at least the following types of tutorial intervention can be explained in terms of why and how they might support learning:
1. A tutor can tell the student how to perform the task.
2. A tutor can state declarative information about the domain.
3. A tutor can provide feedback:
(a) positive, to confirm that a correct but tentative step is in fact correct;
(b) negative, to help a student detect and correct an error.

We first read through the entire corpus and examined it for impressions and trends, as suggested by (Chi, 1997). Our informal assessment convinced us that our minimalist set of tutoring moves was an appropriate starting point. For example, contrary to much that has been written about an idealized socratic type of tutoring where students build knowledge by themselves (Chi et al., 1994), our tutors are rather directive in style, namely, they do a lot of *telling* and *stating*. Indeed our tutors talk a lot, to the tune of producing 93.5% of the total words! We translated the four types above into the following DAs: Direct Procedural Instruction (DPI), Direct Declarative Instruction (DDI), Positive Feedback (+FB), and Negative Feedback (-FB). Besides those 4 categories, we additionally annotated the corpus for Prompt (PT), since our tutors did explicitly invite students to be active in the interaction. We also annotated for Student Initiative (SI), to capture active participation on the part of the student's. SI occurs when the student proactively produces a meaningful utterance, by providing unsolicited explanation (see Figures 6 and 4), or by asking questions. As we had expected, SIs are not as frequent as other moves (see below). However, this is precisely the kind of move that a regression analysis would tease out from others, if it correlates with learning, even if it occurs relatively infrequently. This indeed happens in two models, see Table 8.

Direct Procedural Instruction(DPI) occurs when the tutor directly tells the student what task to perform. More specifically:

- Utterances containing correct steps that lead to the solution of a problem, e.g. see Figure 1.
- Utterances containing high-level steps or subgoals (*it wants us to put the new node that contains G in it, after the node that contains B*).
- Utterances containing tactics and strategies (*so with these kinds of problems, the first thing I have to say is always draw pictures*).
- Utterances where the tutor talked in the first-person but in reality the tutor instructed the student on what to do (*So I'm pushing this value onto a stack. So I'm pushing G back on*).

Direct Declarative Instruction (DDI) occurred when the tutor provided facts about the domain or a specific problem. The key to determine if an utterance is DDI is that the tutor is telling the student something that he or she ostensibly does not already know. Common sense knowledge is not DDI (*ten is less than eleven*). Utterances annotated as DDI include:

- Providing general knowledge about data structures (*the standard format is right child is always greater than the parent, left child is always less than the parent*).
- Telling the student information about a specific problem (*this is not a binary search tree*).
- Conveying the results of a given action (*so now since we've eliminated nine, it's gone*).
- Describing pictures of data structures (*and then there is a link to the next node*).

Prompts (PT) occur when the tutor attempts to elicit a meaningful contribution from the student. We code for six types of tutor prompts, including:

- Specific prompt: An attempt to get a specific response from the student (*that's not b so what do we want to do?*).
- Diagnosing: The tutor attempts to determine the student's knowledge state (*why did you put a D there?*).
- Confirm-OK: The tutor attempts to determine if the student understood or if the student is paying attention (*okay, got that idea?*).
- Fill-in-the-blank: The tutor does not complete an utterance thereby inviting the student to complete the utterance, e.g. see Figure 2.

Up to now we have discussed annotations for utterances that do not explicitly address what the student has said or done. However, many tutoring moves concern providing feedback to the student. Indeed as already known but not often acted upon in ITS interfaces, tutors do not just point out mistakes, but also confirm that the student is making correct steps. While the DAs discussed so far label single utterances, our positive and negative feedback (+FB and -FB) annotations comprise a sequence of consecutive utterances, that starts where the tutor starts providing feedback. We opted for a sequence of utterances rather than for labeling one single utterance because we found it very difficult to pick one single utterance as the one providing feedback, when the tutor may include e.g. an explanation that we consider to be part of feedback. Positive feedback occurs when the student says or does something correct, either spontaneously or after being prompted by the tutor. The tutor acknowledges the correctness of the student's utterance, and possibly elaborates on it with further explanation. Negative feedback occurs when the student says or does something incorrect, either spontaneously or after being prompted by the tutor. The tutor reacts to the mistake and possibly provides some form of explanation.

After developing a first version of the coding manual, we refined it iteratively. During each iteration, two human annotators independently annotated several dialogues for one DA at a time, compared outcomes, discussed disagreements, and fine-tuned the scheme accordingly. This process was repeated until a sufficiently high inter-coder agreement was reached. The Kappa values we obtained in the final iteration of this process are listed in Table 2 (Di Eugenio and Glass, 2004; Artstein and Poesio, 2008). In Table 2, the "Double Coded*" column refers to the sessions that we double coded to calculate the inter-coder agreement. This number does not include the sessions which were double coded when coders were developing the coding manual. The numbers of double-coded sessions differ by DA since it depends on the frequency on the particular DA (recall that we coded for one DA at a time). For example, since Student Initiatives (SI) are not as frequent, we needed to double code more sessions to find a number of SI's high enough to compute a meaningful Kappa (in our whole corpus, there are 1157 SIs but e.g. 4957 Prompts).

Category	Double Coded*	Kappa
DPI	10	.7133
Feedback	5	.6747
DDI	10	.8018
SI	14	.8686
Prompt	8	.9490

Table 2: Inter-Coder Agreement in Corpus

The remainder of the corpus was then independently annotated by the two annotators. For our final corpus, for the double coded sessions we did not come to a consensus label when disagreements arose; rather, we set up a priority order based on topic and coder (e.g., during development of the coding scheme, when coders came to consensus coding, which coder's interpretation was chosen more often), and we chose the annotation by a certain coder based on that order.

As a final important note, given our coding scheme some utterances have more than one label (see Figures 2 and 4), whereas others are not labelled at all. Specifically, most student utterances, and some tutor utterances, are not labelled (see Figures 1 and 4).

3 Method

3.1 Linear Regression Models

In this work, we adopt a multiple regression model, because it can tell us how much variation in learning outcomes is explained by the variation of individual features in the data. The features we use include pre-test score, the length of the tutoring sessions, and DAs, both the single DAs we annotated for and DA *n-grams*, i.e. DA sequences of length n. Pre-test score is always included since the effect of previous knowledge on learning is well established, and confirmed in our data (see all Models 1 in Table 4); indeed multiple linear regression allows us to factor out the effect of previous knowledge on learning, by quantifying the predictive power of features that are added beyond pre-test score.

3.2 n-gram Dialogue Act Model

n-grams (sequences of n units, such as words, POS tags, dialogue acts) have been used to derive language models in computational linguistics for a long time, and have proven effective in tasks like part-of-speech tagging, spell checking.

Our innovation with regard to using DA n-grams is to allow gaps in the sequence. This allows us to extract the sequences that are really effective, and to eliminate noise. Note that from the point of view of an effective sequence, *noise* is anything that does not contribute to the sequence. For example, a tutor's turn may be interrupted by a student's acknowledgments, such as "OK" or "Uh-hah" (see Figure 1). Whereas these acknowledgments perform fundamental functions in conversation such as grounding (Clark, 1992), they may not directly correlate with learning (a hypothesis to test). If we counted them in the sequence, they would contribute two utterances, transforming a 3 DA sequence into a 5 DA sequence. As well known, the higher the n, the sparser the data becomes, i.e., the fewer sequences of length n we find, making the task of discovering significant correlations all the harder. Note that some of the bigrams in (Litman and Forbes-Riley, 2006) could be considered to have gaps, since they pair one student move (say SI) with each tutor move contained in the next tutor turn (eg, in our Figure 6 they would derive two bigrams [SI, FB], and [SI, Prompt]). However, this does not result in a systematic exploration of all possible sequences of a certain length n, with all possible gaps of length up to m, as we do here.

The tool that allows us to leave gaps in sequences is part of Apache Lucene,[1] an open source full text search library. It provides strong capabilities to match and count efficiently. Our counting method is based on two important features provided by Lucene, that we already used in other work (Chen and Di Eugenio, 2010) to detect uncertainty in different types of corpora.

- Synonym matching: We can specify several different tokens at the same position in a field of a document, so that each of them can be used to match the query.
- Precise gaps: With Lucene, we can precisely specify the gap between the matched query and the indexed documents (sequences of DAs in our case) using a special type of query called *SpanNearQuery*.

To take advantage of Lucene as described above, we use the following algorithm to index our corpus.

1. For each Tutor-Topic session, we generate n-gram utterance sequences – note that these are sequences of utterances at this point, not of DAs.
2. We prune utterance sequences where either 0 or only 1 utterance is annotated with a DA, because we are mining sequences with at least 2 DAs. Recall that given our annotation, some utterances are not annotated (see e.g. Figure 1).
3. After pruning, for each utterance sequence, we generate a Lucene document: each DA label on an utterance will be treated as a token, multiple

[1] http://lucene.apache.org/

labels on the same utterance will be treated as "synonyms".

By indexing annotations as just described, we avoid the problem of generating too many combinations of labels. After indexing, we can use SpanNearQuery to query the index. SpanNearQuery allows us to specify the position distance allowed between each term in the query.

Figure 3 is the field of the generated Lucene document corresponding to the utterance sequences in Figure 4. We can see that each utterance of the tutor is tagged with 2 DAs. Those 2 DAs produce 2 tokens, which are put into the same position. The tokens in the same position act as synonyms to each other during the query.

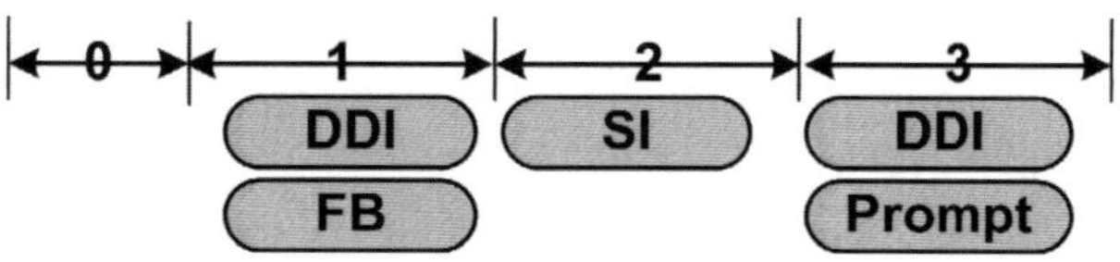

Figure 3: Lucene Document Example for DAs

258: okay.
JAC: its right child is eight. [*DDI, FB*]
258: uh no it has to be greater than ten. [*SI*]
JAC: right so it's not a binary search tree # it's not a b s t, right? [*DDI,Prompt*]

Figure 4: {FB, SI, DDI} is most effective in Trees

4 Experiments and Results

Here we build on our previous results reported in (Di Eugenio et al., 2009). There we had shown that, for lists and stacks, models that include positive and negative feedback are significant and explain more of the variance with respect to models that only include pre-test score, or include pre-test score and session length. Table 4 still follows the same approach, but adds to the regression models the additional DAs, DPI, DDI, Prompt and SI that had not been included in that earlier work. The column M refers to three types of models, Model 1 only includes Pre-test, Model 2 adds session length to Pre-test, and Model 3 adds to Pre-test all the DAs. As evidenced by the table, only DPI provides a marginally significant contribution, and only for lists. Note that length is not included in Model 3's. We did run all the equivalent models to Model 3's including length. The R^2's stay the same (literally, to the second decimal digit), or minimally decrease. However, in all these Model 3+'s that include length no DA is significant, hence we consider them as less explanatory than the Model 3's in Table 4: finding that a longer dialogue positively affects learning does not tell us what happens during that dialogue which is conducive to learning.

Note that the β weights on the pre-test are always negative in every model, namely, students with higher pre-test scores learn less than students with lower pre-test scores. This is an example of the well-known *ceiling effect*: students with more previous knowledge have less *learning opportunity*. Also noticeable is that the R^2 for the Trees models are much higher than for Lists and Stacks, and that for Trees no DA is significant (although there will be significant trigram models that involve DAs for Trees). We have observed that Lists are in general more difficult than Stacks and Trees (well, at least than binary search trees) for students.

Topic	Pre-Test	σ	Gain	σ
Lists	.40	.27	.14	.25
Stacks	.29	.30	.31	.24
Trees	.50	.26	.30	.24

Table 3: Learning gains and t-test statistics

Indeed Table 3 shows that in the CS-tutoring corpus the average learning gain is only .14 for Lists, but .31 for Stacks and .30 for Trees; whereas students have the lowest pre-test score on Stacks, and hence they have more opportunities for learning, they learn as much for Trees, but not for Lists.

We now examine whether DA sequences help us explain why student learn. We have run 24 sets of linear regression experiments, which are grouped as the following 6 types of models.

- With DA bigrams (DA sequences of length 2):
  - Gain $\sim$ DA Bigram
  - Gain $\sim$ DA Bigram + Pre-test Score
  - Gain $\sim$ DA Bigram + Pre-test Score + Session Length
- With DA trigrams (DA sequences of length 3):
  - Gain $\sim$ DA Trigram
  - Gain $\sim$ DA Trigram + Pre-test Score
  - Gain $\sim$ DA Trigram + Pre-test Score + Session Length

For each type of model:

Topic	M	Predictor	β	R^2	P
Lists	1	Pre-test	$-.47$	.20	$< .001$
	2	Pre-test	$-.43$	.29	$< .001$
		Length	.01		$< .001$
	3	Pre-test	$-.500$	.377	$< .001$
		+FB	.020		$< .01$
		-FB	.039		ns
		DPI	.004		$< .1$
		DDI	.001		ns
		SI	.005		ns
		Prompt	.001		ns
Stacks	1	Pre-test	$-.46$	.296	$< .001$
	2	Pre-test	$-.46$	.280	$< .001$
		Length	$-.002$		ns
	3	Pre-test	$-.465$	.275	$< .001$
		+FB	$-.017$		$< .01$
		-FB	$-.045$		ns
		DPI	.007		ns
		DDI	.001		ns
		SI	.008		ns
		Prompt	$-.006$		ns
Trees	1	Pre-test	$-.739$	.676	$< .001$
	2	Pre-test	$-.733$	.670	$< .001$
		Length	.001		ns
	3	Pre-test	$-.712$	.667	$< .001$
		+FB	$-.002$		ns
		-FB	$-.018$		ns
		DPI	$-.001$		ns
		DDI	$-.001$		ns
		SI	$-.001$		ns
		Prompt	$-.001$		ns
All	1	Pre-test	$-.505$	.305	$< .001$
	2	Pre-test	$-.528$	.338	$< .001$
		Length	.06		$< .001$
	3	Pre-test	$-.573$	.382	$< .001$
		+FB	.009		$< .001$
		-FB	$-.024$		ns
		DPI	.001		ns
		DDI	.001		ns
		SI	.001		ns
		Prompt	.001		ns

Table 4: Linear Regression – Human Tutoring

1. We index the corpus according to the length of the sequence (2 or 3) using the method we introduced in section 3.2.
2. We generate all the permutations of all the DAs we annotated for within the specified length; count the number of occurrences of each permutation using Lucene's SpanNearQuery allowing for gaps of specified length. Gaps can span from 0 to 3 utterances; for example, the excerpt in Figure 1 will be counted as a {DPI, DDI} bigram with a gap of length 1. Gaps can be discontinuous.
3. We run linear regressions[2] on the six types of models listed above, generating actual models by replacing a generic DA bi- or tri-gram with each possible DA sequence we generated in step 2.
4. We output those regression results, in which the whole model and every predictor are at least marginally significant ($p < 0.1$).

The number of generated significant models is shown in Figure 5. In the legend of the Figure, B stands for **B**igram DA sequence, T stands for **T**rigram DA sequence, L stands for session **L**ength, P stands for **P**re-test score. Not surprisingly, Figure 5 shows that, as the allowed gap increases in length, the number of significant models increases too, which give us more models to analyze.

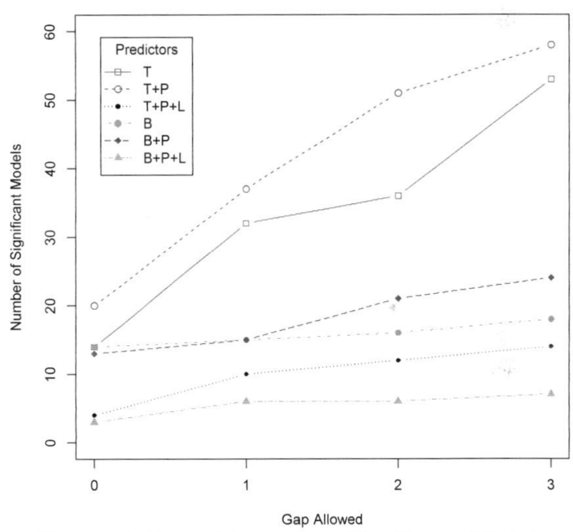

Figure 5: Gaps Allowed vs. Significant Models

Figure 5 shows that there are a high number of significant models. In what follows we will present first of all those that improve on the models that do not use sequences of DAs, as presented in Table 4. Improvement here means not only that the R^2 is higher, but that the model is more appropriate as an approximation of a tutor strategy, and hence, constitutes a better guideline for an ITS. For example, take model 3 for Lists in Table 4. It tells us that positive feedback (+FB) and direct procedural instruction (DPI) positively correlate with learning

[2]We used rJava, http://www.rforge.net/rJava/

gains. However, this obviously cannot mean that our ITS should only produce +FB and DPI. The ITS is interacting with the student, and it needs to tune its strategies according to what happens in the interaction; model 3 doesn't even tell us if +FB and DPI should be used together or independently. Models that include sequences of DAs will be more useful for the design of an ITS, since they point out what sequences of DAs the ITS may use, even if they still don't answer the question, when should the ITS engage in a particular sequence – we have addressed related issues in our work on iList (Fossati et al., 2009; Fossati et al., 2010).

4.1 Bigram Models

{DPI, Feedback} Model Indeed the first significant models that include a DA bigram include the {DPI, Feedback} DA sequence. Note that we distinguish between models that employ Feedback (FB) without distinguishing between positive and negative feedback; and models where the type of feedback is taken into account (+FB, -FB). Table 5 shows that for Lists, a sequence that includes DPI followed by any type of feedback (Feedback, +FB, -FB) produces significant models when the model includes pre-test. Table 5 and all tables that follow include the column *Gap* that indicates the length of the gap within the DA sequence with which that model was obtained. When, as in Table 5, multiple numbers appear in the *Gap* column, this indicates that the model is significant with all those gap settings. We only show the β, R^2 and P values for the gap length which generates the highest R^2 for a model, and the corresponding gap length is in bold font: for example, the first model for Lists in Table 5 is obtained with a gap length = 2. For Lists, these models are not as predictive as Model 3 in Table 4, however we believe they are more useful from an ITS design point of view: they tell us that when the tutor gives direct instruction on how to solve the problem, within a short span of dialogue the tutor produces feedback, since (presumably) the student will have tried to apply that DPI. For Stacks, a {DPI, -FB} model (without taking pre-test into account) significantly correlates ($p < 0.05$) with learning gain, and marginally significantly correlates with learning gain when the model also includes pre-test score. This latter model is actually more predictive than Model 3 for Stacks in Table 4 that includes +FB but not DPI. We can see the β weight is negative for the sequence {DPI, -FB} in the Stacks model. No models including the bigram {DPI, -FB} are significant for Trees.

Topic	Predictor	β	R^2	P	Gap
Lists	DPI, -FB	.039	.235	<.001	**2**, 3
	Pre-test	$-.513$		$< .001$	
	DPI, +FB	.019	.339	<.001	0, **1**, 2, 3
	Pre-test	$-.492$		$< .001$	
	Length	.011		< 0.05	
	DPI, FB	.016	.333	<.05	0, **1**, 2, 3
	Pre-test	$-.489$		$< .001$	
	Length	.011		< 0.05	
Stacks	DPI, -FB	$-.290$	.136	<.05	**0**, 1, 2, 3
	DPI, -FB	$-.187$	.342	<.1	0, **1**, 2, 3
	Pre-test	$-.401$		$< .001$	

Table 5: DPI, Feedback Model

{FB, DDI} Model A natural question arises: since Feedback following DPI results in significant models, are there any significant models which include sequences whose first component is a Feedback move? We found only two that are significant, when Feedback is followed by DDI (Direct Declarative Instruction). Note that here we are not distinguishing between negative and positive feedback. Those models are shown in Table 6. The Lists model is not more effective than the original Model 3 for Lists in Table 4, but the model for Trees is slightly more explanatory than the best model for Trees in that same table, and includes a bigram model, whereas in Table 4, only pre-test is significant for Trees.

Topic	Predictor	β	R^2	P	Gap
Lists	FB, DDI	.1478	.321	<.1	1
	Pre-test	$-.470$		$< .001$	
	Length	.011		$< .05$	
Trees	FB, DDI	.0709	.6953	<.05	0
	Pre-test	$-.7409$		$< .001$	

Table 6: {FB, DDI} Model

4.2 Trigram Models

{DPI, FB, DDI} Model Given our significant bigram models for DPI followed by FB, and FB followed by DDI, it is natural to ask whether the combined trigram model {DPI, FB, DDI} results in a significant model. It does for the topic List, as shown in table 7, however again the R^2 is lower than that of Model 3 in Table 4. This suggests that an effective tutoring sequence is to provide instruction on how to solve the problem (DPI), then Feedback on what the student does, and finally some declarative instruction (DDI).

Topic	Predictor	β	R^2	P	Gap
Lists	DPI, FB, DDI	.156	.371	<.01	1
	Pre-test	−.528		< .001	
	Length	.012		< .05	

Table 7: {DPI, FB, DDI} Model

More effective trigram models include Prompt and SI. Up to now, only one model including sequences of DAs was superior to the simpler models in Table 4. Interestingly, different trigrams that still include some form of Feedback, DPI or DDI, and then either Prompt or SI (Student Initiative) result in models that exhibit slightly higher R^2; additionally in all these models the trigram predictor is highly significant. These models are listed in table 8 (note that the two Trees models differ because in one FB is generic Feedback, irregardless of orientation, in the other it's +FB, i.e., positive feedback). In detail, improvements in R^2 are 0.0382 in topic Lists, 0.12 in topic Stacks and 0.0563 in topic Trees. The highest improvement is in Stacks.

Topic	Predictor	β	R^2	P	Gap
Lists	PT,DPI,FB	.266	.415	<.01	0
	Pre-test	−.463		< .001	
	Length	.011		< .05	
Stacks	DDI,FB,PT	−.06	.416	<.01	1
	Pre-test	−.52		< .001	
Trees	+FB,SI,DDI	.049	.732	<.01	1
	Pre-test	−.746		< .001	
Trees	FB,SI,DDI	.049	.732	<.01	1
	Pre-test	−.746		< .001	

Table 8: Highest R^2 Models

It is interesting to note that the model for Lists add *Prompt* at the beginning to a bigram that had already been found to contribute to a significant model. For Trees, likewise, we add another DA to the bigram {FB,DDI} that had been found to be significant; this time, it is Student Initiative (SI) and it occurs in the middle. This indicates that, after the tutor provides feedback, the student takes the initiative, and the tutor responds with one piece of information the student didn't know (DDI). Of course, the role of Prompts and SI is not surprising, although interestingly they are significant only in association with certain tutor moves. It is well known that students learn more when they build knowledge by themselves, either by taking the initiative (SI), or after the tutor prompts them to do so (Chi et al., 1994; Chi et al., 2001).

LOW: it's backwards # it's got four elements, but they are backwards. [*DDI*]
234: so we have do it again. [*SI*]
LOW: so do it again. [*FB*]
LOW: do what again? [*Prompt*]

Figure 6: {DDI, FB, PT} is most effective in Stacks

4.3 Other models

We found other significant models, specifically, {DDI,DPI} for all three topics, and {-FB,SI} for Lists. However, their R^2 are very low, and much lower than any of the other models presented so far. Besides models that include *only one* DA *sequence* and pre-test score to predict learning gain, we also ran experiments to see if adding multiple DA sequences to pre-test score will lead to significant models – namely, we experimented with models which include two sequences as predictors, say, the two bigrams {-FB,SI} and {FB,DDI}. However, no significant models were found.

5 Conclusions

In this paper, we explored effective tutoring strategies expressed as sequence of DAs. We first presented the CS-Tutoring corpus. By relaxing the DA n-gram definition via the fuzzy matching provided by Apache Lucene, we managed to discover several DA sequences that significantly correlate with learning gain. Further, we discovered models with higher R^2 than models which include only one single DA, which are also more informative from the point of view of the design of interfaces to ITSs.

6 Acknowledgments

This work was mainly supported by ONR (N00014-00-1-0640), and by the UIC Graduate College (2008/2009 Dean's Scholar Award). Partial support is also provided by NSF (ALT-0536968, IIS-0905593).

References

John R. Anderson. 1986. Knowledge compilation: The general learning mechanism. *Machine learning: An artificial intelligence approach*, 2:289–310.

Ron Artstein and Massimo Poesio. 2008. Inter-coder agreement for computational linguistics. *Computational Linguistics*, 34(4):555–596. Survey Article.

Kristy Elizabeth Boyer, Robert Phillips, Amy Ingram, Eun Young Ha, Michael Wallis, Mladen Vouk, and James Lester. 2010. Characterizing the effectiveness of tutorial dialogue with Hidden Markov Models. In *Intelligent Tutoring Systems*, pages 55–64. Springer.

Whitney L. Cade, Jessica L. Copeland, Natalie K. Person, and Sidney K. D'Mello. 2008. Dialogue modes in expert tutoring. In *Intelligent Tutoring Systems*, volume 5091 of *Lecture Notes in Computer Science*, pages 470–479. Springer Berlin / Heidelberg.

Lin Chen and Barbara Di Eugenio. 2010. A lucene and maximum entropy model based hedge detection system. In *Proceedings of the Fourteenth Conference on Computational Natural Language Learning*, pages 114–119, Uppsala, Sweden, July. Association for Computational Linguistics.

Michelene T. H. Chi, Nicholas de Leeuw, Mei-Hung Chiu, and Christian LaVancher. 1994. Eliciting self-explanations improves understanding. *Cognitive Science*, 18(3):439–477.

Michelene T. H. Chi, Stephanie A. Siler, Takashi Yamauchi, and Robert G. Hausmann. 2001. Learning from human tutoring. *Cognitive Science*, 25:471–533.

Min Chi, Kurt VanLehn, and Diane Litman. 2010. The more the merrier? Examining three interaction hypotheses. In *Proceedings of the 32nd Annual Conference of the Cognitive Science Society (CogSci2010)*, Portland,OR.

Michelene T.H. Chi. 1997. Quantifying qualitative analyses of verbal data: A practical guide. *Journal of the Learning Sciences*, 6(3):271–315.

Herbert H. Clark. 1992. *Arenas of Language Use*. The University of Chicago Press, Chicago, IL.

Barbara Di Eugenio and Michael Glass. 2004. The Kappa statistic: a second look. *Computational Linguistics*, 30(1):95–101. Squib.

Barbara Di Eugenio, Trina C. Kershaw, Xin Lu, Andrew Corrigan-Halpern, and Stellan Ohlsson. 2006. Toward a computational model of expert tutoring: a first report. In *FLAIRS06, the 19th International Florida AI Research Symposium*, Melbourne Beach, FL.

Barbara Di Eugenio, Davide Fossati, Stellan Ohlsson, and David Cosejo. 2009. Towards explaining effective tutorial dialogues. In *Annual Meeting of the Cognitive Science Society*, pages 1430–1435, Amsterdam, July.

Martha W. Evens and Joel A. Michael. 2006. *One-on-one Tutoring by Humans and Machines*. Mahwah, NJ: Lawrence Erlbaum Associates.

Davide Fossati, Barbara Di Eugenio, Christopher Brown, Stellan Ohlsson, David Cosejo, and Lin Chen. 2009. Supporting Computer Science curriculum: Exploring and learning linked lists with iList. *IEEE Transactions on Learning Technologies, Special Issue on Real-World Applications of Intelligent Tutoring Systems*, 2(2):107–120, April-June.

Davide Fossati, Barbara Di Eugenio, Stellan Ohlsson, Christopher Brown, and Lin Chen. 2010. Generating proactive feedback to help students stay on track. In *ITS 2010, 10th International Conference on Intelligent Tutoring Systems*. Poster.

Barbara A. Fox. 1993. *The Human Tutorial Dialogue Project: Issues in the design of instructional systems*. Lawrence Erlbaum Associates, Hillsdale, NJ.

Arthur C. Graesser, Natalie K. Person, and Joseph P. Magliano. 1995. Collaborative dialogue patterns in naturalistic one-to-one tutoring. *Applied Cognitive Psychology*, 9:495–522.

Arthur C. Graesser, Shulan Lu, George Tanner Jackson, Heather Hite Mitchell, Mathew Ventura, Andrew Olney, and Max M. Louwerse. 2004. AutoTutor: A tutor with dialogue in natural language. *Behavioral Research Methods, Instruments, and Computers*, 36:180–193.

Mark R. Lepper, Michael F. Drake, and Teresa O'Donnell-Johnson. 1997. Scaffolding techniques of expert human tutors. In K. Hogan and M. Pressley, editors, *Scaffolding student learning: Instructional approaches and issues*. Cambridge, MA: Brookline.

Diane Litman and Kate Forbes-Riley. 2006. Correlations between dialogue acts and learning in spoken tutoring dialogues. *Natural Language Engineering*, 12(02):161–176.

Brian MacWhinney. 2000. *The Childes Project: Tools for Analyzing Talk: Transcription format and programs*, volume 1. Psychology Press, 3 edition.

Johanna D. Moore, Kaska Porayska-Pomsta, Sebastian Varges, and Claus Zinn. 2004. Generating Tutorial Feedback with Affect. In *FLAIRS04, Proceedings of the Seventeenth International Florida Artificial Intelligence Research Society Conference*.

Stellan Ohlsson, Barbara Di Eugenio, Bettina Chow, Davide Fossati, Xin Lu, and Trina C. Kershaw. 2007. Beyond the code-and-count analysis of tutoring dialogues. In *Proceedings of the 13th International Conference on Artificial Intelligence in Education*, pages 349–356, Los Angeles, CA, July. IOS Press.

Stellan Ohlsson. 2008. Computational models of skill acquisition. *The Cambridge handbook of computational psychology*, pages 359–395.

Ron Sun, Paul Slusarz, and Chris Terry. 2005. The Interaction of the Explicit and the Implicit in Skill Learning: A Dual-Process Approach. *Psychological Review*, 112:159–192.

Kurt VanLehn, Arthur C. Graesser, G. Tanner Jackson, Pamela W. Jordan, Andrew Olney, and Carolyn P. Rosé. 2007. When are tutorial dialogues more effective than reading? *Cognitive Science*, 31(1):3–62.

Effect of Word Complexity on L2 Vocabulary Learning

Kevin Dela Rosa
Language Technologies Institute
Carnegie Mellon University
5000 Forbes Ave. Pittsburgh, PA
kdelaros@cs.cmu.edu

Maxine Eskenazi
Language Technologies Institute
Carnegie Mellon University
5000 Forbes Ave. Pittsburgh, PA
max@cs.cmu.edu

Abstract

Research has shown that a number of factors, such as maturational constraints, previous language background, and attention, can have an effect on L2 acquisition. One related issue that remains to be explored is what factors make an individual word more easily learned. In this study we propose that word complexity, on both the phonetic and semantic levels, affect L2 vocabulary learning. Two studies showed that words with simple grapheme-to-phoneme ratios were easier to learn than more phonetically complex words, and that words with two or fewer word senses were easier to learn that those with three or more.

1 Introduction

There is much computer-assisted language learning (CALL) literature that explores effective methods of teaching vocabulary. In recent studies conducted using the REAP system, which finds documents from the internet to teach vocabulary, we have shown that speech synthesis reinforces written text for learning in reading activities (Dela Rosa et al., 2010), and we have also shown that context-sensitive dictionary definitions afford better vocabulary learning for L2 language students (Dela Rosa and Eskenazi, 2011).

One issue that remains to be explored in this context: determining what factors make an individual word easier to learn. We propose that word complexity, on both the phonetic and semantic levels, can affect how easily an L2 vocabulary word can be learned.

In this paper we first discuss past work on factors that impact vocabulary acquisition in intelligent tutoring environments, and then explore work on defining the complexity of a word with respect to vocabulary learning. Next we describe two classroom studies we conducted with ESL college students to test the effect of word complexity on L2 vocabulary learning. Finally we examine our results and suggest future research directions.

2 Background

Many studies have been conducted to investigate the relationship between different variables and second language learning. For example, the age of the foreign language learner is often pointed to as a major factor in determining whether an individual will be successful in learning a new language (Marinova-Todd, 2000).

In the domain of L2 vocabulary instruction, researchers have shown that factors such as maturational constraints, attention, previous language background, and order of acquisition, can all affect L2 vocabulary acquisition (Oxford and Scarcella, 1994). Additionally, another factor that affects L2 vocabulary learning is the number of exposures of a practice item that a student receives during learning activities. In a study on the effects of spacing and retention of vocabulary pairs, Pavlik and Anderson (2005) showed that each time an item is practiced, it receives an increment of

Proceedings of the Sixth Workshop on Innovative Use of NLP for Building Educational Applications, pages 76–80,
Portland, Oregon, 24 June 2011.

strength, but these increments decay as a power function of time. Furthermore, it is generally accepted that reading is beneficial to vocabulary acquisition (Perfetti, 2010).

One group of factors in foreign language vocabulary instruction that has often been overlooked is at the level of the individual word, such as word complexity. In sections 3.2 and 3.3, we describe two simple measures of phonetic and semantic word complexity that were examined during our classroom studies. There have been work on defining the complexity of a word, such as Jakielski's (1998) Index of Phonetic Complexity, but we do not know of work that measures the effect of word complexity on L2 vocabulary learning.

3 Classroom Study Setup

In order to determine the effect that word complexity, in both the phonetic and semantic levels, have on L2 language learners, we conducted two in-vivo studies with ESL students at the English Language Institute of the University of Pittsburgh. The first study focused on the effect of phonetic word complexity on vocabulary learning. The second study explored the effect of semantic word complexity, in the form of the number of senses a word has, on vocabulary learning. Both studies and the tutoring system that was used are described in the next sections.

3.1 Overview of the Tutoring System

The tutoring system, REAP, is a web-based language tutor developed at Carnegie Mellon that harvests documents from the internet for L2 vocabulary learning and reading comprehension (Heilman et al., 2006). It has been used as a testing platform for cognitive science studies. This system has the ability to provide reader-specific passages by consulting profiles that model a reader's reading level, topic interests, and vocabulary goals.

The system's interface has several features that enhance a student's learning experience. One key feature is that it provides users with the ability to listen to the spoken version of any word that appears in a document, making use of the Cepstral Text-to-Speech system (2001) to synthesize words on the fly when clicked on. Additionally, students can look up the definition of any of the words they encounter while reading the documents using an embedded electronic dictionary. The system also automatically highlights focus words, i.e. the words targeted for vocabulary learning in a particular reading.

3.2 Study 1: Phonetic Complexity

In Study 1, we looked at the effect that phonetic complexity, one measure of a word's complexity, has on learning a word, and whether this complexity causes a word to be learned more easily when multimodal input is provided in the form of written text accompanied by spoken text generated through speech synthesis. To measure a word's phonetic complexity, we used the ratio of a word's graphemes to phonemes, where words with a ratio closer to 1 were simpler than those with a ratio much greater or less than 1. Note that for this study, simple letters have been used as the grapheme units.

For example, the word *cat* has a simple one-to-one mapping between its graphemes and phonemes (C A T vs. K AE T), while other words like *borough* and *index* have a more complex relationship (B O R O U G H vs. B ER OW, and I N D E X vs. IH N D EH K S), with grapheme-to-phoneme ratios greater than 1 and less than 1 respectively.

For this study, there were 21 intermediate-level ESL college students at the University of Pittsburgh's English Language Institute whose native languages included Arabic, Chinese and Spanish. Weekly group readings were given as class activities, centered on a total of 18 focus words, followed by practice closed cloze questions (multiple-choice fill-in-the-blank with 5 answer choices provided, and distractors coming from the Academic Word List or words that are similar but do not fit the blank properly) on the focus words that appeared in the particular reading. The focus words used in this study were taken evenly from the following word groups:

- Words with grapheme-to–phoneme ratio equal to 1 [6 words]
- Words with grapheme-to–phoneme ratio greater than 1 [6 words]
- Words with grapheme-to–phoneme ratio less than 1 [6 words]

A pre-test was administered at the beginning of the study, consisting of closed cloze questions about the focus words. A similar set of questions was presented to the students during the post-test, which occurred one week after the last reading activity. Between the pre-test and post-test, 6 reading activities were administered, one per week, each focused on a single document. This activity typically took students 20-30 minutes to complete.

3.3 Study 2: Semantic Complexity

In Study 2, we investigated the effect that multiple word-senses, another measure of word complexity, have on learning a word. There were 21 intermediate-level ESL college students at the University of Pittsburgh's English Language Institute, whose native languages included Arabic, Chinese, Korean, and Spanish. As in Study 1 there was a pre-test, a post-test, and a series of weekly documents to be read featuring the focus words. In total there were 26 focus words, all of which were taken from the Academic Word List and 7 weekly reading activities.

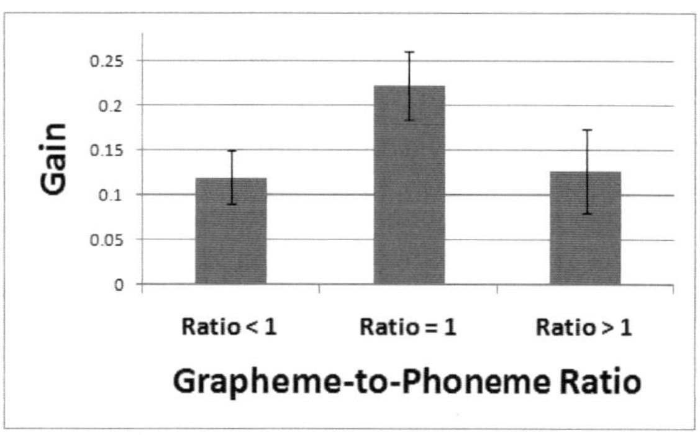

Figure 1: Impact of phonetic complexity on the improvement between pre-test & post-test in Study 1

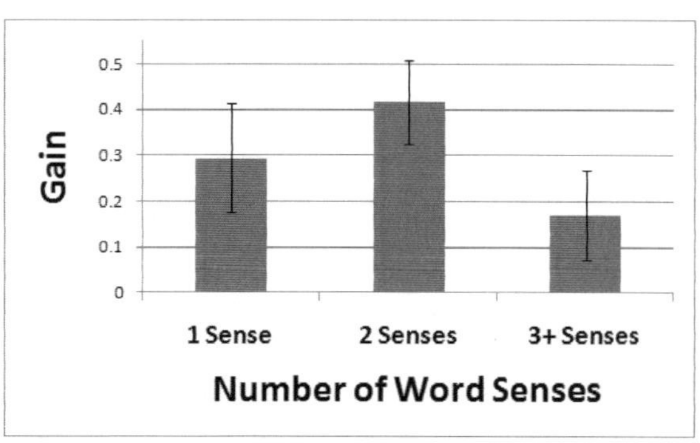

Figure 2: Impact of word sense complexity on the improvement between pre-test & post-test in Study 2

With respect to word complexity, the focus words were divided into the following groups:

- Words with 1 sense [8 words]
- Words with 2 senses [10 words]
- Words with 3 or more senses [8 words]

4 Results

The results of both of our studies showed that the use of the tutoring system significantly helped students improve their performance on the vocabulary tests, as made evident by the average overall gains between the pre-test and post-test ($p < 0.001$). Note that the error bars shown in this section show the standard error. Also note that normalized gain, the measurement being used to describe improvement in both studies, is given the by the following:

If the *post-test score* is greater than the *pre-test score,* then

Normalized gain = (post-test score – pre-test score) / (maximum-possible-score – pre-test score)

Otherwise,

Normalized gain = (post-test score – pre-test score) / (pre-test score)

In Study 1, the average normalized gain between the pre-test and post-test was 0.2563 (± 0.0466). Figure 1 illustrates the differences in vocabulary gain when the gains are separated by word condition type. The average gains per condition are 0.2222, 0.1270, and 0.1191 for the conditions of grapheme-to-phoneme ratio = 1, grapheme-to-phoneme ratio > 1, and grapheme-to-phoneme ratio < 1 respectively.

In Study 2, the average normalized gain between the pre-test and post-test was 0.5323 (± 0.0833). Figure 2 illustrates the impact of word sense complexity on vocabulary gains. With respect to word sense complexity, the average gains per condition are 0.2495, 0.4163, and 0.1699 for the 1-sense, 2-senses, and 3-or-more senses conditions respectively.

5 Discussion

The results of both studies tend to confirm our initial hypotheses and suggest that word complexity, in the forms of phonetic complexity and the number of word senses a word has, does make a significant difference in how easily an L2 vocabulary word is learned.

In Study 1, we see that the 'simple' words (those with grapheme-to-phoneme ratios equal to 1), afford more learning than the more 'complex' words, as made evident by the difference in gains between the pre-test and post-test ($p < 0.04$) shown in Figure 1. This result suggests that the phonetic complexity of a word may play a role in learning that word in an intelligent tutoring environment.

In Study 2, the words with many senses (3 or more) have significantly lower gains than words with 1 or 2 senses ($p < 0.05$). There was no significant difference in gains between words with 1 word sense and words with 2 word senses, as shown in Figure 2. This result seems to suggest that words with 2 or fewer word senses are generally easier for L2 students to learn than those with 3 or more word senses. This could be because a student has a harder time choosing the correct meaning of a word amongst many choices. Fewer choices seem to afford more learning than showing just the right one, which may indicate that by comparing two meanings with the meaning in the document, the student is actively constructing her knowledge of the word. Dela Rosa and Eskenazi (2011) found that giving students only the correct meaning of a polysemous word afforded less learning than giving them several meanings in a ranked order.

6 Conclusion and Future Directions

This paper demonstrates that word complexity can affect how easily an L2 vocabulary word can be learned. We proposed two dimensions of word complexity, one based on the complexity of a word's grapheme to phoneme ratio, and another based on the number of meanings a word has. Two in-vivo studies were conducted with ESL college students to test our hypothesis. Our results suggest that word complexity on both the phonetic and semantic level does have an effect on L2 vocabulary learning.

A future research direction that this work suggests is the search for other measures of word complexity, such as a more complex measure of grapheme to phoneme ratio, for example taking into account the ambiguity of a particular grapheme, or more complex measures of semantic complexity, like one that may take the average number of synonyms a word sense has, to determine their effect on learning using an intelligent tutoring system. This information could help define different ways to teach different words, providing more scaffolding for harder words, for example.

We would also like to investigate whether the average aggregate vocabulary learning trends of different native language groups correlates with different measures of word complexity, and thus might reveal a relation between the structure of L1 and difficulties in L2 vocabulary learning.

Finally we would like to investigate whether providing examples of focus word usage prior to or following a reading activity is beneficial to vocabulary learning.

Acknowledgments

This project is supported through the Pittsburgh Science of Learning Center which is funded by the US National Science Foundation under grant number SBE-0836012. Any opinions, findings, and conclusions or recommendations expressed in this material are those of the authors and do not necessarily reflect the views of the NSF.

The authors would like to thank Betsy Davis, Gregory Mizera, Dawn McCormick, Chris Ortiz, Tamar Bernfeld, and Kimberly Rehak at the University of Pittsburgh's English Language Institute for their participation and input in the classroom studies.

References

Cepstral Text-to-Speech. 2001. http://www.cepstral.com

Kevin Dela Rosa, Gabriel Parent, and Maxine Eskenazi. 2010. Multimodal learning of words: A study on the use of speech synthesis to reinforce written text in L2 language learning. Proceedings of the 2010 ISCA Workshop on Speech and Language Technology in Education.

Kevin Dela Rosa and Maxine Eskenazi. 2011. Impact of Word Sense Disambiguation on Ordering Dictionary Definitions in Vocabulary Learning Tutors. Proceedings of the 24th Florida Artificial Intelligence Research Society Conference.

Michael Heilman, Kevyn Collins-Thompson, Jamie Callan, and Maxine Eskenazi. 2006. Classroom success of an Intelligent Tutoring System for lexical practice and reading comprehension. Proceedings of the 9th International Conference on Spoken Language.

Kathy Jakiellski. 1998. Motor Organization in the Acquisition of Consonant Clusters. PhD Thesis, University of Texas at Austin.

Stefka Marinova-Todd, D. Bradford Marshall, And Catherine Snow. 2000. Three Misconceptions About Age and L2 Learning. TESOL Quarterly, 34(1): 9-34.

Rebecca Oxford and Robin Scarcella. 1994. Second Language Vocabulary Learning Among Adults: State Of The Art In Vocabulary Instruction. System, 22(2): 231-243.

Philip Pavlik and John Anderson. 2005. Practice and forgetting effects on vocabulary memory: An activation-based model of the spacing effect. Cognitive Science, 29 (4): 559-586.

Charles Perfetti. 2010. Decoding, Vocabulary, and Comprehension: The Golden Triangle of Reading Skill. In Bringing Reading Researchers to Life, Margret McKeown & Linda Kucan (editors). Guilford Press, New York, US.

Appendix A. Words Used in Studies

Words from Study 1: condominium, exotic, boost, escapism, yearning, asylum, blatant, denizens, partisan, expats, influx, levy, taxes, lucrative, sector, ostracism, taunts, withdrawal

Words from Study 2: established, incorporated, intervention, coherent, facilitate, induce, relax, designed, flexible, inspected, registered, category, enforce, illustrations, accumulate, hypothesis, period, qualitative, simulations, conducted, debate, domestic, found, concentrate, depression, register

Developing Methodology for Korean Particle Error Detection

Markus Dickinson
Indiana University
md7@indiana.edu

Ross Israel
Indiana University
raisrael@indiana.edu

Sun-Hee Lee
Wellesley College
slee6@wellesley.edu

Abstract

We further work on detecting errors in post-positional particle usage by learners of Korean by improving the training data and developing a complete pipeline of particle selection. We improve the data by filtering non-Korean data and sampling instances to better match the particle distribution. Our evaluation shows that, while the data selection is effective, there is much work to be done with preprocessing and system optimization.

1 Introduction

A growing area of research in analyzing learner language is to detect errors in function words, namely categories such as prepositions and articles (see Leacock et al., 2010, and references therein). This work has mostly been for English, and there are issues, such as greater morphological complexity, in moving to other languages (see, e.g., de Ilarraza et al., 2008; Dickinson et al., 2010). Our goal is to build a machine learning system for detecting errors in post-positional particles in Korean, a significant source of learner errors (Ko et al., 2004; Lee et al., 2009b).

Korean postpositional particles are morphemes that attach to a preceding nominal to indicate a range of linguistic functions, including grammatical functions, e.g., subject and object; semantic roles; and discourse functions. In (1), for instance, *ka* marks the subject (function) and agent (semantic role).[1] Similar to English prepositions, particles can also have modifier functions, adding meanings of time, location, instrument, possession, and so forth.

(1) Sumi-**ka** John-**uy** cip-**eyse** ku-**lul** twu
Sumi-SBJ John-GEN house-LOC he-OBJ two
sikan-**ul** kitaly-ess-ta.
hours-OBJ wait-PAST-END
'Sumi waited for John for (the whole) two hours in his house.'

We treat the task of particle error detection as one of particle selection, and we use machine learning because it has proven effective in similar tasks for other languages (e.g., Chodorow et al., 2007; Oyama, 2010). Training on a corpus of well-formed Korean, we predict which particle should appear after a given nominal; if this is different from the learner's, we have detected an error. Using a machine learner has the advantage of being able to perform well without a researcher having to specify rules, especially with the complex set of linguistic relationships motivating particle selection.[2]

We build from Dickinson et al. (2010) in two main ways: first, we implement a presence-selection pipeline that has proven effective for English preposition error detection (cf. Gamon et al., 2008). As the task is understudied, the work is preliminary, but it nonetheless is able to highlight the primary areas of focus for future work. Secondly, we improve upon the training data, in particular doing a better job of selecting relevant instances for the machine learner. Obtaining better-quality training data is a major issue for machine learning applied to learner language, as the domain of writing is different from news-heavy training domains (Gamon, 2010).

[1] We use the Yale Romanization scheme for writing Korean.

[2] See Dickinson and Lee (2009); de Ilarraza et al. (2008); Oyama (2010) for related work in other languages.

Proceedings of the Sixth Workshop on Innovative Use of NLP for Building Educational Applications, pages 81–86,
Portland, Oregon, 24 June 2011. ©2011 Association for Computational Linguistics

2 Particle error detection

2.1 Pre-processing

Korean is an agglutinative language: Korean words (referred to as *ecels*) are usually composed of a root with a number of functional affixes. We thus first segment and POS tag the text, for both training and testing, using a hybrid (trigram + rule-based) morphological tagger for Korean (Han and Palmer, 2004). The tagger is designed for native language and is not optimized to make guesses for ill-formed input. While the POS tags assigned to the learner corpus are thus often incorrect (see Lee et al., 2009a), there is the more primary problem of segmentation, as discussed in more detail in section 4.

2.2 Machine learning

We use the Maximum Entropy Toolkit (Le, 2004) for machine learning. Training on a corpus of well-formed Korean, we predict which particle should appear after a given nominal; if this is different from what the learner used, we have detected an error. It is important that the data represent the relationships between specific lexical items: in the comparable English case, for example, *interest* is usually found with *in*: ***interest*** *in/*with learning*.

Treating the ends of nominal elements as possible particle slots, we break classification into two steps: 1) Is there a particle? (Yes/No); and 2) What is the exact particle? Using two steps eases the task of actual particle prediction: with a successful classification of negative and positive instances, there is no need to handle nominals that have no particle in step 2. To evaluate our parameters for obtaining the most relevant instances, we keep the task simple and perform only step 1, as this step provides information about the usability of the training data. For actual system performance, we evaluate both steps.

In selecting features for Korean, we have to account for relatively free word order (Chung et al., 2010). We follow our previous work (Dickinson et al., 2010) in our feature choices, using a five-word window that includes the target stem and two words on either side for context (see also Tetreault and Chodorow, 2008). Each word is broken down into: stem, affixes, stem_POS, and affixes_POS. We also have features for the preceding and following noun and verb, thereby approximating relevant selectional properties. Although these are relatively shallow features, they provide enough lexical and grammatical context to help select better or worse training data (section 3) and to provide a basis for a preliminary system (section 4).

3 Obtaining the most relevant instances

We need well-formed Korean data in order to train a machine learner. To acquire this, we use web-based corpora, as this allows us to find data similar to learner language, and using web as corpus (WaC) tools allows us to adjust parameters for new data (Dickinson et al., 2010). However, the methodology outlined in Dickinson et al. (2010) can be improved in at least three ways, outlined next.

3.1 Using sub-corpora

Web corpora can be built by searching for a set of seed terms, extracting documents with those terms (Baroni and Bernardini, 2004). One way to improve such corpora is to use better seeds, namely, those which are: 1) domain-appropriate (e.g., about traveling), and 2) of an appropriate level. In Dickinson et al. (2010), we show that basic terms result in poor quality Korean, but slightly more advanced terms on the same topics result in better-formed data.

Rather than use all of the seed terms to create a single corpus, we divide the seed terms into 13 separate sets, based on the individual topics from our learner corpus. The sub-corpora are then combined to create a cohesive corpus covering all the topics. For example, we use 10 *Travel* words to build a subcorpus, 10 *Learning Korean* words for a different subcorpus, and so forth. This means that terms appropriate for one topic are not mixed with terms for a different topic, ensuring more coherent web documents. Otherwise, we might obtain a *Health Management* word, such as *pyengwen* ('hospital'), mixed with a *Generation Gap* word, such as *kaltung* ('conflict')—in this case, leading to webpages on war, a topic not represented in our learner corpus.

3.2 Filtering

One difficulty with our web corpora is that some of them have large amounts of other languages along with Korean. The keywords are in the corpora, but there is additional text, often in Chinese, English, or Japanese. These types of pages are unreliable for our purposes, as they may not exhibit natural Korean. By using a simple filter, we check whether a majority of the characters in a webpage are indeed from the Korean writing system, and remove pages beneath a certain threshold.

3.3 Instance sampling

Particles are often dropped in colloquial and even written Korean, whereas learners are more often required to use them. It is not always the case that the web pages contain the same ratio of particles as learners are expected to use. To alleviate this over-weighting of having no particle attached to a noun, we propose to downsample our corpora for the machine learning experiments, by removing a randomly-selected proportion of (negative) instances. Instance sampling has been effective for other NLP tasks, e.g., anaphora resolution (Wunsch et al., 2009), when the number of negative instances is much greater than the positive ones. In our web corpora, nouns have a greater than 50% chance of having no particle; in section 3.4, we thus downsample to varying amounts of negative instances from about 45% to as little as 10% of the total corpus.

3.4 Training data selection

In Dickinson et al. (2010), we used a Korean learner data set from Lee et al. (2009b) for development. It contains 3198 ecels, 1842 of which are nominals, and 1271 (≈70%) of those have particles. We use this same corpus for development, to evaluate filtering and down-sampling. Evaluating on (yes/no) particle presence, in tables 1 and 2, recall is the percentage of positive instances we correctly find and precision is the percentage of instances that we classify as positive that actually are. A baseline of always guessing a particle gives 100% recall, 69% precision, and 81.7% F-score.

Table 1 shows the results of the MaxEnt system for step 1, using training data built for the topics in the data with filter thresholds of 50%, 70%, 90%, and 100%—i.e., requiring that percentage of Korean characters—as well as the unfiltered corpus. The best F-score is with the filter set at 90%, despite the size of the filtered corpus being smaller than the full corpus. Accordingly, we use the 90% filter on our training corpus for the experiments described below.

Threshold	100%	90%	70%	50%	Full
Ecel	67k	9.6m	10.3m	11.1m	12.7m
Instances	37k	5.8m	6.3m	7.1m	8.4m
Accuracy	74.75	81.11	74.64	80.29	80.46
Precision	80.03	86.14	79.65	85.41	85.56
Recall	84.50	86.55	84.97	86.15	86.23
F-score	82.20	**86.34**	82.22	85.78	85.89

Table 1: Step 1 (particle presence) results with filters

The results for instance sampling are given in table 2. We experiment with positive to negative sampling ratios of 1.3/1 (≈43% negative instances), 2/1 (≈33%), 4/1 (≈20%), and 10/1 (≈10%). We select the 90% filter, 1.3/1 downsampling settings and apply them to the training corpus (section 3.1) for all experiments below.

P/N ratio	10/1	4/1	2/1	1.3/1	1/1.05
Instances	3.1m	3.5m	4.3m	5m	5.8m
Accuracy	74.75	77.85	80.23	81.59	81.11
Precision	73.38	76.72	80.75	84.26	86.14
Recall	99.53	97.48	93.71	90.17	86.55
F-score	84.47	85.86	86.74	**87.12**	86.34

Table 2: Step 1 (presence) results with instance sampling

One goal has been to improve the web as corpus corpus methodology for training a machine learning system. The results in tables 1 and 2 reinforce our earlier finding that size is not necessarily the most important variable in determining the usefulness or overall quality of data collected from the web for NLP tasks (Dickinson et al., 2010). Indeed, the corpus producing best results (90% filter, 1.3:1 downsampling) is more than 3 million instances smaller than the unfiltered, unsampled corpus.

4 Initial system evaluation

We have obtained an annotated corpus of 25 essays from heritage intermediate learners,[3] with 299 sentences and 2515 ecels (2676 ecels after correcting spacing errors). There are 1138 nominals, with 93 particle errors (5 added particles, 35 omissions, 53 substitutions)—in other words, less than 10% of particles are errors. There are 979 particles after correction. We focus on 38 particles that intermediate

[3]Heritage learners have had exposure to Korean at a young age, such as growing up with Korean spoken at home.

students can be reasonably expected to use. A particle is one of three types (cf. Nam and Ko, 2005): 1) case markers, 2) adverbials (cf. prepositions), and 3) auxiliary particles.[4]

Table 3 gives the results for the entire system on the test corpus, with separate results for each category of particle, (**Case**, **Adv.**, and **Aux.**) as well as the concatenation of the three (**All**). The accuracy presented here is in terms of only the particle in question, as opposed to the full form of root+particle(s). Step 2 is presented in 2 ways: **Classified**, meaning that all of the instances classified as needing a particle by step 1 are processed, or **Gold**, in which we rely on the annotation to determine particle presence. It is not surprising, then, that **Gold** experiments are more accurate than **Classified** experiments, due to step 1 errors and also preprocessing issues, discussed next.

		Step 1	Step 2	
Data	#		Classified	Gold
Case	504	95.83%	71.23%	72.22%
Adv.	205	82.43%	30.24%	32.68%
Aux.	207	89.37%	31.41%	35.74%
All	916	91.37%	53.05%	55.13%

Table 3: Accuracy for step 1 (particle presence) & step 2 (particle selection), with number (#) of instances

Preprocessing For the particles we examine, there are 135 mis-segmented nominals. The problem is more conspicuous if we look at the entire corpus: the tagger identifies 1547 nominal roots, but there are only 1138. Some are errors in segmentation, i.e., mis-identifying the proper root of the ecel, and some are problems with tagging the root, e.g., a nominal mistagged as a verb. Table 4 provides results divided by cases with only correctly pre-processed ecels and where the target ecel has been mis-handled by the tagger. This checks whether the system particle is correct, ignoring whether the whole form is correct; if full-form accuracy is considered, we have no way to get the 135 inaccurate cases correct.

Error detection While our goal now is to establish a starting point, the ultimate, on-going goal of this work is to develop a robust system for automatically detecting errors in learner data. Thus, it is necessary to measure our performance at actually finding the erroneous instances extracted from our test corpus. Table 5 provides results for step 2 in terms of our ability to detect erroneous instances. We report precision and recall, calculated as in figure 1.

[4] Full corpus details will be made available at: `http://cl.indiana.edu/~particles/`.

		Step 1	Step 2	
Data	#		Classified	Gold
Accurate	781	94.24%	55.95%	58.13%
Inaccurate	135	74.81%	36.29%	38.51%

Table 4: Overall accuracy divided by accurate and inaccurate preprocessing

	Case	Adv.	Aux.	All
Precision	28.82%	7.69%	5.51%	15.45%
Recall	87.50%	100%	77.78%	88.00%

Table 5: Error detection (using Gold step 1)

From the set of *erroneous* instances:	
True Positive (TP)	ML class ≠ student class
False Negative (FN)	ML class = student class
From the set of *correct* instances:	
False Positive (FP)	ML class ≠ student class
True Negative (TN)	ML class = student class
Precision (P)	$\frac{TP}{TP+FP}$
Recall (R)	$\frac{TP}{TP+FN}$

Figure 1: Precision and recall for error detection

4.1 Discussion and Outlook

One striking aspect about the results in table 3 is the gap in accuracy between case particles and the other two categories, particularly in step 2. This points at a need to develop independent systems for each type of particle, each relying on different types of linguistic information. Auxiliary particles, for example, include topic particles which—similar to English articles (Han et al., 2006)—require discourse information to get correct. Still, as case particles comprise more than half of all particles in our corpus, the system is already potentially useful to learners.

Comparing the rows in table 4, the dramatic drop in accuracy when moving to inaccurately-processed cases shows a clear need for preprocessing adapted to learner data. While it is disconcerting that nearly 15% (135/916) of the cases have no chance of resulting in a correct full form, the results indicate that we can obtain reliable accuracy (cf. 94.24%) for predicting particle presence across all types of particles, assuming good morphological tagging.

From table 5, it is apparent that we are overguessing errors; recall that only 10% of particles are erroneous, whereas we more often guess a different particle. While this tendency results in high recall, a tool for learners should have higher precision, so that correct usage is not flagged. However, this is a first attempt at error detection, and simply knowing that precision is low means we can take steps to solve this deficiency. Our training data may have too many possible classes in it, and we have not yet accounted for phonological alternations; e.g. if the system guesses *ul* when *lul* is correct, we count a miss, even though they are different realizations of the same morpheme.

To try and alleviate the over-prediction of errors, we have begun to explore implementing a confidence filter. As a first pass, we use a simple filter that compares the probability of the best particle to the probability of the particle the learner provided; the absolute difference in probabilities must be above a certain threshold. Table 6 provides the error detection results for each type of particle, incorporating confidence filters of 10%, 20%, 30%, 40%, 50%, and 60%. The results show that increasing the threshold at which we accept the classifier's answer can significantly increase precision, at the cost of recall. As noted above, higher precision is desirable, so we plan on further developing this confidence filter. We may also include heuristic-based filters, such as the ones implemented in *Criterion* (see Leacock et al., 2010), as well as a language model approach (Gamon et al., 2008).

Finally, we are currently working on improving the POS tagger, testing other taggers in the process, and developing optimal feature sets for different kinds of particles.

Acknowledgments

We would like to thank the IU CL discussion group and Joel Tetreault for feedback at various points.

		Adv	Aux	Case	All
10%	P	10.0%	6.3%	29.9%	16.3%
	R	100%	77.8%	67.8%	73.3%
20%	P	13.5%	7.8%	32.6%	18.0%
	R	100%	77.8%	50.0%	60.0%
30%	P	20.0%	8.3%	36.1%	20.8%
	R	100%	66.7%	39.3%	50.7%
40%	P	19.4%	14.3%	48.6%	26.9%
	R	60.0%	66.7%	30.4%	38.7%
50%	P	23.1%	16.7%	57.9%	32.1%
	R	30.0%	44.4%	19.6%	24.0%
60%	P	40.0%	26.7%	72.3%	45.2%
	R	20.0%	44.4%	14.3%	18.7%

Table 6: Error detection with confidence filters

References

Marco Baroni and Silvia Bernardini. 2004. Bootcat: Bootstrapping corpora and terms from the web. In *Proceedings of LREC 2004*, pages 1313–1316.

Martin Chodorow, Joel Tetreault, and Na-Rae Han. 2007. Detection of grammatical errors involving prepositions. In *Proceedings of the 4th ACL-SIGSEM Workshop on Prepositions*, pages 25–30. Prague.

Tagyoung Chung, Matt Post, and Daniel Gildea. 2010. Factors affecting the accuracy of korean parsing. In *Proceedings of the NAACL HLT 2010 First Workshop on Statistical Parsing of Morphologically-Rich Languages*, pages 49–57. Los Angeles, CA, USA.

Arantza Díaz de Ilarraza, Koldo Gojenola, and Maite Oronoz. 2008. Detecting erroneous uses of complex postpositions in an agglutinative language. In *Proceedings of COLING-08*. Manchester.

Markus Dickinson, Ross Israel, and Sun-Hee Lee. 2010. Building a korean web corpus for analyzing learner language. In *Proceedings of the 6th Workshop on the Web as Corpus (WAC-6)*. Los Angeles.

Markus Dickinson and Chong Min Lee. 2009. Modifying corpus annotation to support the analysis of learner language. *CALICO Journal*, 26(3).

Michael Gamon. 2010. Using mostly native data

to correct errors in learners' writing. In *Human Language Technologies: The 2010 Annual Conference of the North American Chapter of the Association for Computational Linguistics*, pages 163–171. Los Angeles, California.

Michael Gamon, Jianfeng Gao, Chris Brockett, Alexander Klementiev, William Dolan, Dmitriy Belenko, and Lucy Vanderwende. 2008. Using contextual speller techniques and language modeling for esl error correction. In *Proceedings of IJCNLP*. Hyderabad, India.

Chung-Hye Han and Martha Palmer. 2004. A morphological tagger for korean: Statistical tagging combined with corpus-based morphological rule application. *Machine Translation*, 18(4):275–297.

Na-Rae Han, Martin Chodorow, and Claudia Leacock. 2006. Detecting errors in english article usage by non-native speakers. *Natural Language Engineering*, 12(2).

S. Ko, M. Kim, J. Kim, S. Seo, H. Chung, and S. Han. 2004. *An analysis of Korean learner corpora and errors*. Hanguk Publishing Co.

Zhang Le. 2004. *Maximum Entropy Modeling Toolkit for Python and C++*. URL `http://homepages.inf.ed.ac.uk/s0450736/maxent_toolkit.html`.

Claudia Leacock, Martin Chodorow, Michael Gamon, and Joel Tetreault. 2010. *Automated Grammatical Error Detection for Language Learners*. Synthesis Lectures on Human Language Technologies. Morgan & Claypool.

Chong Min Lee, Soojeong Eom, and Markus Dickinson. 2009a. Towards analyzing korean learner particles. Talk given at CALICO '09 Pre-Conference Workshop on Automatic Analysis of Learner Language. Tempe, AZ.

Sun-Hee Lee, Seok Bae Jang, and Sang kyu Seo. 2009b. Annotation of korean learner corpora for particle error detection. *CALICO Journal*, 26(3).

Ki-shim Nam and Yong-kun Ko. 2005. *Korean Grammar (phyocwun kwuke mwunpeplon)*. Top Publisher, Seoul.

Hiromi Oyama. 2010. Automatic error detection method for japanese particles. *Polyglossia*, 18.

Joel Tetreault and Martin Chodorow. 2008. The ups and downs of preposition error detection in esl writing. In *Proceedings of COLING-08*. Manchester.

Holger Wunsch, Sandra Kübler, and Rachael Cantrell. 2009. Instance sampling methods for pronoun resolution. In *Proceedings of RANLP 2009*. Borovets, Bulgaria.

Measuring Language Development in Early Childhood Education: A Case Study of Grammar Checking in Child Language Transcripts

Khairun-nisa Hassanali
Computer Science Department
The University of Texas at Dallas
Richardson, TX, USA
nisa@hlt.utdallas.edu

Yang Liu
Computer Science Department
The University of Texas at Dallas
Richardson, TX, USA
yangl@hlt.utdallas.edu

Abstract

Language sample analysis is an important technique used in measuring language development. At present, measures of grammatical complexity such as the Index of Productive Syntax (Scarborough, 1990) are used to measure language development in early childhood. Although these measures depict the overall competence in the usage of language, they do not provide for an analysis of the grammatical mistakes made by the child. In this paper, we explore the use of existing Natural Language Processing (NLP) techniques to provide an insight into the processing of child language transcripts and challenges in automatic grammar checking. We explore the automatic detection of 6 types of verb related grammatical errors. We compare rule based systems to statistical systems and investigate the use of different features. We found the statistical systems performed better than the rule based systems for most of the error categories.

1 Introduction

Automatic grammar checking and correction has been used extensively in several applications. One such application is in word processors where the user is notified of a potential ungrammatical sentence. This feature makes it easier for the users to detect and correct ungrammatical sentences. Automatic grammar checking can also be beneficial in language learning where students are given suggestions on potential grammatical errors (Lee and Seneff, 2006). Another application of grammar checking is in improving a parser's performance for ungrammatical sentences. Since most parsers are trained on written data consisting mostly of grammatical sentences, the parsers face issues when parsing ungrammatical sentences. Automatic detection and correction of these ungrammatical sentences would improve the parser's performance by detecting the ungrammatical sentences and performing a second parse on the corrected sentences (Caines and Buttery, 2010). From an education perspective, measuring language skills has been extensively explored. There are systems in place that automatically detect and correct errors for second language learners (Eeg-Olofsson and Knuttson, 2003; Leacock et al., 2010).

One method used in measuring language development is the analysis of transcripts of child language speech. Child language transcripts are samples of a child's utterances during a specified period of time. Educators and speech language pathologists use these samples to measure language development. In particular, speech language pathologists score these transcripts for grammatical measures of complexity amidst other measures. Since manual analysis of transcripts is time consuming, many of these grammatical complexity measures require the speech language pathologists to look for just a few examples. The Index of Productive Syntax (IPSyn) (Scarborough, 1990) is one such measure of morphological and syntactic structure developed for measuring language samples of preschool children. The advantage of measures such as IPSyn is that they give a single score that can be used to holistically measure language development. However, they focus on grammatical constructs that the

Proceedings of the Sixth Workshop on Innovative Use of NLP for Building Educational Applications, pages 87–95,
Portland, Oregon, 24 June 2011.

child uses correctly and do not take into account the number and type of grammatical errors that are made by the child.

Educators wishing to measure language development and competence in a child will benefit from having access to the grammatical errors made by a child. Analysis of these grammatical errors will enable educators and speech language pathologists to identify shortcomings in the child's language and recommend intervention techniques customized to the child. Since manual identification of grammatical errors is both cumbersome and time consuming, a tool that automatically does grammar checking would be of great use to clinicians. Additionally, we see several uses of automatic grammar detection. For example, we can use the statistics of grammatical errors as features in building classifiers that predict language impairment. Furthermore, we could also use the statistics of these grammatical errors to come up with a measure of language development that takes into account both grammatical competence and grammatical deficiencies.

In this paper, we use existing NLP techniques to automatically detect grammatical errors from child language transcripts. Since children with Language Impairment (LI) have a greater problem with correct usage of verbs compared to Typically Developing (TD) children (Rice et al., 1995), we focus mainly on verb related errors. We compare rule based systems to statistical systems and investigate the use of different features. We found the statistical systems performed better than the rule based systems for most error categories.

2 Related Work

While there has been considerable work (Sagae et al., 2007) done on annotating child language transcripts for grammatical relations, as far as we know, there has been no work done on automatic grammar checking of child language transcripts. Most of the existing work in automatic grammar checking has been done on written text. Spoken language on the other hand, presents challenges such as disfluencies and false restarts which are not present in written text. We believe that the specific research challenges that are encountered in detecting and correcting child language transcripts warrant a more detailed examination.

Caines and Buttery (2010) focused on identifying sentences with the missing auxiliary verb in the progressive aspect constructions. They used logistic regression to predict the presence of zero auxiliary occurrence in the spoken British National Corpus (BNC). An example of a zero auxiliary construction is "You talking to me?". They first identified constructions with the progressive aspect and annotated the constructions for the following features: subject person, subject case, perfect aspect, presence of negation and use of pronouns. Their model identified zero auxiliary constructions with 96.9% accuracy. They also demonstrated how their model can be integrated into existing parsing tools, thereby increasing the number of successful parses for zero auxiliary constructions by 30%.

Lee and Seneff (2008) described a system for verb error correction using template matching on parse trees in two ways. Their work focused on correcting the error types related to subject-verb agreement, auxiliary agreement and complementation. They considered the irregularities in parse trees caused by verb error forms and used n-gram counts to filter proposed corrections. They used the AQUAINT Corpus of English News Text to detect the irregularities in the parse trees caused by verb error forms. They reported an accuracy of 98.93% for verb errors related to subject-verb agreement, and 98.94% for verb errors related to auxiliary agreement and complementation. Bowden and Fox (2002) developed a system to detect and explain errors made by non-native English speakers. They used classification and pattern matching rules instead of thorough parsing. Their system searched for the verb-related errors and noun-related errors one by one in one sentence by narrowing down the classification of errors. Lee and Seneff (2006) developed a system to automatically correct grammatical errors related to articles, verbs, prepositions and nouns.

Leacock et al. (2010) discuss automated grammatical error detection for English language learners. They focus on errors that language learners find most difficult - constructions that contain prepositions, articles, and collocations. They discuss the existing systems in place for automated grammatical error detection and correction for these and other classes of errors in a number of languages. Addi-

Label	Meaning	Example
0	No error	I like it.
1	Missing auxiliary verb	You talking to me?
2	Missing copulae	She lovely.
3	Subject-auxiliary verb agreement	You is talking to me.
4	Incorrect auxiliary verb used e.g. using does instead of is	She does dead girl.
5	Missing verb	She her a book.
6	Wrong verb usage including subject-verb disagreement	He love dogs.
7	Missing preposition	The book is the table.
8	Missing article	She ate apple.
9	Missing subject before verb	I know loves me.
10	Missing infinitive marker "to"	I give it her.
11	Other errors not covered in 1-10	The put.

Table 1: Different types of errors considered in this study

tionally, they touch on error annotations and system evaluation for grammatical error detection.

3 Data

For the purpose of our experiments, we used the Paradise dataset (Paradise et al., 2005). This dataset contains 677 transcripts corresponding to 677 children aged six that were collected in the course of a study of the relationship of otitis media and child development. The only household language spoken by these children was English. The transcripts in the Paradise set consist of conversations between a child and his/her caretaker. We retained only the child's utterances and removed all other utterances. The Paradise dataset (considering only the child's utterances) contains a total of 108,711 utterances, 394,290 words, and an average Mean Length of Utterance of 3.64. Gabani (2009) used scores on the Peabody Picture Vocabulary Test (Dunn, 1965), total percentage phonemes repeated correctly on a non-word repetition task and mean length of utterance in morphemes to label these transcripts for language impairment. A transcript was labeled as having been produced by a child with LI if the child scored 1.5 or more standard deviations below the mean of the entire sample on at least two of the three tests. Of the 677 transcripts, 623 were labeled as TD and 54 as LI.

We manually annotated each utterance in the transcripts for 10 different types of errors. Table 1 gives the different types of errors we considered along with examples. We focused on these 10 different types of errors since children with LI have problems with the usage of verbs in particular. The list of errors we arrived at was based on the errors we observed in the transcripts. Since an utterance could have more than one error, we annotated each utterance in the transcript for all the errors present in the utterance. While annotating the utterances, we observed that there were utterances that could correspond to multiple types of error. For example, consider the following sentence: "She go to school". The error in this sentence could be an error of a missing auxiliary and a wrong verb form in which case the correct sentence would be "She is going to school"; or it could be a missing modal, in which case the correct form would be "She will go to school"; or it could just be a subject-verb disagreement in which case "She goes to school" would be the correct form. Therefore, although we know that the utterance definitely has an error, it is not always possible to assign a single error. We also observed several utterances had both a missing subject and a missing auxiliary verb error. For example, instead of saying "I am going to play", some children say "Going to play", which misses both the subject and auxiliary verb. In this case, the utterance was annotated as having two errors: missing subject and missing auxiliary. Finally, single word utterances were labeled as being correct.

Table 2 gives the distribution of the errors in the corpus and percentage of TD and LI population that

No	Error Type	Percentage (Count)	% of LI children making error	% of TD children making error
1	Missing auxiliary	8.43% (641)	7%	5%
2	Missing copulae	36.67% (2788)	77.78%	45%
3	Subject-auxiliary agreement	6.31% (480)	40.74%	35%
4	Incorrect auxiliary verb used	0.71%(54)	11.47%	3%
5	Missing verb	5% (380)	29.63%	10%
6	Wrong verb usage	14.59% (1109)	68.5%	50%
7	Missing preposition	5% (380)	7.4%	5%
8	Missing article	3.97% (302)	29.63%	35%
9	Missing subject	7.69% (585)	3.7%	5%
10	Missing infinitive marker "To"	1.58% (120)	7.5%	11.67%
11	Other errors	10.05% (764)	56.7%	23.2%

Table 2: Statistics of Errors

made the error at least once in the entire transcript. As we can see from Table 2, 36.67% of the errors in the corpus are due to missing copulae. Wrong verb usage was the next most common error contributing to 14.59% of the errors in the corpus. We observed that there was a higher percentage of children with LI that made errors on all error categories except for errors related to missing article and missing subject. We observed that on average, the transcripts belonging to children with LI had fewer utterances as compared to transcripts belonging to TD children. Additionally, children with LI used many single word and two word utterances.

One annotator labeled the entire corpus for grammatical errors. To calculate inter-annotator agreement, we randomly selected 386 utterances annotated by the first annotator with different error types. The second annotator was provided these utterances along with the labels given by the first annotator[1]. In case of a disagreement, the second annotator provided a different label/labels. The annotator agreement using the average Cohen's Kappa coeffiecient was 77.7%. Out of the 386 utterances, there were 43 disagreements between the annotators. We found that for some error categories such as the missing auxiliary, there was high inter-annotator agreement of 95.32%, whereas for other categories such as wrong verb usage and missing articles, there was less agreement (64.2% and 65.3% respectively). In particular, we found low inter-annotator agreement on utterances that have errors that could be assigned to multiple categories.

[1]We will perform independent annotation of the errors and calculate inter-annotator agreement based on these independent annotations

4 Experiments

The transcripts were parsed using the Charniak parser (Charniak, 2000). Since the Paradise dataset consists of children's utterances, and many of them have not mastered the language, we observed that processing these transcripts is challenging. As is prevalent in spoken language corpora, these transcripts had disfluencies, false restarts and incomplete utterances, which sometimes pose problems to the parser.

We conducted experiments in detecting errors related to the usage of the -ing participle, subject-auxiliary agreement, missing copulae, missing verb, subject-verb agreement and missing infinitive marker "to". For each of these categories, we constructed one rule based classifier using regular expressions based on the parse tree structure, an alternating decision tree classifier that used rules as features and a naive Bayes multinomial classifier that used a variety of features. For every category, we performed 10 fold cross validation using all the utterances. We used the naive Bayes multinomial classifier and the alternating decision tree classifier from the WEKA toolkit (Hall et al., 2009). Table 3 gives the results using the three classifiers for the different categories of errors, where (P/R) F1 stands for (Pre-

Error	Rule Based System (P/R)F1	Decision Tree Classifier using Rules as features (P/R)F1	Naive Bayes Classifier using a variety of features (P/R)F1
Usage of -ing participle	(0.984/0.978) 0.981	**(0.986/1) 0.993**	(0.736/0.929) 0.821
Missing copulae	(0.885/0.9) 0.892	**(0.912/0.94) 0.926**	(0.82/0.86) 0.84
Missing verb	(0.875/**0.932**) 0.903	(**0.92**/0.89) **0.905**	(0.87/0.91) 0.9
Subject-auxiliary agreement	(0.855/0.932) 0.888	(**0.95**/0.84) 0.892	(0.89/**0.934**) **0.912**
Subject-verb agreement	(0.883/**0.945**) 0.892	(**0.92**/0.877) 0.898	(0.91/0.914) **0.912**
Missing infinitive marker "To"	**(0.97/0.954) 0.962**	(0.94/0.84) 0.887	(0.95/0.88) 0.914
Overall	(0.935/0.923) 0.929	(0.945/0.965) 0.955	**(0.956/0.978) 0.967**

Table 3: Detection of errors using rule based system, alternating decision tree classifier and naive Bayes classifier

No	Feature	Type
1	Verb Adjective	Bigram
2	Auxiliary Noun	Bigram
3	Auxiliary Progressive-verb	Bigram
4	Pronoun Auxiliary	Bigram
5	Wh-Pronoun Progressive verb	Bigram
6	Progressive-verb Wh-adverb	Bigram
7	Adverb Auxiliary	Skip-1
8	Pronoun Auxiliary	Skip-1
9	Wh-adverb Progressive-verb	Skip-1
10	Auxiliary Preposition	Skip-2

Table 4: Top most bigram features useful for detecting misuse of -ing participle

cision/Recall) F1-measure. Below we describe the different experiments we conducted.

4.1 Misuse of the -ing Participle

The -ing participle can be used as a progressive aspect, a verb complementation, or a prepositional complementation. In the progressive aspect, it is necessary that the progressive verb be preceded by an auxiliary verb. When used as a verb complementation, the -ing participle should be preceded by a verb and similiarly when used as a prepositional complement, the -ing participle should be preceded by a preposition.

Rule based system

The -ing participle is denoted by the VBG tag in the Penn tree bank notation. VP and PP correspond to the verb phrase and prepositional phrase structures respectively. The rules that we formed were as follows:

1. Check that the utterance has a VBG tag (if it does not have a VBG tag, it does not contain an -ing participle).
2. If none of the following conditions are met, there is an error in the usage of -ing participle:
   (a) The root of the subtree that contains the -ing participle should be a VP with the head being a verb if used as a verb complementation
   (b) The root of the subtree that contains the -ing participle should be a PP if used as a prepositional complement
   (c) The root of the subtree that contains the -ing participle should be a VP with the head being an auxiliary verb if used as a progressive aspect

Predictive model

The features that we considered were:

1. Bigrams from POS tags
2. Skip bigrams from POS tags

   We used the skip bigrams to account for the fact that there could be other POS tags between an auxiliary verb and the progressive aspect of the verb such as adverbs. A skip-n bigram is a sequence of 2 POS tags with a distance of n between them. We used skip-1 and skip-2 bigrams in this study.

Analysis

As we can see from Table 3, the alternating decision tree classifier with rules as features gave the best results with an F1-measure of 0.993. Table 4 gives the topmost 10 features extracted using feature selection. We got the best results when we used the reduced set of features as opposed to using all bigrams and skip-1 and skip-2 bigrams. We also used the results reported by (Caines and Buttery, 2010) to see if their method was successful in identifying zero auxiliary constructs on our corpus. When we used logistic regression with the coefficients and features used by (Caines and Buttery, 2010), we got a recall of 0%. When we trained the logistic regression model on our data with their features, we got a precision of 1.09%, recall of 53.6% and F1-measure of 2.14%. This leads us to conclude that the features that were used by them are not suitable for child language transcripts. Additionally, we also observed that based on the features they used, in some cases it is difficult to distinguish zero auxiliary constructs from those with auxiliary constructs. For example, "You talking to me?" and "Are you talking to me?" would have the same values for their features, although the former is a zero auxiliary construct and the latter is not.

4.2 Identifying Missing Copulae

A copular verb is a verb that links a subject to its complement. In English, the most common copular verb is "be". Examples of sentences that contain a copular verb is "She is lovely" and "The child who fell sick was healthy earlier". An example of a sentence that misses a copular verb is "She lovely".

Rule based system

The rule that we used was as follows:

If an Adjective Phrase follows a noun phrase, or a Noun phrase follows a noun phrase, the likelihood that the utterance is missing a copular verb is quite high. However, there are exceptions to such rules, for example, "Apple Pie". We formed additional rules to identify such utterances and examined their parse trees to determine the function of the two noun phrases.

Predictive model

The features we used were as follows:

1. Does the utterance contain a noun phrase followed by a noun phrase?
2. Does the utterance contain a noun phrase followed by an adjective phrase?
3. Is the parent a verb phrase?
4. Is the parent a prepositional phrase?
5. Is the parent the root of the parse tree?
6. Is there an auxiliary verb or a verb between the noun phrase and/or adjective phrase?

Analysis

As we can see from Table 3, the alternating decision tree classifier performed the best with an F1-measure of 0.926. Our rules capture simple constructs that are used by young children. The majority of the utterances that missed a copulae consisted of noun phrase and an adjective phrase or a noun phrase and a noun phrase. Hence, the rules based system performed the best. Some of the false positives were due to utterances like "She an apple" where it is unlikely that the missing verb is a copular verb.

4.3 Identifying Missing Verbs

Errors of this type occur when a sentence is missing the verb. For example, the sentence "You can an apple" lacks the main verb after the modal verb "can". Similarly, "I did not it" lacks a main verb after "did not". For the purpose of this experiment, we consider only utterances that contain a modal or an auxiliary verb but do not have a main verb. We also consider utterances that use the verb "do" and detect the main missing verb in such cases.

Rule based system

The rule we used was to check if the utterance contains an auxiliary verb or a modal verb but not a main verb. In this case, the utterance is definitely missing a main verb. In order to identify utterances where the words "did", "do" and "does" are auxiliary verbs, we use the following procedure: If the negation "not" is present after *did/do/does*, then *did/do/does* is an auxiliary verb and needs to be followed by a main verb. In the case of the utterance being a question, the presence of *did/do/does* at the beginning of the utterances indicates the use as an auxiliary verb. In such a case, we need to check for the presence of a main verb. The same holds for the other auxiliary verbs.

Predictive model
We used the following as features:

1. Is an auxiliary verb present?
2. Is a modal verb present?
3. Is a main verb present after the auxiliary verb?
4. Is a main verb present after the modal verb?
5. Type of utterance - interrogative, declarative
6. Is a negation (not) present?

Analysis
As we can see from Table 3, the alternating decision tree classifier using rules as features gave the best result with an F1-measure of 0.905. At present, we handle only a subset of missing verbs and specifically those verbs that contain an auxiliary verb. Since most of the utterances are simple constructs, the alternating decision tree classifier performs well.

4.4 Identifying Subject-auxiliary Agreement

In the case of the subject-auxiliary agreement and subject-verb agreement, the first verb in the verb phrase has to agree with the subject unless the first verb is a modal verb. In the sentence "The girls has bought a nice car", since the subject "The girls" is a plural noun phrase, the auxiliary verb should be in the plural form. While considering the number and person of the subject, we take into account whether the subject is an indefinite pronoun or contains a conjunction since special rules apply to these cases. Indefinite pronouns are words which replace nouns without specifying the nouns they replace. Some indefinite pronouns such as *all*, *any* and *more* take both singular and plural forms. On the other hand, indefinite pronouns like *somebody* and *anyone* always take the singular form.

Rule based system
The rule we used to identify subject-auxiliary agreement was as follows:

1. Extract the number (singular, plural) of the subject and the auxiliary verb in the verb phrase.
2. If the number of the subject and auxiliary verb do not match, there is a subject-auxiliary agreement error.

Predictive model
The features were as follows:

1. Number of subject - singular or plural
2. Type of noun phrase - pronoun or other noun phrase
3. Person of noun phrase - first, second, third
4. Presence of a main verb in the utterance (we are looking at the agreement only for the auxiliary verb)

Analysis
As we can see from Table 3, the naive Bayes multinomial classifier performed the best with an F1-measure of 0.912. We found that our system did not detect the subject-auxiliary agreement correctly if there was an error in the subject such as number agreement.

4.5 Identifying Subject-verb Agreement

In order to achieve subject-verb agreement, the number and person of the subject and verb must agree. The subject-verb agreement applies to the first verb in the verb phrase. We consider cases wherein the first verb is a main verb or contains a modal verb. An example of a sentence that has subject-verb disagreement is "The boy have an ice cream". The number and person of the subject "The boy" and the verb "have" do not match.

Rule based system
The rule we used to identify subject-verb agreement was as follows:

1. Extract the number (singular, plural) and person (first, second, third) of the subject and the first verb in the verb phrase.
2. If the verb is not a modal verb and the number and person of the subject and verb do not match, there is a subject-verb agreement error.

Predictive model
We used the following features to be used in a statistical setup:

1. Type of sentence - interrogative or declarative
2. Number of subject - singular or plural
3. Person of subject if pronoun - first, second or third
4. Number of verb - singular or plural
5. Person of verb - first, second or third
6. Type of verb - modal, main

Analysis
We found that our system did not detect errors in cases where there was a number disagreement. For example, in the sentence "The two dog is playing", our system based on the POS tag would assume that the subject is singular and therefore there is no subject-verb error. One way to improve this would be to detect number disagreement in the subject and correct it before detecting the subject-verb agreement.

4.6 Identifying Missing Infinitive Marker "To"

Errors of this type occur when the sentence lacks the infinitive marker "to". An example of such a sentence would be "She loves sleep". In this case, "She loves to sleep" would be the correct form. On the other hand, this statement is ambiguous since *sleep* could be used as a noun sense or a verb sense. We concentrated on identifying utterances that have the progressive verb followed by the verb in the infinitive form. Examples of such sentences are: "She is going cry". In this case, we can see that the sentence is missing the "to".

Rule based system
If the utterance contains a progressive verb followed by a verb in its infinitive form, it is missing the infinitive marker "to".

Predictive model
The features we used are:

1. Presence of a progressive verb followed by the infinitive
2. Presence of infinitive marker "to" before the infinitive

Analysis
The naive Bayes multinomial classifier performed the best with an F1-measure of 0.967. We encountered exceptions with words like "saying". An example of such a sentence would be "He was saying play". Most of our false positives were due to sentences such as this. We considered a subset of utterances in which the infinitive was used along with the progressive verb. The missing infinitive marker "to" is also found in other utterances such as "I would love to swim" in which case we have two verbs that are in the base form - "love" and "swim".

4.7 Combining the Classifiers

Finally, we perform sentence level binary classification - does the sentence have a grammatical error? Since an utterance can contain more than one error, we serially apply the binary classifiers that we described above for each error category. If any one of the classifiers reports an error in the utterance, we flag the utterance as having a grammatical error. For evaluation, as long as the utterance had any grammatical error, we considered the decision to be correct. As we can see from Table 3, the best result for detecting the overall errors was obtained by serially applying the classifiers that used the features that were not rule based.

5 Conclusions and Future Work

In this paper, we described a study of grammatical errors in child language transcripts. Our study showed that a higher percentage of children with LI made at least one mistake than TD children on most error categories. We created different systems including rule based systems that used parse tree template matching and classifiers to detect errors related to missing verbs, subject-auxiliary agreement, subject verb agreement, missing infinitive marker "to", missing copulae and wrong usage of -ing participle. In all cases, we had a recall higher than 84%. When combining the classifiers to detect sentences with grammatical errors, the classifiers that used features other than rules performed the best with an F1-measure of 0.967.

The error categories that we detect at present are restricted in their scope to specific kind of errors. In future, we plan to enhance our systems to detect other grammatical errors such as missing articles, missing prepositions and missing main verbs in utterances that do not have an auxiliary verb. Furthermore, we will investigate methods to address issues in child language transcripts due to incomplete utterances and disfluencies.

At present, we treat sentences that conform to formal English language as correct. We could enhance our systems to look at dialect specific constructs and grammatical errors made across different demographics. For example, African American children have a different dialect and do not always follow the formal English language while speaking. Therefore, in the context of detecting language impairment, it would be interesting to see whether both TD children and LI children make the same errors that are otherwise considered the norm in the dialect they speak.

Acknowledgments

The authors thank Chris Dollaghan for sharing the Paradise data, and Thamar Solorio for discussions. This research is partly supported by an NSF award IIS-1017190.

References

Mari I. Bowden and Richard K. Fox. 2002. A Diagnostic Approach to the Detection of Syntactic Errors in English for Non-Native Speakers. Technical report, The University of Texas-Pan American.

Andrew Caines and Paula Buttery. 2010. You talking to me?: A predictive model for zero auxiliary constructions. In *Proceedings of the 2010 Workshop on NLP and Linguistics: Finding the Common Ground*, pages 43–51.

Eugene Charniak. 2000. A maximum-entropy-inspired parser. In *Proceedings of the 1st North American chapter of the Association for Computational Linguistics conference*, pages 132–139.

Lloyd M. Dunn. 1965. *Peabody picture vocabulary test.* American Guidance Service Circle Pines, MN.

Jens Eeg-Olofsson and Ola Knuttson. 2003. Automatic grammar checking for second language learners-the use of prepositions. In *Proceedings of NoDaLiDa.*

Keyur Gabani. 2009. Automatic identification of language impairment in monolingual English-speaking children. Master's thesis, The University Of Texas At Dallas.

Mark Hall, Eibe Frank, Geoffrey Holmes, Bernhard Pfahringer, Peter Reutemann, and Ian H. Witten. 2009. The WEKA data mining software: An update. *ACM SIGKDD Explorations Newsletter*, 11(1):10–18.

Claudia Leacock, Martin Chodorow, Michael Gamon, and Joel Tetreault. 2010. Automated Grammatical Error Detection for Language Learners. *Synthesis Lectures on Human Language Technologies*, 3(1):1–134.

John Lee and Stephanie Seneff. 2006. Automatic grammar correction for second-language learners. In *Proceedings of INTERSPEECH-2006*, pages 1978–1981.

John Lee and Stephanie Seneff. 2008. Correcting misuse of verb forms. In *Proceedings of ACL-08:HLT*, pages 174–182.

Jack L. Paradise, Thomas F. Campbell, Christine A. Dollaghan, Heidi M. Feldman, Bernard S. Bernard, D. Kathleen Colborn, Howard E. Rockette, Janine E. Janosky, Dayna L. Pitcairn, Marcia Kurs-Lasky, et al. 2005. Developmental outcomes after early or delayed insertion of tympanostomy tubes. *New England Journal of Medicine*, 353(6):576–586.

Mabel L. Rice, Kenneth Wexler, and Patricia L. Cleave. 1995. Specific language impairment as a period of extended optional infinitive. *Journal of Speech and Hearing Research*, 38(4):850.

Kenji Sagae, Eric Davis, Alon Lavie, Brian MacWhinney, and Shuly Wintner. 2007. High-accuracy annotation and parsing of CHILDES transcripts. In *Proceedings of the Workshop on Cognitive Aspects of Computational Language Acquisition*, pages 25–32.

Hollis S. Scarborough. 1990. Index of productive syntax. *Applied Psycholinguistics*, 11(01):1–22.

GRASP: Grammar- and Syntax-based Pattern-Finder in CALL

Chung-Chi Huang* **Mei-Hua Chen*** **Shih-Ting Huang+** **Hsien-Chin Liou**** **Jason S. Chang+**
*Institute of Information Systems and Applications, NTHU, HsinChu, Taiwan, R.O.C. 300
+Department of Computer Science, NTHU, HsinChu, Taiwan, R.O.C. 300
** Department of Foreign Languages and Literature, NTHU, HsinChu, Taiwan, R.O.C. 300
{u901571,chen.meihua,koromiko1104,hsienchin,jason.jschang}gmail.com

Abstract

We introduce a method for learning to describe the attendant contexts of a given query for language learning. In our approach, we display phraseological information in the form of a summary of *general* patterns as well as lexical bundles anchored at the query. The method involves syntactical analyses and inverted file construction. At run-time, grammatical constructions and their lexical instantiations characterizing the usage of the given query are generated and displayed, aimed at improving learners' deep vocabulary knowledge. We present a prototype system, GRASP, that applies the proposed method for enhanced collocation learning. Preliminary experiments show that language learners benefit more from GRASP than conventional dictionary lookup. In addition, the information produced by GRASP is potentially useful information for automatic or manual editing process.

1 Introduction

Many learners submit word or phrase queries (e.g., "*role*") to language learning sites on the Web to get usage information every day, and an increasing number of services on the Web specifically target such queries. Language learning tools such as concordancers typically accept single-word queries and respond with example sentences containing the words. There are also collocation reference tools such as Sketch Engine and TANGO that provide co-occurring words for the query word. Another collocation tool, JustTheWord further organizes and displays collocation clusters.

Learners may want to submit phrase queries (fixed or rigid collocaions) to learn further how to use the phrase in context, or in other words, to acquire the knowledge on the attendant phraseology of the query. These queries could be answered more appropriately if the tool accepted long queries and returned a concise summary of their surrounding contexts.

Consider the query "*play role*". The best responses for this query are probably not just example sentences, but rather the phraseological tendencies described grammatically or lexically. A good response of such a summary might contain patterns such as "*play* Det Adj *role*" (as in "*play an important role*") and "*play ~ role in* V-ing" (as in "*play ~ role in shaping* ..."). Intuitively, by exploiting simple part-of-speech analysis, we can derive such patterns, inspired by the grammatical theory of Pattern Grammar[1] in order to provide more information on demand beyond what is given in a grammar book.

We present a system, GRASP, that provide a usage summary of the contexts of the query in the form of patterns and frequent lexical bundles. Such rich information is expected to help learners and lexicographers grasp the essence of word usages. An example GRASP response for the query "*play*

[1] Please refer to (Hunston and Francis, 2000).

Proceedings of the Sixth Workshop on Innovative Use of NLP for Building Educational Applications, pages 96–104,
Portland, Oregon, 24 June 2011.

role" is shown in Figure 1. GRASP has retrieved the sentences containing the query in a reference corpus. GRASP constructs these query-to-sentence index in the preparation stage (Section 3).

Type your search query, and push GRASP!
Search query: play role [GRASP]

Mapping query words to (position, sentence) pairs:
"play" occurs in (10,77), (4,90), (6,102), …, and so on.
"role" occurs in (7,90), (12,122), (6,167), …, and so on.

A. In-between pattern grammar:
Distance 3 (1624):
play DT JJ *role* (1364):
e.g., 'play an important role' (259), 'play a major role' (168), …
play DT VBG *role* (123):
e.g., 'play a leading role' (75), 'play a supporting role' (5), …
play DT JJR *role* (40):
e.g., 'play a greater role' (17), 'play a larger role' (8), …
Distance 2 (480):
play DT *role* (63):
e.g., 'play a role' (197), 'play the role' (123), …
play JJ *role* (63):
e.g., 'play important role' (15), 'play different role' (6), …
Distance 1 (6):
play role (6)
B. Subsequent pattern grammar:
play ~ role IN(*in*) DT (707):
e.g., 'play ~ role in the' (520), 'play ~ role in this' (24), …
play ~ role IN(*in*) VBG (407):
e.g., 'play ~ role in shaping' (22), …
play ~ role IN(*in*) NN (166):
e.g., 'play ~ role in society' (7), 'play ~ role in relation' (5), …
C. Precedent pattern grammar:
NN MD *play ~ role* (83):
e.g., 'communication will play ~ role ' (2), …
JJ NNS *play ~ role* (69):
e.g., 'voluntary groups play ~ role' (2), …

Figure 1. An example GRASP search for "play role".

At run-time, GRASP starts with a search query (e.g., "*play role*") submitted by the user. GRASP then retrieves example sentences and generates a summary of representative contexts, using patterns (e.g., "*play ~ role in* V-ing") and lexical bundles (e.g., "*play ~ role in shaping*. In our implementation, GRASP also returns the translations and the example sentences of the lexical instances, so the learner can use their knowledge of native language to enhance the learning process.

2 Related Work

Computer-assisted language learning (CALL) has been an area of active research. Recently, more and more research based on natural language processing techniques has been done to help language learners. In our work, we introduce a language learning environment, where summarized usage information are provided, including how function words and verb forms are used in combination with the query. These usage notes often help contrast the common sources of error in learners' writing (Nicholls, 1999). In our pilot teaching experiment, we found learners have problems using articles and prepositions correctly in sentence composition (as high as 80% of the articles and 60% of the prepositions were used incorrectly), and GRASP is exactly aimed at helping ESL or EFL learners in that area.

Until recently, collocations and usage information are compiled mostly manually (Benson et al., 1986). With the accessibility to large-scale corpora and powerful computers, it has become common place to compile a list of collocations automatically (Smadja, 1993). In addition, there are many collocation checkers developed to help non-native language learners (Chang et al., 2008), or learners of English for academic purposes (Durrant, 2009).

Recently, automatic generation of collocations for computational lexicography and online language learning has drawn much attention. Sketch Engine (Kilgarriff et al., 2004) summarizes a word's grammatical and collocation behavior, while JustTheWord clusters the co-occurring words of single-word queries and TANGO (Jian et al., 2004) accommodates cross-lingual collocation searches. Moreover, Cheng et al. (2006) describe how to retrieve mutually expected words using concgrams. In contrast, GRASP, going one step further, automatically computes and displays the information that reveals the regularities of the contexts of user queries in terms of grammar patterns.

Recent work has been done on incorporating word class information into the analyses of phraseological tendencies. Stubbs (2004) introduces phrase-frames, which are based on lexical ngrams with variable slots, while Wible et al. (2010) describe a database called StringNet, with lexico-syntactic patterns. Their methods of using word class information are similar in spirit to our work. The main differences are that our patterns is anchored with query words directly and generalizes query's contexts via parts-of-speech, and that we present the query's usage summary in terms of function words as well as content word form (e.g., "*play ~ role in* V-ing"), as well as elastic lexical bundles (e.g., "*play ~ role in shaping*"). Additionally, we also use semantic codes (e.g., PERSON) to provide more information in a way similar what is provided in learner dictionaries.

3 The GRASP System

3.1 Problem Statement

We focus on constructing a usage summary likely to explain the contexts of a given linguistic search. The usage summary, consisting of the query's predominant attendant phraseology ranging from pattern grammar to lexical phrases, is then returned as the output of the system. The returned summary, or a set of patterns pivoted with both content and function words, can be used for learners' benefits directly, or passed on to an error detection and correction system (e.g., (Tsao and Wible, 2009) and some modules in (Gamon et al., 2009) as rules. Therefore, our goal is to return a reasonable-sized set of lexical and grammatical patterns characterizing the contexts of the query. We now formally state the problem that we are addressing.

Problem Statement: We are given a reference corpus *C* from a wide range of sources and a learner search query *Q*. Our goal is to construct a summary of word usages based on *C* that is likely to represent the lexical or grammatical preferences on *Q*'s contexts. For this, we transform the words in *Q* into sets of (word position, sentence record) pairs such that the context information, whether lexically- or grammatical-oriented, of the querying words is likely to be acquired efficiently.

In the rest of this section, we describe our solution to this problem. First, we define a strategy for preprocessing our reference corpus (Section 3.2). Then, we show how GRASP generates contextual patterns, comprising the usage summary, at run-time (Section 3.3).

3.2 Corpus Preprocessing

We attempt to find the word-to-sentence mappings and the syntactic counterparts of the L1 sentences expected to speed up run-time pattern generation. Our preprocessing procedure has two stages.

Lemmatizing and PoS Tagging. In the first stage, we lemmatize each sentence in the reference corpus *C* and generate its most probable POS tag sequence. The goal of lemmatization is to reduce the impact of morphology on statistical analyses while that of POS tagging is to provide a way to grammatically describe and generalize the contexts/usages of a linguistic query. Actually, using POS tags is quite natural: they are often used for general description in grammar books, such as *one's* (i.e., possessive pronoun) in the phrase "make up one's mind", *oneself* (i.e., reflexive pronoun) in "enjoy oneself very much", *superlative_adjective* in "the most superlative_adjective", *NN* (i.e., noun) and *VB* (i.e., base form of a verb) in "insist/suggest/demand that NN VB" and so on.

Constructing Inverted Files. In the second stage, we build up inverted files of the lemmas in *C* for quick run-time search. For each lemma, we record the sentences and positions in which it occurs. Additionally, its corresponding surface word and POS tag are kept for run-time pattern grammar generation.

```
procedure GRASPusageSummaryBuilding(query,proximity,N,C)
(1)  queries=queryReformulation(query)
(2)  GRASPresponses= ϕ
     for each query in queries
(3)    interInvList=findInvertedFile(w1 in query)
       for each lemma wi in query except for w1
(4)      InvList=findInvertedFile(wi)
         //AND operation on interInvList and InvList
(5a)     newInterInvList= ϕ ; i=1; j=1
(5b)     while i<=length(interInvList) and j<=lengh(InvList)
(5c)       if interInvList[i].SentNo==InvList[j].SentNo
(5d)         if withinProximity(interInvList[i].
                        wordPosi,InvList[j].wordPosi,proximity)
(5e)           Insert(newInterInvList, interInvList[i],InvList[j])
             else if interInvList[i].wordPosi<InvList[j].wordPosi
(5f)           i++
             else //interInvList[i].wordPosi>InvList[j].wordPosi
(5g)           j++
           else if interInvList[i].SentNo<InvList[j].SentNo
(5h)         i++
           else //interInvList[i].SentNo>InvList[j].SentNo
(5i)         j++
(5j)     interInvList=newInterInvList
       //construction of GRASP usage summary for this query
(6)    Usage= ϕ
       for each element in interInvList
(7)      Usage+={PatternGrammarGeneration(query,element,C)}
(8a)   Sort patterns and their instances in Usage in descending order
                                                     of frequency
(8b)   GRASPresponse=the N patterns and instances in Usage with
                                                highest frequency
(9)    append GRASPresponse to GRASPresponses
(10) return GRASPresponses
```

Figure 2. Generating pattern grammar and usage summary at run-time.

3.3 Run-Time Usage Summary Construction

Once the word-to-sentence mappings and syntactic analyses are obtained, GRASP generates the usage summary of a query using the procedure in Figure 2.

In Step (1) we reformulate the user query into new ones, *queries*, if necessary. The first type of query reformulation concerns the language used in *query*. If it is not in the same language as *C*, we translate *query* and append the translations to *queries* as if they were submitted by the user. The second concerns the length of the query. Since single words may be ambiguous in senses and contexts or grammar patterns are closely associated with words' meanings (Hunston and Francis, 2000), we transform single-word queries into their collocations, particularly focusing on one word sense (Yarowsky, 1995), as stepping stones to GRASP patterns. Notice that, in implementation, users may be allowed to choose their own interested translation or collocation of the *query* for usage learning. The prototypes for first-language (i.e., Chinese) queries and English queries of any length are at A[2] and B[3] respectively. The goal of cross-lingual GRASP is to assist EFL users even when they do not know the words of their searches and to avoid incorrect queries largely because of miscollocation, misapplication, and misgeneralization.

Afterwards, we initialize *GRASPresponses* to collect usage summaries for *queries* (Step (2)) and leverage inverted files to extract and generate each *query*'s syntax-based contexts. In Step (3) we prep *interInvList* for the intersected inverted files of the lemmas in *query*. For each lemma w_i within, we first obtain its inverted file, *InvList* (Step (4)) and perform an AND operation on *interInvList* (intersected results from previous iteration) and *InvList* (Step (5a) to (5j)[4]), defined as follows.

First, we enumerate the inverted lists (Step (5b)) after the initialization of their indices *i* and *j* and temporary resulting intersection *newInterInvList* (Step (5a)). Second, we incorporate a new instance of (position, sentence), based on *interInvList*[*i*] and *InvList*[*j*], into *newInterInvList* (Step (5e)) if the sentence records of the indexed list elements are the same (Step (5c)) and the distance between their words are within *proximity* (Step (5d)). Otherwise, *i* and *j* are moved accordingly. To accommodate the contexts of queries' positional variants (e.g., "*role to play*" and "*role ~ play by*" for the query "play role"), Step (5d) considers the *absolute* distance. Finally, *interInvList* is set for the next AND iteration (Step (5j)).

Once we obtain the sentences containing *query*, we construct its context summary as below. For each *element*, taking the form ([wordPosi(w_1), …, wordPosi(w_n)], *sentence record*) denoting the positions of *query*'s lemmas in the *sentence*, we generate pattern grammar involving replacing words in the sentence with POS tags and words in wordPosi(w_i) with lemmas, and extracting fixed-window[5] segments surrounding *query* from the transformed sentence. The result is a set of grammatical patterns with counts. Their lexical realizations also retrieved and displayed.

The procedure finally generates top *N* predominant syntactic patterns and their *N* most frequent lexical phrases as output (Step (8)). The usage summaries GRASP returns are aimed to accelerate EFL learners' language understanding and learning and lexicographers' word usage navigation. To acquire more semantic-oriented patterns, we further exploit WordNet and majority voting to categorize words, deriving the patterns like "*provide* **PERSON** *with.*"

4 Experimental Results

GRASP was designed to generate usage summarization of a query for language learning. As such, GRASP will be evaluated over CALL. In this section, we first present the setting of GRASP (Section 4.1) and report the results of different consulting systems on language learning in Section 4.2.

4.1 Experimental Setting

We used British National Corpus (BNC) as our underlying reference corpus *C*. It is a British English text collection. We exploited GENIA tagger to obtain the lemmas and POS tags of *C*'s sentences. After lemmatizing and syntactic analyses, all sentences in BNC were used to build up inverted files and used as examples for grammar pattern extraction.

[2] http://140.114.214.80/theSite/bGRASP_v552/

[3] http://140.114.214.80/theSite/GRASP_v552/

[4] These steps only hold for sorted inverted files.

[5] Inspired by (Gamon and Leacock, 2010).

English (E) sentence with corresponding Chinese (C) translation	answer to 1st blank	answer to 2nd blank
C: 環境保護對地球有深遠的影響 E: Environmental protection has ___ impact ___.	a profound	on the Earth
C: 房屋仲介商在賣屋上大賺一筆 E: The real estate agent ___ record profit ___.	made a	on house selling
C: 他們打算在不久將來推出新專輯 E: They plan to release their new album in ___ future	the near	none
C: 他為了再見她一面等了很久 E: He waited for her for a long time in ___ attempt ___ again.	an	to see her

4.2 Results of Constrained Experiments

In our experiments, we showed GRASP[6] to two classes of Chinese EFL (first-year) college students. 32 and 86 students participated, and were trained to use GRASP and instructed to perform a sentence translation/composition task, made up of pretest and posttest. In (30-minute) pretest, participants were to complete 15 English sentences with Chinese translations as hints, while, in (20-minute) posttest, after spending 20 minutes familiarizing word usages of the test candidates from us by consulting traditional tools or GRASP, participants were also asked to complete the same English sentences. We refer to the experiments as constrained ones since the test items in pre- and post-test are the same except for their order. A more sophisticated testing environment, however, are to be designed.

Each test item contains one to two blanks as shown in the above table. In the table, the first item is supposed to test learners' knowledge on the adjective and prepositional collocate of "*have impact*" while the second test the verb collocate *make*, subsequent preposition *on*, and preceding article *a* of "*record profit*". On the other hand, the third tests the ability to produce the adjective enrichment of "in future", and the fourth the in-between article *a* or possessive *his* and the following infinitive of "*in attempt*". Note that as existing collocation reference tools retrieve and display collocates, they typically ignore function words like articles and determiners, which happen to be closely related to frequent errors made by the learners (Nicholls, 1999), and fail to provide an overall picture of word usages. In contrast, GRASP attempts to show the overall picture with appropriate function words and word forms.

We selected 20 collocations and phrases [7] manually from 100 most frequent collocations in BNC whose MI values exceed 2.2 and used them as the target for learning between the pretest and posttest. To evaluate GRASP, half of the participants were instructed to use GRASP for learning and the other half used traditional tools such as online dictionaries or machine translation systems (i.e., Google Translate and Yahoo! Babel Fish). We summarize the performance of our participants on pre- and post-test in Table 1 where *GRASP* denotes the experimental group and *TRAD* the control group.

	class 1		*class 2*		*combined*	
	pretest	posttest	pretest	posttest	pretest	posttest
GRASP	26.4	**41.9**	43.6	**58.4**	38.9	**53.9**
TRAD	27.1	32.7	43.8	53.4	39.9	48.6

Table 1. The performance (%) on pre- and post-test.

We observe in Table 1 that (1) the partition of the classes was quite random (the difference between *GRASP* and *TRAD* was insignificant under pretest); (2) GRASP summaries of words' contexts were more helpful in language learning (across *class 1*, *class 2* and *combined*). Specifically, under the column of the 1st class, GRASP helped to boost students' achievements by 15.5%, almost *tripled* (15.5 vs. 5.6) compared to the gain using *TRAD*; (3) the effectiveness of GRASP in language learning do not confine to students at a certain level. Encouragingly, *both* high- and low-achieving students benefited from GRASP if we think of students in *class 2* and those in *class 1* as the high and the low respectively (due to the performance difference on pretests).

We have analyzed some participants' answers and found that GRASP helped to reduce learners' article and preposition errors by 28% and 8%, comparing to much smaller error reduction rate 7% and 2% observed in *TRAD* group. Additionally, an experiment where Chinese EFL students were asked to perform the same task but using GRASP as well as GRASP with translation information[8]

[6] http://koromiko.cs.nthu.edu.tw/grasp/

[7] Include the 15 test items.

[8] http://koromiko.cs.nthu.edu.tw/grasp/ch

was conducted. We observed that with Chinese translation there was an additional 5% increase in students' test performance. This suggests to some extent learners still depend on their first languages in learning and first-language information may serve as another quick navigation index even when English GRASP is presented.

Overall, we are modest to say that (in the constrained experiments) GRASP summarized general-to-specific usages, contexts, or phraseologies of words are quite effective in assisting learners in collocation and phrase learning.

5 Applying GRASP to Error Correction

To demonstrate the viability of GRASP-retrieved lexicalized grammar patterns (e.g., "*play ~ role* In V-ING" and "*look forward to* V-ING") in error detection and correction, we incorporate them into an extended Levenshtein algorithm (1966) to provide broad-coverage sentence-level grammatical edits (involving substitution, deletion, and insertion) to inappropriate word usages in learner text.

Previously, a number of interesting rule-based error detection/correction systems have been proposed for some specific error types such as article and preposition error (e.g., (Uria et al., 2009), (Lee et al., 2009), and some modules in (Gamon et al., 2009)). Statistical approaches, supervised or unsupervised, to grammar checking have become the recent trend. For example, unsupervised systems of (Chodorow and Leacock, 2000) and (Tsao and Wible, 2009) leverage word distributions in general and/or word-specific corpus for detecting erroneous usages while (Hermet et al., 2008) and (Gamon and Leacock, 2010) use Web as a corpus. On the other hand, supervised models, typically treating error detection/correction as a classification problem, utilize the training of well-formed texts ((De Felice and Pulman, 2008) and (Tetreault et al., 2010)), learner texts, or both pairwisely (Brockett et al., 2006). Moreover, (Sun et al., 2007) describes a way to construct a supervised error detection system trained on well-formed and learner texts neither pairwise nor error tagged.

In contrast to the previous work in grammar checking, our pattern grammar rules are automatically inferred from a general corpus (as described in Section 3) and helpful for correcting errors resulting from the others (e.g., "to close" in "play ~ role to close"), our pattern grammar lexicalizes on *both* content and function words and lexical items within may be contiguous (e.g., "*look forward to* V-ING PRP") or non-contiguous (e.g., "*play ~ role* In V-ING"), and, with word class (POS) information, error correction or grammatical suggestion is provided at sentence level.

5.1 Error Correcting Process

Figure 3 shows how we check grammaticality and provide suggestions for a given text with accurate spelling.

```
procedure GrammarChecking(T,PatternGrammarBank)
(1) Suggestions=""//candidate suggestions
(2) sentences=sentenceSplitting(T)
    for each sentence in sentences
(3)  userProposedUsages=extractUsage(sentence)
     for each userUsage in userProposedUsages
(4)   patGram=findPatternGrammar(userUsage.lexemes,
                     PatternGrammarBank)
(5)   minEditedCost=SystemMax; minEditedSug=""
      for each pattern in patGram
(6)     cost=extendedLevenshtein(userUsage,pattern)
        if cost<minEditedCost
(7)       minEditedCost=cost; minEditedSug=pattern
      if minEditedCost>0
(8)     append (userUsage,minEditedSug) to Suggestions
(9) Return Suggestions
```

Figure 3. Procedure of grammar suggestion/correction.

In Step (1), we initiate a set *Suggestions* to collect grammar suggestions to the user text *T* according to a bank of patterns *PatternGrammarBank*, i.e., a collection of summaries of grammatical usages (e.g., "*play ~ role* In V-ING") of queries (e.g., "play role") submitted to GRASP. Since we focus on grammar checking at sentence level, *T* is heuristically split (Step (2)).

For each *sentence*, we extract user-proposed word usages (Step (3)), that is, the user grammatical contexts of ngram and collocation sequences. Take for example the (ungrammatical) sentences and their corresponding POS sequences "he/PRP play/VBP an/DT important/JJ roles/NNS to/TO close/VB this/DT deals/NNS" and "he/PRP looks/VBZ forward/RB to/TO hear/VB you/PRP". Ngram contexts include "*he* VBP DT", "*play an* JJ NNS", "*this* NNS" for the first sentence and "*look forward to* VB PRP" and "*look forward to hear* PRP" for the second. And collocation contexts for the first sentence are "*play ~ role to VERB*" and "*close ~ deal* ."

For each *userUsage* in the sentence (e.g., "*play ~ role* TO VB" and "*look forward to hear* PRP"), we first acquire the pattern grammar of its lexemes (e.g., "*play role*" and "*look forward to hear*") such as "*play ~ role in* V-ing" and "*look forward to hear from*" in Step (4), and we compare the user-proposed usage against the corresponding predominant, most likely more proper, ones (from Step (5) to (7)). We leverage an extended Levenshtein's algorithm in Figure 4 for usage comparison, i.e. error detection and correction, after setting up *minEditedCost* and *minEditedSug* for the minimum-cost edit from alleged error usage into appropriate one (Step (5)).

```
procedure extendedLevenshtein(userUsage,pattern)
(1) allocate and initialize costArray
      for i in range(len(userUsage))
         for j in range(len(pattern))
            //substitution
            if equal(userUsage[i],pattern[j])
(2a)          substiCost=costArray[i-1,j-1]+0
            elseif sameWordGroup(userUsage[i],pattern[j])
(2b)          substiCost=costArray[i-1,j-1]+0.5
            else
(2c)          substiCost=costArray[i-1,j-1]+1
            //deletion
            if equal(userUsage[i+1],pattern[j+1])
(3a)          delCost=costArray[i-1,j]+smallCost
            else
(3b)          delCost=costArray[i-1,j]+1
            //insertion
            if equal(userUsage[i+1],pattern[j+1])
(4a)          insCost=costArray[i,j-1]+smallCost
            else
(4b)          insCost=costArray[i,j-1]+1
(5)         costArray[i,j]=min(substiCost,delCost,insCost)
(6) Return costArray[len(userUsage),len(pattern)]
```

Figure 4. Extended Levenshtein algorithm for correction.

In Step (1) of the algorithm in Figure 4 we allocate and initialize *costArray* to gather the dynamic programming based cost to transform *userUsage* into a specific *pattern*. Afterwards, the algorithm defines the cost of performing substitution (Step (2)), deletion (Step (3)) and insertion (Step (4)) at i-indexed *userUsage* and j-indexed *pattern*. If the entries *userUsage*[*i*] and *pattern*[*j*] are equal literally (e.g., "VB" and "VB") or grammatically (e.g., "DT" and "PRP$"[9]), no edit is needed, hence, no cost (Step (2a)). On the other hand, since learners tend to select wrong word form and preposition, we make less the cost of the substitution of the same word group, say from "VERB" to "V-ing", "TO" to "In" and "In" to "IN(*on*)" (Step (2b)) compared to a total edit (Step (2c)). In addition to the conventional deletion and insertion (Step (3b) and (4b) respectively), we look ahead to the elements *userUsage*[*i*+1] and *pattern*[*j*+1] considering the fact that "with or without preposition" and "transitive or intransitive verb" often puzzles EFL learners (Step (3a) and (4a)). Only a small edit cost is applied if the next elements in *userUsage* and *Pattern* are "equal". In Step (6) the extended Levenshtein's algorithm returns the minimum cost to edit *userUsage* based on *pattern*.

Once we obtain the costs to transform the *userUsage* into its related frequent patterns, we propose the minimum-cost one as its grammatical suggestion (Step (8) in Figure 3), if its minimum edit cost is greater than zero. Otherwise, the usage is considered valid. At last, the gathered suggestions *Suggestions* to *T* are returned to users (Step (9)). Example edits to the user text "*he play an important roles to close this deals. he looks forward to hear you.*" from our working prototype, EdIt[10], is shown in Figure 5. Note that we exploit context checking of collocations to cover longer span than ngrams', and longer ngrams like fourgrams and fivegrams to (more or less) help semantic checking (or word sense disambiguation). For example, "*hear*" may be transitive or intransitive, but, in the context of "*look forward to*", there is strong tendency it is used intransitively and follows by "*from*", as EdIt would suggest (see Figure 5).

There are two issues worth mentioning on the development of EdIt. First, grammar checkers typically have different modules examining different types of errors with different priority. In our unified framework, we set the priority of checking collocations' usages higher than that of ngrams', set the priority of checking longer ngrams' usages higher than that of shorter, and we do not double check. Alternatively, one may first check usages of all sorts and employ majority voting to determine the grammaticality of a sentence. Second, we further incorporate

[9] ONE'S denotes possessives.

[10] http://140.114.214.80/theSite/EdIt_demo2/

Erroneous sentence	EdIt suggestion	ESL Assistant suggestion
Wrong word form		
… a sunny days …	a sunny NN	a sunny day
every days, I …	every NN	every day
I would said to …	would VB	would say
he play a …	he VBD	none
… should have tell the truth	should have VBN	should have to tell
… look forward to see you	look forward to VBG	none
… in an attempt to seeing you	an attempt to VB	none
… be able to solved this problem	able to VB	none
Wrong preposition		
he plays an important role to close …	play ~ role IN(in)	none
he has a vital effect at her.	have ~ effect IN(on)	effect on her
it has an effect on reducing …	have ~ effect IN(of) VBG	none
… depend of the scholarship	depend IN(on)	depend on
Confusion between intransitive and transitive verb		
he listens the music.	missing "to" after "listens"	missing "to" after "listens"
it affects to his decision.	unnecessary "to"	unnecessary "to"
I understand about the situation.	unnecessary "about"	unnecessary "about"
we would like to discuss about this matter.	unnecessary "about"	unnecessary "about"
Mixture		
she play an important roles to close this deals.	she VBD; an JJ NN; play ~ role IN(in) VBG; this NN	play an important role; close this deal
I look forward to hear you.	look forward to VBG; missing "from" after "hear"	none

Table 2. Three common score-related error types and their examples with suggestions from EdIt and ESL Assistant.

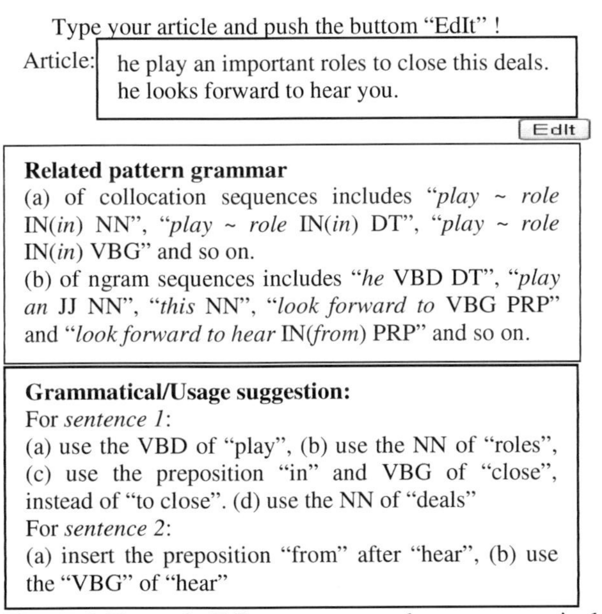

Figure 5. Example EdIt responses to the ungrammatical.

probabilities conditioned on word positions to weigh edit costs. For example, the conditional probability of "VERB" being the immediate follower of "look forward to" is virtually zero, but the probability of "V-ing" is around 0.3.

5.2 Preliminary Results in Error Correction

We examined three common error types in learner text that are highly correlated with essay scores (Leacock and Chodorow, 2003; Burstein et al., 2004), to evaluate EdIt, (see Table 2). In Table 2, the results of a state-of-the-art checker, ESL Assistant (www.eslassistant.com/), are shown for comparison, and information produced by both systems are underscored. As indicated, GRASP retrieves patterns which are potential useful if incorporated into an extension of Levenshtein's algorithm to correct substitution, deletion, and insertion errors in learner.

6 Summary

We have introduced a new method for producing a general-to-specific usage summary of the contexts of a linguistic search query aimed at accelerating learners' grasp on word usages. We have implemented and evaluated the method as applied to collocation and phrase learning and grammar checking. In the preliminary evaluations we show that GRASP is more helpful than traditional language learning tools, and that the patterns and lexical bundles provided are promising in detecting and correcting common types of errors in learner writing.

References

Morton Benson, Evellyn Benson, and Robert Ilson. 1986. *The BBI Combinatory Dictionary of English: A guide to word combinations*. Philadelphia: John Benjamins.

Chris Brockett, William B. Dolan, and Michael Gamon. 2006. Correcting ESL errors using phrasal SMT techniques. In *Proceedings of the ACL*, pages 249-256.

Jill Burstein, Martin Chodorow, and Claudia Leacock. 2004. Automated essay evaluation: the criterion online writing service. *AI Magazine*, 25(3): 27-36.

Yu-Chia Chang, Jason S. Chang, Hao-Jan Chen, and Hsien-Chin Liou. 2008. An automatic collocation writing assistant for Taiwanese EFL learners: a case of corpus-based NLP technology. *CALL*, 21(3): 283-299.

Winnie Cheng, Chris Greaves, and Martin Warren. 2006. From n-gram to skipgram to concgram. *Corpus Linguistics*, 11(4): 411-433.

Martin Chodorow and Claudia Leacock. 2000. An unsupervised method for detecting grammatical errors. In *Proceedings of the NAACL*, pages 140-147.

Rachele De Felice and Stephen G. Pulman. 2008. A classifer-based approach to preposition and determiner error correction in L2 English. In *Proceedings of the COLING*, pages 169-176.

Philip Durrant. 2009. Investigating the viability of a collocation list for students of English for academic purposes. *ESP*, 28(3): 157-169.

John R. Firth. 1957. Modes of meaning. In *Papers in Linguistics*. London: Oxford University Press, pages 190-215.

Michael Gamon, Claudia Leacock, Chris Brockett, William B. Dolan., Jianfeng Gao, Dmitriy Belenko, and Alexandre Klementiev. 2009. Using statistical techniques and web search to correct ESL errors. *CALICO*, 26(3): 491-511.

Michael Gamon and Claudia Leacock. 2010. Search right and thou shalt find ... using web queries for learner error detection. In *Proceedings of the NAACL*.

Matthieu Hermet, Alain Desilets, and Stan Szpakowicz. 2008. Using the web as a linguistic resource to automatically correct lexico-syntatic errors. In *Proceedings of the LREC*, pages 874-878.

Susan Hunston and Gill Francis. 2000. *Pattern Grammar: A Corpus-Driven Approach to the Lexical Grammar of English*. Amsterdam: John Benjamins.

Jia-Yan Jian, Yu-Chia Chang, and Jason S. Chang. 2004. TANGO: Bilingual collocational concordancer. In *ACL Poster*.

Adam Kilgarriff, Pavel Rychly, Pavel Smrz, and David Tugwell. 2004. The sketch engine. In *Proceedings of the EURALEX*, pages 105-116.

Chong Min Lee, Soojeong Eom, and Markus Dickinson. 2009. Toward analyzing Korean learner particles. In *CALICO Workshop*.

Claudia Leacock and Martin Chodorow. 2003. Automated grammatical error detection. In M.D. Shermis and J.C. Burstein, editors, *Automated Essay Scoring: A Cross-Disciplinary Perspective*, pages 195-207.

Vladimir I. Levenshtein. 1966. Binary codes capable of correcting deletions, insertions and reversals. Soviet Physics Doklady, 10, page 707.

Diane Nicholls. 1999. The Cambridge Learner Corpus – error coding and analysis for writing dictionaries and other books for English Learners.

John M. Sinclair. 1987. The nature of the evidence. In J. Sinclair (ed.) *Looking Up*. Collins: 150-159.

Frank Smadja. 1993. Retrieving collocations from text: Xtract. *Computational Linguistics*, 19(1): 143-177.

Michael Stubbs. 2004. At http://web.archive.org/web/20070828004603/http://www.uni-trier.de/uni/fb2/anglistik/Projekte/stubbs/icame-2004.htm.

Guihua Sun, Xiaohua Liu, Gao Cong, Ming Zhou, Zhongyang Xiong, John Lee, and Chin-Yew Lin. 2007. Detecting erroneous sentences using automatically mined sequential patterns. In *Proceedings of the ACL*, pages 81-88.

Joel Tetreault, Jennifer Foster, and Martin Chodorow. 2010. Using parse features for prepositions selection and error detection. In *Proceedings of the ACL*, pages 353-358.

Nai-Lung Tsao and David Wible. 2009. A method for unsupervised broad-coverage lexical error detection and correction. In *NAACL Workshop*, pages 51-54.

Larraitz Uria, Bertol Arrieta, Arantza D. De Ilarraza, Montse Maritxalar, and Maite Oronoz. 2009. Determiner errors in Basque: analysis and automatic detection. *Procesamiento del Lenguaje Natural*, pages 41-48.

David Wible and Nai-Lung Tsao. 2010. StringNet as a computational resource for discovering and investigating linguistic constructions. In *NAACL Workshop*, pages 25-31.

David Yarowsky. 1995. Unsupervised word sense disambiguation rivaling supervised methods. In *Proceedings of the ACL*, pages 189-196.

Generating Example Contexts to Illustrate a Target Word Sense

Jack Mostow
Carnegie Mellon University
RI-NSH 4103, 5000 Forbes Avenue
Pittsburgh, PA 15213-3890, USA
mostow@cs.cmu.edu

Weisi Duan
Carnegie Mellon University
Language Technologies Institute
Pittsburgh, PA 15213-3890, USA
wduan@cs.cmu.edu

Abstract

Learning a vocabulary word requires seeing it in multiple informative contexts. We describe a system to generate such contexts for a given word sense. Rather than attempt to do word sense disambiguation on example contexts already generated or selected from a corpus, we compile information about the word sense into the context generation process. To evaluate the sense-appropriateness of the generated contexts compared to WordNet examples, three human judges chose which word sense(s) fit each example, blind to its source and intended sense. On average, one judge rated the generated examples as sense-appropriate, compared to two judges for the WordNet examples. Although the system's precision was only half of WordNet's, its recall was actually higher than WordNet's, thanks to covering many senses for which WordNet lacks examples.

1 Introduction

Learning word meaning from example contexts is an important aspect of vocabulary learning. Contexts give clues to semantics but also convey many other lexical aspects, such as parts of speech, morphology, and pragmatics, which help enrich a person's word knowledge base (Jenkins 1984; Nagy *et al.* 1985; Schatz 1986; Herman *et al.* 1987; Nagy *et al.* 1987; Schwanenflugel *et al.* 1997; Kuhn and Stahl 1998; Fukkink *et al.* 2001). Accordingly, one key issue in vocabulary instruction is how to find or create good example contexts to help children learn a particular sense of a word. Hand-vetting automatically generated contexts can be easier than hand-crafting them from scratch (Mitkov *et al.* 2006; Liu *et al.* 2009).

This paper describes what we believe is the first system to generate example contexts for a given target sense of a polysemous word. Liu et al. (2009) characterized good contexts for helping children learn vocabulary and generated them for a target part of speech, but not a given word sense. Pino and Eskenazi (2009) addressed the polysemy issue, but in a system for selecting contexts rather than for generating them. Generation can supply more contexts for a given purpose, e.g. teaching children, than WordNet or a fixed corpus contains.

Section 2 describes a method to generate sense-targeted contexts. Section 3 compares them to WordNet examples. Section 4 concludes.

2 Approach

An obvious way to generate sense-targeted contexts is to generate contexts containing the target word, and use Word Sense Disambiguation (WSD) to select the ones that use the target word sense. However, without taking the target word sense into account, the generation process may not output any contexts that use it. Instead, we model word senses as topics and incorporate their *sense indicators* into the generation process – words that imply a unique word sense when they co-occur with a target word.

For example, *retreat* can mean "a place of privacy; a place affording peace and quiet." Indicators for this sense, in decreasing order of Pr(word | topic for target sense), include *retreat, yoga, place, retreats, day, home, center, church, spiritual, life, city, time, lake, year, room, prayer, years, school, dog, park, beautiful, area,* and *stay*. Generated contexts include …*retreat in this bustling* ***city***….

Another sense of *retreat* (as defined in WordNet) is "(military) a signal to begin a withdrawal

Proceedings of the Sixth Workshop on Innovative Use of NLP for Building Educational Applications, pages 105–110,
Portland, Oregon, 24 June 2011.

from a dangerous position," for which indicators include *states, war, united, american, military, flag, president, world, bush, state, Israel, Iraq, international, national, policy, forces, foreign, nation, administration, power, security, iran, force,* and *Russia*. Generated contexts include ...***military** leaders believe that retreat....*

We decompose our approach into two phases, summarized in Figure 1. Section 2.1 describes the Sense Indicator Extraction phase, which obtains indicators for each WordNet synset of the target word. Section 2.2 describes the Context Generation phase, which generates contexts that contain the target word and indicators for the target sense.

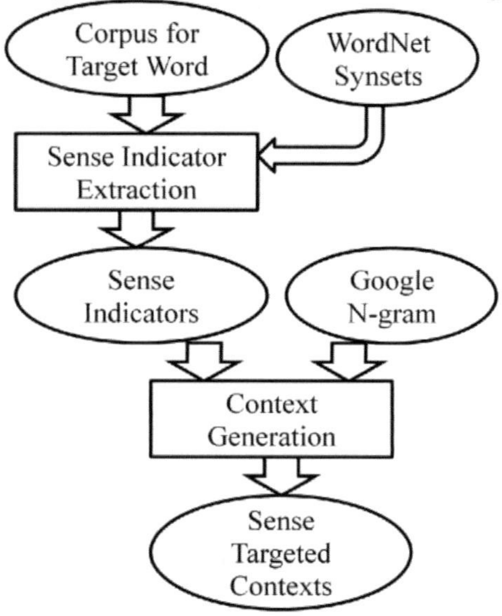

Figure 1: overall work flow diagram

2.1 Sense Indicator Extraction

Kulkarni and Pedersen (2005) and Duan and Yates (2010) performed Sense Indicator Extraction, but the indicators they extracted are not sense targeted. Content words in the definition and examples for each sense are often good indicators for that sense, but we found that on their own they did poorly.

One reason is that such indicators sometimes co-occur with a different sense. But the main reason is that there are so few of them that the word sense often appears without any of them. Thus we need more (and if possible better) sense indicators.

To obtain sense-targeted indicators for a target word, we first assemble a corpus by issuing a Google query for each synset of the target word. The query lists the target word and all content words in the synset's WordNet definition and examples, and specifies a limit of 200 hits. The resulting corpus contains a few hundred documents.

To extract sense indicators from the corpus for a word, we adapt Latent Dirichlet Allocation (LDA) (Blei *et al.* 2003). LDA takes as input a corpus of documents and an integer k, and outputs k latent topics, each represented as a probability distribution over the corpus vocabulary. For k, we use the number of word senses. To bias LDA to learn topics corresponding to the word senses, we use the content words in their WordNet definitions and examples as seed words.

After learning these topics and filtering out stop words, we pick the 30 highest-probability words for each topic as indicators for the corresponding word sense, filtering out any words that also indicate other senses. We create a corpus for each target word and run LDA on it.

Having outlined the extraction process, we now explain in more detail how we learn the topics; the mathematically faint-hearted may skip to Section 2.2. Formally, given corpus C with m documents, let n be the number of topics, and let α_i and β_j be the parameters of the document and topic distributions respectively. LDA assumes this generative process for each document D_i for a corpus C:

1. Choose $\theta_i \sim Dir(\alpha_i)$ where $i \in \{1, \ldots, m\}$
2. Choose $\gamma_j \sim Dir(\beta_j)$ where $j \in \{1, \ldots, n\}$
3. For each word $w_{i,t}$ in D_i where $t \in \{1, \ldots, T\}$, T is the number of words in D_i
   (a) Choose a topic $z_{i,t} \sim Multinomial(\theta_i)$
   (b) Choose a topic $w_{i,t} \sim Multinomial(\gamma_s)$ where $s = z_{i,t}$

In classical LDA, all α_i's are the same. We allow them to be different in order to use the seed words as high confidence indicators of target senses to bias the hyper-parameters of their document distributions.

For inference, we use Gibbs Sampling (Steyvers and Griffiths 2006) with transition probability

$$P(z_{i,t} = z | Z_{c \backslash z_{i,t}}, C, w_{i.t} = w) = \frac{count(w,z) + \beta_{z,w}}{count(z) + \sum_{\boldsymbol{w}} \beta_{z,\boldsymbol{w}}} * \frac{count_i(z) + \alpha_{i,z}}{\sum_{\boldsymbol{z}} count_i(\boldsymbol{Z}) + \sum_{\boldsymbol{z}} \alpha_{i,z}}$$

Here $Z_{c \backslash z_{i,t}}$ denotes the topic assignments to all other words in the corpus except $w_{i,t}$; $count(w,z)$ is the number of times word w is assigned to topic z in the whole corpus; $count(z)$ is the number of words assigned to topic z in the entire corpus;

$count_i(z)$ is the count of tokens assigned to topic z in document D_i; and $\beta_{z,w}$ and $\alpha_{i,z}$ are the hyper-parameters on $\gamma_{z,w}$ and $\theta_{i,z}$ respectively in the two Dirichlet distributions.

For each document D_i that contains seed words of some synset, we bias α_i toward the topic z for that synset by making $\alpha_{i,z}$ larger; specifically, we set each $\alpha_{i,z}$ to 10 times the average value of α_i. This bias causes more words w_{new} in D_i to be assigned to topic z because the words of D_i are likely to be relevant to z. These assignments then influence the topic distribution of z so as to make w_{new} likelier to be assigned to z in any document D_{new}, and thus shift the document distribution in D_{new} towards z. By this time we are back to the start of the loop where the document distribution of D_{new} is biased to z. Thus this procedure can discover more sense indicators for each sense.

Our method is a variant of Labeled LDA (L-LDA) (Ramage 2009), which allows only labels for each document as topics. In contrast, our variant allows all topics for each document, because it may use more than one sense of the target word. Allowing other senses provides additional flexibility to discover appropriate sense indicators.

The LDA method we use to obtain sense indicators fits naturally into the framework of bootstrapping WSD (Yarowsky 1995; Mihalcea 2002; Martinez *et al.* 2008; Duan and Yates 2010), in which seeds are given for each target word, and the goal is to disambiguate the target word by bootstrapping good sense indicators that can identify the sense. In contrast to WSD, our goal is to generate contexts for each sense of the target word.

2.2 Context Generation

To generate sense-targeted contexts, we extend the VEGEMATIC context generation system (Liu *et al.* 2009). VEGEMATIC generates contexts for a given target word using the Google N-gram corpus. Starting with a 5-gram that contains the target word, VEGEMATIC extends it by concatenating additional 5-grams that overlap by 4 words on the left or right.

To satisfy various constraints on good contexts for learning the meaning of a word, VEGEMATIC uses various heuristic filters. For example, to generate contexts likely to be informative about the word meaning, VEGEMATIC prefers 5-grams that contain words related to the target word, i.e., that occur more often in its presence. However, this criterion is not specific to a particular target sense.

To make VEGEMATIC sense-targeted, we modify this heuristic to prefer 5-grams that contain sense indicators. We assign the generated contexts to the senses whose sense indicators they contain. We discard contexts that contain sense indicators for more than one sense.

3 Experiments and Evaluation

To evaluate our method, we picked 8 target words from a list of polysemous vocabulary words used in many domains and hence important for children to learn (Beck *et al.* 2002). Four of them are nouns: *advantage* (with 3 synsets), *content* (7), *force* (10), and *retreat* (7). Four are verbs: *dash* (6), *decline* (7), *direct* (13), and *reduce* (20). Some of these words can have other parts of speech, but we exclude those senses, leaving 73 senses in total.

We use their definitions from WordNet because it is a widely used, comprehensive sense inventory. Some alternative sense inventories might be unsuitable. For instance, children's dictionaries may lack WordNet's rare senses or hypernym relations.

We generated contexts for these 73 word senses as described in Section 2, typically 3 examples for each word sense. To reduce the evaluation burden on our human judges, we chose just one context for each word sense, and for words with more than 10 senses we chose a random sample of them. To avoid unconscious bias, we chose random contexts rather than the best ones, which a human would likelier pick if vetting the generated contexts by hand. For comparison, we also evaluated WordNet examples (23 in total) where available.

We gave three native English-speaking college-educated judges the examples to evaluate independently, blind to their intended sense. They filled in a table for each target word. The left column listed the examples (both generated and WordNet) in random order, one per row. The top row gave the WordNet definition of each synset, one per column. Judges were told: ***For each example, put a 1 in the column for the sense that best fits how the example uses the target word. If more than one sense fits, rank them 1, 2, etc. Use the last two columns only to say that none of the senses fit, or you can't tell, and why.*** (Only 10 such cases arose.)

We measured inter-rater reliability at two levels.

At the fine-grained level, we measured how well the judges agreed on which one sense fit the example best. The value of Fleiss' Kappa (Shrout and Fleiss 1979) was 42%, considered moderate. At the coarse-grained level, we measured how well judges agreed on which sense(s) fit at all. Here Fleiss' Kappa was 48%, also considered moderate.

We evaluated the examples on three criteria.

Yield is the percentage of intended senses for which we generate at least one example – whether it fits or not. For the 73 synsets, this percentage is 92%. Moreover, we typically generate 3 examples for a word sense. In comparison, only 34% of the synsets have even a single example in WordNet.

(Fine-grained) ***precision*** is the percentage of examples that the intended sense fits best according to the judges. Human judges often disagree, so we prorate this percentage by the percentage of judges who chose the intended sense as the best fit. The result is algebraically equivalent to computing precision separately according to each judge, and then averaging the results. Precision for generated examples was 36% for those 23 synsets and 27% for all 67 synsets with generated examples. Although we expected WordNet to be a gold standard, its precision for the 23 synsets having examples was 52% — far less than 100%.

This low precision suggests that the WordNet contexts to illustrate different senses were often not informative enough for the judges to distinguish them from all the other senses. For example, the WordNet example *reduce one's standard of living* is attached to the sense "lessen and make more modest." However, this sense is hard to distinguish from "lower in grade or rank or force somebody into an undignified situation." In fact, two judges did not choose the first sense, and one of them chose the second sense as the best fit.

Coarse-grained precision is similar, but based on how often the intended sense fits the example at all, whether or not it fits best. Coarse-grained precision was 67% for the 23 WordNet examples, 40% for the examples generated for those 23 synsets, and 33% for all 67 generated examples.

Coarse-grained precision is important because fine-grained semantic distinctions do not matter in illustrating a core sense of a word. The problem of how to cluster fine-grained senses into coarse senses is hard, especially if consensus is required (Navigli *et al.* 2007). Rather than attempt to identify a single definitive partition of a target word's synsets into coarse senses, we implicitly define a coarse sense as the subset of synsets rated by a judge as fitting a given example. Thus the clustering into coarse senses is not only judge-specific but example-specific: different, possibly overlapping sets of synsets may fit different examples.

Recall is the percentage of synsets that fit their generated examples. Algebraically it is the product of precision and yield. Fine-grained recall was 25% for the generated examples, compared to only 18% for the WordNet examples. Coarse-grained recall was 30% for the generated examples, compared to 23% for the WordNet examples.

Figure 2 shows how yield, inter-rater agreement, and coarse and fine precision for the 8 target words vary with their number of synsets. With so few words, this analysis is suggestive, not conclusive. We plot all four metrics on the same [0,1] scale to save space, but only the last two metrics have directly comparable values, However, it is still meaningful to compare how they vary. Precision and inter-rater reliability generally appear to decrease with the number of senses. As polysemy increases, the judges have more ways to disagree with each other and with our program. Yield is mostly high, but might be lower for words with many senses, due to deficient document corpora for rare senses.

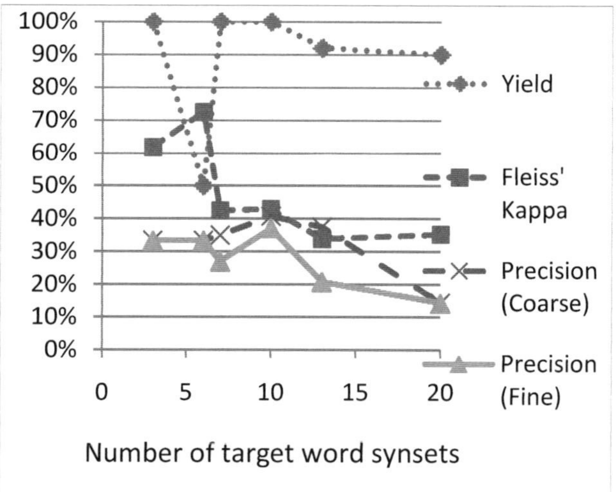

Figure 2: Effects of increasing polysemy

Table 1 compares the generated and WordNet examples on various measures. It compares precision on the same 23 senses that have WordNet examples. It compares recall on all 73 senses. It compares Kappa on the 23 WordNet examples and the sample of generated examples the judges rated.

		Generated	WordNet
Yield		92%	34%
Senses with examples		67	23
Avg. words in context		5.91	7.87
Precision (same 23)	Fine	36%	52%
	Coarse	40%	67%
Recall	Fine	25%	18%
	Coarse	30%	23%
Fleiss' Kappa	Fine	0.43	0.39
	Coarse	0.48	0.49

Table 1: Generated examples vs. WordNet

Errors occur when 1) the corpus is missing a word sense; 2) LDA fails to find good sense indicators; or 3) Context Generation fails to generate a sense-appropriate context.

Our method succeeds when (1) the target sense occurs in the corpus, (2) LDA finds good indicators for it, and (3) Context Generation uses them to construct a sense-appropriate context. For example, the first sense of *advantage* is "the quality of having a superior or more favorable position," for which we obtain the sense indicators *support, work, time, order, life, knowledge, mind, media, human, market, experience, nature, make, social, information, child, individual, cost, people, power, good, land, strategy,* and *company*, and generate (among others) the context *...**knowledge** gave him an advantage....*

Errors occur when any of these 3 steps fails. Step 1 fails for the sense "reduce in scope while retaining essential elements" of *reduce* because it is so general that no good example exists in the corpus for it. Step 2 fails for the sense of *force* in "the force of his eloquence easily persuaded them" because its sense indicators are *men, made, great, page, man, time, general, day, found, side, called,* and *house*. None of these words are precise enough to convey the sense. Step 3 fails for the sense of *advantage* as "(tennis) first point scored after deuce," with sense indicators *point, game, player, tennis, set, score, points, ball, court, service, serve, called, win, side, players, play, team, games, match, wins, won, net, deuce, line, opponent,* and *turn*. This list looks suitably tennis-related. However, the generated context *...the **player** has an advantage...* fits the first sense of *advantage*; here the indicator *player* for the tennis sense is misleading.

4 Contributions and Limitations

This paper presents what we believe is the first system for generating sense-appropriate contexts to illustrate different word senses even if they have the same part of speech. We define the problem of generating sense-targeted contexts for vocabulary learning, factor it into Sense Indicator Extraction and Context Generation, and compare the resulting contexts to WordNet in yield, precision, and recall according to human judges who decided, given definitions of all senses, which one(s) fit each context, without knowing its source or intended sense. This test is much more stringent than just deciding whether a given word sense fits a given context.

There are other possible baselines to compare against, such as Google snippets. However, Google snippets fare poorly on criteria for teaching children vocabulary (Liu *et al.* under revision). Another shortcoming of this alternative is the inefficiency of retrieving all contexts containing the target word and filtering out the unsuitable ones. Instead, we compile constraints on suitability into a generator that constructs only contexts that satisfy them. Moreover, in contrast to retrieve-and-filter, our constructive method (concatenation of overlapping Google 5-grams) can generate novel contexts.

There is ample room for future improvement. We specify word senses as WordNet synsets rather than as coarser-grain dictionary word senses more natural for educators. Our methods for target word document corpus construction, Sense Indicator Extraction, and Context Generation are all fallible. On average, 1 of 3 human judges rated the resulting contexts as sense-appropriate, half as many as for WordNet examples. However, thanks to high yield, their recall surpassed the percentage of synsets with WordNet examples. The ultimate criterion for evaluating them will be their value in tutorial interventions to help students learn vocabulary.

Acknowledgments

This work was supported by the Institute of Education Sciences, U.S. Department of Education, through Grant R305A080157 to Carnegie Mellon University. The opinions expressed are those of the authors and do not necessarily represent the views of the Institute or the U.S. Department of Education. We thank the reviewers and our judges.

References

Isabel L. Beck, Margaret G. Mckeown and Linda Kucan. 2002. Bringing Words to Life: Robust Vocabulary Instruction. NY, Guilford.

David Blei, Andrew Ng and Michael Jordan. 2003. Latent Dirichlet allocation. Journal of Machine Learning Research **3**: 993–1022.

Weisi Duan and Alexander Yates. 2010. Extracting Glosses to Disambiguate Word Senses. Human Language Technologies: The 2010 Annual Conference of the North American Chapter of the Association for Computational Linguistics, Los Angeles.

Ruben G. Fukkink, Henk Blok and Kees De Glopper. 2001. Deriving word meaning from written context: A multicomponential skill. Language Learning **51**(3): 477-496.

Patricia A. Herman, Richard C. Anderson, P. David Pearson and William E. Nagy. 1987. Incidental acquisition of word meaning from expositions with varied text features. Reading Research Quarterly **22**(3): 263-284.

Joseph R. Jenkins, Marcy Stein and Katherine Wysocki. 1984. Learning vocabulary through reading. American Educational Research Journal **21**: 767-787.

Melanie R. Kuhn and Steven A. Stahl. 1998. Teaching children to learn word meaning from context: A synthesis and some questions. Journal of Literacy Research **30**(1): 119-138.

Anagha Kulkarni and Ted Pedersen. 2005. Name discrimination and email clustering using unsupervised clustering and labeling of similar contexts. Proceedings of the Second Indian International Conference on Artificial Intelligence, Pune, India.

Liu Liu, Jack Mostow and Greg Aist. 2009. Automated Generation of Example Contexts for Helping Children Learn Vocabulary. Second ISCA Workshop on Speech and Language Technology in Education (SLaTE), Wroxall Abbey Estate, Warwickshire, England.

Liu Liu, Jack Mostow and Gregory S. Aist. under revision. Generating Example Contexts to Help Children Learn Word Meaning. Journal of Natural Language Engineering.

David Martinez, Oier Lopez de Lacalle and Eneko Agirre. 2008. On the use of automatically acquired examples for all-nouns word sense disambiguation. Journal of Artificial Intelligence Research **33**: 79--107.

Rada Mihalcea. 2002. Bootstrapping large sense tagged corpora. Proceedings of the 3rd International Conference on Languages Resources and Evaluations LREC 2002, Las Palmas, Spain.

R. Uslan Mitkov, Le An Ha and Nikiforos Karamanis. 2006. A computer-aided environment for generating multiple choice test items. Natural Language Engineering **12**(2): 177-194.

William E. Nagy, Richard C. Anderson and Patricia A. Herman. 1987. Learning Word Meanings from Context during Normal Reading. American Educational Research Journal **24**(2): 237-270.

William E. Nagy, Patricia A. Herman and Richard C. Anderson. 1985. Learning words from context. Reading Research Quarterly **20**(2): 233-253.

Roberto Navigli, Kenneth C. Litkowski and Orin Hargraves. 2007. Semeval-2007 task 07: Coarse-grained English all-words task. Proceedings of the 4th International Workshop on Semantic Evaluations, Association for Computational Linguistics**:** 30-35.

Juan Pino and Maxine Eskenazi. 2009. An Application of Latent Semantic Analysis to Word Sense Discrimination for Words with Related and Unrelated Meanings. The 4th Workshop on Innovative Use of NLP for Building Educational Applications, NAACL-HLT 2009 Workshops, Boulder, CO, USA.

Daniel Ramage, David Hall, Ramesh Nallapati, and Christopher D. Manning. 2009. Labeled LDA: A supervised topic model for credit attribution in multi-labeled corpora. Proceedings of the 2009 Conference on Empirical Methods in Natural Language Processing, Association for Computational Linguistics.

Elinore K. Schatz and R. Scott Baldwin. 1986. Context clues are unreliable predictors of word meanings. Reading Research Quarterly **21**: 439-453.

Paula J. Schwanenflugel, Steven A. Stahl and Elisabeth L. Mcfalls. 1997. Partial Word Knowledge and Vocabulary Growth during Reading Comprehension. Journal of Literacy Research **29**(4): 531-553.

Patrick E. Shrout and Joseph L. Fleiss. 1979. Intraclass correlations: Uses in assessing rater reliability. Psychological Bulletin **86**(2): 420-428.

Mark Steyvers and Tom Griffiths. 2006. Probabilistic topic models. Latent Semantic Analysis: A Road to Meaning. T. Landauer, D. McNamara, S. Dennis and W. Kintsch. Hillsdale, NJ, Laurence Erlbaum.

David Yarowsky. 1995. Unsupervised WSD rivaling supervised methods. Proceedings of the 33rd Annual Meeting of the Association for Computational Linguistics, Massachusetts Institute of Technology, Cambridge, MA.

Generating Concept Map Exercises from Textbooks

Andrew M. Olney, Whitney L. Cade, and Claire Williams
Institute for Intelligent Systems
University of Memphis
365 Innovation Drive, Memphis, TN 38152
aolney@memphis.edu

Abstract

In this paper we present a methodology for creating concept map exercises for students. Concept mapping is a common pedagogical exercise in which students generate a graphical model of some domain. Our method automatically extracts knowledge representations from a textbook and uses them to generate concept maps. The purpose of the study is to generate and evaluate these concept maps according to their accuracy, completeness, and pedagogy.

1 Introduction

Concept mapping is an increasingly common educational activity, particularly in K-12 settings. Concept maps are graphical knowledge representations that represent a concept, question or process (Novak and Canas, 2006). A recent meta-analysis of 55 studies involving over five thousand participants found the students *creating* concept maps had increased learning gains (d = .82) and students *studying* concept maps had increased learning gains (d = .37) (Nesbit and Adesope, 2006). In comparison, novice tutoring across many studies have had more modest learning gains (d = .40) (Cohen et al., 1982) – comparable to studying concept maps but not to creating them.

For difficult topics, or for students new to concept mapping, some researchers propose so-called expert skeleton concept maps (Novak and Canas, 2006). These are partially specified concept maps that may have some existing structure and then a "word bank" of concepts, properties, and relations that can be used to fill in the rest of the map. This approach is consistent with concept maps as instructional scaffolds for student learning (O'Donnell et al., 2002). As students increase in ability, they can move from expert skeleton concept maps to self-generated maps.

Because concept maps are essentially knowledge representations based in words, analysis and synthesis of concept maps are theoretically amenable to knowledge-rich computational linguistic techniques. This paper presents an approach to extracting concept maps from textbooks to create educational materials for students. The concept maps can be used as expert skeleton concept maps. The rest of the paper is organized as follows. Section 2 presents a brief overview of concept maps from the AI, psychological, and education literatures and motivates a particular representation used in later sections. Section 3 presents a general technique for extracting concept maps from textbooks and generating graphical depictions of these as student exercises. Section 4 describes a comparative evaluation of maps extracted by the model to gold-standard human generated concept maps. Section 5 discusses these results and their significance for generating concept map exercises for students.

2 Perspectives on Concept Maps

There are many different kinds of concept maps, and each variation imposes different computational demands. One prominent perspective comes from the AI literature in formal reasoning, as an extension of work done a century ago by Pierce on existential graphs (Sowa, 2007; Sowa, 2009). In this formulation (which is now an ISO standard), so-called *con-*

Proceedings of the Sixth Workshop on Innovative Use of NLP for Building Educational Applications, pages 111–119,
Portland, Oregon, 24 June 2011. ©2011 Association for Computational Linguistics

ceptual graphs are interchangeable with predicate calculus. Of particular importance to the current discussion is *grain size*, that is the level of granularity given to nodes and relationships. In these conceptual graphs, grain size is very small, such that each argument, e.g. John, is connected to other arguments, e.g. Mary, through an arbitrary predicate, e.g. John *loves* Mary. Aside from the tight correspondence to logic, grain size turns out to be a relevant differentiator amongst conceptualizations of conceptual graphs amongst different fields, and one that leads to important design decisions when extracting graphs from a text.

Another prominent perspective comes from the psychology literature (Graesser and Clark, 1985), with some emphasis on modeling question asking and answering (Graesser and Franklin, 1990; Gordon et al., 1993). In this formulation of conceptual graphs, nodes *themselves* can be propositions, e.g. "a girl wants to play with a doll," and relations are (as much as possible) limited to a generic set of propositions for a given domain. For example, one such categorization consists of 21 relations including `is-a`, `has-property`, `has-consequence`, `reason`, `implies`, `outcome`, and `means` (Gordon et al., 1993). A particular advantage of limiting relations to these categories is that the categories can then be set into correspondence with certain question types, e.g. definitional, causal consequent, procedural, for both the purposes of answering questions (Graesser and Franklin, 1990) as well as generating them (Gordon et al., 1993).

Finally, concept maps are widely used in science education (Fisher et al., 2000; Mintzes et al., 2005) for both enhancing student learning and assessment. Even in this community, there are several formulations of concept maps. One such widely known map is a hierarchical map (Novak and Canas, 2006; Novak, 1990), in which a core concept/question at the root of the map drives the elaboration of the map to more and more specific details. In hierarchical maps, nodes are not propositions, and the edges linking nodes are not restricted (Novak and Canas, 2006). Alternative formulations to hierarchical maps include cluster maps, MindMaps, computer-generated associative networks, and concept-circle diagrams, amongst others (Fisher et al., 2000).

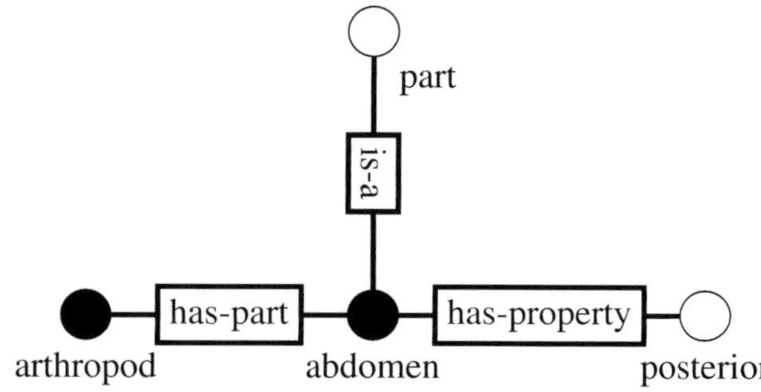

Figure 1: A concept map fragment. Key terms have black nodes.

Of particular interest is the SemNet formulation, which is characterized by a central concept (which has been determined as highly relevant in the domain) linked to other concepts using a relatively prescribed set of relations (Fisher, 2010). End nodes can be arbitrary, and cannot themselves be linked to unless they are another core concept in the domain. Interestingly, in the field of biology, 50% of all links are is-a, part-of, or has-property (Fisher et al., 2000), which suggests that generic relations may be able to account for a large percentage of links in any domain, with only some customization to be performed for specific domains. An example SemNet triple (start node/relation/end node) is "prophase *includes process* chromosomes become visible." Several thousand of such triples are available online for biology, illustrating the viability of this representational scheme for biology (Fisher, 2010).

3 Computational Model

Our approach for extracting concept maps from a biology textbook follows the general SemNet formulation with some elements of the conceptual graphs of Graesser and Clark (1985). There are two primary reasons for adopting this formulation, rather than the others described in Section 2. By using a highly comparable formulation to the original SemNets, one can compare generated graphs with several thousand, expert-generated triples that are freely available. Second, by making just a few modifications to the SemNet formalism, we can create a formalism that is more closely aligned with question answering/question generation, which we believe is a fruitful avenue for future research.

Our concept map representation has two significant structural elements. The first is key terms, shown as black nodes in Figure 1. These are terms in our domain that are pedagogically significant. Only key terms can be the start of a triple, e.g. *abdomen* `is-a` *part*. End nodes can contain key terms, other words, or complete propositions. This structural element is aligned with SemNets. The second central aspect of our representation is labeled edges, shown as boxes in Figure 1. As noted by (Fisher et al., 2000), a small set of edges can account for a large percentage of relationships in a domain. Thus this second structural element aligns better with psychological conceptual graphs (Gordon et al., 1993; Graesser and Clark, 1985), but remains consistent with the spirit of the SemNet representation. The next sections outline the techniques and models used for defining key terms and edges, followed by our method of graph extraction.

3.1 Key Terms

General purpose key term extraction procedures are the subject of current research (Medelyan et al., 2009), but they are less relevant in a pedagogical context where key terms are often already provided in learning materials. For example, both glossaries (Navigli and Velardi, 2008), and textbook indices (Larrañaga et al., 2004) have previously been used as resources in constructing domain models and ontologies. To develop our key terms, we used the glossary and index from a textbook in the domain of biology (Miller and Levine, 2002) as well as the keywords given in a test-prep study guide (Cypress Curriculum Services, 2008). Thus we can skip the keyword extraction step of previous work on concept map extraction (Valerio and Leake, 2008; Zouaq and Nkambou, 2009) and the various errors associated with that process.

3.2 Edge Relations

Since edge relations used in conceptual graphs often depict abstract, domain-independent relationships (Graesser and Clark, 1985; Gordon et al., 1993), it might be inferred that these types of relationships, e.g. `is-a, has-part, has-property`, are exhaustive. While such abstract relationships may be able to cover a sizable percentage of all relationships previous work suggests new content can drive new additions to that set (Fisher et al., 2000). In order to verify the completeness of our edge relations, we undertook an analysis of concept maps from biology.

Over a few hours, we manually clustered 4371 biology triples available on the Internet[1] that span the two topics of molecules & cells and population biology. Although these two topics represent a small subset of biology topics, we hypothesize that as the extremes of levels of description in biology, their relations will be representative of the levels between them.

Consistent with previous reported concept map research in biology (Fisher et al., 2000), our cluster analysis revealed that 50% of all relations were either `is-a`, `has-part`, or `has-property`. Overall, 252 relation types clustered into 20 relations shown in Table 1. The reduction from 252 relation types to 20 clusters generally lost little information because the original set of relations included many specific subclass relationships, e.g. `part-of` had the subclasses `composed of`, `has organelle`, `organelle of`, `component in`, `subcellular structure of`, `has subcellular structure`. In most cases subclassing of this kind is recoverable from information distributed across nodes. For example, if we know that *golgi body* `is-a` *organelle* and we know that *eukaryotic cell* `has-part` *golgi body*, then the original relation *golgi body* `organelle of` *eukaryotic cell* is implied.

Additional edge relations were added based on the psychology literature (Graesser and Clark, 1985; Gordon et al., 1993) as well as adjunct information gleaned from the parser described in the next section, raising the total number of edge relations to 30. As indicated by Table 1 a great deal of overlap exists between the clustered edge relations and those in the psychological literature. However, neither goal-oriented relationships nor logical relationships (and/or) were included as these did not seem appropriate for the domain (a cell divides because it must, not because it "wants to"). We also removed general relations that overlapped with more specific ones, e.g. *temporal* is replaced by *before, during, after*. We hypothesize that the edge relation scheme

[1] `http://www.biologylessons.sdsu.edu`

Relation	Clustered	Gordon	Adjunct	Relation	Clustered	Gordon	Adjunct
after		*		has-consequence	*	*	*
before		*		has-part	*	*	
combine	*			has-property	*	*	
connect	*	*		implies		*	
contain	*	*		isa	*	*	
contrast	*			lack	*		
convert	*			location	*		*
definition	*			manner		*	*
direction			*	not			*
during	*	*		possibility			*
enable	*			produce	*		
example	*			purpose			*
extent			*	reciprocal			*
follow	*			require	*		
function	*			same-as	*	*	

Table 1: Edge relations from cluster analysis, Gordon et al. (1993), and parser adjunct labels

in Table 1 would be portable to other domains, but some additional tuning would be necessary to capture fine-grained, domain specific relationships.

3.3 Automatic Extraction

According to the representational scheme defined above, triples always begin with a key term that is connected by a relation to either another key term or a propositional phrase. In other words, each key term is the center of a radial graph. Triples beginning and ending with key terms bridge these radial graphs. The automatic extraction process follows this representational scheme. Additionally, the following process was developed using a biology glossary and biology study guide as a development data set, so training and testing data were kept separate in this study.

We processed a high school biology text (Miller and Levine, 2002), using its index and glossary as sources of key terms as described above, using the LTH SRL[2] parser. The LTH SRL parser is a semantic role labeling parser that outputs a dependency parse annotated with PropBank and NomBank predicate/argument structures (Johansson and Nugues, 2008; Meyers et al., 2004; Palmer et al., 2005). For each word token in a parse, the parser returns information about the word token's part of speech, lemma, head, and relation to the head. Moreover, it uses PropBank and NomBank to identify predicates in the parse, either verbal predicates (PropBank) or nominal predicates (NomBank), and their associated arguments. A slightly abbreviated example parse corresponding to the concept map in Figure 1 is shown in Table 2.

In Table 2 the root of the sentence is "is," whose head is token 0 (the implied root token) and whose dependents are "abdomen" and "part," the subject and predicate, respectively. Predicate "part.01," being a noun, refers to the Nombank predicate "part" roleset 1. This predicate has a single argument of type A1, i.e. *theme*, which is the phrase dominated by "of," i.e. "of an arthopod's body." Predicate "body.03" refers to Nombank predicate "body" roleset 3 and also has a single argument of type A1, "arthopod," dominating the phrase "an arthopod's." Potentially each of these semantic predicates represents a relation, e.g. *has-part*, and the syntactic information in the parse also suggests relations, e.g. ABDOMEN *is-a*.

The LTH parser also marks adjunct arguments. For example, consider the sentence "During electron transport, H+ ions build up in the intermembrane space, making it positively charged." There are four adjuncts in this sentence: "During electron trans-

[2]The Swedish "Lunds Tekniska Högskola" translates as "Faculty of Engineering"

port" is a temporal adjunct, "in the intermembrane space" is a locative adjunct, "making it positively charged" is an adverbial adjunct, and "positively" is a manner adjunct. The abundance of these adjuncts led to the pragmatic decision to include them as edge relation indicators in Table 1.

After parsing, four triple extractor algorithms are applied to each sentence, targeting specific syntactic/semantic features of the parse, `is-a`, adjectives, prepositions, and predicates. Each extractor first attempts to identify a key term as a possible start node. The search for key terms is greedy, attempting to match an entire phrase if possible, e.g. "abiotic factor" rather than "factor," by searching the dependents of an argument and applying morphological rules for pluralization. If no key term can be found, the prospective triple is discarded. Potentially, some unwanted loss can occur at this stage because of unresolved anaphora. However, it appears that the writing style of the particular textbook used, Miller and Levine (2002), generally minimizes anaphoric reference.

As exemplified by Figure 1 and Table 2, several edge relations are handled purely syntactically. The `is-a` extractor considers when the root verb of the sentence is "be," but not a helping verb. `Is-a` relations can create a special context for processing additional relations. For example, in the sentence, "An abdomen is a posterior part of an arthropod's body," "posterior" modifies "part," but the desired triple is *abdomen* `has-property` *posterior*. This is an example of the adjective extraction algorithm running in the context of an `is-a` relation: rather than always using the head of the adjective as the start of the triple, the adjective extractor considers whether the head is a predicate nominative. Prepositions can create a variety of edge relations. For example, if the preposition has part of speech IN and has a LOC dependency relation to its head (a locative relation), then the appropriate relation is *location*, e.g. "by migrating whales in the Pacific Ocean." becomes *whales* `location` *in the Pacific Ocean*.

The predicates from PropBank and NomBank use specialized extractors that consider both their argument structure as well as the specific sense of the predicate used. As illustrated in some of the preceding examples, not all predicates have an A0. Likewise not all predicates have patient/instrument roles like A1 and A2. Ideally, every predicate would start with A0 and end with A1, but the variability in predicate arguments makes simple mapping unrealistic. To assist the predicate extractors, we created a manual mapping between predicates, arguments, and edge relations, for every predicate that occurred more that 40 times in the textbook. Table 3 lists the four most common predicates and their mappings.

Predicate	Edge Relation	Start	End
have.03	HAS_PROPERTY	A0	Span
use.01	USE	A0	Span
produce.01	PRODUCE	A0	Span
call.01	HAS_DEFINITION	A1	A2

Table 3: Predicate map examples

The label "Span" in the last column indicates that the end node of the triple should be the text dominated by the predicate. Consider the example, "The menstrual cycle has four phases" has AO *cycle* and A1 *phases*. Using just A0 and A1, the extracted triple would be *menstrual cycle* `has-property` *phases*. Using the span dominated by the predicate yields *menstrual cycle* `has-property` *four phases*, which is more correct in this situation. As can be seen in this example, end nodes based on predicate spans tend to contain more words and therefore have closer fidelity to the original sentence.

After triples are extracted from the parse, they are filtered to remove triples that are not particularly useful for generating concept map exercises. Filters are applied on the back end rather than during the extraction process because the triples discarded at this stage might be usefully used for other applications such as student modeling or question generation. The first three filters used are straightforward and require little explanation: the repetition filter, the adjective filter, and the nominal filter. The repetition filter considers the number of words in common between the start and end nodes. If the number of shared words is more than half the words in the end node, the triple is filtered. This helps alleviate redundant triples such as *cell* `has-property` *cell*. The adjective filter removes any triple whose key term is an adjective. These triples violate the assumption by the question generator that all key terms are nouns.

Id	Form	Lemma	POS	Head	Dependency Relation	Predicate	Arg 1	Arg 2
1	abdomen	abdomen	NN	2	SBJ	_	_	_
2	is	be	VBZ	0	ROOT	_	_	_
3	a	_	DT	5	NMOD	_	_	_
4	posterior	posterior	JJ	5	NMOD	_	_	_
5	part	part	NN	2	PRD	part.01	_	_
6	of	_	IN	5	NMOD	_	A1	_
7	an	_	DT	8	NMOD	_	_	_
8	arthropod	arthropod	NN	10	NMOD	_	_	A1
9	s	_	POS	8	SUFFIX	_	_	_
10	body	body	NN	6	PMOD	body.03	_	_
11	.	_	.	2	P	_	_	_

Table 2: A slightly simplified semantic parse

`Has-property` edge relations based on adjectives were also filtered because they tend to overgenerate. Finally the nominal filter removes all NomBank predicates except *has-part* predicates, since these often have Span end nodes and so contain themselves, e.g. *light* `has-property` *the energy of sunlight.*

The final filter uses likelihood ratios to establish whether the relation between start and end nodes is meaningful, i.e. something not likely to occur by chance. This filter measures the association between the start and end node using likelihood ratios (Dunning, 1993) and a χ^2 significance criterion to remove triples with insignificant association. As a first step in the filter, words from the end node that have low log entropy are removed prior to calculation. This penalizes non-distinctive words that occur in many contexts. Next, the remaining words from start and end nodes are pooled into bags of words, and the likelihood ratio calculated. By transforming the likelihood ratio to be χ^2 distributed (Manning and Schütze, 1999), and applying a statistical significance threshold of .0001, triples with a weak association between start and end nodes were filtered out. The likelihood ratio filter helps prevent sentences related to specific examples from being integrated into concept maps for a general concept. For example, the sentence "In most houses, heat is supplied by a furnace that burns oil or natural gas." from the textbook is part of a larger discussion about homeostatis. An invalid triple implied by the sentence is *heat* `has-property` *supplied by a furnace*. Since *heat* and *furnace* do not have a strong association in the textbook overall, the likelihood ratio filter would discard this triple.

After filtering, triples belonging to a graph are rendered to image files using the NodeXL[3] graphing library. In each image file, a key term defines the center of a radial graph. To prevent visual clutter, triples that have the same edge type can be merged into a single node as is depicted in Figure 2.

4 Evaluation

A comparison study using gold-standard, human generated maps was performed to test the quality of the concept maps generated by the method described in Section 3. The gold-standard maps were taken from Fisher (2010). Since these maps cover only a small section of biology, only the corresponding chapters from Miller and Levine (2002), chapters two and seven, were used to generate concept maps. All possible concept maps were generated from these two chapters, and then 60 of these concept maps that had a corresponding map in the gold-standard set were selected for evaluation.

Two judges having background in biology and pedagogy were recruited to rate both the gold standard and generated maps. Each map was rated on the following three dimensions: the coverage/completeness of the map with respect to the key term (*Coverage*), the accuracy of the map (*Accuracy*), and the pedagogical value of the map (*Pedagogy*). A consistent four item scale was used for

[3] `http://nodexl.codeplex.com/`

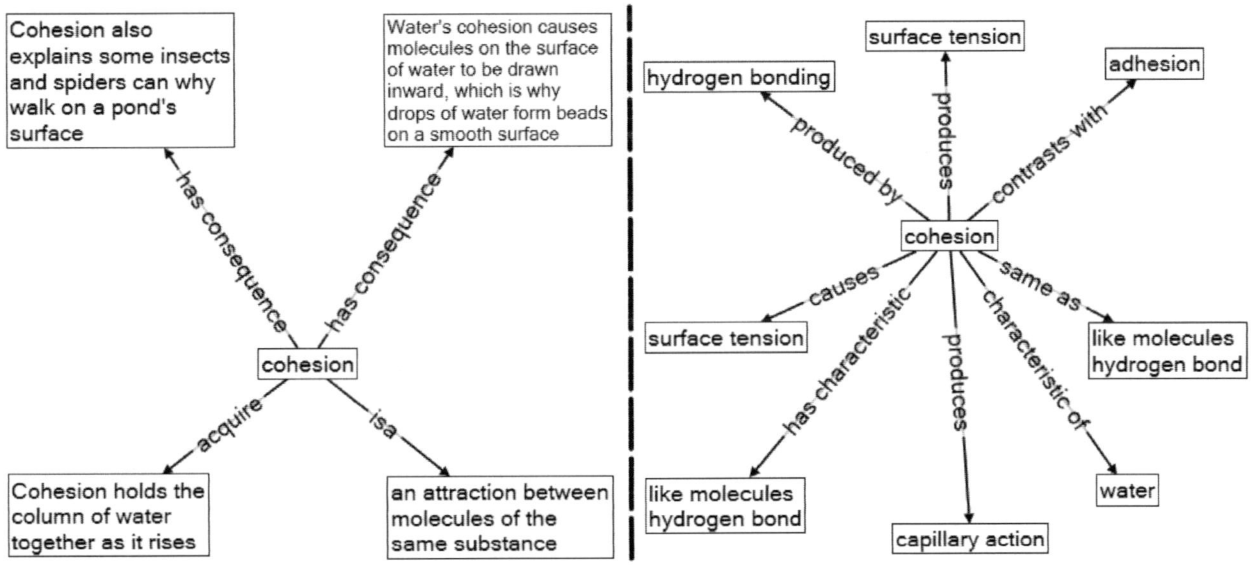

Figure 2: Comparison of computer and human generated concept maps for "cohesion." The computer generated concept map is on the left, and the human generated map is on the right.

all ratings dimensions. An example of the four item scale is shown in Table 4.

Score	Criteria
1	The map covers the concept.
2	The map mostly covers the concept.
3	The map only slightly covers the concept.
4	The map is unrelated to the concept.

Table 4: Rating scale for coverage

Judges rated half the items, compared their scores, and then rated the second half of the items. Inter-rater reliability was calculated on each of the three measures using Cronbach's α. Cronbach's α is more appropriate than Cohen's κ because the ratings are ordinal rather than categorical. A Cronbach's α for each measure is presented in Table 5. Most of the reliability scores in Table 5 are close to .70, which is typically considered satisfactory reliability. However, reliability for accuracy was poor at α = .41.

Scale	Cronbach's α
Coverage	.75
Accuracy	.41
Pedagogy	.71

Table 5: Inter-rater reliability

	Computer		Human	
Scale	Mean	SD	Mean	SD
Coverage	2.47	.55	1.67	.82
Accuracy	1.87	.67	1.47	.55
Pedagogy	2.53	.74	1.83	.90

Table 6: Inter-rater reliability and mean ratings for computer and human generated maps

Means and standard deviations were computed for each measure per condition as shown in Table 6. In general, the means for the computer generated maps were in between 2 and 3 on the respective scales, while the human generated maps were between 1 and 2. The outlier is accuracy for the computer generated maps, which was significantly higher than for the other scales. However, since the inter-rater reliability for this scale was relatively low, the mean for accuracy requires closer analysis. Inspection of the individual means for each judge revealed that judge A had the same mean accuracy for both human and computer generated maps, ($M = 1.73$), while judge B rated the human maps higher ($M = 1.2$) and the computer generated maps lower ($M = 2$). Thus it is reasonable to use this more conservative lower mean, ($M = 2$), as the estimate of accuracy for the computer-generated concept maps.

Wilcoxon signed ranks tests pairing computer and human generated maps based on their key terms were computed for each of the three scales. There was a significant effect for coverage, $Z = 2.95$, $p < .003$, a significant effect for accuracy, $Z = 2.13$, $p < .03$, and a significant effect for pedagogy $Z = 2.46$, $p < .01$.

Since the purpose of the computer generated maps is to help students learn, pedagogy is clearly the most important of the three scales. In order to assess how the other scales were related to pedagogy, correlations were calculated. Accuracy and pedagogy were strongly correlated, $r(28) = .57$, $p < .001$. Coverage and pedagogy were even more strongly correlated, $r(28) = .86$, $p < .001$.

The strong relationship between coverage and pedagogy suggests that the number of the triples in the map might be strongly contributing to the judges ratings. An inspection of the number of triples in the human maps compared to the computer generated maps reveals that there are approximately 3.5 times as many triples in the human maps as the computer generated maps. To further explore this relationship, a linear regression was conducted using the log of number of triples in each graph to predict the mean pedagogy score for that graph. The log number of triples in a graph significantly predicted pedagogy ratings, $b = -.96$, $t(28) = -3.47$, $p < .002$. The log number of triples in the graph explained a significant proportion of variance in pedagogy ratings, $r^2 = .30$, $F(1, 28) = 12.02$, $p < .002$.

These results are encouraging on two fronts. First, the computer generated maps are on average "mostly accurate." Secondly, the computer generated maps fare less well for coverage and pedagogy, but these two scale are highly correlated, suggesting that judges are using a criterion largely based on completeness when scoring maps. The strength of the log number of triples in a graph as a predictor of pedagogy likewise indicates that increasing the number of triples in each graph, which would require access to a larger sample of texts on these topics, would increase the pedagogical ratings for the computer generated maps. However, while gaps in the maps would be problematic if the students were using the maps as an authoritative source for study, gaps are perfectly acceptable for expert skeleton concept maps.

5 Conclusion

In this paper we have presented a methodology for creating expert skeleton concept maps from textbooks. Our comparative analysis using human generated concept maps as a gold standard suggests that our maps are mostly accurate and are appropriate for use as expert skeleton concept maps.

Ideally student concept maps that extend these skeleton maps would be automatically scored and feedback given as is already done in intelligent tutoring systems like Betty's Brain and CIRCSIM Tutor(Biswas et al., 2005; Evens et al., 2001). Both of these systems use expert-generated maps as gold standards by which to evaluate student maps. Therefore automatic scoring of our expert skeleton concept maps would require a more complete map in the background.

In future work we will examine increasing the number of knowledge sources to see if this will increase the pedagogical value of the concept maps and allow for automatic scoring. However, increasing the knowledge sources will also likely lead to an increase not only in total information but also in redundant information. Thus extending this work to include more knowledge sources will likely require incorporating techniques from the summarization and entailment literatures to remove redundant information.

Acknowledgments

The research reported here was supported by the Institute of Education Sciences, U.S. Department of Education, through Grant R305A080594 and by the National Science Foundation, through Grant BCS-0826825, to the University of Memphis. The opinions expressed are those of the authors and do not represent views of the Institute or the U.S. Department of Education or the National Science Foundation.

References

Gautam Biswas, Daniel Schwartz, Krittaya Leelawong, and Nancy Vye. 2005. Learning by teaching: A new agent paradigm for educational software. *Applied Artificial Intelligence*, 19:363–392, March.

Peter A. Cohen, James A. Kulik, and Chen-Lin C. Kulik. 1982. Educational outcomes of tutoring: a meta analysis of findings. *American Educational Research Journal*, 19:237–248.

LLC Cypress Curriculum Services. 2008. *Tennessee Gateway Coach, Biology*. Triumph Learning, New York, NY.

Ted Dunning. 1993. Accurate methods for the statistics of surprise and coincidence. *Computational Linguistics*, 19:61–74, March.

Martha W. Evens, Stefan Brandle, Ru-Charn Chang, Reva Freedman, Micheal Glass, Yoon Hee Lee, Leem Seop Shim, Chong Woo Woo, Yuemei Zhang, Yujian Zhou, Joel A. Michael, and Allen A. Rovick. 2001. CIRCSIM-Tutor: An intelligent tutoring system using natural language dialogue. In *Proceedings of the 12th Midwest AI and Cognitive Science Conference (MAICS 2001)*, pages 16–23, Oxford, OH.

Kathleen M. Fisher, James H. Wandersee, and David E. Moody. 2000. *Mapping biology knowledge*. Kluwer Academic Pub.

Kathleen Fisher. 2010. Biology Lessons at SDSU. http://www.biologylessons.sdsu.edu, January.

Sallie E. Gordon, Kimberly A. Schmierer, and Richard T. Gill. 1993. Conceptual graph analysis: Knowledge acquisition for instructional system design. *Human Factors: The Journal of the Human Factors and Ergonomics Society*, 35(3):459–481.

Arthur C. Graesser and Leslie C. Clark. 1985. *Structures and procedures of implicit knowledge*. Ablex, Norwood, NJ.

Arthur C. Graesser and Stanley P. Franklin. 1990. Quest: A cognitive model of question answering. *Discourse Processes*, 13:279–303.

Richard Johansson and Pierre Nugues. 2008. Dependency-based syntactic-semantic analysis with PropBank and NomBank. In *CoNLL '08: Proceedings of the Twelfth Conference on Computational Natural Language Learning*, pages 183–187, Morristown, NJ, USA. Association for Computational Linguistics.

Mikel Larrañaga, Urko Rueda, Jon A. Elorriaga, and Ana Arruarte Lasa. 2004. Acquisition of the domain structure from document indexes using heuristic reasoning. In *Intelligent Tutoring Systems*, pages 175–186.

Christopher D. Manning and Hinrich Schütze. 1999. *Foundations of Statistical Natural Language Processing*. MIT Press, Cambridge, MA.

Olena Medelyan, Eibe Frank, and Ian H. Witten. 2009. Human-competitive tagging using automatic keyphrase extraction. In *Proceedings of the 2009 Conference on Empirical Methods in Natural Language Processing*, pages 1318–1327, Singapore, August. Association for Computational Linguistics.

Adam Meyers, Ruth Reeves, Catherine Macleod, Rachel Szekely, Veronika Zielinska, Brian Young, and Ralph Grishman. 2004. The NomBank project: An interim report. In A. Meyers, editor, *HLT-NAACL 2004 Workshop: Frontiers in Corpus Annotation*, pages 24–31, Boston, Massachusetts, USA, May 2 - May 7. Association for Computational Linguistics.

Kenneth R. Miller and Joseph S. Levine. 2002. *Prentice Hall Biology*. Pearson Education, New Jersey.

Joel J. Mintzes, James H. Wandersee, and Joseph D. Novak. 2005. *Assessing science understanding: A human constructivist view*. Academic Press.

Roberto Navigli and Paola Velardi. 2008. From glossaries to ontologies: Extracting semantic structure from textual definitions. In *Proceeding of the 2008 conference on Ontology Learning and Population: Bridging the Gap between Text and Knowledge*, pages 71–87, Amsterdam, The Netherlands, The Netherlands. IOS Press.

John C. Nesbit and Olusola O. Adesope. 2006. Learning with concept and knowledge maps: A meta-analysis. *Review of Educational Research*, 76(3):413–448.

Joeseph D. Novak and Alberto J. Canas. 2006. The theory underlying concept maps and how to construct them. Technical report, Institute for Human and Machine Cognition, January.

Joeseph D. Novak. 1990. Concept mapping: A useful tool for science education. *Journal of Research in Science Teaching*, 27(10):937–49.

Angela O'Donnell, Donald Dansereau, and Richard Hall. 2002. Knowledge maps as scaffolds for cognitive processing. *Educational Psychology Review*, 14:71–86. 10.1023/A:1013132527007.

Martha Palmer, Daniel Gildea, and Paul Kingsbury. 2005. The Proposition Bank: An annotated corpus of semantic roles. *Comput. Linguist.*, 31(1):71–106.

John F. Sowa. 2007. Conceptual graphs. In F. Van Harmelen, V. Lifschitz, and B. Porter, editors, *Handbook of knowledge representation*, pages 213–237. Elsevier Science, San Diego, USA.

John F. Sowa. 2009. Conceptual graphs for representing conceptual structures. In P. Hitzler and H. Scharfe, editors, *Conceptual Structures in Practice*, pages 101–136. Chapman & Hall/CRC.

Alejandro Valerio and David B. Leake. 2008. Associating documents to concept maps in context. In A. J. Canas, P. Reiska, M. Ahlberg, and J. D. Novak, editors, *Proceedings of the Third International Conference on Concept Mapping*.

Amal Zouaq and Roger Nkambou. 2009. Evaluating the generation of domain ontologies in the knowledge puzzle project. *IEEE Trans. on Knowl. and Data Eng.*, 21(11):1559–1572.

Readability Annotation: Replacing the Expert by the Crowd

Philip van Oosten
LT[3], Language and Translation Technology Team, University College Ghent
Groot-Brittanniëlaan 45, 9000 Ghent, Belgium
Department of Applied Mathematics and Computer Science, Ghent University
Krijgslaan 281 (S9), 9000 Ghent, Belgium
philip.vanoosten@hogent.be

Véronique Hoste
LT[3], Language and Translation Technology Team, University College Ghent
Groot-Brittanniëlaan 45, 9000 Ghent, Belgium
Department of Linguistics, Ghent University
Blandijnberg 2, 9000 Ghent, Belgium
veronique.hoste@hogent.be

Abstract

This paper investigates two strategies for collecting readability assessments, an *Expert Readers* application intended to collect fine-grained readability assessments from language experts and a *Sort by Readability* application designed to be intuitive and open for everyone having internet access. We show that the data sets resulting from both annotation strategies are very similar. We conclude that crowdsourcing is a viable alternative to the opinions of language experts for readability prediction.

1 Introduction

The task of automatically determining the readability of texts has a long and rich tradition. This has not only resulted in a large number of readability formulas (Flesch, 1948; Brouwer, 1963; Dale and Chall, 1948; Gunning, 1952; McLaughlin, 1969), but also to the more recent tendency of using insights from NLP for automatic readability prediction (Schwarm and Ostendorf, 2005; Collins-Thompson and Callan, 2004; Pitler and Nenkova, 2008). Potential applications include the selection of reading material for language learners, automatic essay scoring, the selection of online text material for automatic summarization, etc.

One of the well-known bottlenecks in data-driven NLP research is the lack of sufficiently large data sets for which annotators provided labels with sufficient agreement. Also readability research is faced with the crucial obstacle that very few corpora of generic texts exist of which reliable readability information is available (Tanaka-Ishii et al., 2010). When constructing such a corpus, the inherent subjectivity of the concept of readability cannot be ignored. The ease with which a given reader can correctly identify the message conveyed in a text is, among other things, inextricably related to the reader's background knowledge of the subject at hand (McNamara et al., 1993). The construction of a corpus, which can serve as a gold standard against which new scoring or ranking systems can be tested, thus requires a multifaceted approach taking into account both the properties of the text under evaluation and those of the readers. In recent years, a tendency seems to have arisen to also explicitly address this subjective aspect of readability. Pitler and Nenkova (2008), for example, base their readability prediction method exclusively on the extent to which readers found a text to be "well-written" and Kate et al. (2010) take the assessments supplied by a number of experts as their gold standard, and test their readability prediction method as well as assessments by novices against these expert opinions.

In this paper, we report on two methodologies to construct a corpus of readability assessments, which can serve as a gold standard against which new scoring or ranking systems can be tested. Both methodologies were used for collecting readability assessments of Dutch and English texts. Since these data collection experiments for English only recently started, the focus in this paper will be on

Proceedings of the Sixth Workshop on Innovative Use of NLP for Building Educational Applications, pages 120–129,
Portland, Oregon, 24 June 2011. ©2011 Association for Computational Linguistics

Dutch. By collecting multiple assessments per text, the goal was to level out the reader's background knowledge and attitude. We will both report on a data collection experiment designed for language experts and a simple crowdsourcing experiment.

We will introduce inter-annotator agreement and calculate K scores in different settings. We will show that from the two readability assessment applications, two very similar data sets are obtained, with calculations of Pearson correlations of at least 87 %, and conclude that the simple crowdsourcing results are a viable alternative to the assessments resulting from expert labelings.

In section 2, we describe the data from language experts and how those data can be converted to relative assessments. Section 3 outlines a simpler crowsourcing application and its correspondences with the experts. Finally, in section 4, we draw conclusions and give a short summary of future work.

2 Readability assessment by the expert reader

Since readability prediction was initially primarily designed to identify reading material suited to the reading competence of a given individual, most of the existing data sets are drawn from textbooks and other sources intended for different compentence levels (François, 2009; Heilman et al., 2008). For Dutch, for example, the only large-scale experimental readability research (Staphorsius and Krom, 1985; Staphorsius, 1994) is limited to texts for elementary school children.[1] For English, the situation is similar as for Dutch, viz. a predominant focus on educational corpora. Recently, an evaluation was designed by LDC in the framework of the DARPA Machine Reading Program (Kate et al., 2010). For this purpose a more general corpus was assembled which was not tailored to a specific audience, genre or domain. Unfortunately, the data are not available for further use. Our research focus is similar and we report on the collection of readability assessments for a corpus of Dutch text, which will be used for training and evaluating a readability prediction system.

2.1 Source data

In order to acquire useful data for the construction of a gold standard, we implemented the *Expert Readers* application intended for language experts. The texts for the application were chosen from the Lassy corpus (van Noord, 2009), which is syntactically annotated, and which is currently being enhanced with several layers of semantic annotations (Schuurman et al., 2009). These annotations will allow us in the future to determine the impact of various semantic, syntactic and pragmatic factors on text readability. The small subcorpus consists of 105 texts of between about 100 and 200 words. Most of the texts are extracted from a larger context, but all are meaningful by themselves. All texts are in Dutch and most of them originate from Wikipedia or newspapers. Further, the corpus contains parts of domain-specific and official documents, manuals, patient information leaflets and others. The texts in the subcorpus have no readability levels assigned, but they are carefully selected in order to obtain texts with a multitude of readability levels. Because of the lack of a prior readability assessment, the selection was purely based on careful, yet intuitive judgment.

2.2 Application set-up

The *Expert Readers* application[2] is designed to collect readability assessments from language experts. They can express their opinion by ranking texts on a scale of 0 (easy) to 100 (difficult), which allows them to compare the texts with each other while at the same time assigning absolute scores. These fine-grained assessments committed by experts are grouped into *submission batches*, holding a number of texts which have been ranked and to which a score has been assigned. For each submitted text, we know who sent it when, with which score and along with which other texts in the same submission batch. The experts can also make use of a so-called frame of reference, in which texts are kept available over different submission batches. The same

[1]Staphorsius (1994), for instance, who conducted the only large-scale experimental readability research in the Dutch-speaking regions, based his research entirely on cloze-testing. A cloze-test is a reading comprehension test introduced by Rankin (1959) in which test subjects are required to fill in automatically deleted words in an unseen text. It is unclear whether such tasks are actually suitable to estimate the readability of a text.

[2]The Expert Readers application is accessible at the password-protected link `http://lt3.hogent.be/tools/expert-readers-nl/`.

text can occur only once per batch, but can be presented again to the same expert in other batches. Apart from the readability scores and the rankings in the batches, the experts can also enter comments on what makes each text more or less readable. That allows for qualitative analysis. We did not ask more detailed questions about certain aspects of readability, because we wanted to avoid influencing the text properties experts pay attention to. Neither did we inform the experts in any way how they should judge readability. Any presumption about which features are important readability indicators was thus avoided. Our main interest is to design a system that is robust enough to model readability as generally as possible.

In the context of our experiments, we regard people as language experts if they are native readers professionally involved with the Dutch language. Our current pool of active experts consists of 34 teachers, writers and linguists, who have contributed a total of 1862 text scores over 108 submission batches. The experts were all volunteers and were not paid for their work. Their instructions consisted of an explanation of how the application works on paper and an instruction movie of a couple of minutes. The sizes of the submission batches range from 5 to all available texts. Batches with less than 5 texts were omitted from the data.

2.3 Text scores converted to text pairs

The Expert Readers application provided a rich, but highly fine-grained output. At first sight, a straightforward and intuitive way to work with the *Expert Readers* data would be to use, for example, the mean readability score assigned to each text. Pitler and Nenkova (2008) and Kate et al. (2010), for example, average out results collected from different readers. However, problems with this approach immediately arise. Results from Anderson and Davison (1986), for example, show for their data set that if the data on which readability formulas are based, were not aggregated on the school grade level but considered at the individual level, their predictive power would drop from around 80% to an estimated 10%.

We observed a similar tendency in the results of the expert readers application: Figure 1 illustrates that different experts employ different standards to assign readability scores to texts. Being given the

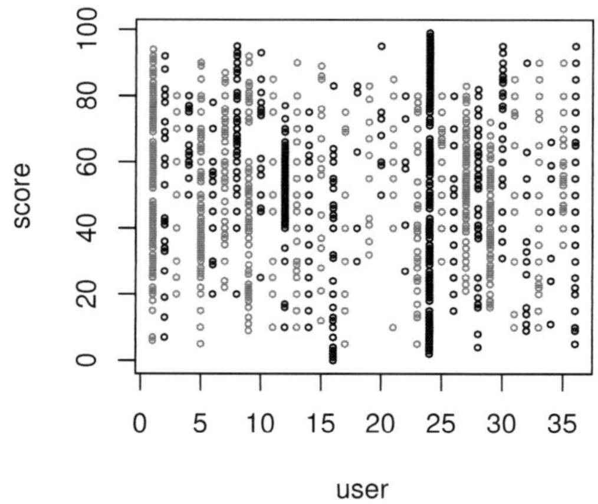

Figure 1: Different scoring strategies for a subset of experts, showing all text scores aggregated across batches

choice to label texts with marks between 0 and 100, some annotators decided to use a more coarse-grained labeling strategy (e.g. by using multiples of 10 or 20), whereas others used a fine-grained scoring (all marks between 0 and 100). Furthermore, some people seem to be reluctant to assign either high or low scores, or both, while some others use the full range of possible scores.

Moreover, the experts delivered their data in several batches. The texts presented in each submission batch were selected randomly, which implies that the annotator could have been confronted with predominantly less readable or predominantly more readable texts, which may have affected his scoring.

Furthermore, since each text being added to a batch makes it increasingly difficult for an annotator to position this text to the already scored texts, we can assume that the greater the number of texts in a batch, the more effort the annotator did to position each text correctly in the batch. We decided to only take into account submission batches in which at least 5 texts were compared to each other. Figure 2 clearly shows the variability in the scores assigned to the texts.

There is by no means a notion of a single statistical distribution that allows for a useful interpretation of the means of the scores. Since it is far from trivial to use the absolute scores assigned by the experts, we transformed their assessments to a relative scale. A resulting text pair then consists

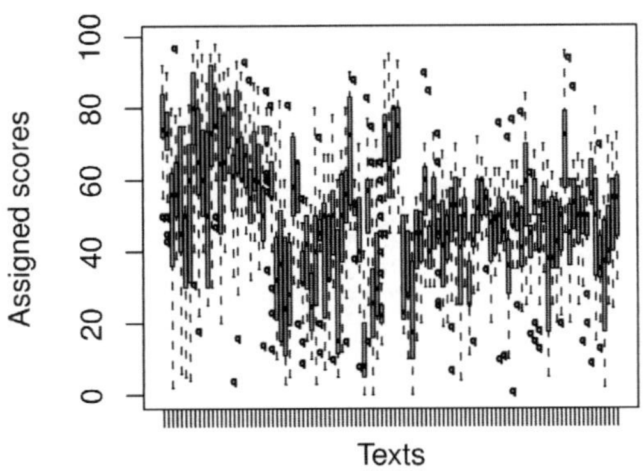

Figure 2: Box plots showing the minimum, first quantile, median, third quantile, the maximum and the outliers for the scores assigned to each text

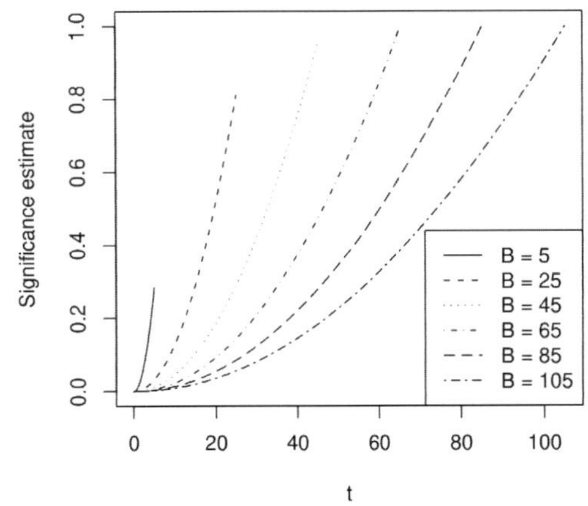

Figure 3: S as a function of t for 6 different values of B

of two texts, accompanied with an assessment that designates which of the two texts is easier than the other one, and to what degree. The identification of text pairs is straightforward, since in each batch, each pair of distinct texts presents a text pair, leading to $\frac{n\times(n-1)}{2}$ pairs per batch. For the transformation from the position of the texts in a batch to a relative assessment for each text pair, we need to fit the batch size and number of texts scored in between two texts in the same batch to a measure that indicates the difference in readability between two texts. In order to do so, a possible formula to map the significance of the difference in readability is the following:

$$S = \left(\frac{t}{B}\right)^2 \times \left(1 - \exp\left(-\frac{B}{10}\right)\right)$$

in which S is the significance of the difference in readability, B is the batch size and t is the number of texts scored in between two texts.

The quadratic function $\left(\frac{t}{B}\right)^2$ in the first factor expresses that, in order to achieve a greater significance, the value of t must be more than proportionally higher. Because of the quadratic function, more texts must be scored in between two texts in order to get a higher significance estimate. If the quadratic part would be the only factor, the two outer texts in each batch would always get the highest possible significance estimate. However, the second factor, $1 - \exp\left(-\frac{B}{10}\right)$ ensures that small batches are less likely to result in text pairs with a great difference in readability. Figure 3 illustrates S as a function of t for different batch sizes.

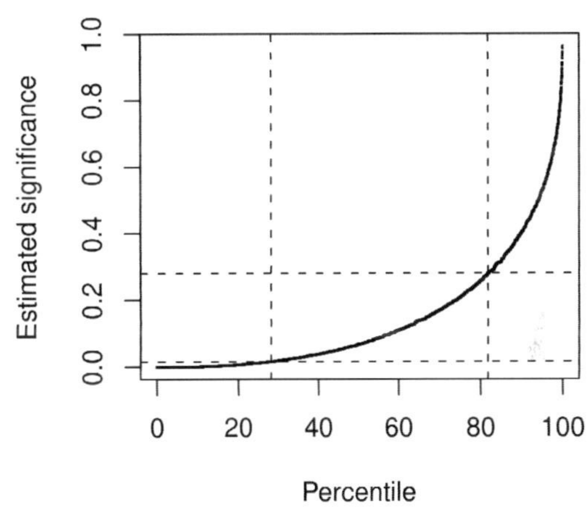

Figure 4: The relative cumulative frequency of the estimated significance scores

A plot of which percentile of the text scores generated from the batches results in which significance of the difference in readability is shown in Figure 4. The text pairs plotted on the lower left of the figure will be regarded as text pairs for which the annotators assess the readability of both texts in the pair as equal. The text pairs plotted in the middle of the figure will be regarded as assessed with a somewhat different readability and those plotted in the upper right part will be interpreted as text pairs with much difference in readability.

3 From the expert to the crowd

Based on the assumption that the readability of a text can be conceptualized as the extent to which the text is perceived to be readable by the community of language users, we also investigated whether a crowdsourcing approach could be a viable alternative to expert labeling. Crowdsourcing has already been used with success for NLP applications such as WSD (Snow et al., 2008) or anaphora resolution[3]. By redesigning readability assessment as a crowdsourcing application, we hypothesize that no background in linguistics is required to judge the readability of a given text. The *Sort by Readability* application[4] is designed as a simple crowdsourcing application to be used by as many users as possible. The site is accessible to anyone having internet access and very inutitive; the users are not required to provide personal data. A screenshot of the crowdsourcing application is shown in Figure 5.

Two texts are displayed simultaneously and the user is asked to tick one of the following statements "Left: much more difficult – Right: much easier", "Left: somewhat more difficult – Right: somewhat easier", "Both equally difficult", "Left: somewhat easier – Right: somewhat more difficult", "Left: much easier Right: much more difficult". The assessments were performed on the same data set that was used for the Expert readers application. The respondents were not paid for their work and initially recruited among friends and students. The only instructions they were given were the following two sentences on the landing page of the application:

> Using this tool, you can help us compose a readability corpus. You are shown two texts of which you can decide which is the more difficult and which is the easier one.

We assume that most respondents are native speakers of the Dutch language.

At the time of writing, 8568 comparisons were performed.

[3]http://www.phrasedetectives.org

[4]The Sort by Readability application can be accessed through the following link: `http://lt3.hogent.be/tools/sort-by-readability-nl/`.

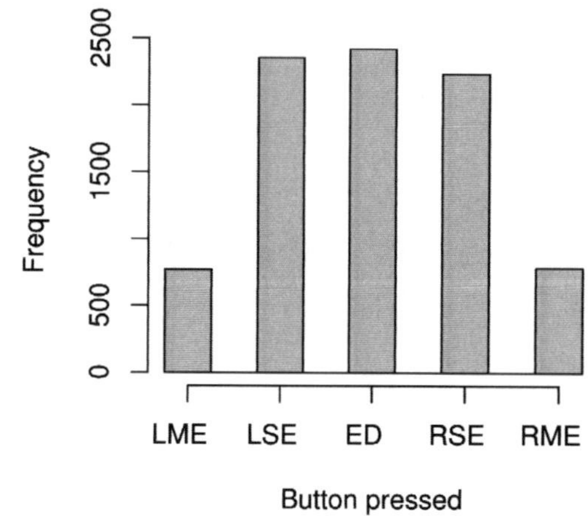

Figure 6: The number of times each button is pressed in the Sort by Readability application. The buttons from left to right are LME ("Left: much easier – Right: much more difficult"), LSE ("Left: somewhat easier – Right: somewhat more difficult"), ED ("Both equally difficult"), RSE ("Left: somewhat more difficult – Right: somewhat easier") and RME ("Left: much more difficult – Right: much easier").

The number of times each button in the crowdsourcing application was pressed is displayed in Figure 6. The number of times the text on the left was found easier is almost exactly the same as the number of times for the right one. That means that users of the crowdsourcing application are generally not biased towards finding texts on one side easier than on the other side. Most of the times two texts were compared, people found that there was a difference in readability. Only in 28.2% of the cases, people assessed both texts as equally difficult. In 53.6% of the cases, the crowd assigned a slight difference in readability and in 18.2%, the readability was assessed as very different. Note that not everyone evaluated the same text pairs. Moreover, nobody evaluated all the possible text pairs.

Figure 7 shows for both the *Expert readers* and *Sort by Readability* application the relationship between the proportions with which each text is assessed as easier (both much and somewhat easier), equally readable or more difficult (both much and somewhat more difficult) than any other text. In all scatter plots, the texts occur in a sickle-shaped form. The plots for both data sets look very similar, but there is less variability for the Expert Read-

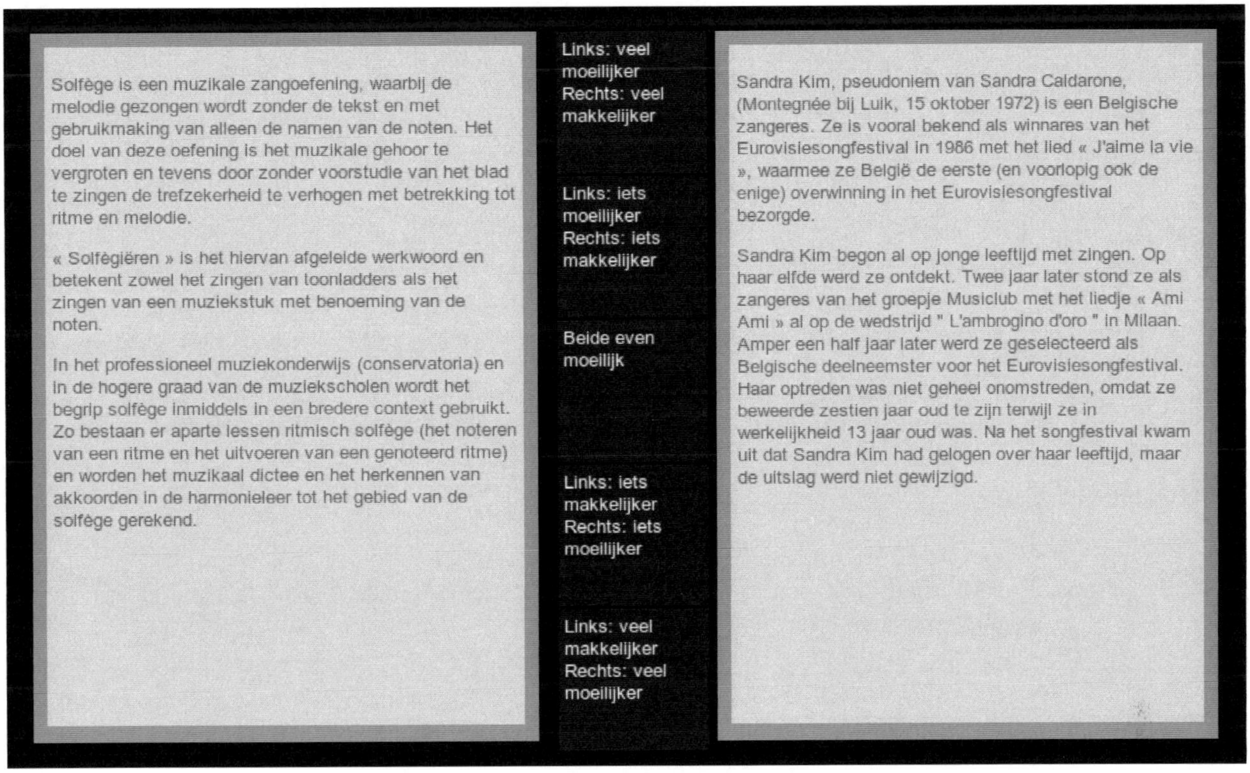

Figure 5: A screenshot of the *Sort by Readability* application.

ers data. That may indicate that the Expert Readers application actually helps people to provide assessments more consistently than the Sort by Readability application. Despite these small variations, we can conclude that from the two readability assessment applications, two very similar data sets are obtained.

3.1 Inter-annotator agreement

For most NLP tasks, there is a tradition to calculate some measure of inter-annotator agreement (IAA). If this measure is high enough, the data are deemed acceptable to serve as a gold standard. If not, the underlying annotation guidelines can be adapted or further specified in order to improve the future agreement between annotators. In readability research, however, this practice does not seem to have gained much ground. Given that many readability prediction methods (e.g. (Flesch, 1948; Staphorsius, 1994)) were developed before it became commonplace, it is not surprising that inter-annotator agreement played no great part in the development of those readability formulas. However, also in the more recent classification-based work on readability prediction, we are not aware of such efforts. Determining inter-annotator agreement for both our annotation tasks is far from trivial. In both applications, not all texts received an equal number of assessments, as shown in Figures 8 and 9. Since this evidently leads to a varying number of assessments per text pair (ranging from 1 to 25 for Expert Readers and from 1 to 8 for Sort by Readability), we took this into account in the calculation of the inter-annotator agreement. Further, our definition of readability does not allow annotation guidelines. We explicitly avoided to influence people on what their view on readability should be, because we assume that their collective view is what defines the readability of a given text. Annotation guidelines would make the definition recursive. Inter-annotator agreement is therefore implemented as a descriptive statistic. It is not used to further guide the annotation process.

We calculated the IAA both for the text pairs from the Sort by Readability application and the mapped text pairs resulting from the Expert Readers data. To convert the significance levels of the Expert Read-

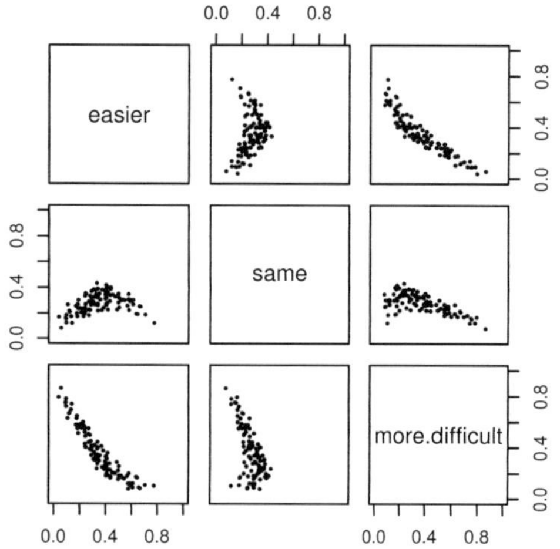

(a)

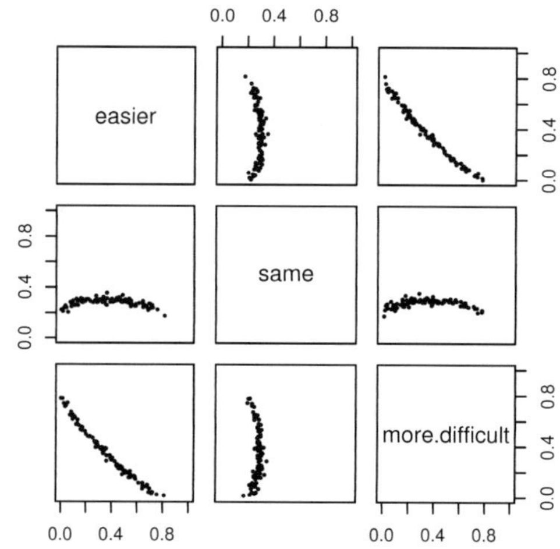

(b)

Figure 7: Proportion of times each text was assessed as easier, equally difficult or more difficult than any other text: (a) for the Sort by Readability data and (b) for the Expert Readers data.

Data set	# text pairs	Setup	K
Experts	1 – 10	standard	30 %
Experts	11 – 25	standard	31 %
Experts	1 – 25	standard	30 %
Experts	1 – 10	no same	56 %
Experts	11 – 25	no same	75 %
Experts	1 – 25	no same	60 %
Experts	1 – 10	much difference	95 %
Experts	11 – 25	much difference	98 %
Experts	1 – 25	much difference	96 %
Experts	1 – 10	adjacent	50 %
Experts	11 – 25	adjacent	65 %
Experts	1 – 25	adjacent	54 %
Experts	1 – 10	merged	35 %
Experts	11 – 25	merged	41 %
Experts	1 – 25	merged	37 %
Crowd	1 – 8	standard	44 %
Crowd	1 – 8	no same	66 %
Crowd	1 – 8	much difference	88 %
Crowd	1 – 8	adjacent	59 %
Crowd	1 – 8	merged	50 %

Table 1: Kappa statistics for all the different setups. The second column shows the number of times a text pair must have been labeled in order to be taken into account.

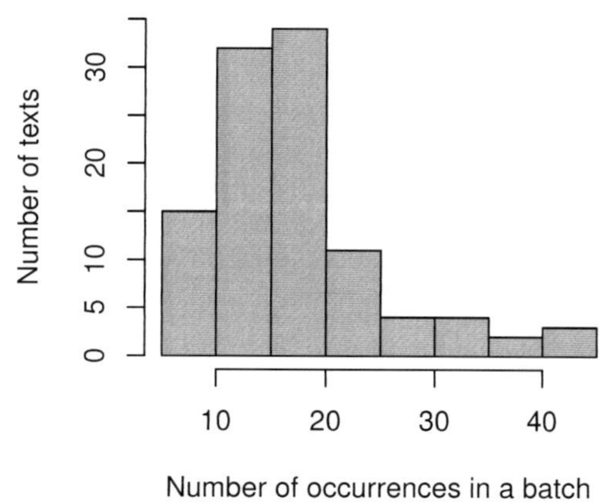

Figure 8: The distribution of the texts, according to the number of submission batches in which they occurred. Only batches with >5 texts were taken into account.

ers text pairs as shown in Figure 4 to classes of text pairs like in the Sort by Readability data, we can choose boundary values for the classes. As boundary values, we chose the significance estimates leading to equal proportions of equally difficult, somewhat different or much different text pairs for both data sets. The only possible alternative would be to choose ad hoc boundaries. Projection of the number of times each button is pressed in the Sort by

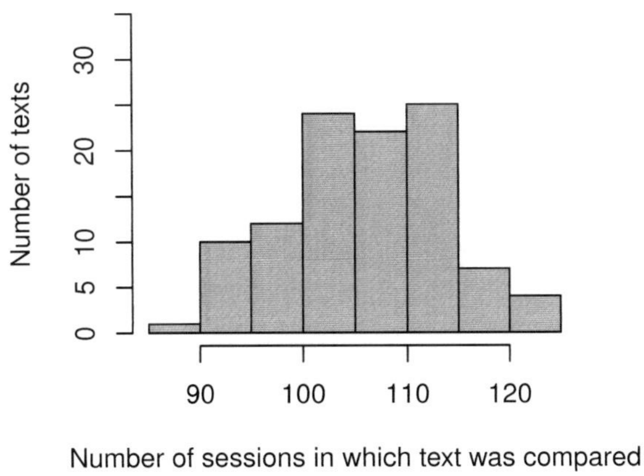

Figure 9: Distribution of the number of sessions each text was seen in for the Sort by Readability application

Readability application[5] on the Expert Readers data set, leads to the boundary values displayed as dashed lines in Figure 4. 28 % of the text pairs in both applications are thus labeled as equally readable, while 18 % of the pairs are labeled with much difference in difficulty. Those partitions correspond with boundary values of 0.016 and 0.29 for S, respectively.

We used K as proposed by Carletta (1996) as a measure for the agreement between annotators. K is given by the following formula:

$$K = \frac{P(A) - P(E)}{1 - P(E)}$$

in which $P(A)$ is the probability that two annotators make the same decision and $P(E)$ is the probability that the same decision is made coincidently. For $P(A)$, we take into account the number of times two annotators agree about a text pair and the number of times they disagree. The trivial case, when there is total agreement, simply because a text pair is annotated only once, was not taken into account for the calculation of the kappa statistic. $P(E)$ is empirically estimated in the standard way.

We calculate K in 5 different settings. In the *standard* setting, each of the five possible assessments for a text in a text pair is regarded as a separate class, without ordering of the classes.

In a second calculation of inter-annotator agreement, we considered a click on an adjacent button for the same text pair as agreement. By doing so, we took into account that the choice between "easier" and "much easier" and between "more difficult" "much more difficult" , respectively, is less straightforward than the distinction between "easier" and "more difficult". Furthermore, the boundary between "both equally difficult" and "somewhat easier/more difficult" could also be considered less transparent.

In a third calculation, named *merged*, the classes "easier" and "much easier" on one hand, and "more difficult" and "much more difficult" on the other hand are merged, resulting in three different classes.

Finally, we examine two cases in which a part of the text pairs are omitted, viz. *no same* and *much difference*. In both cases, a binary classification is performed. $P(E)$ now equals 0.5 for both classes, because there are two possible outcomes, with equal probability. For *no same*, the button in the middle was discarded. The "easier" and "much easier" classes were merged, as well as the "more difficult" and "much more difficult" classes. In the *much difference* setting, only the texts labeled as much easier or much more difficult were taken into account.

The results of all these calculations are shown in Table 1. The second column indicates a range of a number of text pairs, which determines how many times a text pair must have been labeled in order to be taken into account for the calculation of K. The results are variable, depending on how K was calculated. For the Expert Readers, we consistently observe higher K values when more labelings are required per text pair.

One possibility to get an idea of how similar the two data sets are is by calculating correlation metrics, such as the Pearson correlation coefficient. In order to calculate that, a numerical value acquired from both data sets must be attached to each text. For each text, we attached two values per data set, viz. the proportions of times the text was assessed either as easier or as more difficult than any other text. The correlations between the 4 resulting values per text are shown in Table 2. From those results, it is clear that the data sets are very similar.

There are different viable alternatives to construct a gold standard from the data sets. The type of gold standard that is needed depends on the learning task to be performed. For regression, for example, the

[5]See Figure 6

	Crowd easier	Crowd more difficult	Experts easier	Experts more difficult
Crowd – easier	100 %	-93 %	88 %	-87 %
Crowd – more difficult	-93 %	100 %	-87 %	89 %
Experts – easier	88 %	-87 %	100 %	-99 %
Experts – more difficult	-87 %	89 %	-99 %	100 %

Table 2: Pearson correlations between 4 different metrics calculated based on the assessments by experts or the crowd. The metrics are the proportions of times a text is assessed either as easier or as more difficult than any other text.

most suitable gold standard consists of an assignment of a readability score to each individual text. Those readability scores can for example be the proportion of times each text was assessed as easier than any other text. Other possibilities to assign scores can also lead to a gold standard for regression. Binary classification is an example of a different learning task, for which the data set doesn't need to be transformed. For two texts, a binary classifier attempts to determine which is the easiest and which the most difficult one. Further research will focus on how the data sets resulting from both annotation strategies can be transformed into gold standards.

4 Concluding remarks

We have implemented two web applications to collect assessments about the readability of texts in a selected corpus: an application intended for language experts and a crowdsourcing tool. Although both English and Dutch are targeted, we focused on the results that were obtained for Dutch. In order to compare the resulting readability assessments, we viewed the data as text pairs, for which a relative assessment is given. A comparison of both data sets revealed that they are very similar, a similarity which was numerically confirmed by an analysis with Pearson's correlation coefficient. Finally, we gave examples of how gold standards for different learning tasks canbe constructed from the data sets.

We introduced the problem of inter-annotator agreement into the field of readability prediction and calculated inter-annotator agreement for both data sets in five different ways. We show that for the text pairs which were assessed > 10 times, higher K scores are obtained in each of the different settings, which strengthens our confidence that readability can be learned from our data sets.

We conclude that both data sets are valuable and that crowdsourcing is a viable alternative to readability assessments by language experts.

Future work includes a further extension and analysis of the data sets. Further analysis could also reveal the ideal way to extract a gold standard from the data sets. We will also continue to investigate the impact of different linguistic features on automatic readability prediction (van Oosten et al., 2010).

Acknowledgments

This research was funded by the University College Ghent Research Fund.

We would like to thank all volunteers who cooperated with our research by using our web applications.

References

Richard C. Anderson and Alice Davison. 1986. Conceptual and Empirical Bases of Readability Formulas. Technical Report 392, University of Illinois at Urbana-Champaign, October.

R. H. M. Brouwer. 1963. Onderzoek naar de leesmoeilijkheden van Nederlands proza. *Pedagogische Studiën*, 40:454–464.

Jean Carletta. 1996. Assessing Agreement on Classification Tasks: The Kappa Statistic. *Computational Linguistics*, 22(2):249–254.

Kevin Collins-Thompson and Jamie Callan. 2004. A language modeling approach to predicting reading difficulty. In *Proceedings of HLT / NAACL 2004*, Boston, USA, May.

Edgar Dale and Jeanne S. Chall. 1948. A formula for predicting readability. *Educational research bulletin*, 27:11–20.

Rudolph Flesch. 1948. A new readability yardstick. *Journal of Applied Psychology*, 32(3):221–233, June.

Thomas François. 2009. Combining a Statistical Language Model with Logistic Regression to Predict the Lexical and Syntactic Difficulty of Texts for FFL.

In *Proceedings of the EACL 2009 Student Research Workshop*.

Robert Gunning. 1952. *The technique of clear writing*. McGraw-Hill, New York.

Michael Heilman, Kevyn Collins-Thompson, and Maxine Eskenazi. 2008. An Analysis of Statistical Models and Features for Reading Difficulty Prediction. In *The Third Workshop on Innovative Use of NLP for Building Educational Applications*.

Rohit J. Kate, Xiaoqiang Luo, Siddharth Patwardhan, Martin Franz, Radu Florian, Raymond J. Mooney, Salim Roukos, and Chris Welty. 2010. Learning to Predict Readability using Diverse Linguistic Features. In *23rd International Conference on Computational Linguistics*.

G. Harry McLaughlin. 1969. SMOG grading – a new readability formula. *Journal of Reading*, pages 639–646.

Danielle S. McNamara, Eileen Kintsch, Nancy Butler Songer, and Walter Kintsch. 1993. Are good texts always better? Interactions of text coherence, background knowledge, and levels of understanding in learning from text. Technical report, Institute of Cognitive Science, University of Colorado.

Emily Pitler and Ani Nenkova. 2008. Revisiting Readability: A Unified Framework for Predicting Text Quality. In *EMNLP*, pages 186–195. ACL.

Earl F. Rankin. 1959. The cloze procedure: its validity and utility. *Eighth Yearbook of the National Reading Conference*, 8:131–144.

Ineke Schuurman, Véronique Hoste, and Paola Monachesi. 2009. Cultivating Trees: Adding Several Semantic Layers to the Lassy Treebank in SoNaR. In *Proceedings of the 7th International Workshop on Treebanks and Linguistic Theories*, Groningen, The Netherlands.

Sarah E. Schwarm and Mari Ostendorf. 2005. Reading Level Assessment Using Support Vector Machines and Statistical Language Models. In *Proceedings of the 43rd Annual Meeting of the ACL*, pages 523–530, Ann Arbor, June. Association of Computational Linguistics.

Rion Snow, Brendan O'Connor, Daniel Jurafsky, and Andrew Y. Ng. 2008. Cheap and fast—but is it good?: evaluating non-expert annotations for natural language tasks. In *Proceedings of the Conference on Empirical Methods in Natural Language Processing*, EMNLP '08, pages 254–263, Stroudsburg, PA, USA. Association for Computational Linguistics.

Gerrit Staphorsius and Ronald S.H. Krom. 1985. *Cito leesbaarheidsindex voor het basisonderwijs: verslag van een leesbaarheidsonderzoek*. Number 36 in Specialistisch bulletin. Cito Arnhem, april.

Gerrit Staphorsius. 1994. *Leesbaarheid en leesvaardigheid. De ontwikkeling van een domeingericht meetinstrument*. Cito, Arnhem.

Kumiko Tanaka-Ishii, Satoshi Tezuka, and Hiroshi Terada. 2010. Sorting Texts by Readability. *Computational Linguistics*, 36(2):203–227.

Gertjan J.M. van Noord. 2009. Large Scale Syntactic Annotation of written Dutch (LASSY), January.

Philip van Oosten, Dries Tanghe, and Véronique Hoste. 2010. Towards an Improved Methodology for Automated Readability Prediction. In Nicoletta Calzolari, Khalid Choukri, Bente Maegaard, Joseph Mariani, Jan Odijk, Stelios Piperidis, and Daniel Tapias, editors, *Proceedings of the seventh International Conference on Language Resources and Evaluation (LREC'10)*, Valletta, Malta, May. European Language Resources Association (EL.

Story Assembly in the R^{2}aft Dyslexia Fluency Tutor

Arthur Ward
Department of Biomedical Informatics
University of Pittsburgh
Pittsburgh, Pa., 15232
akw13@pitt.edu

Rebecca Crowley
Department of Biomedical Informatics
University of Pittsburgh
Pittsburgh, Pa., 15232
CrowleyRS@upmc.edu

Abstract

To overcome their substantial barriers to fluent reading, students with dyslexia need to be enticed to read more, and to read texts with carefully controlled lexical content. We describe and show examples from a prototype of the new R^{2}aft story assembly engine, which generates an interactive text that has A) variable plot and B) lexical content which is individualized by decoding pattern.

1 Introduction

Dyslexia is a specific disability which prevents students from reading at a level commensurate with their general intelligence. It is also the most common learning disability, affecting as many as 15 (NICHD, 2011) or 20% of the population (Shaywitz, 2003).

We have recently started a new Intelligent Tutoring System project to address dyslexia. The R^{2}aft tutor (**R**epeated **R**eading **A**daptive **F**luency **T**utor) is intended to improve reading fluency among students with dyslexia. An important part of the R^{2}aft tutor will be its story assembly engine TASA (**T**ext **A**nd **S**tory **A**ssembler), which will generate the text to be read. In this paper, we will discuss how the special characteristics of dyslexia influenced the design of TASA, and describe the prototype system.

Research has shown that phonological processing is the core deficit in dyslexia, but one which can be addressed by intensive training in phonemic awareness and phonics (e.g. (Torgesen et al., 2001)). Because dyslexic readers have difficulty distinguishing individual phonemes within a word, they also have great difficulty learning the relationships between written letter patterns and the sounds they make. These decoding patterns, which are often absorbed intuitively by normal readers, must be explicitly taught to dyslexic readers. For example, the words "tramped" and "padded" both end in "ed," but are pronounced differently. In "tramped" "ed" makes a "t" sound (the "ed_t" pattern), while in "padded" it makes an "ed" sound (the "ed_ed" pattern). [1] A dyslexic reader must receive explicit training on hundreds of decoding patterns such as these. In addition, to improve fluency a dyslexic reader must practice these patterns extensively, in large amounts of connected text.

Unfortunately, this practice is difficult to obtain. "Decodable texts" which use a constrained vocabulary are available (e.g. (Bloomfield et al., 1998)), however, professional dyslexia tutors report that these booklets often do not meet the individual vocabulary needs of their students. In addition, students with dyslexia typically *hate* to read (Shaywitz, 2003), and do little to acquire the necessary practice in connected text.

This analysis suggests that a successful fluency tutor should address two sets of issues. It should address vocabulary issues to ensure that the student gets practice on appropriate decoding patterns. It also should address motivational issues, to entice students to read more text. As described below, TASA addresses the vocabulary issue by using templates whose slots allow for lexical individualization. It aims to improve motivation by generating a variable plot line, and allowing students to make

[1] These examples are taken from (Bloomfield et al., 1998).

Proceedings of the Sixth Workshop on Innovative Use of NLP for Building Educational Applications, pages 130–135,
Portland, Oregon, 24 June 2011.

plot choices that affect the unfolding story. There are several reasons to expect that allowing dyslexic students to interactively shape plot events will improve their motivation. For example the popular "Choose Your Own Adventure" books (e.g. (Montgomery, 1982)), allow their readers to choose paths in a branching narrative. Also, "Interactive Fiction" type text adventures (Montfort, 2003) which allow the reader to control the protagonist, enjoy continuing popularity.[2] Furthermore, a study with the REAP ESL vocabulary tutor suggests that presenting more interesting stories can improve learning (Heilman et al., 2010).

Authoring a branching narrative entirely by hand, however, is an unattractive option. Even a small story could require authoring hundreds of plot branches. Reducing this burden would allow authoring the large volume of text needed by our readers.

The dyslexia tutoring domain therefore suggests three design goals for our story generation engine.

1. **Lexical Individualization:** It should allow us to fine tune lexical content to feature the decoding patterns required by each student.
2. **Interactivity:** It should allow student plot choices to influence the story being read.
3. **Tractable Authoring:** It should help reduce the burden of authoring multiple story branches.

2 Story Representation

As described above, the dyslexia domain requires detailed control over lexical content in our reading, and our approach to motivational issues involves interactive text. Both of these considerations argue against the use of pre-existing texts as are used, for example, in the Listen (Mostow, 2011) or REAP (Brown and Eskenazi, 2004) systems. Instead, we investigate generating our own stories.

The literature on story analysis and generation can be usefully divided into approaches which model the structure of the story itself, versus approaches which model some of the processes involved in story creation. The latter often simulate the author (e.g. (Dehn, 1981), the reader (Bailey, 1999), or the story world (Meehan, 1976). They also typically require large amounts of real-world knowledge to generate even simple stories. Given our need to produce a large amount of practice text, this approach seems untenable.

Instead, we take the first mentioned approach of modeling story structure. To do this, we will require a formalism which will allow us to represent, manipulate and re-combine pre-written stories. Early work in story grammars used elegant hierarchical tree structures to *analyze* plot structure. (see (Graesser et al., 1991) for an overview of this work). In general, these structures seem underspecified for *generating* stories.

We turn instead to the causal network theory of Trabasso and van den Broek (1985). This formalism does not enforce strict hierarchies, but represents text as a sequence of nodes. The nodes represent categories such as "Setting," "Goal," "Event," "Reaction" or "Outcome," and are connected in sequence by temporal and causal links.

This formalism provides guidelines about legal node sequences. It also enforces several constraints on the type of text we can represent. For example, the text base must be generated in strict temporal and causal order, we cannot represent flashbacks or other types of transformed narrative. Also, each node generates text, we cannot represent events which do not appear in the textbase.

3 The Story

Our prototype story is a rehash of several standard themes common in young reader fiction. A young protagonist moves to a new house with a parent (the genre seems to require that one parent be missing). This protagonist is shown to be weak and fearful in various ways. The protagonist discovers some source of inspiration which leads him/her to attempt some endeavor. After many setbacks the protagonist becomes accomplished at this endeavor, then at the climax uses his/her new strength/skill to save the parent from certain doom.

Our prototype story was developed to instantiate these themes each in several ways. For example, the initial source of inspiration comes in two options. The first source will be found in a springhouse at the rear of the protagonist's new home. The alternate source is found in a locked room of the main house. There are also several options for the resulting en-

[2] However, see (Glassner, 2004, pg 239) for a discussion of the difficulties of branching narrative.

deavor and several options for the final climax. Pursuant to our goal of presenting an *interactive* text, most of these plot variations will be determined at runtime by reader choice.

For example, toward the beginning of the story, the protagonist is found in his/her new bedroom, with a goal to explore the unfamiliar house. Here the reader chooses what to investigate, with the next plot fork being determined by whether the "springhouse" or the "locked door" is chosen.

This story is written in text form, then deconstructed into a causal network in the following way. An analyst examines the initial story text, and divides it into chunks. Following the Trabasso framework described in Section 2, each chunk is required to be temporally and causally subsequent to the previous chunk, and to depict elements such as a "setting," "event," "goal," "attempt" "reaction" or "outcome." The story chunk described above, for example, is labeled as a goal node. The subsequent chunk in which the protagonist begins to explore, is labeled as an "attempt." After this analysis, the resulting chunks are instantiated as production system rules, as described below.

4 The TASA Prototype

Our prototype **TASA** system is instantiated as a set of facts and rules in the Clips expert system shell (Giarratano and Riley, 1994). Expert systems typically consist of a set of *if-then rules*, plus a set of *facts* asserted in memory. Rules whose *if* portions are satisfied by facts are activated and placed on an *agenda*. A rule on the agenda is then selected and fired, according to some salience scheme. Rules typically assert new, or modify old facts in memory. These facts then cause more rules to activate and fire, and the cycle continues until the agenda is empty. In our system, we write rules which append text to the accumulating story when the story world is in a particular state.

The **TASA** system includes three types of facts: user-model, story-world, and lexicon facts.

User-model facts include details about the student's age and gender, as well as about targeted decoding patterns for that individual student.

Figure 1 shows an abbreviation of a student fact. This fact records information about the current student user such as age and gender. It also records the set of decoding patterns that should be selected in the text. The "ed_t" pattern is shown.

```
(student
    (decodePat ed_t)
    (age 9)
    (gender m))
```

Figure 1: Abbreviated student fact, requesting "ed_t" pattern

Story-world facts include the text so far, as well as the relevant story state. The story state is much less detailed than is required for the story generation systems described in Section 2, and simply includes information about the location, goals and mood of characters, and the locations and status of certain objects, as seems necessary to prevent rules from appending text in inappropriate places. It prevents, for example, text about unlocking a door from being appended when the door is open. Facts belonging to the same world state are co-indexed (with the "worldHist" variable shown in Figure 1), so that when a rule modifies the world state, the entire set of world facts can be re-asserted into memory with an updated index. This allows several different plot branches to be developed in memory simultaneously, without context-breaching intrusions from each other.

```
(character
    (charID clif_1)
    (worldHist 0)
    (role protag)
    (firstName Clif)
    (gender m)
    (goal explore_springHouse)
    (location bedroom)
    (subjPronoun he)
    (objPronoun him)
    (posPronoun his)
    (age 9))
```

Figure 2: Abbreviated story-world fact for protagonist

Figure 2 abbreviates a "protagonist" story-world fact. Among other things, this fact contains the protagonist's current location and goal, as well as appropriate forms for pronominal reference. Note also that the protagonist's age and gender have been set to match those of the current student user.

The **Lexicon facts** are a large set of words known

to the system. Each word is associated with both a synonym and a decoding pattern. This allows the system to locate all appropriate substitutions for a target word which also exhibit a targeted decoding pattern.

```
(decodeSet
      (decodePat ed_ed)
      (word padded)
      (syn walked))
(decodeSet
      (decodePat ed_t)
      (word tramped)
      (syn walked))
```

Figure 3: Example Lexicon Facts

Figure 3 shows several example lexicon facts. They allow the system, for example, to locate words which can substitute for "walked" and which display the "ed_ed" decoding pattern. Note that organizing our lexicon by substitutable synonyms allows the prototype to dispense with representing things like tense and number. Other senses of "walked," if needed, would be listed with an index, ie. "walked_2."

In the final system, we expect to implement the 70 to 80 decoding patterns commonly featured in Orton-Gillingham (Orton-Gillingham, 2011) based instructional materials. Based on discussions with professional dyslexia tutors, we hope to provide at least five examples of each pattern, requiring a lexicon of above 400 words. In addition, we hope to show each example word in several sentence contexts, which brings the number of expected sentence templates well into the thousands.

As mentioned above, each node from the story analysis is instantiated as one or more rules in this expert system. If a rule matches a story-world state and fires, it appends text to the story so far. Each rule also changes the story-world in some feature which is modelled by the system and matched in the rule's *if* part. For example a rule should leave the protagonist in a different place or in a different mood than in the previous chunk. This is a practical requirement to prevent the same rule from repeatedly firing when the story-world facts are re-asserted.

The *then* portions of these rules contain templates which are used to generate text. Each template includes slots which are to be filled by appropriate words from the lexicon. Because one template typically does not exhaust all the ways to express the rule's intended message, the analyst typically writes several forms of the rule, which increases the range of potential word use.

Given this structure of rules and facts, the production rule paradigm is appealing for its ability to meet all three of our design goals: plot variety, lexical individualization, and tractable authoring. By modularizing chunks of text and associating them with appropriate story-world conditions (in their *if* parts), we can make a system able to generate plot forks by matching two potential child nodes to the previous story node. We can achieve lexical individualization by writing rules which match not only story world facts, but also student model facts about targeted decoding patterns. Authoring burden is reduced by the ability of existing rules to add text in new situations. We give examples of each of these features below.

As an example of how this works in our prototype system, consider the plot node described above. The protagonist is in the bedroom. If the reader chooses to investigate the springhouse, a rule like the following is activated. [3]

```
(defrule walkAcrossYard_1
      (Code which binds state variables omitted here)
      ?prot ← (character (charID ?proID)
                  (worldHist ?rh)
                  (location ?proLoc&bedroom)
                  (goal explore_springHouse)
                  (firstName ?proFn))
            (student (decodePat ?dp))
            (decodeSet (decodePat ?dp)(syn walked)(word ?wlkd))
⇒
(Code which duplicates state variables omitted here)
      (text (str-cat ?txt ?proFn " " ?wlkd " across the back yard to the springhouse. ")))
```

Figure 4: Rule describing walk to springhouse

Figure 4 abbreviates a rule which fires if A) the protagonist is in the bedroom with goal to explore the springhouse, and B) the current student needs a decoding pattern ?dp which is available in a synonym of "walked." If these conditions are met, then

[3]For clarity, example rules are extensively pruned from the Clips rule syntax.

(below the ⇒) the rule fills a sentence template with the name of the protagonist and the appropriate synonym of walked.

For example, if the protagonist's name is set to "Clif," (as in Figure 2) and the decoding rule "ed_t" is targeted (as in Figure 1), this rule will produce a sentence for each matching synonym of "walked," (one of which is shown in Figure 3) including:

> Clif tramped across the back yard to the springhouse.

If the targeted pattern had instead been "ed_ed," this rule would produce sentences like "Clif padded across the back yard to the springhouse."

When the rule fires, the story world is changed to place Clif at the springhouse door, which causes additional rules to be activated. Still assuming the "ed_ed" decoding rule is active, one subsequent rule appends a sentence as follows:

> Clif hunted across the back yard to the springhouse. He pounded on the door, and listened for an answer.

Alternatively, if the source of inspiration in the story is set to be in the locked room, TASA produces a different variety of sentences including:

> Clif padded across the room toward the locked door. He pounded on the door, and listened for an answer.

Note from Figure 3 that "padded" is in the lexicon as another synonym for "walked" that follows the "ed_ed" decoding pattern. Also note that in this example the second sentence was produced by the same rule that provided the second sentence in the previous example, which had been written for a different branch of the plot. Together, these examples show how TASA can provide both plot variation and lexical individualization. They also demonstrate the feature of text reuse, which we expect will become more prevalent as the rule base grows larger.

5 Future Work

In our ongoing work we are re-implementing the prototype system in the Drools expert system shell (Bali, 2009). Drools provides for the inclusion of Java code in instantiated story-world facts, which will allow us to offload the substantial portion of our prototype rules devoted to updating and maintaining the story state. In addition we are greatly expanding our rule-base as we instantiate more of the prototype story. In the course of this work we will also evaluate moving to a more expressive story formalism, such as Graesser's Conceptual Graph Structures (Graesser et al., 1991) which can represent additional relationships between nodes.

In addition, we will evaluate improved ways to select the best text from the many options output by the system. Rather than simply comparing the number of targeted decoding patterns (as we do now) we will experiment with other evaluation metrics such as cohesion (Graesser et al., 2004), or methods which have been useful in essay evaluation (e.g. : (Higgins et al., 2004)).

After sufficient story development, we intend to evaluate the effect of interactive text on students' motivation to read. This evaluation will collect motivational survey results and "voluntary" reading times, and compare them between students using interactive and non-interactive versions of the system.

Acknowledgments

This work was supported by the National Library of Medicine Training Grant 5 T15 LM007059. We also thank Carol Utay for several productive conversations about dyslexia tutoring.

References

Paul Bailey. 1999. Searching for Storiness: Story-Generation from a Reader's Perspective. *Proceedings of the AAAI Fall 99 Symposium on Narrative Intelligence.*

Michal Bali. 2009. *Drools JBoss Rules 5.0 Developer's Guide.* Packt Publishing Ltd., Birmingham, B27 6PA, UK.

Leonard Bloomfield, Clarence Barnhart, Robert Barnhart, and Cynthia Barnhart. 1998. *Let's Read 7 Revised Edition.* Educators Publishing Service, Inc., Cambridge, MA, USA.

Jonathan Brown and Maxine Eskenazi. 2004. Retrieval of authentic documents for reader-specific lexical practice. In *In Proceedings of InSTIL/ICALL Symposium.*

Natalie Dehn. 1981. Story generation after tale-spin. In *In IJCAI-81*, pages 16–18.

Joseph Giarratano and Gary Riley. 1994. *Expert Systems: Principles and Programming*. PWS Publishing Co., Boston, MA, USA.

Andrew Glassner. 2004. *Interactive Storytelling: Techniques for 21st Century Fiction*. A.K. Peters, Nantick, MA.

Arthur Graesser, Jonathan Golding, and Debra Long. 1991. Narrative representation and comprehension. In Rebecca Barr, Michael Kamil, Peter Mosenthal, and P. David Pearson, editors, *Handbook of Reading Research, vol. 2*, pages 171 –205. Longman Publishing Group, White Plains, NY.

Arthur Graesser, Danielle McNamara, Max Louwerse, and Zhiqiang Cai. 2004. Coh-metrix: Analysis of text on cohesion and language. *Behavior Research Methods, Instruments, and Computers*, 36:193–202.

Michael Heilman, Kevyn Collins-Thompson, Jamie Callan, Maxine Eskenazi, Alan Juffs, and Lois Wilson. 2010. Personalization of reading passages improves vocabulary acquisition. *International Journal of Artificial Intelligence in Education*, 20:73–98, January.

D. Higgins, J. Burstein, D. Marcu, and C. Gentile. 2004. Evaluating multiple aspects of coherence in student essays. *Proceedings of the Annual Meeting of HLT/NAACL*, pages 185 – 192.

James Meehan. 1976. *The Metanovel: Writing Stories by Computer*. Doctor of philosophy, Yale University, New Haven, Conn.

Nick Montfort. 2003. *Twisty Little Passages: an approach to interactive fiction*. MIT Press, Cambridge, Massachusetts.

R. A. Montgomery. 1982. *The Abominable Snowman*. Chooseco, LLC., Waitsfield, Vermont.

Jack Mostow. 2011. Project listen: A reading tutor that listens. http://www.cs.cmu.edu/ listen/.

NICHD. 2011. What are learning disabilities? http://www.nichd.nih.gov/health/topics/learning_disabilities.cfm.

Orton-Gillingham. 2011. Institute for multi-sensory education. http://www.orton-gillingham.com/.

Sally E. Shaywitz. 2003. *Overcoming Dyslexia: a new and complete science-based program for reading problems at any level.* Vintage Books, New York.

Joseph Torgesen, Ann Alexander, Richard Wagner, Carol Rashotte, Kytja Voeller, and Tim Conway. 2001. Intensive remedial instruction for children with severe reading disabilities: immediate and long-term outcomes from two instructional approaches. *Journal of Learning Disabilities*, 34:33–58,78.

Tom Trabasso and Paul van den Broek. 1985. Causal thinking and the representation of narrative events. *Journal of Memory and Language*, 24:612 – 630.

Predicting Change in Student Motivation by Measuring Cohesion between Tutor and Student

Arthur Ward
Department of Biomedical Informatics
University of Pittsburgh
Pittsburgh, Pa., 15232
akw13@pitt.edu

Diane Litman
Department of Computer Science, LRDC
University of Pittsburgh
Pittsburgh, Pa., 15260
litman@cs.pitt.edu

Maxine Eskenazi
Language Technologies Institute
Carnegie Mellon University
Pittsburgh, Pa., 15213
max@cmu.edu

Abstract

We apply a previously reported measure of dialog cohesion to a corpus of spoken tutoring dialogs in which motivation was measured. We find that cohesion significantly predicts changes in student motivation, as measured with a modified MSLQ instrument. This suggests that non-intrusive dialog measures can be used to measure motivation during tutoring.

1 Introduction

Motivation is widely believed to be an important factor in learning, and many studies have found relationships between motivation and educational outcomes. For example Pintrich and DeGroot (1990) found that students' motivational state was a significant predictor of classroom performance. In addition, pedagogically significant behaviors such as dictionary lookup in the REAP (Brown and Eskenazi, 2004) vocabulary tutor have been shown to be positively correlated with motivation assessments (DelaRosa and Eskenazi, 2011). Also, in a separate study with the REAP tutor, attempts to manipulate reading motivation by presenting more interesting stories were shown to improve vocabulary learning (Heilman et al., 2010).

In addition to influencing learning outcomes, motivational state may also affect which interventions will be effective during tutoring. For example, Ward and Litman (2011) have shown that motivation can significantly affect which students benefit from a reflective reading following interactive tutoring with a the Itspoke (Litman and Silliman, 2004) tutor.

An accurate way to measure student motivation during tutoring could therefore be valuable to Intelligent Tutoring System (ITS) researchers. Several self-report instruments have been developed which measure various aspects of motivation (e.g. (Pintrich and DeGroot, 1990; McKenna and Kear, 1990)). However, these instruments are too intrusive to be administered *during* tutoring, for fear of fatally disrupting learning. We would prefer a non-intrusive measure which would allow an ITS to detect when student motivation is decreasing so as to launch a motivational intervention. Similarly, the ITS should be able to detect when motivation is increasing again, to determine if the intervention worked. As mentioned above, such a measure might also allow an ITS to determine when it would be effective to use certain instructional tactics.

In this work we investigate *cohesion* as a non-intrusive measure of motivation for natural language dialog based ITS. As defined more precisely below, our measure of cohesion quantifies lexical and semantic similarity between tutor and student dialog utterances. We hypothesize that this measure of lexical similarity may be related to motivation in part because other measures of dialog similarity have been shown to be related to task success. For example, there is evidence that perceived similarity between a student's own speech rate and that of a recorded task request increases the student's feelings of immediacy, which are in turn linked to greater compliance with the request to perform a task (Buller and Aune, 1992). [1] In addition, Ward and Litman (2006; 2008) investigated a measure of lexical similarity between

[1] In this experiment, the task was to watch a series of videos.

Proceedings of the Sixth Workshop on Innovative Use of NLP for Building Educational Applications, pages 136–141,
Portland, Oregon, 24 June 2011. ©2011 Association for Computational Linguistics

the tutor and student partners in a tutoring dialog which was shown to be correlated with task success in several corpora of tutorial dialogs.

Measures of cohesion have also been used in a variety of NLP tasks such as measuring text readability (e.g. (Pitler and Nenkova, 2008)), measuring stylistic differences in text (Mccarthy et al., 2006), and for topic segmentation in tutorial dialog (Olney and Cai, 2005).

Given the previously mentioned results relating motivation to educational task success, these links between task success and cohesion lead us to hypothesize a direct correlation between motivation and cohesion when using the Itspoke tutor.

We will first briefly describe the Itspoke tutor, and the corpus of tutoring dialogs used in this study. We will then describe the instrument we used to measure motivation both before and immediately after tutoring, then we will describe the algorithm used to measure cohesion in the tutoring dialogs. Finally, we show results of correlations between the measure of motivation and the measure of cohesion. We will find that the *change* in motivation is significantly correlated with dialog cohesion.

2 Itspoke System and Corpus

Itspoke (**I**ntelligent **T**utoring **SPOKE**n dialog system) is a spoken dialog tutoring system which teaches qualitative physics. It provides a spoken dialog interface to the Why2-Atlas (VanLehn et al., 2002) tutor, and has recently been re-implemented using the TuTalk (Jordan et al., 2007) dialog platform. The Itspoke tutor presents a problem in qualitative physics, and asks the student an initial question. The student answers the question, and the dialog continues until all points have been covered to the tutor's satisfaction.

The corpus used in the current work was collected in a previous study (Ward and Litman, 2011), using novice subjects who had never taken a college physics course. Before tutoring, students were given a motivation survey which will be described in Section 3. They then engaged Itspoke in five tutoring dialogs as described above. Immediately after tutoring they were given the motivation questionnaire again, with tenses changed as appropriate.

166 subjects were recruited by flyer, by advertisement during an undergraduate psychology course, or from the University of Pittsburgh's psychology subject pool. Of these, 40 were dismissed after pretest as "middle third" knowledge students, following extreme groups design (Feldt, 1961). Extreme groups design was adopted to increase the power of a "high" vs "low" knowledge comparison, which is reported elsewhere (Ward, 2010). Another 27 students were not used for various reasons including incomplete data. This left a corpus of 99 subjects who each participated in 5 tutorial dialogs.

Speaker	Utterance
Tutor	To see which vehicle's **change** in motion is greater, we use the definition of **acceleration**. What is the definition of acceleration?
Student	**Change** in **velocity**.
Tutor	Excellent. Acceleration is defined as the amount **velocity changes** per unit time.

Table 1: Dialog turns, with Token, Stem, and Semantic Similarity Matches in **bold** (as discussed in Section 4).

Table 1 shows an exchange from one of these dialogs. The tutor asks a question about the current problem, which the student then answers. The tutor restates the answer, and (later in the dialog) proceeds on to the next point of discussion.

3 Motivation Measure

In this study we measure motivation using a reduced version of the "Motivated Strategies for Learning Questionnaire (MSLQ)" developed by Pintrich and DeGroot (1990). This version of the MSLQ is also based on work by Roll (2009), who adapted it for use in an IPL (Invention as Preparation for Learning (Schwartz and Martin, 2004)) tutoring environment. Our motivational survey is shown in Figure 1.

Questions one and two address "self-regulation," particularly the students' tendency to manage and control their own effort. Question one is on a reversed scale relative to the other questions, so responses to it were inverted. Question three addresses "self-efficacy," the students' expectation of success on the task. Questions four and five address "intrinsic value," the students' beliefs about the importance and interest of the task.

These dimensions of motivation are theoretically

Please read the following statements and then click a number on the scale that best matches how true it is of you. 1 means "not at all true of me" whereas 7 means "very true of me".

1. I think that when the tutor is talking I will be thinking of other things and won't really listen to what is being said.
2. If I could take as much time as I want, I would spend a lot of time on physics tutoring sessions.
3. I think I am going to find the physics tutor activities difficult.
4. I think I will be able to use what I learn in the physics tutor sessions in my other classes.
5. I think that what I will learn in the physics tutor sessions is useful for me to know.

Figure 1: Pre-tutoring Motivational Survey

distinct. However, except for question three (the self-efficacy question), responses to these questions were all very significantly correlated with each other in our survey ($p < .01$).

Table 2 shows values of Cronbach's Alpha (Cronbach, 1951) for various subsets of the motivation questions. Alpha measures the internal consistency of responses to a multi-point questionnaire, and is a function of the number of test items and the correlation between them. Higher values are thought to indicate that the various test items are measuring the same underlying latent construct. For this study we omit Question 3, maximizing Alpha at .716. This is just above the commonly accepted (Gliem and Gliem, 2003) threshold for reliability in such an instrument.

As mentioned above, this instrument was administered both before and (with suitable tense changes) immediately after tutoring. We will report correlations using mean scores on the pre- and post-tutoring measures, as well as for the *change*-in-motivation score, calculated as post-minus-pre.

Questions	Alpha
1, 2, 3, 4, 5	0.531
1, 2, 4, 5	0.716
2, 4, 5	0.703
4, 5	0.683

Table 2: Alpha reliability scores for various subsets of questions.

4 Semantic Cohesion Measure

In this work we measure cohesion between tutor and student using the "semantic cohesion" measure first reported by Ward and Litman (2008). This measure counts the number of "cohesive ties" (Halliday and Hasan, 1976) between adjacent tutor and student dialog turns. A cohesive tie can be the repetition of an exact word or word stem, or the use of two words with similar meanings in adjacent turns. Stop words are excluded, and cohesive ties are counted in both the student-to-tutor and the tutor-to-student directions. For example, in the dialog shown in Table 1, the final tutor turn repeats the word "velocity" from the previous student turn. This repetition would be counted as an *exact* cohesive tie. Similarly, the tutor uses the word "changes" following the student's use of "change." This would be counted as a stem repetition cohesive tie.

Finally, the student's use of "velocity" will be counted as a cohesive tie because of its semantic similarity to "acceleration," from the preceding turn. The algorithm therefore counts four ties in Table 1. As described more completely in (Ward and Litman, 2008), semantic similarity cohesive ties are counted by measuring two words' proximity in the WordNet (Miller et al., 1990) hierarchy. We use a simple path distance similarity measure, as implemented in NLTK (Loper and Bird, 2002). This measure counts the number of edges N in the shortest path between two words in WordNet, and calculates similarity as $1 / (1 + N)$. Our implementation of this semantic similarity measure allows setting a threshold θ, such that only word pairs with stronger-than-threshold similarity are counted. Table 3 shows some semantic similarity pairs counted with a threshold of 0.3.

We obtain a normalized cohesion score for each dialog by dividing the tie count by the number of turns in the dialog. We then sum the line normalized counts over all the dialogs for each student, resulting in a per-student cohesion measure.

motion-contact
man-person
decrease-acceleration
acceleration-change
travel-flying

Table 3: Example Semantic ties: $\theta = 0.3$

5 Results

We ran correlations between the change-in-motivation score described in Section 3 and the semantic similarity measure of cohesion described in Section 4. We report results for a semantic similarity threshold of .3 for consistency with (Ward and Litman, 2008), however the pattern of results is not sensitive to this threshold. Significant results were obtained for all thresholds between .2 and .5, in .1 increments. [2] In addition, we report results for the motivation measure with the third question removed for consistency with (Ward and Litman, 2011). However the pattern of results is not sensitive to this exclusion, either. Significant results were also obtained using the entire questionnaire.

In all cases, the change in motivation was found to be significantly and positively correlated with the cohesiveness of the tutoring dialog. More lexical similarity between tutor and student was predictive of increased student motivation. As shown in the middle row of Table 4, the correlation with motivational change, using a threshold of .3 and the reduced motivation measure was r(97)= .21, p = 0.03.

Motivation Measure	Cor.	pValue
pre-Tutoring	0.02	0.86
Change	0.21	**0.03**
post-Tutoring	0.19	0.055

Table 4: Cohesion - Motivation Correlations. N = 99. $\theta = 0.3$

Interestingly, as shown in the top and bottom rows of Table 4, neither motivation before tutoring r(97) = .02, p=.86, nor after tutoring r(97) = .19, p = .055, was significantly correlated with cohesion, although the post-tutoring measure achieves a strong trend.

Pre- and post-tutoring mean motivation levels were, however, significantly correlated with each other (R(97) = .69, $p < .0001$). Mean motivation levels also showed a non-significant improvement from 4.31 before tutoring to 4.44 after tutoring.

6 Discussion and Future Work

We have brought forward evidence that cohesion in tutorial dialog, as measured in this paper, is correlated with changes in student motivation. This suggests that dialog cohesion may be useful as a non-intrusive measure of motivational fluctuations.

As discussed in Section 1, other researchers have investigated various types of cohesion, and their relationship to things such as task success and learning. In addition, work has been done investigating the role of motivation in learning. However, we believe ours is the first work relating dialog cohesion directly to user motivation.

The presence of a correlation between cohesion and motivation leaves open the possibility that more motivated students are experiencing greater task success in the tutor, and so generating more cohesive dialogs. [3] Note, however, that the very non-significant correlation between *pre*-dialog motivation and dialog cohesion argues against this possibility. Instead, it seems that some process is both creating dialog cohesion and *improving* student motivation. The lack of significance in the post-dialog/motivation correlation may be due to data sparsity.

In future work, we hope to investigate other dialog features which may be even better predictors of student motivation. As mentioned in Section 1, we became interested in dialog similarity metrics partly because of their association with task success. These kinds of associations between task success and dialog have also been shown for dialog *entrainment*.

In this discussion we will use the term "entrainment" for the phenomenon in which conversational partners' speech features become more similar to each other at many levels, including word choice, over the course of a dialog. [4] As mentioned above, we use the term "cohesion" for *overall* similarity of word choice between speakers in a dialog, perhaps resulting from entrainment.

Users appear to entrain strongly with dialog systems. For example, Brennan (1996) has found that users are likely to adopt the terms used by a WOZ dialog system, and that this tendency is at least as strong as with human dialog partners. Similarly, Parent and Eskenazi (2010) showed that users of the Let's Go (Raux et al., 2005) spoken dialog system quickly entrain to its lexical choices.

[2] Note from the path distance formula that thresholds between .5 and 1 are impossible

[3] We thank an anonymous reviewer for prompting this discussion.

[4] This definition conflates studies of priming, alignment, convergence and accommodation.

As with measures of dialog similarity, dialog entrainment has been found to be related to satisfaction and success in task oriented dialogs. For example, Reitter and Moore (2007) found that lexical and syntactic repetition predicted task success in the MapTask corpus. Similarly, Ward and Litman (2007) found that lexical and acoustic-prosodic entrainment are correlated with task success in the Itspoke dialog system. Interestingly, in that work entrainment was more strongly correlated with task success than a measure of dialog cohesion similar to the one used in the current paper. This raises the question of whether such a measure of dialog entrainment might also be a better predictor of motivation than the current measure of cohesion. We hope in future work to further investigate this possibility.

Finally, because we are interested in predicting motivation during tutoring, our dialog metrics may be improved by making them sensitive to the educational domain. For example, exploratory work with our tutor has suggested that a measure of cohesion which only counts cohesive ties between physics terms is better correlated with certain measures of learning than a measure which counts non-physics terms. This suggests that measures of cohesion or entrainment which recognize educational domain words may also improve correlations with motivation.

Acknowledgments

This work was supported by the ONR (N00014-07-1-0039), by the NSF (0631930 and 0914615), and by the LRDC and ISP at the University of Pittsburgh.

References

Susan E. Brennan. 1996. Lexical entrainment in spontaneous dialog. In *International Symposium on Spoken Dialog*, pages 41–44.

Jonathan Brown and Maxine Eskenazi. 2004. Retrieval of authentic documents for reader-specific lexical practice. In *In Proceedings of InSTIL/ICALL Symposium.*

David Buller and R.Kelly Aune. 1992. The effects of speech rate similarity on compliance: Application of communication accommodation theory. *Western Journal of Communication*, 56:37–53.

Lee Cronbach. 1951. Coefficient alpha and the internal structure of tests. *Psychometrika*, 16(3):297–334.

Kevin DelaRosa and Maxine Eskenazi. 2011. Self-assessment of motivation: Explicit and implicit indicators of l2 vocabulary learning. *Proceedings 15th International Conference on Artificial Intelligence Education (AIED).*

Leonard Feldt. 1961. The use of extreme groups to test for the presence of a relationship. *Psychometrika*, 26(3):307–316.

Joesph Gliem and Rosemary Gliem. 2003. Calculating, interpreting, and reporting cronbach's alpha reliability coefficient for likert-type scales. *Midwest Research to Practice in Adult, Continuing and Community Education.*

M. A. K. Halliday and Ruqaiya Hasan. 1976. *Cohesion in English.* English Language Series. Pearson Education Limited.

Michael Heilman, Kevyn Collins-Thompson, Jamie Callan, Maxine Eskenazi, Alan Juffs, and Lois Wilson. 2010. Personalization of reading passages improves vocabulary acquisition. *International Journal of Artificial Intelligence in Education*, 20:73–98, January.

Pamela Jordan, Brian Hall, Michael Ringenberg, Yui Cui, and Carolyn Rosé. 2007. Tools for authoring a dialogue agent that participates in learning studies. In *Proc. of Artificial Intelligence in Ed., AIED*, pages 43–50.

D. Litman and S. Silliman. 2004. ITSPOKE: An intelligent tutoring spoken dialogue system. In *Companion Proc. of the Human Language Technology Conf: 4th Meeting of the North American Chap. of the Assoc. for Computational Linguistics.*

Edward Loper and Steven Bird. 2002. Nltk: The natural language toolkit. In *In Proceedings of the ACL Workshop on Effective Tools and Methodologies for Teaching Natural Language Processing and Computational Linguistics. Philadelphia: Association for Computational Linguistics.*

Philip M. Mccarthy, Gwyneth A. Lewis, David F. Dufty, and Danielle S. Mcnamara. 2006. Analyzing writing styles with coh-metrix. In *In Proceedings of the Florida Artificial Intelligence Research Society International Conference (FLAIRS.*

M.C. McKenna and D.J. Kear. 1990. Measuring attitude toward reading: A new tool for teachers. *The Reading Teacher*, 43(8):626–639.

George A. Miller, Richard Beckwith, Christiane Fellbaum, Derek Gross, and Katherine J. Miller. 1990. Introduction to WordNet: An on-line lexical database. *International Journal of Lexicography (special issue)*, 3 (4):235–312.

Andrew Olney and Zhiqiang Cai. 2005. An orthonormal basis for topic segmentation in tutorial dialog. In *Pro-*

ceedings of the Human Language Technology Conference and Conference on Empirical Methods in Natural Language Processing (HLT/EMNLP), pages 971–978. Vancouver, October.

Gabriel Parent and Maxine Eskenazi. 2010. Lexical entrainment of real users in the let's go spoken dialog system. In *Proceedings Interspeech-2010*, pages 3018 – 3021, Makuhari, Chiba, Japan.

Paul Pintrich and Elisabeth DeGroot. 1990. Motivational and self-regulated learning components of classroom academic performance. *Journal of Educational Psychology*, 82(1):33–40.

Emily Pitler and Ani Nenkova. 2008. Revisiting readability: A unified framework for predicting text quality. In *Proceedings of Empirical Methods in Natural Language Processing (EMNLP)*, pages 186 – 195.

Antoine Raux, Brian Langner, Dan Bohus, Alan W Black, and Maxine Eskenazi. 2005. Lets go public! taking a spoken dialog system to the real world. In *Proceedings Interspeech-2005*, pages 885 – 888, Lisbon, Portugal.

David Reitter and Johanna D. Moore. 2007. Predicting success in dialogue. In *In Proceedings of the 45th Annual Meeting of the Association of Computational Linguistics (ACL)*, pages 808 – 815, Prague, Czech Republic.

Ido Roll. 2009. *Structured Invention Tasks to Prepare Students for Future Learning: Means, Mechanisms, and Cognitive Processes.* Doctor of philosophy, Carnegie Mellon University, 5000 Forbes Ave. Pittsburgh, Pa.

Daniel Schwartz and Taylor Martin. 2004. Inventing to prepare for future learning: The hidden efficiency of encouraging original student production in statistics instruction. *Cognition and Instruction*, 22:129 – 184.

K. VanLehn, P. Jordan, C. Rose, D. Bhembe, M. Boettner, A. Gaydos, M. Makatchev, U. Pappuswamy, M. Ringenberg, A. Roque, S. Siler, and Srivastava R. 2002. The architecture of why2-atlas: A coach for qualitative physics essay writing. In *Proc. 6th Int. Conf. on Intelligent Tutoring Systems*, pages 158–167.

Arthur Ward and Diane Litman. 2006. Cohesion and learning in a tutorial spoken dialog system. In *Proceedings of the 19th International FLAIRS Conference (FLAIRS-19)*, pages 533–538, May.

Arthur Ward and Diane Litman. 2007. Dialog convergence and learning. In *Proceedings 13th International Conference on Artificial Intelligence Education (AIED)*, Los Angeles, Ca.

Arthur Ward and Diane Litman. 2008. Semantic cohesion and learning. In *Proceedings 9th International Conference on Intelligent Tutoring Systems (ITS)*, pages 459–469, Ann Arbor, June.

Arthur Ward and Diane Litman. 2011. Adding abstractive reflection to a tutorial dialog system. *Proceedings 24th International FLAIRS (Florida Artificial Intelligence Research Society) Conference.*

Arthur Ward. 2010. *Reflection and Learning Robustness in a Natural Language Conceptual Physics Tutoring System.* Doctor of philosophy, University of Pittsburgh, Pittsburgh, PA. 15260.

Using Semantic Distance to Automatically Suggest Transfer Course Equivalencies

Beibei Yang
University of Massachusetts Lowell
One University Avenue
Lowell, MA 01854
byang1@cs.uml.edu

Jesse M. Heines
University of Massachusetts Lowell
One University Avenue
Lowell, MA 01854
heines@cs.uml.edu

Abstract

Semantic distance is the degree of closeness between two pieces of text determined by their meaning. Semantic distance is typically measured by analyzing a set of documents or a list of terms and assigning a metric based on the likeness of their meaning or the concept they represent. Although related research provides some semantic-based algorithms, few applications exist. This work proposes a semantic-based approach for automatically identifying potential course equivalencies given their catalog descriptions. The method developed by Li et al. (2006) is extended in this paper to take a course description from one university as the input and suggest equivalent courses offered at another university. Results are evaluated and future work is discussed.

1 Introduction

Hundreds of students transfer to University of Massachusetts Lowell (UML) each year. As part of that process, courses taken at students' previous educational institutions must be evaluated by UML for transfer credit. Course descriptions are usually short paragraphs of less than 200 words. To determine whether an incoming course can be transferred, the undergraduate and graduate transfer coordinators from each department must manually compare its course description to the courses offered at UML. This process can be tedious and time-consuming. Although the publicly available *course transfer dictionary* (Figure 1) for students transferring to UML lists equivalent courses from hundreds of institutions, it is not always up to date and the data set is sparse and non-uniformed.

This work proposes an approach to automatically identify course equivalencies by analyzing the course descriptions and comparing their semantic distance. The course descriptions are first pruned and unrelated contexts are removed. Given a course from another university, the algorithm measures word, sentence, and paragraph similarities to suggest a list of potentially equivalent courses offered by UML. This work has two goals: (1) to efficiently and accurately suggest equivalent courses to reduce the workload of transfer coordinators, and (2) to explore new applications using semantic distance to move toward the Semantic Web, i.e., to turn existing resources into knowledge structures.

Ext. Course Title	Ext. Course #	UML Course #	UML Course Title
Cultural Anthropology	ANT 101	48.102	Social Anthropology
Art Appreciation	ART 101	58.101	Art Appreciation
Art History I	ART 105	58.203	History Of Art:Preh-Med
Art History II	ART 106	58.204	Hist Of Art II:Ren - Mod
Asian Art	ART 108	58.205	Studies In World Art
Color And Design	ART 113	70.101	Art Concepts I (studio)
Intro To Sculpture&3-D Design	ART 115	70.299	Studio Art 200 electives
Printmaking	ART 117	70.267	Printmaking
Drawing I	ART 121	70.255	Drawing I

Figure 1. A subset of the transfer dictionary for students transferred from an external institution to UML.

Proceedings of the Sixth Workshop on Innovative Use of NLP for Building Educational Applications, pages 142–151,
Portland, Oregon, 24 June 2011. ©2011 Association for Computational Linguistics

2 Related Research

Semantic distance measures have been used in applications such as automatic annotation, keyword extraction, and social network extraction (Matsuo et al., 2007). It is important to note that there are two kinds of semantic distance: *semantic similarity* and *semantic relatedness*. Semantic relatedness is more generic than semantic similarity in that it includes all classical and non-classical semantic relations such as holonymy[1], meronymy[2], and antonymy[3], where semantic similarity is limited to relations such as hyponymy[4] and hypernymy[5] (Budanitsky and Hirst, 2006). The terms semantic distance, semantic relatedness, and semantic similarity are sometimes used interchangeably by different authors in the literature related to this topic. The relative generality of the three terms is illustrated in Figure 2.

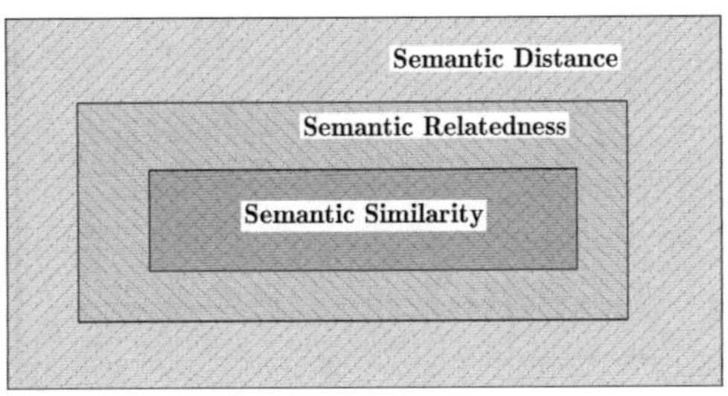

Figure 2. The relations of semantic distance, semantic relatedness, and semantic similarity as described by Budanitsky and Hirst (2006).

Related work in semantic distance measurement can be roughly divided into three categories: (1) lexicographic resource based methods, (2) corpus based methods, and (3) hybrid methods.

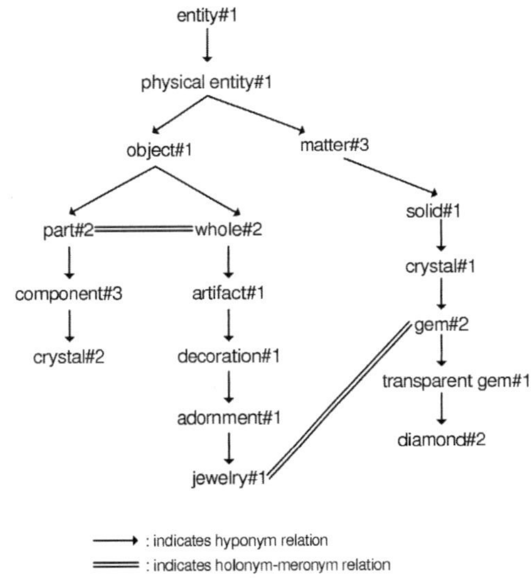

Figure 3. A fragment of WordNet's taxonomy.

Lexicographic resource based methods typically calculate semantic distance based on WordNet[6]. In related work (Rada et al., 1989; Wu and Palmer, 1994; Leacock and Chodorow, 1998; Hirst and St-Onge, 1998; Yang and Powers, 2005), lexicographic resource based methods use one or more edge-counting (also known as shortest-path) techniques in the WordNet taxonomy (Figure 3). In this technique, concept nodes are constructed in a hierarchical network and the minimum number of hops between any two nodes represents their semantic distance (Collins and Quillian, 1969). The measure by Hirst and St-Onge (1998) is based on the fact that the target concepts are likely more distant if the target path consists of edges that belong to many different relations. The approach by Leacock and Chodorow (1998) combines the shortest path with maximum depth so that edges lower down in the is-a hierarchy correspond to smaller semantic distances than the ones higher up. Yang and Powers (2005) further suggest that it is necessary to consider relations such as holonymy and meronymy.

A corpus-based method typically calculates co-occurrence on one or more corpora to deduce semantic closeness (Sahami and Heilman, 2006; Cilibrasi and Vitanyi, 2007; Islam and Inkpen, 2006; Mihalcea et al., 2006). Using this technique, two words

[1] A *holonym* is a word that names the whole of which a given word is a part. For example, "hat" is a holonymy for "brim" and "crown."

[2] A *meronym* is a word that names a part of a larger whole. For example, "brim" and "crown" are meronyms of "hat."

[3] A *antonym* is a word that expresses a meaning opposed to the meaning of another word. For example, "big" is an antonym of "small."

[4] A *hyponym* is a word that is more specific than a given word. For example, "nickel" is a hyponym of "coin."

[5] A *hypernym* is a word that is more generic than a given word. For example, "coin" is a hypernym of "nickel."

[6] http://wordnet.princeton.edu/

are likely to have a short semantic distance if they co-occur within similar contexts (Lin, 1998).

Hybrid methods (including distributional measures) combine lexicographic resources with corpus statistics (Jiang and Conrath, 1997; Mohammad and Hirst, 2006; Li et al., 2003; Li et al., 2006). Related work shows that hybrid methods generally outperform lexicographic resource based and corpus based methods (Budanitsky and Hirst, 2006; Curran, 2004; Mohammad and Hirst, 2006; Mohammad, 2008).

Li et al. (2006) proposed a hybrid method based on WordNet and the Brown corpus to incorporate semantic similarity between words, semantic similarity between sentences, and word order similarity to measure overall sentence similarity. The semantic similarity between words is derived from WordNet based on path lengths and depths of lowest common hypernyms. The semantic similarity between two sentences is defined as the cosine coefficient of two vectors that are derived from building two semantic vectors and collecting the information content for each term from the Brown corpus. The word order similarity is then determined by the normalized difference in word order of each sentence. Finally, the overall sentence similarity is defined as the weighted sum of the semantic similarity between sentences and the word order similarity.

3 Proposed Method

This work proposes a variant of the hybrid method by Li et al. (2006) to identify course equivalencies by measuring the semantic distance between course descriptions. Our approach has three modules: (1) semantic distance between words, (2) semantic distance between sentences, and (3) semantic distance between paragraphs. Their word order similarity and overall sentence similarity modules are found to *decrease* the accuracy (See Section 4). Therefore, these methods are not used in our approach. This work modifies the semantic similarity between words and the semantic similarity between sentences modules developed by Li et al. (2006) and adds semantic distance between paragraphs tailored to the domain of identifying equivalent courses. Experiments show that these modifications maximized accuracy.

3.1 Semantic Distance Between Words

Given a concept c_1 of word w_1, and a concept c_2 of word w_2, the semantic distance between the two words (SDBW) is a function of the path length between the two concepts and the depth of their lowest common hypernym.

The path length p from c_1 to c_2 is determined by one of five cases. This work adds holonymy and meronymy relations to the method by Li et al. (2006) to measure the semantic relatedness:

1. c_1 and c_2 are in the same synonym set (synset).
2. c_1 and c_2 are not in the same synset, but the synset of c_1 and the synset of c_2 contain one or more common words.
3. c_1 is either a holonym or a meronym of c_2.
4. c_1 is neither a holonym nor a meronym of c_2, but the synset of c_1 contains one or more words that are either holonyms or meronyms of one or more words in the synset that c_2 belongs to.
5. c_1 and c_2 do not satisfy any of the previous four cases.

If c_1 and c_2 belong to case 1, p is 0. If c_1 and c_2 belong to cases 2, 3, or 4, p is 1. In case 5, p is the number of links between the two words. Therefore, the semantic distance of c_1 and c_2 is an exponential decaying function of p, where α is a constant (Li et al., 2006):

$$f_1(p) = e^{\alpha p} \quad (\alpha \in [-1, 0]). \tag{1}$$

Let h be the depth of the lowest common hypernym of c_1 and c_2 in the WordNet hierarchy. f_2 is a monotonically increasing function of h (Li et al., 2006):

$$f_2(h) = \frac{e^{\beta h} - e^{-\beta h}}{e^{\beta h} + e^{-\beta h}} \quad (\beta \in [0, 1]). \tag{2}$$

The values of α and β are given in Section 4.

The semantic distance between concepts c_1 and c_2 is defined as:

$$f_{word}(c_1, c_2) = f_1(p) \cdot f_2(h), \tag{3}$$

where f_1 and f_2 are given by Equations 1 and 2. The values of both f_1 and f_2 are between 0 and 1 (Li et al., 2006).

WordNet is based on concepts, not words. Words with different meanings are considered different "words" and are marked with sense tags (Budanitsky and Hirst, 2006). Unfortunately, common corpora (as well as course descriptions) are not sense-tagged. Therefore, a mapping between a word and a certain sense must be provided. Such mapping is called word sense disambiguation (WSD), which is the ability to identify the meaning of words in context in a computational manner (Navigli, 2009). We consider two strategies to perform the WSD: (1) compare all senses of two words and select the maximum score, and (2) apply the first sense heuristic (McCarthy et al., 2004). We will show that the overall performance of the two strategies is about the same.

To improve accuracy, the *parts of speech*[7] (POS) of two words have to be the same before visiting the WordNet taxonomy to determine their semantic distance. Therefore, "book" as in "read a book" and "book" as in "book a ticket" are considered different. We do not distinguish the plural forms of POS from singular forms. Therefore, POS such as "NN" (the singular form of a noun) and "NNS"(the plural form of a noun) are considered the same.

The SDBW module also considers the *stemmed* forms of words. Without considering stemmed words, two equivalent course titles such as "networking" and "data communication" are misclassified as semantically distant because "networking" in WordNet is solely defined as socializing with people, not as a computer network. The stemmed word "network" is semantically closer to "data communication."

Algorithm 1 shows how to determine the semantic distance between two words w_1 and w_2.

The SDBW module uses WordNet as a lexical knowledge base to determine the semantic closeness between words. The path lengths and depths in the WordNet IS-A hierarchy may be used to measure how strongly a word contributes to the meaning of a sentence. However, this approach has a problem. Because WordNet is a manually created lexical resource, it does not cover all the words that appear in a sentence, even though some of these words are commonly seen in literature. Words not defined in WordNet are misclassified as semantically distant when compared with any other words. This is a huge problem for identifying equivalent courses. For example, course names "propositional logic" and "logic" are differentiated solely by the word "propositional," which is not defined in WordNet[8]. The semantic distance measurement between *sentences* therefore cannot be simplified to all pairwise comparisons of words using WordNet. A corpus must be introduced to assess the semantic relatedness of words in sentences.

Algorithm 1 Semantic Distance Between Words

1: If two words w_1 and w_2 have different POS, consider them semantically distant. Return 0.
2: If w_1 and w_2 have the same POS and look the same but do not exist in WordNet, consider them semantically close. Return 1.
3: Using either maximum scores or the first sense heuristic to perform WSD, measure the semantic distance between w_1 and w_2 using Equation 3.
4: Using the same WSD strategy as the previous step, measure the semantic distance between the stemmed w_1 and the stemmed w_2 using Equation 3.
5: Return the larger of the two results in steps (3) and (4), i.e., the score of the pair that is semantically closer.

3.2 Semantic Distance Between Sentences

To measure the semantic distance between sentences, Li et al. (2006) join two sentences S_1 and S_2 into a unique word set S, with a length of n:

$$S = S_1 \cup S_2 = \{w_1, w_2, \dots w_n\}. \quad (4)$$

A semantic vector SV_1 is computed for sentence S_1 and another semantic vector SV_2 for sentence S_2. Given the number of words in S_1 as t, Li et al. (2006) define the value of an entry of SV_1 for sentence S_1 as:

$$SV_{1i} = \hat{s_{1i}} \cdot I(w_i) \cdot I(w_{1j}), \quad (5)$$

where $i \in [1, n]$, $j \in [1, t]$, $\hat{s_{1i}}$ is an entry of the lexical semantic vector $\hat{s_1}$ derived from S_1, w_i is a word in S, and w_{1j} is semantically the closest to w_i

[7] We use the part-of-speech tags from the Penn Treebank project: http://www.ling.upenn.edu/courses/Fall_2003/ling001/penn_treebank_pos.html.

[8] WordNet 3.0 is used in our implementation and experiments.

in S_1. $I(w_i)$ is the information content (IC) of w_i in the Brown corpus and $I(w_{1j})$ is the IC of w_{1j} in the same corpus.

Our work redefines the semantic vector as:

$$SV_{1i} = \hat{s_{1i}} \cdot (TFIDF(w_i)+\epsilon) \cdot (TFIDF(w_{1j})+\epsilon). \quad (6)$$

There are two major modifications in our version. First, we replace the information content with the Term Frequency–Inverse Document Frequency (TFIDF) weighting scheme, which is a bag-of-words model (Joachims, 1997). In the TFIDF formula, each term i in document D is assigned weight m_i:

$$m_i = tf_i \cdot idf_i = tf_i \cdot \log \frac{N}{df_i}, \quad (7)$$

where tf_i is the frequency of term i in D, idf_i is the inverse document frequency of term i, N is the total number of documents, and df_i is the number of documents that contain i (Salton and Buckley, 1987). Our approach uses a smoothing factor ϵ to add a small mass[9] to the TFIDF.

Second, we compute TFIDF over our custom course description corpus instead of the Brown corpus. The course description corpus is built from crawling the course catalogs from two universities' websites. These two modifications find inner relations of words from the course description data domain, rather than from the various domains provided by the Brown corpus.

The semantic distance of S_1 and S_2 is the cosine coefficient of their semantic vectors SV_1 and SV_2 (Li et al., 2006):

$$f_{sent}(S_1, S_2) = \frac{SV_1 \cdot SV_2}{||SV_1|| \cdot ||SV_2||}. \quad (8)$$

Although Li et al. (2006) do not remove *stop words*[10], it is found that the removal of stop words remarkably improves accuracy to identify equivalent courses. (See Section 4.)

While building and deriving the lexical semantic vectors $\hat{s_1}$ for sentence S_1 and $\hat{s_2}$ for sentence S_2, it is found that some words from the joint word list S (Equation 4) which are not stop words, but are very generic, in turn rank as semantically the closest words to most other words. These generic words cannot be simply regarded as domain-specific stop words in that a generic word in a pair of courses may not be generic in another pair. To discourage these generic words, we introduce a *ticketing algorithm* as part of the process to build a lexical semantic vector. Algorithm 2 shows the steps to build the lexical semantic vector[11] $\hat{s_1}$ for sentence S_1. Similarly, we follow these steps to build $\hat{s_2}$ for S_2.

Algorithm 2 Lexical Semantic Vector $\hat{s_1}$ for S_1

1: **for all** words $w_i \in S$ **do**
2: if $w_i \in S_1$, set $\hat{s_{1i}} = 1$ where $\hat{s_{1i}} \in \hat{s_1}$.
3: if $w_i \notin S_1$, the semantic distance between w_i and each word $w_{1j} \in S_1$ is calculated (Section 3.1). Set $\hat{s_{1i}}$ to the highest score if the score exceeds a preset threshold δ ($\delta \in [0, 1]$), otherwise $\hat{s_{1i}} = 0$.
4: Let $\gamma \in [1, n]$ be the maximum number of times a word $w_{1j} \in S_1$ is chosen as semantically the closest word of w_i. Let the semantic distance of w_i and w_{1j} be d, and f_{1j} be the number of times that w_{1j} is chosen. If $f_{1j} > \gamma$, set $\hat{s_{1i}} = d/\gamma$ to give a penalty to w_{1j}. This step is called *ticketing*.
5: **end for**

3.3 Semantic Distance Between Paragraphs

Although Li et al. (2006) claim that their approach is for measuring the semantic similarity of sentences and short texts, test cases show that the accuracy of their approach is not satisfactory on course descriptions. We introduce the semantic distance measure between paragraphs to address this problem.

Given course descriptions P_1 and P_2, the first step is to remove generic data and prerequisite information. Let P_1 be a paragraph consisting of a set of n sentences, and P_2 be a paragraph of m sentences, where n and m are positive integers. For s_{1i} ($s_{1i} \in P_1, i \in [1, n]$) and s_{2j} ($s_{2j} \in P_2, j \in [1, m]$), the semantic distance between paragraphs P_1 and P_2 is defined as a weighted mean:

[9] In our experiments, ϵ=0.01.

[10] Stop words (such as "the", "a", and "of") are words that appear in almost every document, and have no discrimination value for contexts of documents. Porter et al.'s English stop words list (http://snowball.tartarus.org/algorithms/english/stop.txt) are adapted in this work.

[11] In our experiments, we chose δ=0.2.

$$f_{para}(P_1, P_2) = \frac{\sum_{i=1}^{n} (\max_{j=1}^{m} f_{sent}(s_{1i}, s_{2j})) \cdot N_i}{\sum_{i=1}^{n} N_i}, \quad (9)$$

where N_i is the sum of the number of words in sentences s_{1i} ($s_{1i} \in P_1$) and s_{2j} ($s_{2j} \in P_2$), and $f_{sent}(s_{1i}, s_{2j})$ is the semantic distance between sentences s_{1i} and s_{2j} (Section 3.2). Algorithm 3 summarizes these steps. Optionally the *deletion* flag can be enabled to speed up the computation. Empirical results show that accuracy is about the same whether or not the *deletion* flag is enabled.

Algorithm 3 Semantic Distance for Paragraphs

1: If *deletion* is enabled, given two course descriptions, select the one with fewer sentences as P_1, and the other as P_2. If *deletion* is disabled, select the first course description as P_1, and the other as P_2.
2: **for** each sentence $s_{1i} \in P_1$ **do**
3: Calculate the semantic distance between sentences (Section 3.2) for s_{1i} and each of the sentences in P_2.
4: Find the sentence pair $\langle s_{1i}, s_{2j} \rangle$ ($s_{2j} \in P_2$) that scores the highest. Save the highest score and the total number of words of s_{1i} and s_{2j}. If *deletion* is enabled, remove sentence s_{2j} from P_2.
5: **end for**
6: Collect the highest score and the number of words from each run. Use their weighted mean (Equation 9) as the semantic distance between P_1 and P_2.

We introduce θ to denote how much we weigh course titles over course descriptions. Course titles are compared using the semantic distance measurement discussed in Section 3.2. Given title T_1 and description P_1 of course C_1, and title T_2 and description P_2 of course C_2, the semantic distance of the two courses is defined as:

$$f_{course}(C_1, C_2) = \theta \cdot f_{sent}(T_1, T_2) + (1 - \theta) \cdot f_{para}(P_1, P_2). \quad (10)$$

4 Implementation and Experimental Results

The method proposed in this paper is fully implemented using Python and NLTK (Bird et al., 2009). The WordNet interface built into NLTK is used to retrieve lexical information for word similarities. In our experiments, the default parameters are: $\alpha = -0.2$, $\beta = 0.45$ (Li et al., 2006), $\gamma = 2$, and $\theta = 0.7$. The γ and θ values are found empirically to perform well.

A course description corpus must be built for the experiments. The UMass Lowell (UML) course transfer dictionary lists courses that are equivalent to those from hundreds of other institutions (see Figure 1, shown in Section 1). We only used the transfer dictionary as a test corpus rather than a training corpus to keep the algorithm simple and efficient. Middlesex Community College (MCC) is picked as an external institution in our experiments. The transfer dictionary lists over 1,400 MCC courses in different majors. We remove the rejected courses, elective courses, and those with missing fields from the transfer dictionary. Referring to the equivalencies from the transfer dictionary, we crawl over 1,500 web pages from the course catalogs of both UML and MCC to retrieve over 200 interconnected courses that contain both course names and descriptions. Two XML files are created, one for UML and one for MCC courses. Given an MCC course, the goal is to suggest the most similar UML course. A fragment of the MCC XML file is shown below. Each course entry has features such as course ID, course name, credits, description, and the ID of its equivalent course at UML. The UML XML file has the same layout except that the *equivalence* tag is removed and the root tag is *uml*.


```
<mcc>
  <course>
    <courseid>ART 113</courseid>
    <coursename>Color and Design</coursename>
    <credits>3</credits>
    <description>Basic concepts of composition
    and color theory. Stresses the process and
    conceptual development of ideas in two
    dimensions and the development of a strong
    sensitivity to color.</description>
    <equivalence>70.101</equivalence>
  </course>
  ...
</mcc>
```

After the integrity check, the MCC XML file contains 108 courses and the UML XML file contains 89 courses. The reason there are more MCC courses than UML courses is that the transfer dictionary allows multiple courses from MCC to be transferred to the same UML course.

To monitor the accuracy change over different numbers of documents, we randomly select equivalent courses to create two smaller data sets for UML and MCC respectively in the XML format. The random number of courses in each XML file is shown in Table 1. These three pairs of XML data sets are used both as the corpora and as the test data sets.

XML Datasets	MCC Courses	UML Courses	Total
Small	25	24	49
Medium	55	50	105
Large	108	89	197

Table 1. Number of courses in the data sets

Consider the small data set as an illustration. Each of the 25 MCC courses is compared with all 24 UML courses. All words are converted to lowercase and punctuation is removed. We also remove both *general stop words*[12] (such as "a" and "of") and *domain-specific stop words*[13] (such as "courses," "students," and "reading"). We do not remove words based on high or low occurrence because that is found empirically to *decrease* accuracy. Using the algorithms discussed in Section 3, a score is computed for each comparison. After comparing an MCC course to all UML courses, the 24 UML courses are sorted by score in descending order. The course equivalencies indicated by the transfer dictionary are used as the benchmark. In each run we mark the rank of the real UML course that is equivalent to the given MCC course as indicated by the transfer dictionary. We consider the result of each run correct when the equivalent course indicated by the transfer dictionary is in the top 3 of the sorted list. After doing this for all the 25 MCC courses, we calculate the overall accuracy and the average ranks of the real equivalent courses.

Empirical results show that accuracy drops when some inseparable phrases naming *atomic keywords* (such as "local area networks," "data communications," and "I/O") are tokenized. To address this problem, a list of 40 atomic keywords is constructed manually.

Our approach is compared against two baselines: TFIDF only (Equation 7), and the method by Li et al. (2006). Since the method by Li et al. (2006) does not measure semantic distance between paragraphs, we consider each course description as a sentence. Figure 4 shows that the accuracy of our approach outperforms the TFIDF and Li et al. (2006) approaches over the three sets of documents from Table 1. It is interesting to note that while the accuracies of the TFIDF and Li et al. (2006) approaches *decrease* as the number of documents increases, the accuracy of our approach *increases* when the number of documents increases from 105 to 195. This observation is counter-intuitive and therefore requires further analysis in future work.

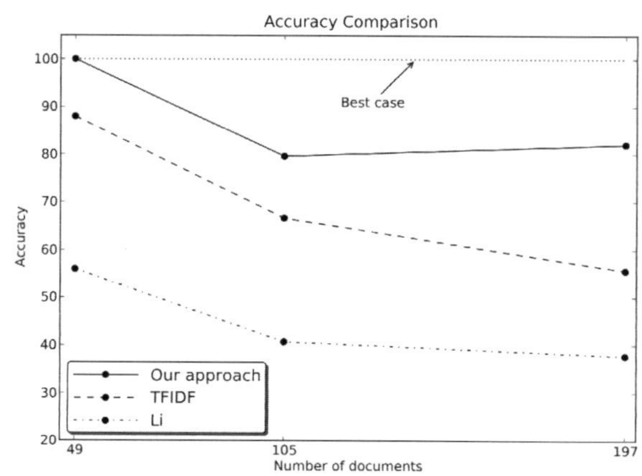

Figure 4. Accuracy of our approach compared to the TFIDF and Li et al. (2006) approaches.

For each of the three different approaches, we note the average ranks of the real equivalent courses indicated by the transfer dictionary. Figure 5 shows that our approach outperforms the TFIDF and Li et al. (2006) approaches. It also shows that the average rank in our approach does not increase as fast as the other two.

The word order similarity module in the Li et al. (2006) approach tokenizes two sentences into a list of unique words. Each of the two sentences is converted into a numbered list where each entry in the list is the index of the corresponding word in the joint set. The word order similarity between these

[12]A list of English stop words in NLTK is used in our experiments.

[13]A list of domain-specific stop words is created manually.

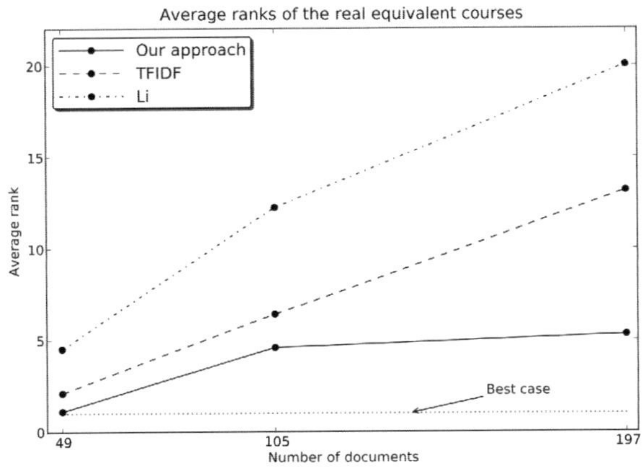

Figure 5. Average ranks of the real equivalent courses.

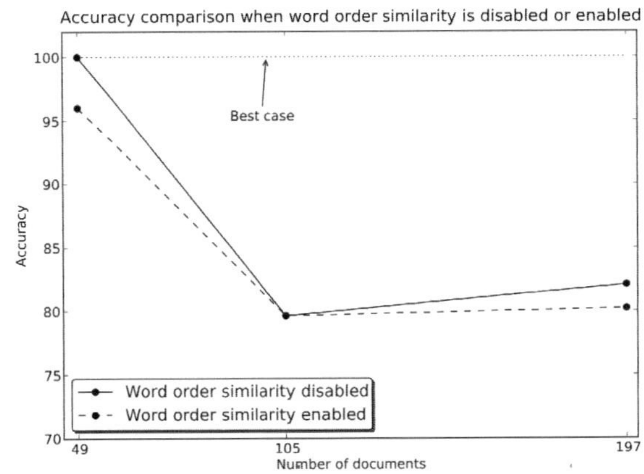

Figure 6. The accuracy of our approach when enabling or disabling word order similarity.

two sentences is in turn the normalized difference of their word orders. We experiment with enabling and disabling word order similarity to compare accuracy (Figure 6) and speed. Empirical results show that disabling word order similarity increases the accuracy of our approach and the speed is over 20% faster. Therefore, the word order similarity module by Li et al. (2006) is removed from our approach.

We then compare the two WSD strategies as described in Section 3.1: (1) always select the maximum score on all senses of two words (Max), and (2) apply the first sense heuristic. As Figure 7 and Figure 8 suggest, the accuracy of Max is higher than the first sense heuristic, but the average rank of the first sense heuristic is better than Max. Therefore, the overall performance of the two strategies is about the same.

We also experiment with enabling and disabling ticketing (Section 3.2). Results show that both accuracy and average ranks are improved when ticketing is enabled.

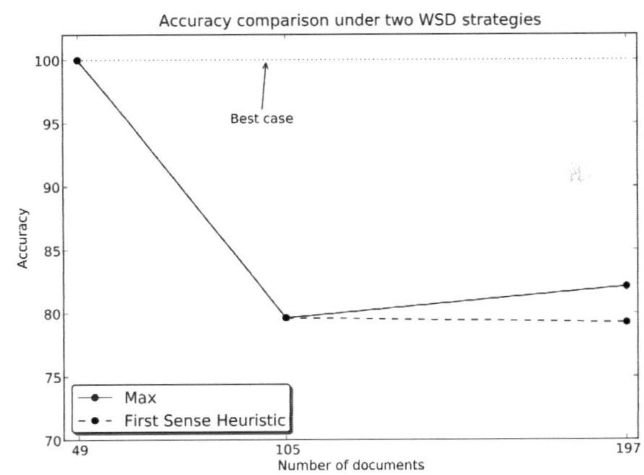

Figure 7. Accuracy comparison under two WSD strategies.

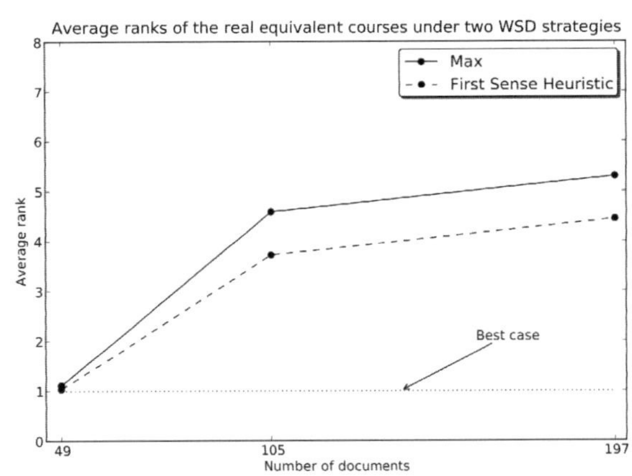

Figure 8. Average ranks of the real equivalent courses under two WSD strategies.

5 Future Refinements

This paper presents a novel application of semantic distance to suggesting potential equivalencies for a course transferred from an external university. It proposes a hybrid method that incorporates semantic distance measurement for words, sentences, and paragraphs. We show that a composite weighting scheme based on a lexicographic resource and a bag-of-words model outperforms previous work to identify equivalent courses. In practice, it is not common for two sentences in the course description corpus to have the exact same word order. Therefore, word order similarity is not very useful for identifying course equivalencies. Empirical results suggest that WSD and POS are helpful to increase accuracy, and that it is necessary to remove general and domain-specific stop words. The ticketing algorithm (Algorithm 2) also improves accuracy.

UML's transfer dictionary is only used as a test corpus in this paper. Alternatively, a set of examples might be constructed from the transfer dictionary to automatically learn equivalent properties without compromising the time complexity. Analyzing transfer dictionaries from other universities might help as well.

Meta data such as course levels, textbooks, and prerequisites can also be used as indicators of course equivalencies, but unfortunately these data are not available in the resources we used. Obtaining these data would require a great deal of manual work, which runs counter to our goal of devising a simple and straightforward algorithm for suggesting course equivalencies with a reasonable time complexity.

WordNet is selected as the lexical knowledge base for determining the semantic closeness between words, but empirical results indicate that WordNet does not cover all the concepts that exist in course descriptions. To address this issue, a domain-specific ontology could be constructed.

We plan to test our approach against other semantic distance measures in addition to the approach by Li et al. (2006), such as the work by Mihalcea et al. (2006) and Islam and Inkpen (2007).

Other directions for future work include: (1) optimizing performance and the exploration of more elegant WSD algorithms, (2) testing the sensitivity of results to values of γ and θ, (3) testing courses from a larger number of universities, (4) proposing robust methodologies that tolerate poorly formed texts, (5) adding more data to the course description corpus, and (6) making the course description corpus publicly available to the research community.

Acknowledgments

The authors thank Dr. Karen M. Daniels for reviewing drafts of this paper. We also appreciate correspondence with Dr. Yuhua Li at the early stage of our work. Last, but not least, we thank the reviewers for their insightful comments that guided improvement of the contents of this paper.

References

Steven Bird, Ewan Klein, and Edward Loper. 2009. Natural Language Processing with Python. *O'Reilly Media, Inc.* Sebastopol, CA, USA

Alexander Budanitsky and Graeme Hirst. 2006. Evaluating WordNet-based Measures of Lexical Semantic Relatedness. *Computational Linguistics*, volume 32.

Rudi L. Cilibrasi and Paul M. B. Vitanyi. 2007. The Google Similarity Distance. *IEEE Transactions on Knowledge and Data Engineering*. 19(3):370 – 383

Allan M. Collins and M. Ross Quillian. 1969. Retrieval Time from Semantic Memory. *Journal of Verbal Learning and Verbal Behavior*, volume 8.

James R. Curran. 2004. From Distributional to Semantic Similarity. Ph.D. Thesis. University of Edinburgh, Edinburgh, U.K.

Graeme Hirst and David St-Onge. 1998. Lexical chains as representations of context for the detection and correction of malapropisms. In Christiane Fellbaum, editor, WordNet: An Electronic Lexical Database. *The MIT Press, Cambridge, MA*, pages 305–332.

Aminul Islam and Diana Inkpen. 2006. Second Order Co-occurrence PMI for Determining the Semantic Similarity of Words. *Proceedings of the International Conference on Language Resources and Evaluation (LREC 2006)*, Genoa, Italy, pages 1033–1038.

Aminul Islam and Diana Inkpen. 2007. Semantic Similarity of Short Texts. *Proceedings of the International Conference on Recent Advances in Natural Language Processing (RANLP)*, Bulgaria, September 2007.

Jay J. Jiang and David W. Conrath. 1997. Semantic similarity based on corpus statistics and lexical taxonomy. *Proceedings of International Conference on Research in Computational Linguistics (ROCLING X)*, Taiwan, pages 19–33.

Thorsten Joachims. 1997. A Probabilistic Analysis of the Rocchio Algorithm with TFIDF for Text Categorization. *Proceedings of International Conference on Machine Learning (ICML)*.

Claudia Leacock and Martin Chodorow. 1998. Using Corpus Statistics and WordNet Relations for Sense Identification. *Computational Linguistics*, 24(1):147–165.

Yuhua Li, Zuhair A. Bandar, and David McLean. 2003. An Approach for Measuring Semantic Similarity between Words Using Multiple Information Sources.

IEEE Transactions on Knowledge and Data Engineering, volume 15, pages 871–882. IEEE Computer Society.

Yuhua Li, David McLean, Zuhair A. Bandar, James D. O'Shea, and Keeley Crockett. 2006. Sentence Similarity Based on Semantic Nets and Corpus Statistics. *IEEE Transactions on Knowledge and Data Engineering* volume 18. IEEE Computer Society. Los Alamitos, CA, USA.

Dekang Lin. 1998a. Extracting Collocations from Text Corpora. *Workshop on Computational Terminology*, Montreal, Canada.

Yutaka Matsuo, Junichiro Mori, Masahiro Hamasaki, Takuichi Nishimura, Hideaki Takeda, Koiti Hasida, and Mitsuru Ishizuka. 2007. POLYPHONET: An Advanced Social Network Extraction System from the Web. *Web Semantics*, volume 5(4). Elsevier Science Publishers B.V., Amsterdam, The Netherlands.

Rada Mihalcea, Courtney Corley, and Carlo Strapparava. 2006. Corpus-based and Knowledge-based Measures of Text Semantic Similarity. *Proceedings of the American Association for Artificial Intelligence (AAAI 2006)*, Boston.

Diana McCarthy, Rob Koeling, Julie Weeds, and John Carroll. 2004. Using Automatically Acquired Predominant Senses for Word Sense Disambiguation. *In Proceedings of the ACL SENSEVAL-3 Workshop*. Barclona, Spain. pp 151-154.

Saif Mohammad. 2008. Measuring Semantic Distance Using Distributional Profiles of Concepts. Ph.D. Thesis. University of Toronto, Toronto, Canada.

Saif Mohammad and Graeme Hirst. 2006. Determining Word Sense Dominance Using a Thesaurus. *In Proceedings of the 11th conference of the European chapter of the Association for Computational Linguistics (EACL-2006)*, April 2006, Trento, Italy.

Roberto Navigli. 2009. Word Sense Disambiguation: A Survey. *ACM Computing Surveys*, 41(2):1–69.

Roy Rada, Hafedh Mili, Ellen Bicknell, and Maria Blettner. 1989. Development and Application of a Metric on Semantic Nets. *IEEE Transactions on Systems, Man, and Cybernetics*, volume 19.

Philip Resnik. 1995. Using Information Content to Evaluate Semantic Similarity in a Taxonomy. *In Proceedings of the 14th International Joint Conference on Artificial Intelligence (IJCAI '95)*, volume 1. Morgan Kaufmann Publishers Inc., San Francisco, CA, USA.

Mehran Sahami and Timothy D. Heilman. 2006. A Web-based Kernel Function for Measuring the Similarity of Short Text Snippets. *In Proceedings of the 15th International Conference on World Wide Web (WWW '06)*. ACM. New York, NY, USA.

Gerard Salton and Chris Buckley. 1987. Term Weighting Approaches in Automatic Text Retrieval. *Technical report*. Ithaca, NY, USA.

Ian H. Witten and Eibe Frank. 2005. Data Mining: Practical machine learning tools and techniques, 2nd Edition. *Morgan Kaufmann*, San Francisco, CA, USA, pages 161–171.

Zhibiao Wu and Martha Palmer. 1994. Verb Semantics And Lexical Selection. *In Proceedings of the 32nd annual meeting on Association for Computational Linguistics (ACL '94)*. Association for Computational Linguistics, Stroudsburg, PA, USA.

Dongqiang Yang and David M. W. Powers. 2005. Measuring semantic similarity in the taxonomy of WordNet. *In Proceedings of the 28th Australasian conference on Computer Science (ACSC '05)*, volume 38. Australian Computer Society, Darlinghurst, Australia.

Non-scorable Response Detection for Automated Speaking Proficiency Assessment

Su-Youn Yoon, Keelan Evanini, Klaus Zechner
Educational Testing Service
660 Rosedale Road, Princeton, NJ, USA
{syoon,kevanini,kzechner}@ets.org

Abstract

We present a method that filters out non-scorable (NS) responses, such as responses with a technical difficulty, in an automated speaking proficiency assessment system. The assessment system described in this study first filters out the non-scorable responses and then predicts a proficiency score using a scoring model for the remaining responses.

The data were collected from non-native speakers in two different countries, using two different item types in the proficiency assessment: items that elicit spontaneous speech and items that elicit recited speech. Since the proportion of NS responses and the features available to the model differ according to the item type, an item type specific model was trained for each item type. The accuracy of the models ranged between 75% and 79% in spontaneous speech items and between 95% and 97% in recited speech items.

Two different groups of features, signal processing based features and automatic speech recognition (ASR) based features, were implemented. The ASR based models achieved higher accuracy than the non-ASR based models.

1 Introduction

We developed a method that filters out non-scorable (NS) responses as a supplementary module to an automated speech proficiency assessment system. In this study, the method was developed for a telephony-based assessment of English proficiency for non-native speakers. The examinees' responses were collected from several different environmental conditions, and many of the utterances contain background noise from diverse sources. In addition to the presence of noise, many responses have other sub-optimal characteristics. For example, some responses contain uncooperative behavior from the speakers, such as non-English speech, whispered speech, and non-responses. These types of responses make it difficult to provide a valid assessment of a speaker's English proficiency. Therefore, in order to address the diverse types of causes for these problematic responses, we used a two step approach: first, these problematic responses were filtered out by a "filtering model," and only the remaining responses were scored using the automated scoring model.

The overall architecture of our method, including the automated speech proficiency scoring system, is as follows: for a given spoken response, the system performs speech recognition, yielding a word hypothesis and time stamps. In addition to word recognition, the system computes pitch and power to generate prosodic features; the system calculates descriptive statistics such as the mean and standard deviation of pitch and power at both the word level and response level. Given the word hypotheses and pitch/power features, it derives features for automated proficiency scoring. Next, the non-ASR based features are calculated separately using signal processing techniques. Finally, given both sets of features, the filtering model identifies NS responses.

This paper will proceed as follows: we will review previous studies (Section 2), present the data

Proceedings of the Sixth Workshop on Innovative Use of NLP for Building Educational Applications, pages 152–160,
Portland, Oregon, 24 June 2011.

(Section 3), and then describe the structure of the filtering model (Section 4). Next, the results will be presented (Section 5), followed by a discussion (Section 6), and we will conclude with a summary of the importance of the findings (Section 7).

2 Previous Work

Higgins et al. (2011) developed a "filtering model" that is conceptually similar to the one in this paper. The model was trained and tested on a corpus containing responses from non-native speakers to an English proficiency assessment. This system used a regression model based on four features which were originally designed for automated speech proficiency scoring: the number of distinct words in the speech recognition output, the average speech recognizer confidence score, the average power of the speech signal, and the mean absolute deviation of the speech signal power. This model was able to identify responses which were also identified as NS responses by human raters with an approximately 98% accuracy when a false positive rate (the proportion of responses without technical difficulties that were incorrectly flagged as problematic) was lower than 1%.

Although there are few other studies which are directly related to the task of filtering out non-scorable responses in the domain of automated speech proficiency assessment, several signal processing studies are related to this work. Traditionally, the Signal to Noise Ratio (SNR) has been used to detect speech with a large amount of background noise. This method measures the ratio between the total energy of the speech signal and the total energy of the noise; if the SNR is low, then the speech contains loud background noise. A low SNR results in lower intelligibility and increases the difficulty for both human and automated scoring. Furthermore, spectral characteristics can be also applied to detect speech with loud background noise, since noise has different spectral characteristics than speech (noise tends to have no or few peaks in the spectral domain). If a response contains loud background noise, then the spectral characteristics of the speech may be obscured by noise and it may have similar characteristics with the noise. These differences in spectral characteristics have been used in audio information retrieval Lu and Hankinson (1998).

Secondly, responses without valid speech can be identified using Voice Activity Detection (VAD). VAD is a technique which distinguishes human speech from non-speech. When speech is clean, VAD can be calculated by simply computing the zero-crossing rate which signals the existence of cyclic waves such as vowels. However, if the response also contains loud background noises, more sophisticated methods are required. In order to remove the influence of noise, Chang and Kim (2003), Chang et al. (2006), Shin et al. (2005) and Sohn et al. (1999) estimated the characteristics of the noise spectrum and the distribution of noise, and compensated for them when speech is identified. The performance of these systems is heavily-influenced by the accuracy of estimating characteristics of the background noise.

In this study, we used a set of ASR based features and non-ASR based features. ASR based features were similar to the ones used by Zechner et al. (2009). In addition to the features based on ASR hypotheses, the ASR based feature set contained basic pitch and power related features since the ASR system in this study also produced pitch and power measurements in order to generate prosodic features. The non-ASR based features were comprised of four groups of features based on signal processing techniques such as SNR, VAD, and pitch and power. Features related to pitch and power were included in both the ASR based features and the non-ASR based features. Since the non-ASR based features were originally implemented as an independent module from the ASR-based system (it was implemented for the case where the appropriate recognizer is unavailable), there is some degree of overlap between the two feature sets.

3 Data

The data for this experiment were drawn from a prototype of a telephony-based English language assessment. Non-native speakers of English each responded to 40 test items designed to evaluate their level of English proficiency. The test was composed of items that elicited both spontaneous speech (hereafter SS) and recited speech (hereafter RS). In this study, 8 items (four SS and four RS) were used for each speaker.

Participants used either a cell phone or a land line to complete the assessment, and the participants were compensated for their time. The motivation level of the participants was thus lower than in the case of an actual high stakes assessment, where a participant's performance could have a substantial impact on their future. In addition, the data collection procedure was less controlled than in an operational testing environment; for example, some recordings exhibited higher levels of ambient noise than others. These two facts led to the quality of some of the responses being lower than would be expected in an operational assessment.

The data for this study were collected from participants in two countries: India and China. For India, 4900 responses from 638 speakers were collected. For China, 5565 responses from 702 speakers were collected (some of the participants did not provide responses to all 8 test items). Each response is approximately 45 sec in duration.

After the data was collected, all of the responses were given scores on a three-point scale by trained raters. The raters also labeled responses as "non-scorable" (NS), when appropriate. NS responses are ones that could not be given a score according to the rubrics of the three-point scale. These were due to either a technical difficulty obscuring the content of the response or an inappropriate response from the participant.

The proportion of NS responses differs markedly between the two countries. 852 of the responses in the India data set (17% of the total) were labeled as NS, compared to 1548 responses (28%) in the China data set.

Table 1 provides the different types of NS responses that were annotated by the raters, along with the relative frequency of each NS category compared to the others.

Excluding the category "Other", background noise, non-responses, and unrelated topic were the most frequent types of NS response for both data sets. However, the relative proportions of each type differed somewhat between the two countries. For example, the most frequent NS type in India was background noise; 33% of NS responses were of this type, 1.7 times higher than in China.

The proportion of unrelated topic responses was also high in both countries, but it was much higher in the China data set: it was 19% in the responses from India and 40% for China (more than twice as high as in India). All responses which were not directly related to the prompt fell into this category. For SS items, the majority included responses about a different topic. For RS items, responses in which the speakers read different prompts were classified into this category.

The responses were divided into training and testing for NS response detection. Due to the significant difference in the proportion of NS responses and relative frequencies of NS types in the two data sets, filtering models were trained separately for each country. In addition, since the proportions of NS responses and the available features varied according to the item type, training and testing data were further classified by item types. The proportions of NS responses and the sizes of the partitions, along with the percent of NS responses in each item type, are shown in Table 2.

NS Type	India (%)	China (%)
Background noise	33.2	19.6
Other	25.0	15.4
Unrelated response	18.9	40.1
Non-response	10.6	8.8
Non-English speech	4.9	6.4
Too soft	2.8	1.0
Background speech	2.0	1.9
Missing samples	1.5	4.0
Too loud	0.8	0.1
Cheating	0.3	2.7

Table 1: Different types of NS responses and their relative frequency, in % of all NS for each country (ranked by frequency of occurrence in India)

Data Partition	India		China	
	# of responses	NS (%)	# of responses	NS (%)
SS-train	1114	31.6	1382	32.2
SS-eval	1271	27.5	1391	33.8
RS-train	1253	8.0	1392	22.4
RS-eval	1275	4.8	1400	22.9

Table 2: Item-type specific training and evaluation data

The partitions for testing the filtering model were selected to maximize the number of speakers with complete sets of responses; however, this constraint was not able to be met for the training partitions in the India data set (due to insufficient data). This explains the lower proportion of NS responses in the India test partitions, since speakers with complete sets of responses were less likely to provide bad responses. As Table 2 shows, NS responses were more frequent among SS items than RS items: the proportion of NS responses in SS items was four times higher than in RS items in India and 1.5 times in China.

4 Method

4.1 Overview

In this study, two different sets of features were used in the model training process; ASR-based features and non-ASR based features. For each item-type, an item-type-specific filtering model was developed using these two sets of features.

4.2 Feature generation

4.2.1 ASR based features

For this feature set, we used the features from an automated speech proficiency scoring system. This scoring system used an ASR engine containing word-internal triphone acoustic models and item-type-specific language models. Separate acoustic models were trained for the data sets from the two countries. The acoustic training data for the two models consisted of 45.5 hours of speech from India and 123.1 hours of speech from China. In addition, separate language models were trained for the SS and RS items for each country; for the RS items, the language models also incorporated the texts of the prompts.

A total of 61 features were available. Among these features, many features were conceptually similar but based on different normalization methods. These features showed a strong intercorrelation. For this study, 30 features were selected and classified into four groups according to their characteristics: basic features, fluency features, ASR-confidence features, and Word Error Rate (WER) features.

The basic features are related to power and pitch, and they capture the overall distribution of pitch and power values in a speaker's response using mean and variance calculations. These features are relevant since NS responses may have an abnormal distribution in energy. For instance, non-responses contain very low energy. In order to detect these abnormalities in speech signal, pitch and power related features were calculated.

The fluency features measure the length of a response in terms of duration and number of words. In addition, this group contains features related to speaking rate and silences, such as mean duration and number of silence. In particular, these features are effective in identifying Non-responses which contain zero or only a few words.

The ASR-confidence group contains features predicting the performance of the speech recognizer. Low speech recognition accuracy may be indicated by low confidence scores.

Finally, the WER group provides features estimating the similarity between the prompts and the recognition output. In addition to the conventional word error rate (WER), term error rate (TER) was also implemented for the filtering model. TER is a metric commonly used in spoken information retrieval, and it only accounts for errors in content words. This measure may be more effective in identifying NS responses than conventional WER; for instance, the overlap in function words between off-topic responses and prompts can be correctly ignored. TER was calculated according to the following formula:

$$dif(W_c) = \begin{cases} 0 \ if C_{ref}(W_c) < C_{hyp}(W_c) \\ C_{ref}(W_c) - C_{hyp}(W_c) \ otherwise \end{cases}$$
$$TER = \frac{\sum_{c \in WC} dif(W_c)}{\sum_{c \in WC} C_{ref}(W_c)} \quad (1)$$

where $C_{ref}(W_c)$ is the number of occurrences of the word W_c in reference, $C_{hyp}(W_c)$ is the number of occurrences of the word W_c in hypothesis, and WC is the set of content words in reference.

Formula 1 differs from the conventional method

Group	List of features
Basic	mean/standard deviation/minimum/maximum of power, difference between maximum and minimum in power, mean/standard deviation/minimum/maximum of pitch, difference between maximum and minimum in pitch
Fluency	duration of whole speech part, number of words, speaking rate (word per sec), mean/standard deviation of silence duration, number of silences, silences per sec and silences per word
ASR score	mean of confidence score, normalized Acoustic Model score by word length, normalized Language Model score by number of words
Word Error Rate	the word accuracy between prompt and ASR word hypothesis, correct words per minute, term error rate

Table 3: List of ASR based features

of calculating TER in two ways. Firstly, content words which occurred only in the word hypothesis are ignored in the formula. Secondly, if a word occurred in the word hypothesis more frequently than in the reference, the difference is ignored. These modifications were made to address characteristics of the responses in the data. On the one hand, speakers occasionally inserted a few words such as "too difficult" at the end of a response. In addition, a few speakers repeated words contained in the prompt multiple times. The two modifications to TER address both of these issues.

All features from the four groups are summarized in Table 3.

4.2.2 Non-ASR based features

A total of 12 features from four different groups were implemented using non-ASR based methods such as VAD and SNR. These features are listed in Table 4.

Feature Category	Feature
VAD	proportion of voiced frames in response, number and total duration of voiced regions
Syllable	number of syllables
Amplitude	maximum, minimum, mean, standard deviation
SNR	SNR, speech peak

Table 4: List of non-ASR based features

VAD related features were implemented using the ESPS speech analysis program. For every 10 millisecond interval, the voice frame detector determined whether the interval was voiced or not. Three features were implemented using this voiced interval information: the number of voiced intervals, ratio of voiced intervals in the entire response, and the total duration of voiced intervals.

In addition, the number of syllables was estimated based on the flow of energy. The energy of the syllable tends to reach its peak in the nucleus and the dip in the boundaries. By counting the number of such fluctuations in energy measurements, the number of syllables can be estimated. The Praat script from De Jong and Wempe (2009) was used for this purpose.

In order to detect the abnormalities in energy, amplitude based features were calculated. These features were similar to the basic features in ASR based features.

Finally, if a response contains loud background noise, the ratio of speech to noise is low. SNR, the mean noise level, and the peak speech level were computed using the NIST audio quality assurance package (NIST, 2009).

The VAD and syllable feature groups were designed to estimate the number of syllables, the proportion of speech to non-speech, and the total duration of speech intervals. These features were similar to the number of words and duration of speech features in the ASR-based feature set. Despite the conceptual similarity, these features were implemented since the two types of features were calculated using different characteristics of the spoken response.

The VAD and syllable features are based on the flow of energy and the zero crossing rate and the ASR-based features are based on the speech recognition. In particular, the speech recognizer tends to generate word hypotheses even for responses that contain no speech input, but VAD does not have such a tendency. Due to this difference, VAD based features may be more robust in the responses with no valid speech.

4.3 Model building

For each response, both ASR features and non-ASR features were calculated. In contrast to non-ASR features, which were available for all responses, ASR features (except the Basic group) were unavailable for some responses, namely, responses for which the ASR system did not generate any word hypotheses because no tokens received scores above the rejection threshold. This causes a missing value problem; about 7% of the responses did not have a complete set of attributes.

Missing values are a common problem in machine learning. One of the popular approaches is to replace a missing value with a unique value such as the attribute's mean. Ding and Simonoff (2008) proposed a method that replaces a missing value with an arbitrary unique value. This method is preferable when missing of a value depends on the target value and this relationship holds in both training and test data.

In this study, the missing values were replaced with unique values due to the relationship between the missing values and the target label; if the speech recognizer did not produce any word hypotheses, the response was highly likely to be a NS response. 63% of the responses where the speech recognizer failed to generate word hypotheses were NS responses. Since all ASR-based features were continuous values, we used two real values: 0.0 for fluency features and ASR features and 100.0 for word error rate features. The fluency features and ASR features tend to be 0.0 while the word error rate features tend to be 100.0 when the responses are NS responses.

A total of 42 features were used in the model building. The only exception was WER; since WER features were only available for the model based on recited speech, they were calculated only for RS items. Decision tree models were trained using the J48 algorithm (WEKA implementation of C4.5) of WEKA machine learning toolkit (Hall et al., 2009).

5 Results

For each item-type, three models were built to investigate the impact of each feature group: a model using non-ASR features, a model using ASR features, and a model using both features (the "Combined" model). Tables 5 and 6 present the accuracy of the SS models and Tables 7 and 8 present the accuracy of the RS models. In all tables, the baseline was calculated using majority voting, and represented a system in which no responses were classified as NS; since the majority class was scorable, the baseline using the majority voting did not predict any response as non-scorable response. Therefore, precision, recall, F-score are all 0 in this case.

Model	Acc.	Pre.	Rec.	F-score
Baseline	72.5	0	0	0
Non-ASR	77.0	0.645	0.364	0.465
ASR	79.0	0.683	0.444	0.538
Combined	78.6	0.657	0.461	0.542

Table 5: Performance of the SS model in India

Model	Acc.	Pre.	Rec.	F-score
Baseline	66.2	0	0	0
Non-ASR	68.9	0.601	0.240	0.343
ASR	72.9	0.718	0.326	0.448
Combined	72.9	0.720	0.323	0.446

Table 6: Performance of the SS model in China

Model	Acc.	Pre.	Rec.	F-score
Baseline	94.8	0	0	0
Non-ASR	95.7	0.684	0.210	0.321
ASR	97.2	0.882	0.484	0.625
Combined	96.8	0.769	0.484	0.594

Table 7: Performance of the RS model in India

In both item-types, the models using ASR-based features achieved the best performance. The SS model achieved 79% accuracy in India and 73% accuracy in China, representing improvements of approximately 7% over the baseline. In both data sets, the RS model achieved high accuracies: 97% accuracy in India and 96% accuracy in China. In India,

Model	Acc.	Pre.	Rec.	F-score
Baseline	77.1	0	0	0
Non-ASR	78.3	0.555	0.268	0.361
ASR	95.6	0.942	0.860	0.899
Combined	95.1	0.912	0.872	0.892

Table 8: Performance of the RS model in China

this represents a 2.4% improvement over the baseline. Although the absolute value of this error reduction is not very large, the relative error reduction is 46%. In China, the improvement was more salient; there was 18% improvement over baseline, corresponding to a relative error reduction of 78%.

Additional experiments were conducted to determine the robustness of the filtering models to evaluation data from a country not included in the training data. The evaluation sets from both item types (SS and RS) in both countries (India and China) were processed using three different models: 1) a model trained using the ASR-based features for the responses from the same country (the "Same" condition, whose results are identical to the "ASR" results in Tables 5 - 8), 2) a model trained using the ASR-based features for the responses from the other country (the "Different" condition), and 3) a model trained using the ASR-based features for the responses from both countries (the "Both" condition). Table 9 presents the accuracy results for these four sets of experiments.

Model	India		China	
	SS	RS	SS	RS
Same	79.0	97.2	72.9	95.6
Different	80.1	95.4	73.5	93.8
Both	80.0	96.5	74.0	95.9

Table 9: Accuracy results using training and evaluation data from different countries

These results show that the models are quite robust to evaluation data from a different country. In all cases, there is at most a small decline in performance when training data from the other country is used (in the case of the SS responses, there is even a slight increase in performance). Table 9 also shows that the RS models performed worse in the Different Country condition (compared to the Same Country condition) than the SS models. This difference is likely due to the difference in the number of NS responses among the RS data in the two countries (as shown in Table 2). However, the decline is still relatively small, suggesting that it would be reasonable to extend the filtering models to responses from additional countries that were not seen in the training data.

6 Discussion

Approximately 40 features were available for the model building, but not all features had a significant impact on the detection of NS responses. For each item-type, the importance of features were further investigated using a logistic regression analysis. The training data of India and China were combined, and a stepwise logistic regression analysis was performed using the SPSS statistical analysis program.

For each item-type, the top 3 features are presented in Table 10; the features are presented in the same order selected in the models.

Model	RS	SS
ASR	TER, speaking rate, s.d. of pitch	mean of confidence scores, speaking rate, s.d. of power
Non-ASR	number of syllables, number and duration of voiced regions	number of syllables, s.d. and mean of amplitude
Combined	TER, speaking rate, s.s.dd. pitch	mean of confidence scores, speaking rate, number of voiced regions

Table 10: Top 3 features in stepwise logistic regression model

For the RS items, TER was the best feature and it was the top feature for both the ASR feature based model and the combined model. The top 3 features in the combined model were the same as the ASR feature based model, and non-ASR features were not selected. In non-ASR based features, the number of syllables was the best feature, followed by the VAD based features.

For the SS items, the top 2 features were the same in both the ASR feature based model and the combined model. The combined model selected one non-ASR based feature, namely, a VAD based feature. As with the RS items, the number of syllables was the best feature, followed by the energy related feature.

These results show the importance of WER features. Most of the current features are designed for signal level abnormalities such as responses with large background noise or non-responses. For instance, fluency features and VAD features are effective for non-response detection, since they can determine whether the responses contain valid speech or not. SNR and pitch/power related features are useful for identifying responses with large background noise. However, no features except the WER group can identify content-level abnormalities such as unrelated topic and non-English responses. The high proportion of these two types of responses (24% in India and 46% in China) may be the major explanation for the lower accuracy of the model for SS responses than for RS responses. In the future, content-related features should also be developed for spontaneous speech.

The features selected the first time in the logistic model differed according to item-types. The results support the item-type-specific model approach adopted in this paper; item-type-specific models can assign strong weights to the item-type-specific features that are most important.

As shown in Tables 5 - 8, the combination of non-ASR and ASR features could not achieve any further improvement over the model consisting only of ASR based features. However, in all cases, the non-ASR based model did lead to some improvement over the baseline. The magnitude of this improvement was greater in SS items than RS items; in particular, it was greatest among the SS items in the India data set. This difference may be due to the different distributions of the NS types among the data sets. The non-ASR based features can cover only limited types of NS responses such as non-responses and responses with background noise, and the proportion of these types is much higher among the SS responses from India.

In addition, in RS items, the poor performance of the combined model may be related to the high performance of TER. The stepwise regression analysis showed that the combined model did not select any of non-ASR based features.

7 Conclusion

In this study, filtering models were implemented as a supplementary module to an automated proficiency scoring system. Due to the difference in the available features and proportion of NS responses, item-type specific models were trained.

The item-types heavily influenced the overall characteristics of the filtering models. First, the proportion of NS responses was significantly different according to item-type; it was much higher in spontaneous speech items than recited speech items. Secondly, the word error rate feature group was only available for recited speech. Although the word error rate feature group contained three features, they improved the performance of the filtering model significantly.

ASR feature based models outperformed non-ASR feature based models, but non-ASR based features may be useful for new tests. Finally, experiments demonstrated that the country-specific models using the ASR-based features are relatively robust to responses from a different country. This result suggests that this approach can generalize well to speakers from different countries.

In this study, large numbers of features (42 for RS items and 39 for SS items) were used in the model training, but some features were conceptually similar and not all of them were significantly important; the logistic regression analsysis using traning data showed that there was no significant improvement after selecting 5 features for RS items and 13 features for SS items. Use of non-significant features in the model training may result in the overfitting problems. In future research, the features will be classified into subgroups based on their conceptual similarities; groups of features with high intercorrelations will be reduced to include only the best performing feature in each group. Thus, based on careful pre-selection procedures, only high performing features will be selected, and the model will be retrained.

In addition, many different types of NS responses were lumped into one big category (NS); this may increase the confusion between scorable and non-scorable responses and decrease the model's performance. Some of NS types have very different characteristics compared to other NS types and this fact caused critical differences in the feature values. For instance, non-responses contained zero or close to zero words, whereas non-English responses and off-topic responses typically had a word count similar to scorable responses. This difference may reduce the effectiveness of this feature. In order to avoid this type of problem, we will classify NS types into small numbers of subgroups and build a seperate model for each subgroup.

References

Joon-Hyuk Chang and Nam Soo Kim. 2003. Voice activity detection based on complex Laplacian model. *Electronics Letters*, 39(7):632–634.

Joon-Hyuk Chang, Nam Soo Kim, and Sanjit K. Mitra. 2006. Voice activity detection based on multiple statistical models. *IEEE Transactions on Signal Processing*, 54(6):1965–1976.

Nivja H. De Jong and Ton Wempe. 2009. Praat script to detect syllable nuclei and measure speech rate automatically. *Behavior research methods*, 41(2):385–390.

Yufeng Ding and Jeffrey S. Simonoff. 2008. An investigation of missing data methods for classification trees. *Statistics Working Papers Series*.

Mark Hall, Eibe Frank, Geoffrey Holmes, Bernhard Pfahringer, Peter Reutemann, and Ian H. Witten. 2009. The WEKA Data Mining Software: An Update. In *SIGKDD Explorations*, volume 11.

Derrick Higgins, Xiaoming Xi, Klaus Zechner, and David Williamson. 2011. A three-stage approach to the automated scoring of spontaneous spoken responses. *Computer Speech and Language*, 25:282–306, April.

Guojun Lu and Templar Hankinson. 1998. A technique towards automatic audio classification and retrieval. In *Proceedings of the 4th International Conference on Signal Processing*, volume 2, pages 1142–1145.

NIST. 2009. The NIST SPeech Quality Assurance (SPQA) Package Version 2.3. from `http://www.nist.gov/speech/tools/index.htm`.

Jong Won Shin, Hyuk Jin Kwon, Suk Ho Jin, and Nam Soo Kim. 2005. Voice activity detection based on generalized gamma distribution. In *Proceedings of the IEEE International Conference on Acoustics, Speech, and Signal Processing*, pages 781–784.

Jongseo Sohn, Nam Soo Kim, and Wonyong Sung. 1999. A statistical model-based voice activity detection. *IEEE Signal Processing Letter*, 6(1):1–3.

Klaus Zechner, Derrick Higgins, Xiaoming Xi, and David M. Williamson. 2009. Automatic scoring of non-native spontaneous speech in tests of spoken English. *Speech Communication*, 51(10):883–895.

Non-English Response Detection Method for Automated Proficiency Scoring System

Su-Youn Yoon and Derrick Higgins
Educational Testing Service
660 Rosedale Road, Princeton, NJ, USA
{syoon,dhiggins}@ets.org

Abstract

This paper presents a method for identifying non-English speech, with the aim of supporting an automated speech proficiency scoring system for non-native speakers.

The method uses a popular technique from the language identification domain, a single phone recognizer followed by multiple language-dependent language models. This method determines the language of a speech sample based on the phonotactic differences among languages.

The method is intended for use with non-native English speakers. Therefore, the method must be able to distinguish non-English responses from non-native speakers' English responses. This makes the task more challenging, as the frequent pronunciation errors of non-native speakers may weaken the phonetic and phonotactic distinction between English responses and non-English responses. In order to address this issue, the speaking rate measure was used to complement the language identification based features in the model.

The accuracy of the method was 98%, and there was 45% relative error reduction over a system based on the conventional language identification technique. The model using both feature sets furthermore demonstrated an improvement in accuracy for speakers at all English proficiency levels.

1 Introduction

We developed a non-English response identification method as a supplementary module for the automated speech proficiency scoring of non-native speakers. The method can identify speech samples of test takers who try to game the system by speaking in their native languages. For the items that elicited spontaneous speech, fluency features such as speaking rate have been one of the most important features in the automated scoring. By speaking in their native languages, speakers can generate fluent speech, and the automated proficiency scoring system may assign a high score. This problem has been rarely recognized, and none of research has focused on it as to the authors' knowledge. In order to address this issue, the automated proficiency scoring system in this study first filters out the responses in non-English languages, and for the remaining responses, it predicts the proficiency score using a scoring model.

Non-English detection is strongly related to language identification(Lamel and Gauvain, 1993; Zissman, 1996; Li et al., 2007); language identification is the process of determining which language a spoken response is in, while non-English detection makes a binary decision whether the spoken response is in English or not. Due to the strong similarity between the two tasks, the language identification method was used here for non-English response detection.

In contrast to previous research, the method described here was intended for use with non-native speakers, and the English responses for model training and evaluation were accordingly collected from non-native speakers. Among other differences, non-native speakers' speech tends to display non-standard pronunciation characteristics which can

Proceedings of the Sixth Workshop on Innovative Use of NLP for Building Educational Applications, pages 161–169,
Portland, Oregon, 24 June 2011. ©2011 Association for Computational Linguistics

make the task of language identification more challenging. For instance, when native Korean speakers speak English, they may replace some English phonemes not in their language with their native phones, and epenthesize vowels within consonant clusters. Such processes tend to reduce the phonetic and phonotactic distinction between English and other languages. The frequency of these pronunciation errors is influenced by speakers' native language and proficiency level, with lower-proficiency speakers likely to exhibit the greatest degree of divergence from standard pronunciation. Language identification method may not effectively distinguish non-fluent speakers' English responses from non-English responses. In order to address these non-native speech characteristics, the model described here includes the speaking rate feature, which has been found to be an indicator of speaking proficiency in previous research(Strik and Cucchiarini, 1999; Zechner et al., 2009). Non-fluent speakers' English responses can be distinguished from non-English responses by slow speaking rate.

This paper will proceed as follows: we first review previous studies in section 2, then describe the data in section 3, and present the experiment in section 4. The results and discussion are presented in section 5, and the conclusions are presented in section 6.

2 Previous Work

Many previous studies in language identification focused on phonetic and phonotactic differences among languages. The frequencies of phones and phone sequences differ according to languages and some phone sequences occur only in certain languages. The literature in language identification captured this characteristic using the likelihood score of speech recognizers, which signals the degree of a match between the test sentences and speech recognizer models. Both the language model (hereafter, LM) and acoustic model (hereafter, AM) of a phone recognizer are optimized for the acoustic characteristics and the phoneme distribution of the training data. If a spoken response is recognized using a recognizer trained on a different language, it may result in a low likelihood score due to a mismatch between the test sentences and the models.

Lamel and Gauvain (1993) trained multiple language-dependent-phone-recognizers and selected the language with the highest matching score as the input language (hereafter, parallel PRLM). For instance, if the test data contained English and Hindi speech data, the English-phone-recognizer and the Hindi-phone-recognizer were trained independently. In the test, the given speech samples were recognized using two phone recognizers, and the language that had a higher matching score was selected. However, training multiple phone recognizers was time-consuming and labor intensive; therefore, Zissman (1996) proposed a system using single-language phone recognition followed by multiple language-dependent language modeling (hereafter, PRLM). PRLM was able to achieve comparable performance to parallel PRLM for long speech (longer than 30 seconds), and in a two-language situation, the error rate was between 5 and 7%.

Instead of language-dependent LM, Li et al. (2007) used vector space modeling (VSM). They applied metrics frequently used in information retrieval. As with the PRLM method, the speech was converted into phone sequences using the phone recognizer, and cooccurrence statistics such as term frequency (TF) and inverse document frequency (IDF) were calculated. The method outperformed the PRLM approach for long speech.

These methods can be challenging and time-consuming to implement, as they require implementation of methods beyond those typically available in a standard word-based recognition system. In particular, the application of the phone recognizer increases the processing time substantially. Because of this problem, Lim et al. (2004) presented a method based on the features that were readily available for speech recognizers: a confidence score and the cross-entropy of the LM. The confidence scoring method measured the acoustic match between the word hypotheses and the real sound, while the cross-entropy measured how well a sentence matched a given language model. If the test sentence was recognized by the speech recognizer in a different language, the phonetic and lexical mismatches between two languages resulted in a low confidence score and a high cross-entropy. Using this methodology, Lim et al. (2004) achieved 99.8% accuracy in their three-way classification task.

The current study can be distinguished from the previous studies in the following points. First of all, special features were implemented to model non-native speech since the method was developed for non-native speech. In our study, the data contained non-native speakers' English speech, characterized by inaccurate pronunciation. It resulted in a mismatch between the speech-recognizer models and test sentences, even for utterances in English. In particular, the mismatch was more salient in non-fluent speakers' speech, which comprised a high proportion of our data. In order to address this issue, speaking rate, which has achieved good performance in the estimation of non-native speakers' speaking proficiency (Strik and Cucchiarini, 1999; Zechner et al., 2009), was implemented as an additional feature. Secondly, in contrast to previous studies that determined which language the speech was in, we made a binary decision whether the speech was in English or not. Finally, the method was developed as part of a language assessment system.

3 Data

The OGI Multi-language corpus (Muthusamy et al., 1992), a standard language identification development data set, was used in the training and evaluation of the system. It contains a total of 1,957 calls from speakers of 10 different languages (English, Farsi, French, German, Japanese, Korean, Mandarin Chinese, Spanish, Tamil, and Vietnamese). The corpus was composed of short speech and long speech; the short files contained approximately 10 seconds speech, while the long files contained speech ranged from 30 seconds to 50 seconds.

The method described here was implemented to distinguish non-English responses from non-native speakers' English responses. Therefore, the English data used to train and evaluate the model for non-English response detection was collected from non-native speakers. In particular, responses to the English Practice Test (EPT) were used. The EPT is an online practice test which allows students to gain familiarity with the format of a high-stakes test of English proficiency and receive immediate feedback on their test responses based on automated scoring methods. The speaking section of the EPT assessment consists of 6 items in which speakers are prompted to provide open-ended responses of 45-60 seconds in length. The scoring scale of each item is discrete from 1 to 4, where 4 indicates high speaking proficiency and 1 low proficiency.

The non-English detection task is composed of two major components: training of PRLM, and training of the classifier which makes a binary decision about whether a speech sample is in the English language, given PRLM-based features and the speaking rate.

The OGI corpus was used in training of both PRLM and the classifier; a total of 9,033 short files from the OGI corpus were used in PRLM training, and 158 long files were used in classifier training. (The small number of long files in the OGI corpus limited the number of samples comparable in length to our English-language data described below, so that only these 158 OGI samples could be used in classifier training and evaluation.) For English, only short samples were selected for use in this experiment.

In addition, a total of 3,021 EPT responses were used in classifier training. As the English proficiency levels of speakers may have an influence on the accuracy of non-English response detection, the EPT responses were selected to include similar numbers of responses for each score level. Responses were classified into four groups according to their proficiency scores and 1000 responses were randomly selected from each group. For score 1 and 4, where the number of available responses was smaller than 1000, all available responses were selected. Ultimately, 156 responses for score 1, 1000 responses for score 2 and score 3, and 865 responses for score 4 were selected.

The resultant training and evaluation data sets are summarized in Table 1.

Due to the lack of non-Engilsh responses in EPT data, 158 non-English utterances in OGI data were used in both training and evaluation of non-English detection. EPT responses were collected from many different countries, and speakers with 75 different native languages were participated in the data collection. Due to the large variations, many of their native languages were not covered by OGI data. However, all 9 languages in OGI data were in top 15 L1 languages and covered approximately 60% of speakers'

Partition name	Purpose	Number of English files	Number of non-English files
PRLM-train	Training of Language-dependent LM	1,716 (OGI)	7,317 (OGI)
EN-detection	Training and evaluation of non-English detection classifier	3,021 (EPT)	158 (OGI)

Table 1: Data partition

native languages.

4 Experiment

4.1 Overview

Due to the efficiency in processing time and implementation, a PRLM was implemented instead of a parallel PRLM. However, the difference between PRLM and parallel PRLM in this study may not be significant since PRLM has been shown to be comparable to parallel PRLM for test samples longer than 30 seconds, and the duration of test instances in this study was longer than 30 seconds. In addition to PRLM, speaking rate was calculated as a feature.

4.2 PRLM based features

The PRLM based method in this study is composed of three parts: training of a phone recognizer, training of language-dependent LMs, and generation of PRLM-based features. In contrast to the conventional language identification approach that only focused on identifying the language with the highest matching score, 6 additional features were implemented to capture the difference between English model and other models.

Phone recognizer: An English triphone acoustic model was trained on 30 hours of non-native English speech (EPT data) using the HTK toolkit (Young et al., 2002). The model contained 43 monophones and 4,887 triphones. Due to the difference in the sampling rate of EPT (11,025 Hz) and the OGI corpus (8,000 Hz), the EPT data was down-sampled to 8,000 Hz and the acoustic model was trained using the down-sampled data. In order to avoid the influence of English in phone hypothesis generation, a triphone bigram language model with a uniform probability distribution was used as the LM. (All possible combinations of two triphones were generated and a uniform probability was assigned to each combination.) The phone recognition accuracy rate was 42.7% on the 94 held-out EPT test samples. This phone recognizer was used in phone hypothesis generation for all data; the same recognizer was used for all languages.

Language-dependent LMs: For responses in the PRLM-train partition, phone hypothesis was generated using the English recognizer. Instead of the manual transcription, a language-dependent phone bigram LM was trained using the phone hypothesis. In order to avoid a data sparseness problem, triphones were converted into monophones by removing left and right context phones, and a bigram LM with closed vocabulary was trained. 10 language-dependent bigram LMs, including one for English, were trained.

PRLM based feature generation: For each response in the EN-detection partition, phone hypothesis was generated, and triphones were converted into monophones. Given monophone hypothesis, an LM score was calculated for each language using a language-dependent LM. A total of 10 LM scores were calculated.

Since the LM score increases as the number of phones increases, the LM score was normalized by the number of phones in each response, in order to avoid the influence of hypothesis length. 7 features were generated based on these normalized LM scores:

- MaxLanguage: The language with the maximum LM score
- SecondLanguage: The language with the second-largest LM score.
- MaxScore: Normalized LM score of the MaxLanguage.

- MaxDifference: Difference between normalized English LM score and MaxScore
- MaxRatio: Ratio between normalized English LM score and MaxScore
- AverageDifference: Difference between normalized English LM score and the average of normalized LM scores for languages other than English
- AverageRatio: Ratio between normalized English LM score and the average of normalized LM scores for languages other than English

Among above 6 features, 4 features (MaxDifference, MaxRatio, AverageDifference, and AverageRatio) were designed to measure the difference between matching of a test responses with English model and it with the other models. These features may be particularly effective when MaxLanguage of the English response is not English; these values will be close to 0 when the divergence due to non-native characteristics result in only slightly better match with other language than that with English.

4.3 Speaking rate calculation

The speaking rate was calculated as a feature relevant to establishing speakers' proficiency level, as established in previous research. Speaking rate was calculated from the phone hypothesis as the number of phones divided by the duration of responses (cf. Strik and Cucchiarini (1999)).

4.4 Model building

For each response, both PRLM-based features and speaking rate were calculated, and a decision tree model was trained to predict binary values (0 for English and 1 for non-English) using the J48 algorithm (WEKA implementation of C4.5) of the WEKA machine learning toolkit (Hall et al., 2009).

Due to the limited number of non-English responses in the EN-detection partition, three-fold cross validation was performed during classifier training and evaluation. The 3,179 responses were partitioned into three sets to include approximately same numbers of non-English responses and English responses for each proficiency score group. Each partition contained 52 $\sim$ 53 non-English responses and 1007 English responses. In each fold, the decision tree was trained using two of these partitions and tested on the remaining one.

5 Evaluation

First, the accuracy of the PRLM method was evaluated based on multiple forced-choice experiments with two alternatives using OGI data; in addition to non-English responses in EN-detection partition, English responses from the OGI data were used in this experiment. For each response (in English and one other language), phone hypothesis was generated and two normalized LM scores were calculated using the English LM and the LM for the other language. The MaxLanguage was hypothesized as the source language of the speech. The same experiment was performed for 9 combinations of English and other languages. Each experiment was comprised of 17 English utterances and 17 non-English utterances[1]. The majority class baseline was thus 0.5. The mean accuracy of the 9 experiments in this study was 0.943, which is comparable to (1996)'s performance: in his study, the best performing PRLM exhibited an average accuracy of 0.950. This initial evaluation used the same data and feature as Zissman (1996). (Of the seven PRLM-based features listed above, only MaxLanguage was used in (1996)'s study.)

Table 2 summarizes the evaluation results of the non-English response detection experiments using three-fold cross-validation within the EN-detection partition. In order to investigate the impact of different types of features, the features were classified into four sets—**MaxLanguage** only, **PRLM** (encompassing all PRLM features), **SpeakingRate**, and **all**—and models were trained using each set. The baseline using majority voting demonstrated an accuracy of 0.95 by classifying all responses as English responses.

All models achieved improvements over baseline. In particular, the model using all features achieved a 66% relative error reduction over the baseline of 0.95. Furthermore, the all-features model outperformed the model based only on PRLM or speaking

[1]Due to the languages where the available responses were only 17, the same 17 English responses were used in the all experiment although 18 responses were available

Features	Acc.	Pre.	Rec.	F-score
Base-line	0.950	0.000	0.000	0.000
Max-Language	0.969	0.943	0.411	0.572
PRLM	0.966	0.675	0.633	0.649
Speaking-Rate	0.962	0.886	0.278	0.415
All	0.983	0.909	0.746	0.816

Table 2: Performance of non-English response detection

rate; the accuracy of the all-features model was approximately 1-2% higher than other models in absolute value and represented approximately a 45-50% relative error reduction over these models.

The PRLM-based model had higher overall accuracy than the speaking rate-based model, and the difference was even more salient by the F-score measure: the PRLM-based model achieved an F-score approximately 24% higher than the speaking rate-based model.

The model based on all PRLM features did not achieve a higher accuracy than the model based on only MaxLanguage. However, there was a clear improvement in F-score by using the additional features. The PRLM-based model achieved an F-score approximately 8% higher than the model based only on MaxLanguage.

In order to investigate the influence of speakers' proficiency on the accuracy of non-English detection, the responses in EN-detection were divided into 4 groups according to proficiency score, and the performance was calculated for each score group; the performance of each score group was calculated using subset comprised of all non-English responses and English responses with the corresponding scores.

A majority class baseline (classifying all responses as English) was again used. Table 3 summarizes the results observed, by score level, for the baseline model and for four different models used in Table 2. Note that the baseline is lower in Table 3 than in Table 2, because the ratio of English to non-English responses is lower for each of the subsets of the EN-detection partitions used for the evaluations

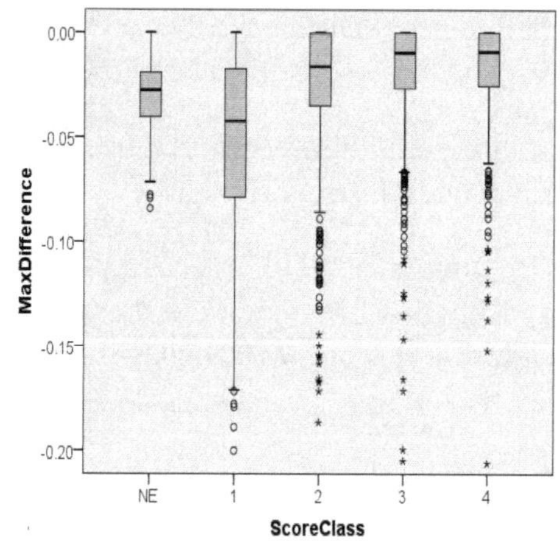

Figure 1: Relationship between proficiency score and MaxDifference

at a given score level.

For all score groups, the model using all features achieved high accuracy. The model's accuracy on all data sets except for score group 1 was approximately 0.96 and the F-score approximately 0.85. The accuracy on score group 1 was 0.87, relatively lower than other score groups. This is largely due to the smaller number of English responses available at score level 1, and the consequent lower baseline on this data set. However, the relative error reduction was much larger; it was 74% for score group 1.

For all score groups, the PRLM-based models outperformed MaxLanguage based models and speaking rate based models. Additional PRLM features improved the performance over the models only based on MaxLanguage (conventional language identification method). In addition, the combination of both types of features resulted in further improvement.

The consistent improvement of the model using both PRLM and speaking rate features suggests a compensatory relationship between these features. In order to investigate this relationship in further detail, two representative features, MaxDifference and AverageDifference were selected, and boxplots were created. Figure 1 and Figure 2 show the relationship between proficiency score and PRLM features. In these figures, the label 'NE' is used to indicate the non-English group, while the labels 1, 2, 3, and 4 correspond to each score group.

Figure 1 shows that MaxDifference decreases as

Score	Features	Acc.	Pre.	Rec.	F-score
1	Baseline	0.497	0.000	0.000	0.000
	MaxLanguage	0.696	0.970	0.411	0.577
	PRLM	0.792	0.936	0.633	0.752
	SpeakingRate	0.636	1.000	0.278	0.432
	All	0.869	0.992	0.746	0.851
2	Baseline	0.865	0.000	0.000	0.000
	MaxLanguage	0.919	0.983	0.411	0.579
	PRLM	0.930	0.811	0.633	0.709
	SpeakingRate	0.901	1.000	0.278	0.432
	All	0.962	0.971	0.746	0.843
3	Baseline	0.865	0.000	0.000	0.000
	MaxLanguage	0.920	1.000	0.411	0.582
	PRLM	0.939	0.903	0.633	0.738
	SpeakingRate	0.901	0.983	0.278	0.430
	All	0.963	0.976	0.746	0.845
4	Baseline	0.846	0.000	0.000	0.000
	MaxLanguage	0.908	0.987	0.411	0.579
	PRLM	0.936	0.934	0.633	0.752
	SpeakingRate	0.882	0.896	0.278	0.417
	All	0.955	0.956	0.746	0.837

Table 3: Performance of non-English detection according to speakers' proficiency level

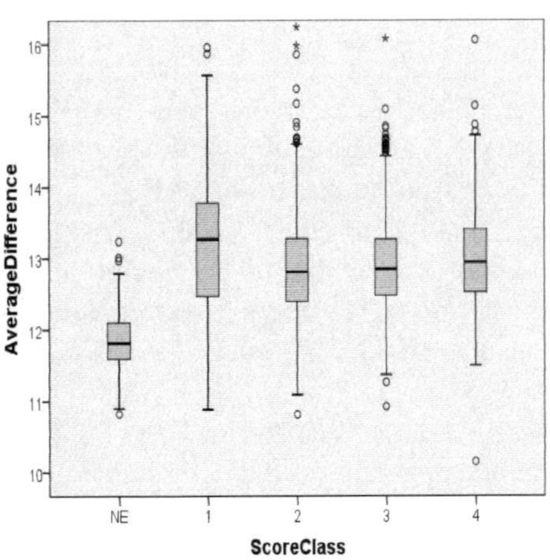

Figure 2: Relationship between proficiency score and AverageDifference

the speaker's proficiency decreases, although the feature displays a large variance. The feature mean for non-English responses is lower than for score groups 2, 3, and 4, but the distinction between non-English and English becomes smaller as the proficiency score decreases. The feature mean for score group 1 is even lower than for non-English responses. This obscures the distinction between English responses and non-English responses at lower score levels.

As Figure 2 shows, AverageDifference is relatively stable across score levels, compared to MaxDifference. Although the mean feature value decreases as the proficiency score decreases, the decrease is smaller than for MaxDifference. In addition, the mean feature values of the English groups are consistently higher than those for non-English responses.

Figure 3 shows the relationship between proficiency score and speaking rate.

For the speaking rate feature, the distinction between non-English and English responses increases as speakers' proficiency level decreases, as shown

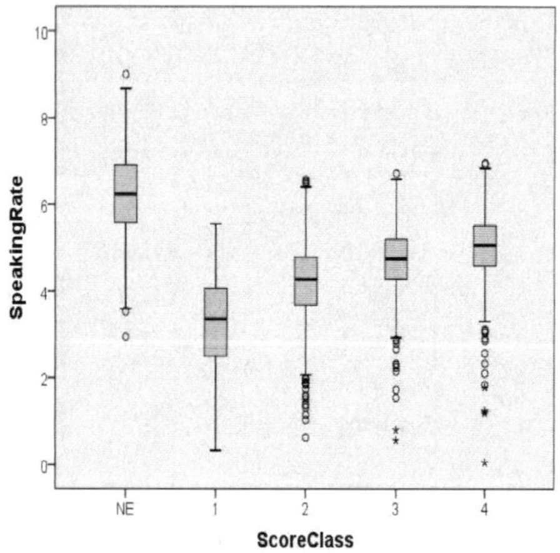

Figure 3: Relationship between proficiency score and SpeakingRate

in Figure 3. The speaking rate of non-English responses is the highest among all groups compared, and the speaking rate decreases for English responses as the speaker's proficiency score decreases. Thus, the PRLM features tend to display better discrimination between English and non-English responses at the higher end of the proficiency scale, while the SpeakingRate feature provides better discrimination at the lower end of the scale. By combining both feature classes, we are able to produce a model which outperforms both a PRLM-based model and a model using speaking rate alone.

6 Conclusion

In this study, we presented a non-English response detection method for non-native speakers' speech. A decision tree model was trained using PRLM-based features and speaking rate.

The method was intended for use as a supplementary module of an automated speech proficiency scoring system. The characteristics of non-native English speech (frequent pronunciation errors) reduced the phonetic distinction between English responses and non-English responses, and correspondingly, the differences between the feature values for non-English and English speech decreased as well.

In order to address this issue, a speaking rate feature was added to the model. This feature was specialized for second language (L2) learners' speech, as speaking rate has previously proved useful in estimating non-native speakers' speaking proficiency. In contrast to PRLM-based features, the speaking rate feature showed increasing discrimination between non-English and English speech samples as speakers' proficiency level decreased. The complementary relationship between PRLM-based features and speaking rate led to an improvement in the model when these features were combined. Improvements resulting from the combined feature set extended across speakers at all proficiency levels studied in the context of this paper.

The speaking rate becomes less effective if test takers speak slowly in their native languages. However, the test takers are unlikely to use this strategy, since it will result in a low score although they can game the system.

Due to lack of non-English responses in EPT data, non-English utterances were extracted from OGI data. Since the features in this study were not directly related to acoustic scores, the acoustic differences between EPT and OGI data may not give significant impact on the results. However, in order to avoid any influence by differences between corpora, the non-English responses will be collected using EPT setup and the evaluation will be performed using new data in future.

References

Mark Hall, Eibe Frank, Geoffrey Holmes, Bernhard Pfahringer, Peter Reutemann, and Ian H. Witten. 2009. The WEKA Data Mining Software: An Update. In *SIGKDD Explorations*, volume 11.

Lori F. Lamel and Jean-Luc Gauvain. 1993. Cross-lingual experiments with phone recognition. In *Proceedings of the IEEE International Conference on Acoustics, Speech, and Signal Processing*, volume 2, pages 507–510.

Haizhou Li, Bin Ma, and Chin-Hui Lee. 2007. A vector space modeling approach to spoken language identification. *Audio, Speech and Language Processing*, 15:271 – 284.

Boon Pang Lim, Haizhou Li, and Yu Chen. 2004. Language identification through large vocabulary continuous speech recognition. In *Proceedings of the 2004 International Symposium on Chinese Spoken Language Processing*, pages 49 – 52.

Yeshwant K. Muthusamy, Ronald A. Cole, and Beatrice T. Oshika. 1992. The OGI multi-language telephone speech corpus. In *Proceedings of the Inter-*

national Conference on Spoken Language Processing, pages 895–898.

Helmer Strik and Catia Cucchiarini. 1999. Automatic assessment of second language learners' fluency. In *Proceedings of the 14th International Congress of Phonetic Sciences*, pages 759–762, San Francisco, USA.

Steve Young, Gunnar Evermann, Dan Kershaw, Gareth Moore, Julian Odell, Dave Ollason, Dan Povey, Valtcho Valtchev, and Phil Woodland. 2002. *The HTK Book (for HTK Version3.2)*. Microsoft Corporation and Cambridge University Engineering Department.

Klaus Zechner, Derrick Higgins, Xiaoming Xi, and David M. Williamson. 2009. Automatic scoring of non-native spontaneous speech in tests of spoken english. *Speech Communication*, 51(10):883 – 895.

Marc A. Zissman. 1996. Comparison of four approaches to automatic language identification of telephone speech. *Speech and Audio Processing*, 4:31 – 44.

Bilingual Random Walk Models for Automated Grammar Correction of ESL Author-Produced Text

Randy West and **Y. Albert Park**
Department of Computer Science & Engineering
University of California, San Diego
La Jolla, CA 92093-0533
{rdwest,yapark}@cs.ucsd.edu

Roger Levy
Department of Linguistics
University of California, San Diego
La Jolla, CA 92093-0533
rlevy@ucsd.edu

Abstract

We present a novel noisy channel model for correcting text produced by English as a second language (ESL) authors. We model the English word choices made by ESL authors as a random walk across an undirected bipartite dictionary graph composed of edges between English words and associated words in an author's native language. We present two such models, using cascades of weighted finite-state transducers (wFSTs) to model language model priors, random walk-induced noise, and observed sentences, and expectation maximization (EM) to learn model parameters after Park and Levy (2011). We show that such models can make intelligent word substitutions to improve grammaticality in an unsupervised setting.

1 Introduction

How do language learners make word choices as they compose text in a language in which they are not fluent? Anyone who has attempted to learn a foreign language can attest to spending a great deal of time leafing through the pages of a bilingual dictionary. However, dictionaries, especially those without a wealth of example sentences or accompanying word sense information, can often lead even the most scrupulous of language learners in the wrong direction. Consider an example: the English noun "head" has several senses, e.g. the physical head and the head of an organization. However, the Japanese *atama* can only mean the physical head or mind, and likewise *shuchou*, meaning "chief," can only map to the second sense of head. A native English speaker and Japanese learner faced with the choice of these two words and no additional explanation of which Japanese word corresponds to which sense is liable to make a mistake on the flip of a coin.

One could of course conceive of more subtle examples where the semantics of a set of choices are not so blatantly orthogonal. "Complete" and "entire" are synonyms, but they are not necessarily interchangeable. "Complete stranger" is a common two-word phrase, but "entire stranger" sounds completely strange, if not entirely ungrammatical, to the native English speaker, who will correct "entire" to "complete" in a surprisingly automatic fashion. Thus, correct word choice in non-native language production is essential not only to the preservation of intended meaning, but also to fluent expression of the correct meaning.

The development of software to correct ESL text is valuable for both learning and communication. A language learner provided instant grammaticality feedback during self-study is less likely to fall into patterns of misuse, and the comprehension difficulties one may encounter when corresponding with non-native speakers would be ameliorated by an automated system to improve text fluency. Additionally, since machine-translated text is often ungrammatical, automated grammar correction algorithms can be deployed as part of a machine translation system to improve the quality of output.

We propose that word choice production errors on the part of the language learner can be modeled as follows. Given an observed word and an undirected bipartite graph with nodes representing

Proceedings of the Sixth Workshop on Innovative Use of NLP for Building Educational Applications, pages 170–179,
Portland, Oregon, 24 June 2011. ©2011 Association for Computational Linguistics

words in one of two languages, i.e. English and the sentence author's native tongue, and edges between words in each language and their dictionary translation in the other (see Figure 1 for an example), there exists some function $f \mapsto [0,1]$ that defines the parameters of a random walk along graph edges, conditioned on the source word. By composing this graph with a language model prior such as an n-gram model or probabilistic context-free grammar, we can "correct" an observed sentence by inferring the most likely unobserved sentence from which it originated.

More concretely, given that we know f, we can compute $\text{argmax}_{\boldsymbol{w}'} p(\boldsymbol{w}'|\boldsymbol{w}, f, \theta)$, where $\boldsymbol{w}$ is the observed sentence, θ is the language model, and $\boldsymbol{w}'$ is the "corrected," unobserved sentence. Under this view, some $\boldsymbol{w}'$ drawn from the distribution θ is subjected to some noise process f, which perturbs the sentence author's intended meaning and outputs $\boldsymbol{w}$. We perform this computation in the standard way from the statistical machine translation (SMT) literature (Brown et al., 1993), namely by using Bayes' theorem to write

$$p(\boldsymbol{w}'|\boldsymbol{w}, f, \theta) = \frac{p(\boldsymbol{w}'|\theta)p(\boldsymbol{w}|\boldsymbol{w}', f, \theta)}{p(\boldsymbol{w}|\theta)}$$

Since the denominator of the RHS is independent of $\boldsymbol{w}'$, we can rewrite our argmax as

$$\underset{\boldsymbol{w}'}{\text{argmax}}\, p(\boldsymbol{w}'|\theta)p(\boldsymbol{w}|\boldsymbol{w}', f, \theta)$$

We have now decomposed our original equation into two manageable parts, a prior belief about the grammaticality of an unobserved sentence $\boldsymbol{w}'$, which we can compute using a language model θ learned separately using standard supervised techniques (in particular, n-gram estimation), and the probability of the observed sentence $\boldsymbol{w}$ given $\boldsymbol{w}'$, f, and θ. Together, these constitute a noisy channel model from information theory (Shannon, 1948). All that remains is to learn an appropriate f, for which we will employ unsupervised methods, namely expectation maximization.

The rest of this paper is organized as follows. In Section 2, we will discuss related work. In Section 3, we will present the implementation, methodology and results of two experiments with different f. In Section 4, we will discuss our experimental results, and we will conclude in Section 5.

2 Related Work

The literature on automated grammar correction is mostly focused on rule-based methods and error identification rather than correction. However, there has been a recent outgrowth in the application of machine translation (MT) techniques to address the problem of single-language grammar correction. Park and Levy (2011) propose a noisy channel model for learning to correct various types of errors, including article and preposition errors, word-form errors, and spelling mistakes, to which this paper is an extension. As the present work builds on Park and Levy's basic model, we will reserve a more detailed discussion of their work for Section 3.

Brockett et al. (2006) use phrasal SMT techniques to identify and correct mass noun errors of ESL students with some success, but they correct no other production error classes to our knowledge.

Lee and Seneff (2006) learn a method to aid ESL students in language acquisition by reducing sentences to their canonical form, i.e. a lemmatized form devoid of articles, prepositions, and auxiliaries, and then building an over-specified lattice by reinserting all word inflections and removed word classes. They then score this lattice using a trigram model and PCFG. While this method has many advantages, it does not take into account the full context of the original sentence.

Kok and Brockett (2010) use random walks over bi- and multilingual graphs generated by aligning English sentences with translations in 10 other European languages to learn paraphrases, which they then evaluate in the context of the original sentence. While their approach shares many high-level similarities with ours, both their task, paraphrasing correct sentences, and the details of their methodology are divergent from the present work.

Désilets and Hermet (2009) employ round-trip machine translation from L1 to L2 and back again to correct second language learner text by keeping track of the word alignments between translations. They operate on a very similar hypothesis to that of this work, namely that language learners make overly-literal translations when the produce text in their second language. However, they go about correcting these errors in a very different way than the present work, which is novel to the best of

Figure 1: Example English-Korean dictionary graph for a subset of the edges out of the English *head*, *leader*, and *chief*.

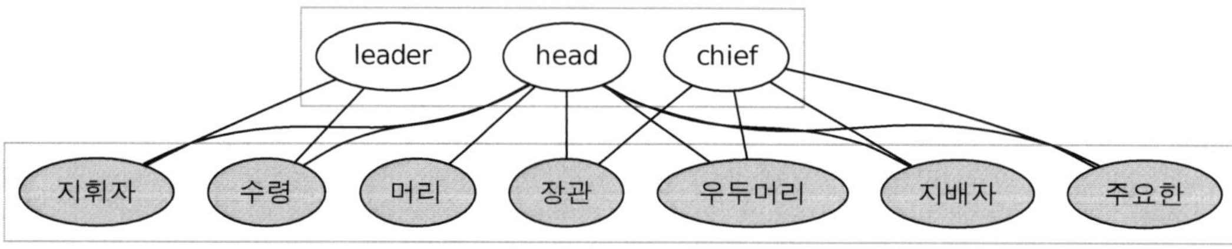

our knowledge, and their technique of using error-annotated sentences for evaluation makes a comparison difficult.

3 Model Implementation and Experiments

We present the results of two experiments with different random walk parametrizations. We begin by describing our dataset, then proceed to an overview of our model and experimental procedures, and finally detail the experiments themselves.

3.1 Dataset

We use the dataset of Park and Levy (2011), a collection of approximately 25,000 essays comprised of 478,350 sentences scraped from web postings made by Korean ESL students studying for the Test of English as a Foreign Language (TOEFL). Of these, we randomly select 10,000 sentences for training, 504 as a development set, and 1017 held out for final model evaluation.

Our English-Korean dictionary is scraped from `http://endic2009.naver.com`, a widely-used and trusted online dictionary source in South Korea. We are unfortunately unaware of any freely available, downloadable English-Korean dictionary databases.

3.2 Model and Experimental Procedures

3.2.1 Overview

The bulk of our experimental methodology and machinery is borrowed from Park and Levy (2011), so we will summarize that portion of it only briefly here. At a high level, there are three major components to the model of a sentence: a language prior, a noise model, and an observed sentence. Each of these is implemented as a wFST and composed together into a single transducer whose accepting paths represent all possibilities of transducing from an (unobserved) input sentence to the (observed) output sentence, with the path weight being associated probability. See Figure 2 for an example.

3.2.2 Language Model

For our language model, we use a Kneser-Ney smoothed trigram model learned from a version of the British National Corpus modified to use Americanized spellings (Chen and Goodman, 1996; Burnard, 1995). The implementation of an n-gram model as a wFST requires that each state represent a context, and so one must necessarily instantiate arcs for all words in the alphabet from each state. In order to reduce model size and minimize memory usage, it is standard practice to remove relatively uninformative higher-order n-grams from the model, but under the wFST regime one cannot, for example, remove some trigrams from a bigram context without removing all of them. Instead, we retain only the 1,000 most informative bigram *contexts*, as measured by the Kullback-Leibler divergence between each bigram context and its unigram counterpart. This is in contrast to standard cutoff models, which remove n-grams occurring less than some cutoff number of times in the corpus.

3.2.3 Noise Models

The structure of the noise wFST differs for each noise model; for our model of word-choice error, we can use a single initial/final state with arcs labeled with unobserved words as input, observed words as output, and a weight defined by the function f that governs the parameters of a random walk across our dictionary graph (again, see Figure 2 for an example). We will reserve the definition of f, which is

Figure 2: Example wFSTs for the sentence "head chief". From top to bottom, the pictured transducers are the observed sentence s, a noise model n with parameter λ, a unigram language model l representing the normalized frequency of each word, and the fully composed model, $l \circ n \circ s$.

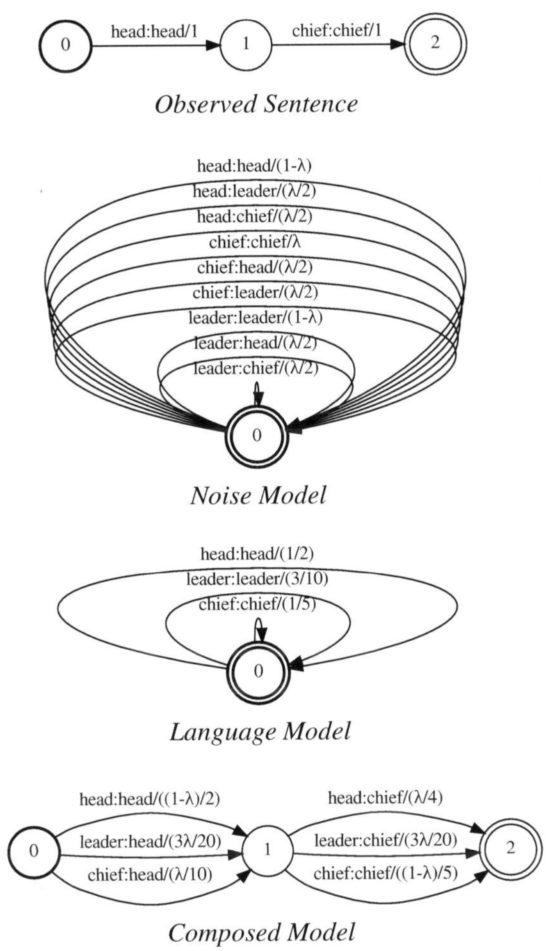

different for each experiment, for Section 3.3.

We have thus far proceeded by describing the construction of an ideal noise model that completely implements the dictionary graph described previously. However, due to the size of the dictionary graph, such a model would be computationally prohibitive[1]. Moreover, we must handle the non-trivial peculiars of arbitrary lookups in a roughly lemmatized dictionary and preservation of word forms through random walks, which we discuss now.

[1] The maximum degree of the dictionary graph is 515, meaning that the upper bound on the number of paths in a random walk of length 2 is $515^2 = 265,225$!

Among its various capabilities, the CELEX database (Baayen et al., 1995) provides interfaces for mapping arbitrary English words to their lemmas, querying for lemma syntactic (sub)classes, and discovering the morphological inflectional features of arbitrary words. We use these capabilities in conjunction with unigram frequencies from our language model and a standard stop word filter to build abridged sets of random walk candidates as in Algorithm 1.

Algorithm 1 Build an abridged set of random walk candidates C for an observed word w s.t. each $c_i \in C$ has syntactic and morphological characteristics similar to w and is in the top m such candidates as sorted by word frequency.

Let $G = (V, E)$ be the undirected dictionary graph, m the max candidates per word, B the set of stop words, I the set of inflectional features of w, and C the set of random walk candidates for w, initially $\{\}$
if $w \in B$ **then**
  return $\{\}$
end if
for lemmas l of w **do**
  Let S be the set of syntactic classes of l
  for l' generated from a random walk of length 2 in G from l **do**
    if $S \cap \{$syntactic classes of $l'\} \neq \{\}$ **then**
      for words w' related to l' **do**
        if $I \cap \{$inflectional features of $w'\} \neq \{\} \wedge w' \notin B$ **then**
          $C \leftarrow C \cup \{w'\}$
        end if
      end for
    end if
  end for
end for
if $|C| > m$ **then**
  $C \leftarrow$ top m members of C by word frequency
end if
return C

3.2.4 Sentence Models

Sentences are simply identity transducers, i.e. wFSTs with $n + 1$ states for a sentence of length n and a single arc between each state $0 \leq i < n$ and state $i+1$ labeled with input and output token i from the sentence and weight 1.

3.2.5 Training and Decoding

For training, we hold language model parameters constant and use expectation maximization (Dempster et al., 1977) to learn noise model parameters as follows. We replace language model input symbols and sentence model output symbols with the empty symbol ϵ and use the V-expectation semiring of Eisner (2002) to annotate noise model arcs with initial parameter values. This is our M-step. Then, we compose the language, noise, and sentence models, which produces a transducer with only ϵ-labeled arcs, and use ϵ-removal to move expectation information into a single state from which we can easily read off expected noise model parameter counts thanks to the V-expectation semiring's bookkeeping (Eisner, 2002; Mohri, 2001). We repeat this process over a batch of training sentences and add the results together to yield a final vector of expected counts. This is our E-step. Finally, we normalize the expected parameter counts to recompute our parameters and rebuild the noise model in a repetition of the M-step. This process goes back and forth from E- to M-step until the parameters converge within some threshold.

The decoding or inference process is performed in a similar fashion, the main difference being that we use the negative log Viterbi semiring for computing shortest paths instead of the V-expectation semiring. We first build a new noise model for each sentence using the parameter values learned during training. Then, the language, noise, and sentence models (sans ϵ substitutions) are composed together, and the shortest path is computed.

3.2.6 wFST Implementation

All wFST manipulation is performed using OpenFST (Allauzen et al., 2007), an open source weighted finite-state transducer library written in C++. Additionally, we use the V-expectation semiring code of Dreyer et al. (2008) for training.

3.2.7 Evaluation

The most probable unobserved sentence $\boldsymbol{w}'$ from which the observed sentence $\boldsymbol{w}$ was generated under our model, $\text{argmax}_{\boldsymbol{w}'} p(\boldsymbol{w}'|\theta)p(\boldsymbol{w}|\boldsymbol{w}', f, \theta)$, can be read off from the input of the transducer produced during the decoding process. In order to evaluate its quality versus the observed ESL sentence, we use the `METEOR`[2] and `BLEU` evaluation metrics for machine translation (Lavie and Agarwal, 2007; Papineni et al., 2002). This evaluation is performed using a set of human-corrected sentences gathered via Amazon Mechanical Turk, an online service where workers are paid to perform a short task, and further filtered for correctness by an undergraduate research assistant. 8 workers were assigned to correct each sentence from the development and evaluation sets described in Section 3.1, and so after filtering we had 8 or fewer unique corrected versions per sentence available for evaluation. We note that the use of `METEOR` and `BLEU` is justified inasmuch as the process of grammar correction is translation from an ungrammatical "language" to a grammatical one (Park and Levy, 2011). However, it is far from perfect, as we shall see shortly.

While human evaluation is far too costly to attempt at every step during development, it is very worthwhile to examine our corrections through a human eye for final evaluation, especially given the somewhat tenuous suitability of `METEOR` and `BLEU` for our evaluation task. In order to facilitate this, we designed a simple task, again using Amazon Mechanical Turk, where native English speakers are presented with side-by-side ESL and corrected sentences and asked to choose which is more correct. Workers are instructed to "judge whether the corrected sentence improves the grammaticality and/or fluency of the ESL sentence without changing the ESL sentence's basic meaning." They are then presented with two questions per sentence pair:

1. *Question:* "Between the two sentences listed above, which is more correct?"
   Answer choices: "ESL sentence is more correct," "Corrected sentence is more correct," "Both are equally correct," and, "The sentences are identical."

[2] Although the `METEOR` "synonymy" module may initially seem appropriate to our evaluation task, we find that it does little to improve or clarify evaluation results. For that reason, and moreover since we do not wish for differing forms of the same lemma to be given equal weight in a grammar correction task, we instead use the "exact" module for all evaluation in this paper.

2. *Question:* "Is the meaning of the corrected sentence significantly different from that of the ESL sentence?"
   Answer choices: "Yes, the two sentences do not mean the same thing," and, "No, the two sentences have roughly the same meaning."

Each task is 10 sentences long, 3 of which are identical filler sentences. When a worker mislabels more than one sentence as identical in any single task, the results for that task are thrown out and resubmitted for another worker to complete. We additionally require that each sentence pair be judged by 5 unique, U.S.-based workers.

3.3 Experiments

3.3.1 Experiment 1

Motivation and Noise Model For our first experiment, we assume that the probability of arriving at some word $w' \neq w$ after a random walk of length 2 from an observed word w is uniform across all w. This is perhaps not the most plausible model, but it serves as a baseline by which we can evaluate more complex models.

More concretely, we use a single parameter λ modeling the probability of walking two steps along the dictionary graph from an observed English word w to its Korean definition(s), and then back to some other English word $w' \neq w$. Since we treat unobserved words as transducer input and observed words as output, λ is normalized by $|\{w|w \neq w'\}|$, i.e. the number of edges with different input and output per input word, and $p(w|w) = 1 - \lambda$ such that $\sum_w p(w|w') = 1$.

Initialization and Other Settings We train two variations on the same model, setting m from Algorithm 1, i.e. the maximum number of allowed random walk candidates per word, to 5 and 10. We initialize λ to 0.01 for each.

Results We find that both variations converge after roughly 10 iterations[3]. The parameters learned are slightly lower than the initialization value ($\lambda =$ 0.01), 0.007246 for the 5 candidate variation and 0.009528 for the 10 candidate variation. We interpret the parameter value disparity between the two model variations as follows. The larger the number of random walk candidates available for each observed word, the more likely that at least one of the candidates has a high probability in the sentence context, so it makes sense that the 10 candidate variation would yield a higher value for λ. Moreover, recalling that λ is normalized by the number of observed words $|\{w|w \neq w'\}|$ reachable from each unobserved candidate word w', it is reasonable that a higher value of λ would need to be learned in order to distribute enough probability mass to candidates that are highly probable in the sentence context.

The METEOR and BLEU scores for this Experiment are summarized in Table 1, and the final parameter values after 10 iterations are listed in Table 2. We discuss these in greater detail in Section 4.

Table 1: METEOR and BLEU scores for all experiments.

	METEOR	BLEU
ESL baseline	0.820802	0.715625
Exp. 1, 5 candidates	0.816055	0.708871
Exp. 1, 10 candidates	0.815703	0.708284
Exp. 2, 5 candidates	0.815162	0.707549
Exp. 2, 10 candidates	0.814533	0.706587

Table 2: Final parameter values after 10 iterations for Experiment 1 with 5 and 10 word random walk candidate limits.

	Max 5 Candidates	Max 10 Candidates
λ	0.007246	0.009528

3.3.2 Experiment 2

Motivation and Noise Model For our second experiment, we hypothesize that there is an inverse relationship between unobserved word frequency and random walk path probability. We motivate this by observing that when a language learner produces a common word, it is likely that she either meant to use that word or used it in place of a rarer word that she did not know. Likewise, when she uses a rare word, it is likely that she chose it above any of the

[3]Running on a Linux server with two quad-core Intel Xeon processors and 72GB of memory, training for all models in this paper takes around 4 hours per model. Note that decoding is a much quicker process, requiring less than one second per sentence.

common words that she knows. If the word that she chose was erroneous, then, it is most likely that she did not mean to use a common word but could have meant to use a different rare word with a subtle semantic difference. Hence, we should always prefer to replace observed words, regardless of their frequency, with rare words unless the language model overwhelmingly prefers a common word.

In order to model this hypothesis, we introduce a second parameter $\alpha < 0$ to which power the unigram frequency of each unobserved word w', $\text{freq}(w')$, is raised. The resulting full model is $p(w|w')_{w \neq w'} = \frac{\text{freq}(w')^{\alpha}\lambda}{|\{w|w \neq w'\}|}$ and $p(w|w) = 1 - \text{freq}(w)^{\alpha}\lambda$. We approximate the full model to simple coin flips by bucketing the unique word frequencies from the language model and initializing each bucket using its average frequency and some appropriate initial values of α and λ, leaving us with a number of parameters equal to the number of frequency buckets.

Initialization and Other Settings We train two variations on the same model, setting m from Algorithm 1 to 5 and 10. We initialize λ to 0.01 and α to -0.1 for each and use 10 frequency buckets.

Results As in Experiment 1, we find that both model variations converge after roughly 10 iterations. The random walk parameters learned for both variations in the highest frequency bucket, $\text{freq}(w')^{\alpha}\lambda \approx 0.004803$ and 0.004845 for 5 and 10 candidates, respectively, seem to validate our hypothesis that we should prefer rare unobserved words. However, the parameters learned for the proceeding buckets do not indicate the smooth positive slope that we might have hoped for, which we discuss further in Section 4. The 10 candidate variation learns consistently higher parameter values than the 5 candidate variation, and we interpret this disparity in the same way as in Experiment 1.

The METEOR and BLEU scores for this Experiment are summarized in Table 1, and the final parameter values after 10 iterations are listed in Table 3. We discuss these in greater detail in Section 4.

Table 3: Final parameter values after 10 iterations for Experiment 2 with 5 and 10 word random walk candidate limits.

Word Frequency (high to low)	Max 5 Candidates	Max 10 Candidates
Bucket 1	0.004803	0.004845
Bucket 2	0.031505	0.052706
Bucket 3	0.019211	0.036479
Bucket 4	0.006871	0.013130
Bucket 5	0.002603	0.005024
Bucket 6	0.000032	0.000599
Bucket 7	0.001908	0.003336
Bucket 8	0.000609	0.002771
Bucket 9	0.001256	0.002014
Bucket 10	0.006085	0.006828

4 Discussion

At first glance, the experimental results are less than satisfactory. However, METEOR and BLEU do not tell the whole story. At a high level, these metrics work by computing the level of agreement, e.g. unigram and bigram precision, between the sentence being evaluated and a pool of "correct" sentences (Lavie and Agarwal, 2007; Papineni et al., 2002). When the correct sentences agree strongly with each other, the evaluated sentence is heavily penalized for any departures from the correct sentence pool. This sort of penalization can occur even when the model-corrected sentence is a perfectly valid correction that just had the misfortune of choosing a different replacement word than the majority of the human workers. For example, one ESL sentence in our evaluation set reads, *progress of medical science helps human live longer.* All four of our models correct this to *progress of medical science helps people live longer*, but none of the workers correct to "people," instead opting for "humans." This issue is exacerbated by the fact that Mechanical Turk workers were instructed to change each ESL sentence as little as possible, which helps their consistency but hurts these particular models' evaluation scores.

With the exception of some mostly harmless but ultimately useless exchanges, e.g. changing "reduce mistakes" to "reduce errors," the models actually do fairly well when they correct ungrammatical words and phrases. As we alluded to in Section 1, all four model variations correct the sentence *to begin with, i'd rather not room with someone who is a entire stranger to me* from our development set to *to be-*

gin with, i'd rather not room with someone who is a complete stranger to me. But only 2 out of 5 human workers make this correction, 2 retain "entire," and 1 removes it altogether. As another example, all model variations correct *however, depending merely on luck is very dangerous* from our evaluation set to *however, depending solely on luck is very dangerous*. However, only 1 worker corrects "merely" to "solely," with the others either preferring to retain "merely" or leaving it out entirely.

None of this is to say that the models suffer only from an unfortunate difference in correction bias relative to the workers, or even that the models make good corrections a majority of the time. In fact, they make a range of false-positive corrections as well[4]. These seem to fall into three major categories: slight preferences for similar words that don't fit in the overall context of the sentence or change its meaning in an undesired way, e.g. changing "roommate" to "lodger" in *you and your roommate must devide [sic] the housework*, strong preferences for very common words in the local context that render the corrected sentence ungrammatical, e.g. changing "compose" to "take" in *first, during childhood years, we compose our personality*, and misinterpretations of ambiguous parts of speech that cause nouns to be replaced with verbs, etc., e.g. changing "circumstance" to "go" in ... *that help you look abound your circumstance and find out* ....

Many of these issues can be blamed at least partially on the myopia of the language model, which, for example, vastly prefers "go and find" to "circumstance and find." However, they can also be attributed to the motivational intuition for Experiment 2, which states that we should avoid replacing observed words with common alternatives. While Table 3 does demonstrate that the models in Experiment 2 learn this preference to a degree for the highest frequency bucket, the proceeding buckets do not exhibit a smooth upwards slope analogous to the function being approximated. Indeed, the words in bucket 2 are preferred an order of magnitude more than those in bucket 1. This can be traced to the truncation policy of Algorithm 1, which selects only the highest frequency words from an over-sized set of random walk candidates. While it is unclear how to intelligently select a good candidate set of manageable size, a policy that butts heads with our intuition about which words we should be correcting is clearly not the right one.

The differences between the models themselves are somewhat more difficult to interpret. The 5 and 10 candidate variations of Experiment 1 and those of Experiment 2 correct 103, 108, 115, and 130 sentences out of 1017, respectively, and at least one model differs from the others on 123 of those sentences (they all agree on 42 sentences). These disagreements are of all types: sometimes only a single model corrects or vice versa, sometimes two models are pitted against the other two, and occasionally all four will choose a different word, but none of these inconsistencies seem to follow any sort of pattern, e.g. the two five candidate models agreeing more often than the other two or the like.

Interestingly, however, the models tend to be in agreement on the sentences that they correct the most effectively. We explore this more concretely in Table 4, in which we manually judge the quality of sentence corrections versus the agreement between models. Specifically, we judge a set of sentence corrections as *Good* if all of the corrections made between models improve sentence grammaticality, *Harmless* if the corrections do not significantly improve or reduce grammaticality, and *Bad* if at least one of the corrections is either ungrammatical or changes the sentence meaning. We note that *Bad* corrections for the most part do not take grammatical sentences and make them ungrammatical, only perturb them in some other erroneous fashion. Clearly, there is a strong correlation between corrected sentence quality and model agreement. We conclude from this observation that the models are all learning to correct the most unambiguously incorrect sentences in a consistent way, but where some deal of ambiguity remains, they are subject to random differences inherent in each's construction.

To round out our evaluation of correction quality, we presented the corrected sentences from all 4 model variations to human workers for judgment using the task detailed in Section 3.2.7. The results

[4]Although Type I errors are of course undesirable, Gamon et al. (2009) suggest that learners are able to effectively distinguish between good and bad corrections when presented with possible error locations and scored alternatives. Such an interactive system is beyond the scope of this paper but nonetheless feasible without significant model modification.

Table 4: Manual judgments of model-corrected sentence quality between experiments. If all models are in agreement, a sentence is marked as *Same*, and *Different* otherwise. We judge a set of sentence corrections as *Good* if all of the corrections made between models improve sentence grammaticality, *Harmless* if the corrections do not significantly improve or reduce grammaticality, and *Bad* if at least one of the corrections is either ungrammatical or changes the sentence meaning. Only corrected sentences are listed.

Model Agreement	Judgment	# of Sentences	% of Total
Same	Good	6	14.3%
	Harmless	11	26.2%
	Bad	25	59.5%
	Total	42	–
Different	Good	4	3.3%
	Harmless	34	27.6%
	Bad	85	69.1%
	Total	123	–

Figure 3: Human judgments of corrected sentences gathered using Mechanical Turk. The items listed in the legend are answers to the questions *Between the [original (ESL) and corrected] sentences, which is more correct? / Is the meaning of the corrected sentence significantly different from that of the ESL sentence?* See Section 3.2.7 for methodological details and Section 4 for results discussion.

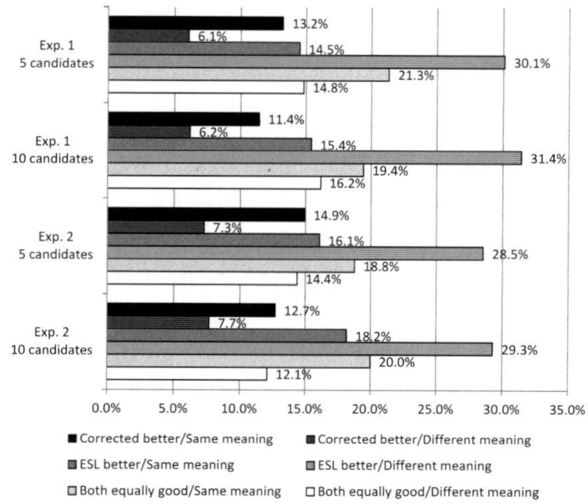

of this effort are detailed in Figure 3. The workers are perhaps a bit more generous with their judgments than we are, but overall, they tend towards the same results that we do in our manual evaluation. Aside from the conclusions already presented, the worker judgments do expose one interesting finding: When the corrected sentence is judged to be at least as grammatical as the ESL sentence, it also tends to preserve the ESL sentence's meaning. However, when the ESL sentence is judged more correct, the meaning preservation trend is reversed. This observation leads us to believe that incorporating some measure of semantic distance into our random walk function f might prove effective.

5 Conclusion and Future Work

We have presented a novel noisy channel model for correcting a broad class of language learner production errors. Although our experimental results are mixed, we believe that our model constitutes an interesting and potentially very fruitful approach to ESL grammar correction. There are a number of opportunities for improvement available. Using a richer language model, such as a PCFG, would undoubtedly improve our results. Noting that ESL errors tend to occur in groups within sentences and are often interdependent, the addition of other noise models, such as those detailed in Park and Levy (2011), would further improve things by allowing the language model to consider a wider range of corrected contexts around each word. Our random walk model itself could also be improved by incorporating observed word frequency information or some notion of semantic difference between observed and unobserved words, or by learning separate parameters for different word classes. Somewhat counterintuitively, a structured reduction of dictionary richness could also yield better results by limiting the breadth of random walk candidates. Finally, a more intelligent heuristic for truncating large sets of random walk candidates would likely foster improvement.

Acknowledgments

We would like to thank three anonymous reviewers for their insightful comments and suggestions, and Markus Dreyer for providing us with his expectation semiring code. Additionally, we are grateful to the San Diego Supercomputer Center for allowing us access to DASH.

References

Cyril Allauzen, Michael Riley, Johan Schalkwyk, Wojciech Skut, and Mehryar Mohri. 2007. Openfst: a general and efficient weighted finite-state transducer library. In *Proceedings of the 12th international conference on Implementation and application of automata*, CIAA'07, pages 11–23, Berlin, Heidelberg. Springer-Verlag.

Harald R. Baayen, Richard Piepenbrock, and Leon Gulikers. 1995. *The CELEX Lexical Database. Release 2 (CD-ROM).* Linguistic Data Consortium, University of Pennsylvania, Philadelphia, Pennsylvania.

Chris Brockett, William B. Dolan, and Michael Gamon. 2006. Correcting esl errors using phrasal smt techniques. In *Proceedings of the 21st International Conference on Computational Linguistics and the 44th annual meeting of the Association for Computational Linguistics*, ACL-44, pages 249–256, Stroudsburg, PA, USA. Association for Computational Linguistics.

Peter F. Brown, Vincent J. Della Pietra, Stephen A. Della Pietra, and Robert L. Mercer. 1993. The mathematics of statistical machine translation: parameter estimation. *Comput. Linguist.*, 19:263–311, June.

Lou Burnard. 1995. *Users Reference Guide British National Corpus Version 1.0.* Oxford University Computing Services, UK.

Stanley F. Chen and Joshua Goodman. 1996. An empirical study of smoothing techniques for language modeling. In *Proceedings of the 34th annual meeting on Association for Computational Linguistics*, ACL '96, pages 310–318, Stroudsburg, PA, USA. Association for Computational Linguistics.

Arthur P. Dempster, Nan M. Laird, and Donald B. Rubin. 1977. Maximum likelihood from incomplete data via the EM algorithm (with discussion). *Journal of the Royal Statistical Society B*, 39:1–38.

Alain Désilets and Matthieu Hermet. 2009. Using automatic roundtrip translation to repair general errors in second language writing. pages 198–206. MT Summit XII.

Markus Dreyer, Jason R. Smith, and Jason Eisner. 2008. Latent-variable modeling of string transductions with finite-state methods. In *Proceedings of the Conference on Empirical Methods in Natural Language Processing*, EMNLP '08, pages 1080–1089, Stroudsburg, PA, USA. Association for Computational Linguistics.

Jason Eisner. 2002. Parameter estimation for probabilistic finite-state transducers. In *Proceedings of the 40th Annual Meeting on Association for Computational Linguistics*, ACL '02, pages 1–8, Stroudsburg, PA, USA. Association for Computational Linguistics.

Michael Gamon, Claudia Leacock, Chris Brockett, William B Dolan, Jianfeng Gao, Dmitriy Belenko, and Alexandre Klementiev. 2009. Using statistical techniques and web search to correct esl errors. *CALICO Journal*, 26:491–511.

Stanley Kok and Chris Brockett. 2010. Hitting the right paraphrases in good time. In *Human Language Technologies: The 2010 Annual Conference of the North American Chapter of the Association for Computational Linguistics*, HLT '10, pages 145–153, Stroudsburg, PA, USA. Association for Computational Linguistics.

Alon Lavie and Abhaya Agarwal. 2007. Meteor: an automatic metric for mt evaluation with high levels of correlation with human judgments. In *Proceedings of the Second Workshop on Statistical Machine Translation*, StatMT '07, pages 228–231, Stroudsburg, PA, USA. Association for Computational Linguistics.

John Lee and Stephanie Seneff. 2006. Automatic grammar correction for second-language learners. ICSLP.

Mehryar Mohri. 2001. Generic ϵ-removal algorithm for weighted automata. In Shen Yu and Andrei Paun, editors, *Implementation and Application of Automata*, volume 2088 of *Lecture Notes in Computer Science*, pages 230–242. Springer Berlin / Heidelberg.

Kishore Papineni, Salim Roukos, Todd Ward, and Wei-Jing Zhu. 2002. Bleu: a method for automatic evaluation of machine translation. In *Proceedings of the 40th Annual Meeting on Association for Computational Linguistics*, ACL '02, pages 311–318, Stroudsburg, PA, USA. Association for Computational Linguistics.

Y. Albert Park and Roger Levy. 2011. Automated whole sentence grammar correction using a noisy channel model. ACL '11. Association for Computational Linguistics. In Press.

C. E. Shannon. 1948. A mathematical theory of communication. *Bell Systems Technical Journal*, 27:623–656.

High-Order Sequence Modeling for Language Learner Error Detection

Michael Gamon
Microsoft Research
One Microsoft Way
Redmond, WA 98052
mgamon@microsoft.com

Abstract

We address the problem of detecting English language learner errors by using a discriminative high-order sequence model. Unlike most work in error-detection, this method is agnostic as to specific error types, thus potentially allowing for higher recall across different error types. The approach integrates features from many sources into the error-detection model, ranging from language model-based features to linguistic analysis features. Evaluation results on a large annotated corpus of learner writing indicate the feasibility of our approach on a realistic, noisy and inherently skewed set of data. High-order models consistently outperform low-order models in our experiments. Error analysis on the output shows that the calculation of precision on the test set represents a lower bound on the real system performance.

1. Introduction

Systems for automatic detection and correction of errors in native writing have been developed for many decades. Early in the development of these systems, the approach was exclusively based on knowledge engineering. Hand-crafted grammars would analyze a sentence and would contain special mechanisms for rule or constraint relaxation that allow ungrammatical sentences to produce a parse, while at the same time indicating that a grammatical error is present. More recently, data-driven methods have assumed prominence and there has been an emerging area of research into the challenge of detecting and correcting errors in learner language (for an overview see Leacock et al. 2010). Data-driven methods offer the familiar set of advantages: they can be more flexible than a manually maintained set of rules and they tend to cope better with noisy input. Drawbacks include the inability to handle linguistically more complex errors that involve long distance dependencies such as subject-verb agreement. Learner errors as a target for error detection and correction pose a particular challenge but also offer some unique opportunities. The challenge lies in the density of errors (much higher than in native writing), the variety of errors (a superset of typical native errors) and the generally more non-idiomatic writing. On the other hand, the availability of annotated corpora, often comprised of manually corrected learner essays or scripts, provides a big advantage for the evaluation and training of data-driven systems.

Data-driven systems for English learner error detection and correction typically target a specific set of error types and contain a machine learned component for each error type. For example, such a system may have a classifier that determines the correct choice of preposition given the lexical and syntactic part-of-speech (POS) context and hence can aid the learner with the notoriously difficult problem of identifying an appropriate preposition. Similarly, a classifier can be used to predict the correct choice of article in a given context. Such targeted systems have the advantage that they often achieve relatively high precision at, of course, the cost of recall. However, while there are a few major learner error categories, such as prepositions and articles, there is also a long tail of content word and other errors that is not amenable to a targeted approach.

In this paper, we depart from the error-specific paradigm and explore a sequence modeling approach to general error detection in learner writing. This approach is completely agnostic as to the error type. It attempts to predict the location of an

Proceedings of the Sixth Workshop on Innovative Use of NLP for Building Educational Applications, pages 180–189,
Portland, Oregon, 24 June 2011. ©2011 Association for Computational Linguistics

error in a sentence based on observations gathered from a supervised training phase on an error-annotated learner corpus. Features used here are based on an *n*-gram language model, POS tags, simple string features that indicate token length and capitalization, and linguistic analysis by a constituency parser. We train and evaluate the method on a sizeable subset of the corpus. We show the contribution of the different feature types and perform a manual error analysis to pinpoint shortcomings of the system and to get a more accurate idea of the system's precision.

2. Related work

Error-specific approaches comprise the majority of recent work in learner error detection. Two of the most studied error types in learner English are preposition and article errors since they make up a large percentage of errors in learner writing (16% and 13% respectively in the *Cambridge Learner Corpus*, without considering spelling and punctuation errors). The most widely used approach for detecting and correcting these errors is classification, with lexical and POS features gleaned from a window around the potential preposition/article site in a sentence. Some recent work includes Chodorow et al. (2007), De Felice and Pulman (2008), Gamon (2010), Han et al. (2010), Izumi et al. (2004), Tetreault and Chodorow (2008), Rozovskaya and Roth (2010a, 2010b). Gamon et al. (2008) and Gamon (2010) used a language model in addition to a classifier and combined the classifier output and language model scores in a meta-classifier. These error-specific methods achieve high precision (up to 80-90% on some corpora) but only capture highly constrained error types such as preposition and determiner errors.

There has also been research on error-detection methods that are not designed to identify a specific error type. The basic idea behind these error-agnostic approaches is to identify an error where there is a particularly unlikely sequence compared to the patterns found in a large well-formed corpus. Atwell (1986) used low-likelihood sequences of POS tags as indicators for the presence of an error. Sjöbergh (2005) used a chunker to detect unlikely chunks in native Swedish writing compared to the chunks derived from a large corpus of well-formed Swedish writing. Bigert and Knutsson (2002) employed a statistical method to identify a variety of errors in Swedish writing as rare sequences of morpho-syntactic tags. They significantly reduced false positives by using additional methods to determine whether the unexpected sequence is due to phrase or sentence boundaries or due to rare single tags. Chodorow and Leacock (2000) utilized mutual information and chi-square statistics to identify typical contexts for a small set of targeted words from a large well-formed corpus. Comparing these statistics to the ones found in a novel sentence, they could identify unlikely contexts for the targeted words that were often good indicators of the presence of an error. Sun et al. (2007) mined for patterns that consist of POS tags and function words. The patterns are of variable length and can also contain gaps. Patterns were then combined in a classifier to distinguish correct from erroneous sentences. Wagner et al. (2007) combined parse probabilities from a set of statistical parsers and POS tag *n*-gram probabilities in a classifier to detect ungrammatical sentences. Okanohara and Tsujii (2007) differed from the previous approaches in that they directly used discriminative language models to distinguish correct from incorrect sentences, without the direct modeling of error-indicating patterns. Park and Levy (2011) use a noisy channel model with a base language model and a set of error-specific noise models for error detection and correction.

In contrast to previous work, we cast the task as a sequence modeling problem. This provides a flexible framework in which multiple statistical and linguistic signals can be combined and calibrated by supervised learning. The approach is error-agnostic and can easily be extended with additional statistical or linguistic features.

3. Error detection by sequence modeling

Errors consist of a sub-sequence of tokens in a longer token sequence. They can be identified by a combination of internal and contextual features, the latter requiring a notion of Markov window (a window around a token in which relevant information is likely to be found). This is similar to tasks such as named entity recognition (NER) or part-of-speech tagging, where sequence modeling has proven to be successful.

We choose a Maximum Entropy Markov Model (MEMM, McCallum et al. 2000) as the modeling technique. In NER, the annotation convention uses three labels for a token "O" (outside of NE), "B" (beginning of NE), and "I" (inside of NE). For our purpose we reduced the set of labels to just "O" and "I" since most of the errors are relatively short.

Conditional Random Fields (Lafferty et al. 2001) are considered to be superior to MEMMs in learning problems affected by label bias (Bottou 1991). In our scheme, however, there are only two states "O" and "I", and both states can transition to each other. Since there are no states with asymmetric transition properties that would introduce a bias towards states with fewer transitions, label bias is not a problem for us.

Figure 1 shows the structure of our MEMM with a Markov order of five (the diagram only shows the complete set of arcs for the last state). The input sentence contains the token sequence *the past year I was stayed ...* with the error *was stayed*. Instead of using the tokens themselves as observations, we chose to use POS tags assigned by an automatic tagger (Toutanova et al. 2003). This choice was motivated by data sparseness. Learning a model that observes individual lexical items and predicts a sequence of error/non-error tags would be ideal, but given the many different error types and triggering contexts for an error, such a model would require much more training data. A large set of features that serve as constraints on the state transition models are extracted for each state. These features are described in Section 5.

Note that the model structure would lend itself to a factorial conditional random field (McCallum et al. 2003) which allows the joint labeling of POS tags and state labels. This would, however, require training data that is labeled for both errors and POS tags.

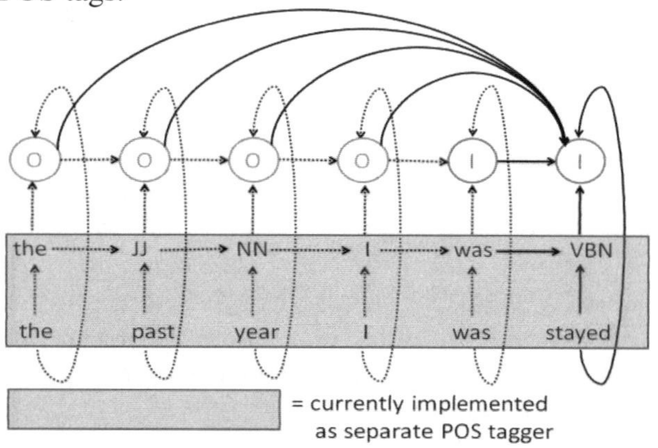

Figure 1: MEMM model for error detection, the full set of dependencies is only shown for the last state.

4. Detecting errors in the Cambridge Learner Corpus

The learner corpus used to train and evaluate the system is the *Cambridge Learner Corpus* (CLC). It consists of essays (scripts) written as part of the University of Cambridge *English for Speakers of Other Languages* (ESOL) examinations. The corpus contains about 30 million words of learner English. All errors are annotated and include, when possible, a single suggested correction. Errors are categorized into 87 error types.

We performed a number of preprocessing steps on the data. On the assumption that learners have access to a spell checker, errors that were marked as spelling errors were corrected based on the annotations. Confused words (*their/there*) were treated in the same way, given that they are corrected by a modern proofing tool such as the one in Microsoft Word. In addition, British English spelling conventions were changed to those of American English. Sentences containing errors that had no suggested rewrite were eliminated. Finally, only lexical errors are covered in this work. For punctuation and capitalization we removed the error annotations, retaining the original (erroneous) punctuation and capitalization.

We grouped the remaining 60 error classifications into eight categories: Content word, Inflectional morphology, Noun phrase errors, Preposition errors, Multiple errors, Other errors involving content words, Other errors involving function words and Derivational morphology. The distribution of error categories is shown in Table 1.

Error Class	Freq	Pct
Content word insertion, deletion or choice	185,201	21%
Inflectional morphology and agreement of content words	157,660	18%
Noun phrase formation: Determiners and quantifiers	130,829	15%
Preposition error	124,902	14%
Multiple: Adjacent and nested annotations	113,615	13%
Other content word errors	79,596	9%
Other function word errors: anaphors and conjunctions	65,034	7%
Derivational morphology of content words	39,213	4%

Table 1: Error types in the CLC.

The *multiple* error class includes any combination of error types where the error annotations are either nested or adjacent. The other categories are more focused: the errors are of a particular class and their adjacent context is correct, although there may be another error annotation a single token away. *Content word* errors involve the insertion, deletion and substitution of nouns, verbs, adjectives and adverbs. Further analysis of this error category on a random sample of 200 instances reveals that the majority (72%) of content word errors involve substitutions, while deletions account for 10% of the errors and insertions for 18%. Most substitutions (63%) involve the wrong choice of a word that is somewhat semantically related to the correct choice. *Inflectional morphology* includes all inflection errors for content words as well as subject-verb agreement errors. The inflectional errors include many cases of what might be considered spelling errors, for example **dieing/dying*. Similarly, the *derivational morphology* errors include all derivational errors for content words – and also include many errors that may be considered as spelling errors. *Noun formation* errors include all annotations involving determiners and quantifiers: inflection, derivation, countability, word form and noun-phrase-internal agreement. *Preposition* errors include all annotations that involve prepositions: insertion, deletion, substitution and a non-preposition being used in place of a preposition. There are two other categories: those involving the remaining function words (anaphors and conjunctions) and those involving remaining content words (collocation, idiom, negative formation, argument structure, word order, etc.).

It is important to highlight the challenges inherent in this data set. First of all, the problem is highly skewed since only 7.3% of tokens in the test set are involved in an error. Second, since we included correct learner sentences in the development and test sets in the proportion they occur in the overall corpus, only 47% of sentences in the test set contain error annotations, greatly increasing the likelihood of false positives.

5. Features

5.1 Language model features

The language model (LM) features comprise a total of 29 features. Each of these features is calculated from *n*-gram probabilities observed at and around the current token. All LM features are based on scores from a 7-gram language model with absolute discount smoothing built from the Gigaword corpus (Gao et al. 2001, Nguyen et al. 2007).

We group the language model features conceptually into five categories: basic features, ratio features, drop features, entropy delta features and miscellaneous. All probabilities are log probabilities, and n in the n-grams ranges from 1 to 5. All features are calculated for each token w of the tokens $w_0 \ldots w_i$ in a sentence.

Basic LM features consist of two features: the unigram probability of w and the average n-gram probability of all n-grams in the sentence that contain w.

Ratio features are based on the intuition that errors can be characterized as involving tokens that have a very low ratio of higher order n-gram probabilities to lower order n-gram probabilities. In other words, these are tokens that are part of an unlikely combination of otherwise likely smaller n-grams. These features are calculated as the ratio of the average x-gram probability of all x-grams containing w to the average y-gram probability of all y-grams containing w. The values for x and y are: 5 and 1, 4 and 1, 3 and 1, 2 and 1, 5 and 4, 4 and 3, 3 and 2.

Drop features measure either the drop or increase in n-gram probability across token w. For example, the *bigram drop* at w_i is the delta between the bigram probability of the bigram starting at $i\text{-}1$ to the bigram probability of the bigram starting at i. Drop features are calculated for n-grams with $2 \leq n \leq 5$.

Entropy delta features offer another way to look at the changes of n-gram probability across a token w. *Forward entropy* for w_i is defined as the entropy of the string $w_i \ldots w_n$ where n is the index of the last token in the sentence. We calculate the entropy of an n-gram as the language model probability of string $w_i \ldots w_n$ divided by the number of tokens in that string. *Backward entropy* is calculated analogously for $w_0 \ldots w_i$. For n-grams with $1 \leq n \leq 5$, we also calculate, at each index i into the token array, the delta between the n-gram entropy of the n-gram starting at i and the n-gram starting at $i+1$ (*forward sliding entropy*). Similarly the delta between the n-gram entropy of the n-gram starting at i and the n-gram starting at $i\text{-}1$ (*backward sliding entropy*) is calculated.

There are four miscellaneous language model features. Three of them, *minimum ratio to random*, *average ratio to random*, and *overall ratio to random* address the fact that a "good" n-gram is likely to have a much higher probability than an n-gram with the same tokens in random order. For all n-grams where $2 \leq n \leq 5$ we calculate the ratio between the n-gram probability and the sum of the unigram probabilities. For a token w_i we produce the *minimum ratio to random* (the minimum ratio of all n-grams including w) and the *average ratio to random* (the average of all ratios of the n-grams including w). *Overall ratio to random* is obtained by looping through each n-gram where $2 \leq n \leq 5$ that includes w_i and summing the n-gram probabilities (*sum1*) as well as the unigram probabilities of all unigrams in these n-grams (*sum2*). The ratio feature is then *sum1/sum2*. The final feature addresses the intuition that an erroneous word may cause n-grams that contain the word to be less likely than adjacent but non-overlapping n-grams. *Overlap to adjacent ratio* is the sum of probabilities of n-grams including w_i, divided by the sum of probabilities of n-grams that are adjacent to w_i but do not include it.

Note that this use of a host of language model features is substantially different from using a single language model score on hypothesized error and potential correction to filter out unlikely correction candidates as in Gamon et al. (2008) and Gamon (2010).

5.2 String features

String features capture information about the characters in a token and the tokens in a sentence. Two binary features indicate whether a token is capitalized (initial capitalization or all capitalized), one feature indicates the token length in characters and one feature measures the number of tokens in the sentence.

5.3 Linguistic Analysis features

Each sentence is linguistically analyzed by a PCFG-LA parser (Petrov et al., 2006) trained on the Penn Treebank (Marcus et al., 1993). A number of features are extracted from the constituency tree to assess the syntactic complexity of the whole sentence, the syntactic complexity of the local environment of a token, and simple constituency information for each token. These features are: label of the parent and grandparent node, number of sibling nodes, number of siblings of the parent, presence of a governing head node, label of the governing head node, and length of path to the root. An additional feature indicates whether the POS tag assigned by the parser does not match the tag assigned by the POS tagger, which may indicate a tagging error.

6. Experiments

6.1 Design

For our experiments we use three different mutually exclusive random subsets of CLC. 50K sentences are used for training of the models (larger data sets exceeded the capabilities of our MEMM trainer). In this set, we only include sentences that contain at least one annotated error. We also experimented using a mix of error-free and erroneous sentences, but the resulting models turned out to be extremely skewed towards always predicting the majority state "O" (no error). 20K sentences (including both erroneous and correct sentences) are used for parameter tuning and testing, respectively.

Each token in the data is annotated with one of the states "O" or "I". Performance is measured on a per token basis, i.e. each mismatch between the predicted state and the annotated state is counted as an error, each match is counted as a correct prediction.

We use the development set to tune two parameters: the size of the Markov window and a prior to prevent overfitting. The latter is a Gaussian prior (or quadratic regularizer) where the mean is fixed to zero and the variance is left as a free parameter. We perform a grid search to find values for the parameters that optimize the model's *F1* score on the development data.

In order to be able to report precision and recall curves, we use a technique similar to the one described in Minkov et al. (2010): we introduce an artificial feature with a constant value at training time. At test time we perform multiple runs, modifying the weight on the artificial feature. This weight variation influences the model's prior propensity to assign each of the two states, allowing us to measure a precision/recall tradeoff.

6.2 Performance of feature sets

Figure 2 illustrates the performance of three different feature sets and combinations. The baseline is using only language model features and standard POS tags, which tops out at about 20% precision. Adding the string features discussed in the previous section, and *partially lexicalized* (*PL*) POS tags, where we used POS tags for content word tokens and the lexicalized token for function words, we get a small but consistent improvement. We obtain the best performance when all features are used, including the linguistic analysis features (DepParse). We found that a high-order model with a Markov window size of 14 performed best for all experiments with a top *F1* score. *F1* at lower orders was significantly worse. Training time for the best models was less than one hour.

6.3 Predicting error types

In our next experiment, we tried to determine how the sequence modeling approach performs for individual error types. Here we trained eight different models, one for each of the error types in Table 1. As in the previous experiments, the development and test files contained error-free sentences. The optimal Markov window size ranged from 8 to 15. Note that our general sequence model described in the previous sections does not recognize different error types, so it was necessary to train one model per error type for the experiments in this section.

Figure 3 shows the results from this series of experiments. We omit the results for *other content word error, other function word* and *multiple errors* in this graph since these relatively ill-defined error classes performed rather poorly. As Figure 3 illustrates, derivational errors and preposition errors achieve by far the best results. The fact that the individual precision never reaches the level of the general sequence model (Figure 2) can be attributed to the much smaller overall set of errors in each of the eight training sets. In Figure 4 we compare the sequence modeling results for prepositions with results from the preposition component of the current version of the system described in Gamon (2010) on the same test set. That system consists of a preposition-specific classifier, a language model and a meta-classifier that combines evidence from the classifier and the language model. The sequence model approach outperforms the classifier of that system, but the full system including language model and meta-classifier achieves much higher precision than the sequence modeling approach.

6.4 Learning curve experiments

An obvious question that arises is how much training data we need for an error detection sequence model, i.e. how does performance degrade as we decrease the amount of training data from the 50K error-annotated sentences that were used in the previous experiments. To this end we produced random subsets of the training data in 20% increments. For each of these training sets, we determined the resulting *F1* score by first performing parameter tuning on the development set and then measuring precision and recall of the best model on the test set. Results are shown in Figure 5: at 20% of training data, precision starts to increase at the cost of recall. At 80% of the training data, recall starts to trend up as well. This upward trend of both precision and recall indicates that increasing the amount of training data is likely to further improve results.

6.5 Error analysis

The precision values obtained in our experiments are low, but they are also based on the strictest possible measure of accuracy: an error prediction is only counted as correct if it exactly matches a location and annotation in the CLC. A manual analysis of 400 randomly selected sentences containing "false positives", where the system had 29% precision and 10% recall, by the strictest calculation, showed that 14% of the "false positives" identified an error that was either not annotated in CLC or was an error type not covered by the system such as punctuation or case (recall from Section 4 that for these errors we removed the error annotations but retained the original string). An additional 16% were adjacent to an error annotation. 12% had error annotations within 2-4 tokens from the predicted error. Foreign language and other unknown proper names comprised an additional 6%. Finally, 9% were due to tokenization problems or all-upper case input that throws off the POS tagger. Thus the precision reported in Figure 2 through Figure 6 is really a lower bound. 30% of the "false positives" either identify, or are adjacent to, an error.

Sentence length has a strong influence on the accuracy of the sequence model. For sentences less than 7 tokens long, average precision is approximately 7%, whereas longer sentences average at 29% precision. This observation fits with the fact that high-order models perform best in the task, i.e. the more context a model can access, the more reliable its predictions are. Shorter sentences are also less likely to contain an error: only 12% of short sentences contain an error, as opposed to 46% of sentences of seven tokens or longer.

For sentences that are at least 7 tokens long, error predictions on the first and last two tokens (the last token typically being punctuation) have an average precision of 22% as compared to an average of 30% at all other positions. Other unreliable error predictions include those involving non-alphabetic characters (quotes, parentheses, symbols, numbers) with 1% precision and proper name tags with 10% precision. Many of the predictions on NNP tags identify, by and large, unknown or foreign names (*Cricklewood*, *Cajamarca*). Ignoring system flags on short sentences, symbols and NNP tags would improve precision with little cost to recall.

We also experimented with a precision/recall metric that is less harsh but at the same time realistic for error detection. For this "soft metric" we count correct and incorrect predictions at the error level instead of the token level. An error is defined as a consecutive sequence of n error tags, where $n \geq 1$.

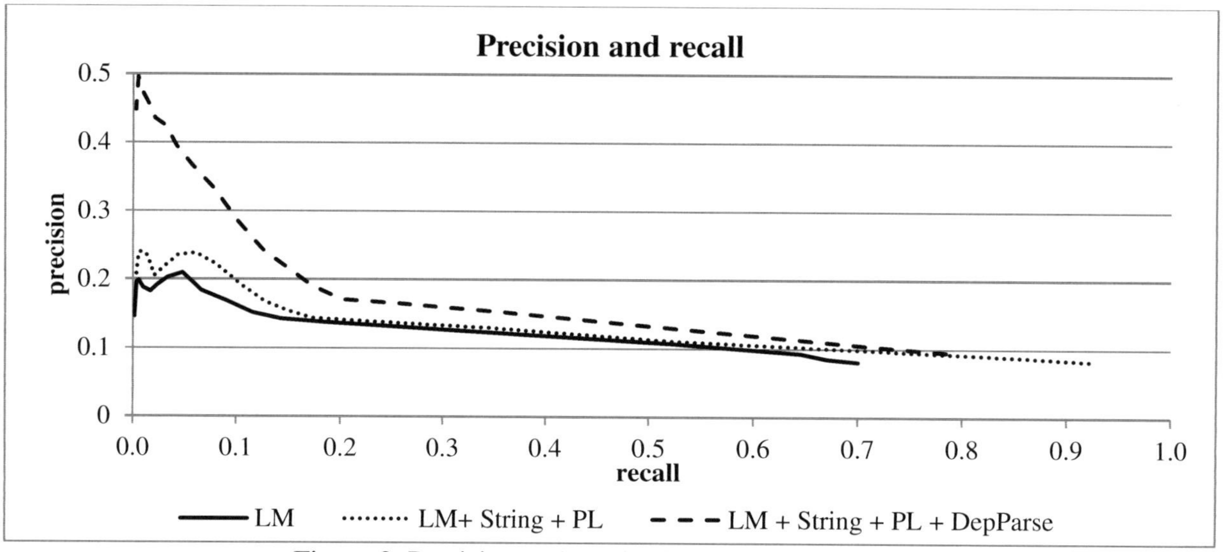

Figure 2: Precision and recall of different feature sets.

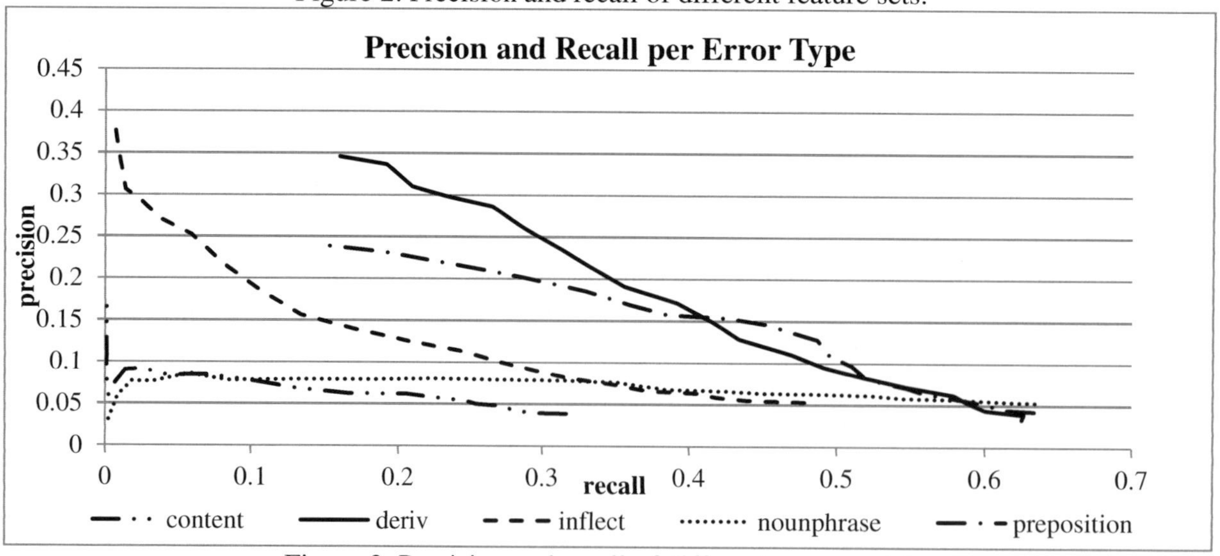

Figure 3: Precision and recall of different error models.

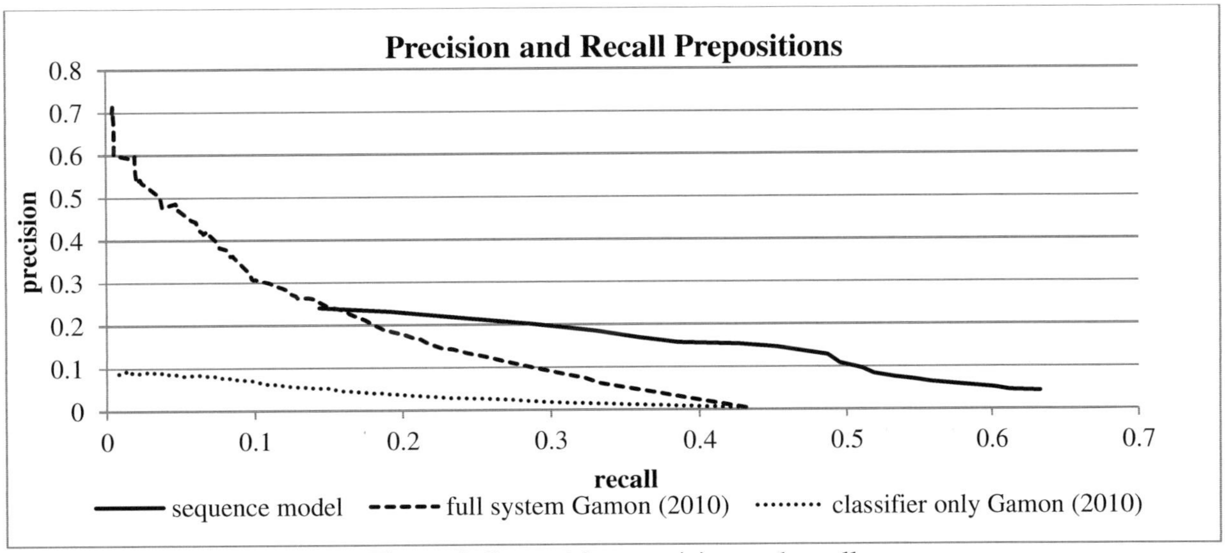

Figure 4: Preposition precision and recall.

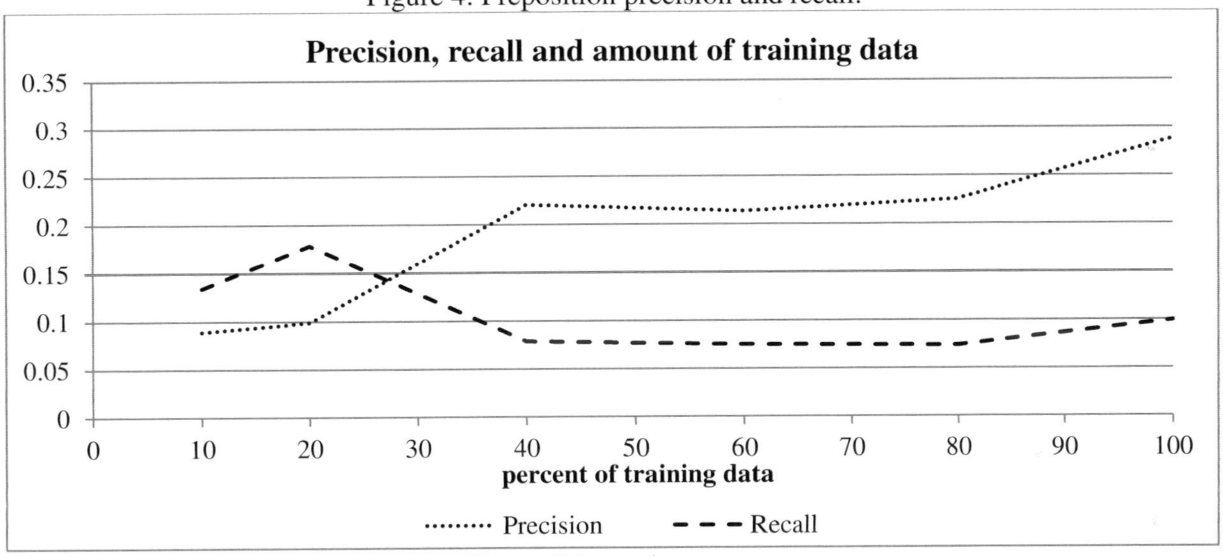

Figure 5: Learning curve.

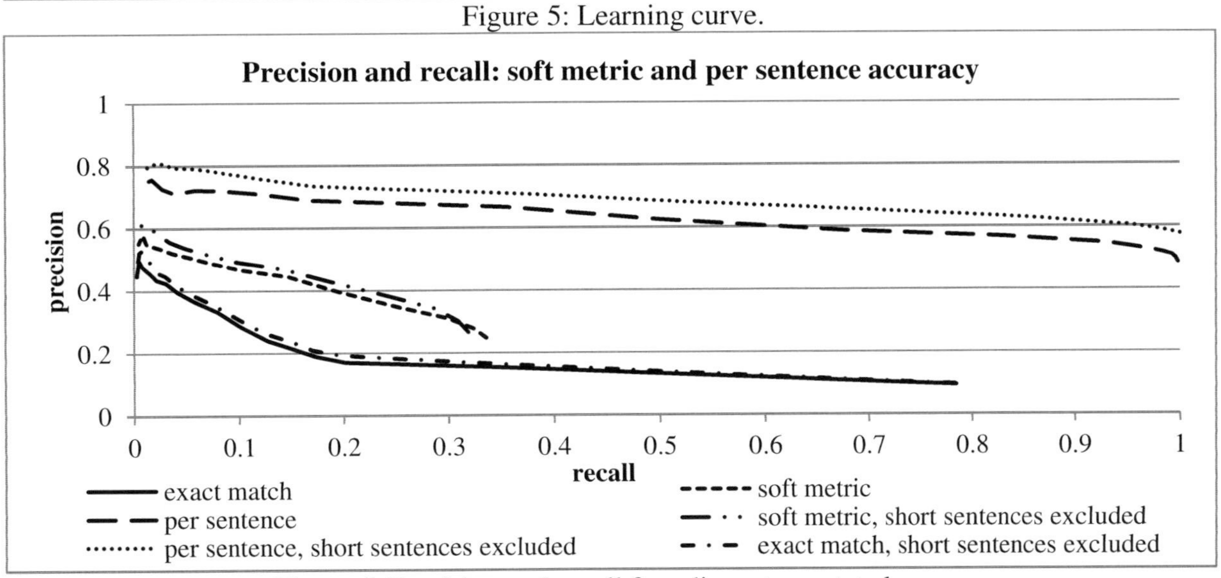

Figure 6: Precision and recall for adjacent annotated error

A predicted error counts as being correct with respect to an annotated error if the following two criteria are met:

a) At least one predicted error token is part of an annotated error or is directly adjacent to an annotated error
b) No more than two predicted error tokens fall outside the annotated error.

Criterion (a) establishes that predicted and annotated error are overlapping or at least directly adjacent. Criterion (b) ensures that the predicted error is "local" enough to the annotated error and does not include too much irrelevant context, but it still allows an annotated error to be flanked by predicted error tokens. Figure 6 illustrates the precision/recall characteristics of the best model when using this soft metric as compared to the strict metric. We also included a "per sentence" metric in Figure 6, where we measure precision and recall at the level of identifying a sentence as containing an error or not, in other words when using the model as a detector for ungrammatical sentences. In addition we show for each of the three metrics how the results change if short sentences (shorter than 7 tokens) are excluded from the evaluation.

7. Conclusion and future work

We have shown that a discriminative high order sequence model can be used to detect errors in English learner writing. This enables a general approach to error detection, at the cost of requiring annotated data. High-order models outperform lower order models significantly for this problem.

It is obvious that there are several avenues to pursue in order to improve upon these initial results. Two possibilities that we would like to highlight are the model structure and the feature set. As mentioned in Section 3, instead of using a separate POS tagger we could follow McCallum et al. (2003) and design a model that jointly predicts two sequences: POS tags and error tags. As for feature sets, we conducted some preliminary additional experiments where we added a second set of language model features, based on a different language model, namely the Microsoft web n-gram model (Wang et al. 2010). The addition of these features raised both precision and recall.

Finally, an error detection system is only of practical use if it is combined with a component that suggests possible corrections. For future work, we envision a combination of generic error detection with a corpus-based lookup system that finds alternative strings that have been observed in similar contexts. All these alternatives can then be scored by a language model in the original context of the user input, allowing only those suggestions to be shown to the user that achieve a better language model score than the original input. This combination of error detection and error correction has the advantage that the error detection component can be used to provide recall, i.e. it can be allowed to operate at a lower precision level. The error correction component, on the other hand, then reduces the number of false flags by vetting potential corrections by language model scores.

Acknowledgments

We would like to thank Claudia Leacock for the manual error analysis, Michel Galley for detailed comments on an earlier draft and Chris Quirk for discussions and help around the MEMM model implementation. The idea of the *ratio to random* language model features is Yizheng Cai's. We also greatly benefited from the comments of the anonymous reviewers.

References

Eric Steven Atwell. 1986. How to detect grammatical errors in a text without parsing it. In *Proceedings of EACL*, pp. 38-45.

Léon Bottou. 1991. Une approche théorique de l'apprentissage connexionniste: Applications à la reconnaissance de la parole. Doctoral dissertation, Université de Paris XI.

Johnny Bigert and Ola Knutsson. 2002. Robust error detection: a hybrid approach combining unsupervised error detection and linguistic knowledge. In *Proceedings of the Second Workshop on Robust Methods in Analysis of Natural Language Data*, pp. 10-19.

Martin Chodorow and Claudia Leacock. 2000. An unsupervised method for detecting grammatical errors. In *Proceedings of NAACL*, pp. 140-147.

Martin Chodorow, Joel Tetreault and Na-Rae Han. 2007. Detection of grammatical errors involving prepositions. In *Proceedings of the Fourth ACL-SIGSEM Workshop on Prepositions*, pp. 25-30.

Rachele De Felice and Stephen G. Pulman. 2008. A classifier-based approach to preposition and determiner error correction in L2 English. In *Proceedings of COLING*, pp. 169-176.

Michael Gamon, Jianfeng Gao, Chris Brockett, Alexandre Klementiev, William Dolan, Dmitriy Belenko and Lucy Vanderwende. 2008. Using Contextual Speller Techniques and Language Modeling for ESL Error Correction. In *Proceedings of IJCNLP*.

Michael Gamon. 2010. Using mostly native data to correct errors in learners' writing. In *Proceedings of NAACL*.

Jianfeng Gao, Joshua Goodman, and Jiangbo Miao. 2001. The use of clustering techniques for language modeling--Application to Asian languages. Computational Linguistics and Chinese Language Processing, 6(1), 27-60.

Na-Rae Han, Joel Tetreault, Soo-Hwa Lee and Jin-Young Ha. 2010. Using error-annotated ESL data to develop an ESL error correction system. In *Proceedings of LREC*.

Emi Izumi, Kiyotaka Uchimoto and Hitoshi Isahara. 2004. SST speech corpus of Japanese learners' English and automatic detection of learners' errors. *International Computer Archive of Modern English Journal*, 28:31-48.

John Lafferty, Andrew McCallum and Fernando Pereira. 2001. Conditional random fields: Probabilistic models for segmenting and labeling sequence data. In *Proceedings of ICWSM*, pp. 282-289.

Claudia Leacock, Martin Chodorow, Michael Gamon and Joel Tetreault. 2010. *Automated Grammatical Error Detection for Language Learners*. Morgan and Claypool.

Mitchell P. Marcus, Beatrice Santorini and Mary Ann Marcinkiewicz. 1993. Building a large annotated corpus of English: The Penn Treebank. *Computational Linguistics* 19:313-330.

Andrew McCallum, Dayne Freitag and Fernando Pereira. 2000. Maximum entropy Markov models for information extraction and segmentation. In *Proceedings of ICML*, pp. 591-598.

Andrew McCallum, Khashayar Rohanimanesh and Charles Sutton. 2003. Dynamic Conditional Random Fields for jointly labeling multiple sequences. In *Proceedings of NIPS Workshop on Syntax, Semantics and Statistics*.

Einat Minkov, Richard C. Wang, Anthony Tomsaic and William C. Cohen. 2010. NER systems that suit user's preferences: Adjusting the Recall-Precision trade-off for entity extraction. In *Proceedings of NAACL*, pp. 93-96.

Patrick Nguyen, Jianfeng Gao, and Milind Mahajan. 2007. MSRLM: A scalable language modeling toolkit (MSR-TR-2007-144). Redmond, WA: Microsoft.

Daisuke Okanohara and Jun'ichi Tsujii. 2007. A discriminative language model with pseudo-negative samples. In *Proceedings of ACL*, pp. 73-80.

Y. Albert Park and Roger Levy. 2011. Automated whole sentence grammar correction using a Noisy Channel Model. In *Proceedings of ACL 2011*.

Slav Petrov, Leon Barrett, Romain Thibaux and Dan Klein. 2006. Learning accurate, compact, and interpretable tree annotation. In *Proceedings of COLING/ACL*, pp. 443-440.

Alla Rozovskaya and Dan Roth. 2010a. Training Paradigms for correcting errors in grammar and usage. In *Proceedings of NAACL-HLT*.

Alla Rozovskaya and Dan Roth. 2010b. Generating confusion sets for context-sensitive error correction. In *Proceedings of EMNLP*.

Jonas Sjöbergh. 2005. Chunking: An unsupervised method to find errors in text. In *Proceedings of the 15th NODALIDA conference*.

Guihua Sun, Xiaohua Liu, Gao Cong, Ming Zhou, Zhongyang Xiong, John Lee and Chin-Yew Lin. 2007. Detecting erroneous sentences using automatically mined sequential patterns. In *Proceedings of ACL*, pp. 81-88.

Joel Tetreault and Martin Chodorow. 2008. The ups and downs of preposition error detection in ESL writing. In *Proceedings of COLING*, pp. 865-872.

Kristina Toutanova, Dan Klein, Chris Manning, and Yoram Singer. 2003. Feature-rich part-of-speech tagging with a cyclic dependency network. In *Proceedings of NAACL*, pp. 252-259.

Joachim Wagner, Jennifer Foster, and Josef van Genabith. 2007. Judging grammaticality: Experiments in sentence classification. *In Proceedings of EMNLP & CONLL*, pp 112-121.

Kuansan Wang, Christopher Thrasher, Evelyne Viegas, Xialong Li, and Paul Hsu. 2010. An Overview of Microsoft web n-gram corpus and applications. In: *Proceedings of NAACL 2010*.

Author Index